Roman Conquests: North Africa

To Esther (again)

You remain

My power, my pleasure, my pain

ROMAN CONQUESTS: NORTH AFRICA

Nic Fields

Pen & Sword
MILITARY

First published in Great Britain in 2010 by
Pen & Sword Military
An imprint of
Pen & Sword Books Ltd
47 Church Street
Barnsley
South Yorkshire
S70 2AS

Copyright © Nic Fields, 2010

ISBN 978 1 84415 970 3

The right of Nic Fields to be identified as Author of this work has been asserted by them in accordance with the Copyright, Designs and Patents Act 1988.

A CIP catalogue record for this book is
available from the British Library

All rights reserved. No part of this book may be reproduced or transmitted in any form or by any means, electronic or mechanical including photocopying, recording or by any information storage and retrieval system, without permission from the Publisher in writing.

Typeset in 10 on 12pt Times New Roman by
Acredula

Printed and bound in England
By the MPG Books Group

Pen & Sword Books Ltd incorporates the Imprints of Pen & Sword Aviation, Pen & Sword Family History, Pen & Sword Maritime, Pen & Sword Military, Wharncliffe Local History, Pen & Sword Select, Pen & Sword Military Classics, Leo Cooper, Remember When, Seaforth Publishing and Frontline Publishing

For a complete list of Pen & Sword titles please contact
PEN & SWORD BOOKS LIMITED
47 Church Street, Barnsley, South Yorkshire, S70 2AS, England
E-mail: enquiries@pen-and-sword.co.uk
Website: www.pen-and-sword.co.uk

Contents

Acknowledgements vi
Maps vii
List of Illustrations xiv
Prologue.. xv
Chronology xxvii
  1. From emporium to empire 1
  2. Army and navy 9
  3. First contact 25
  4. Picking a fight 33
  5. Between the wars 45
  6. Hannibal's revenge 49
  7. Zama, a lesson learnt 60
  8. A military superpower 68
  9. Hannibal's retreat 73
10. The final act 77
11. The horse lords 86
12. Mobile warfare 94
13. Iugurtha's gamble 103
14. Sallust on Iurgurtha 114
Epilogue... 121
Appendix 1 124
Appendix 2 134
Notes 145
Bibliography 181
Index 186

Acknowledgements

When our thoughts turn to Carthage we automatically think of suicidal Dido and her fatal love affair, and, of course, the unlucky Hannibal and his elephants. Dido's relationship with Aeneas is one of the best-known love stories of all time and countless writers, poets, painters and composers have been inspired by it. Similarly, Hannibal's passage of the Alps, along with the charge of the Light Brigade and Custer's last stand, has stirred the imagination of humankind. They were, however, only two dramatic details on a much larger canvas of historical (mythical) events. And for that discovery, I am forever indebted to John Lazenby and his stimulating teaching.

I offer my sincere thanks to Philip Sidnell of Pen & Sword Books for his Herculean patience with my extreme (glacial, in truth) slowness and philosophical peculiarities. I am grateful, as well, to Elizabeth James for her careful and helpful reading and for her understanding of the finer points of the Latin language. I should like to offer a big thank you to Graham Sumner and Ian Hughes; the first for his artwork, the second for his mapwork. This volume is far richer as a result of their artistic talents and labours. Finally, trite though it may seem, my greatest thanks (as ever) go to Esther, who, once again, has been with me on this project all along the (rocky) way.

Maps

LIST OF MAPS

1. The Roman Empire at its greatest extent, with North Africa highlighted viii
2. The Mediterranean basin, 8th-6th centuries BC ix
3. The Western Mediterranean basin, 3rd century BC x
4. The Eastern Mediterranean basin, 3rd century BC xi
5. Carthage and its hinterland xii
6. Carthage, 2nd century BC xiii
7. The Battle of Zama 64
8. The Burning of the Camps 89

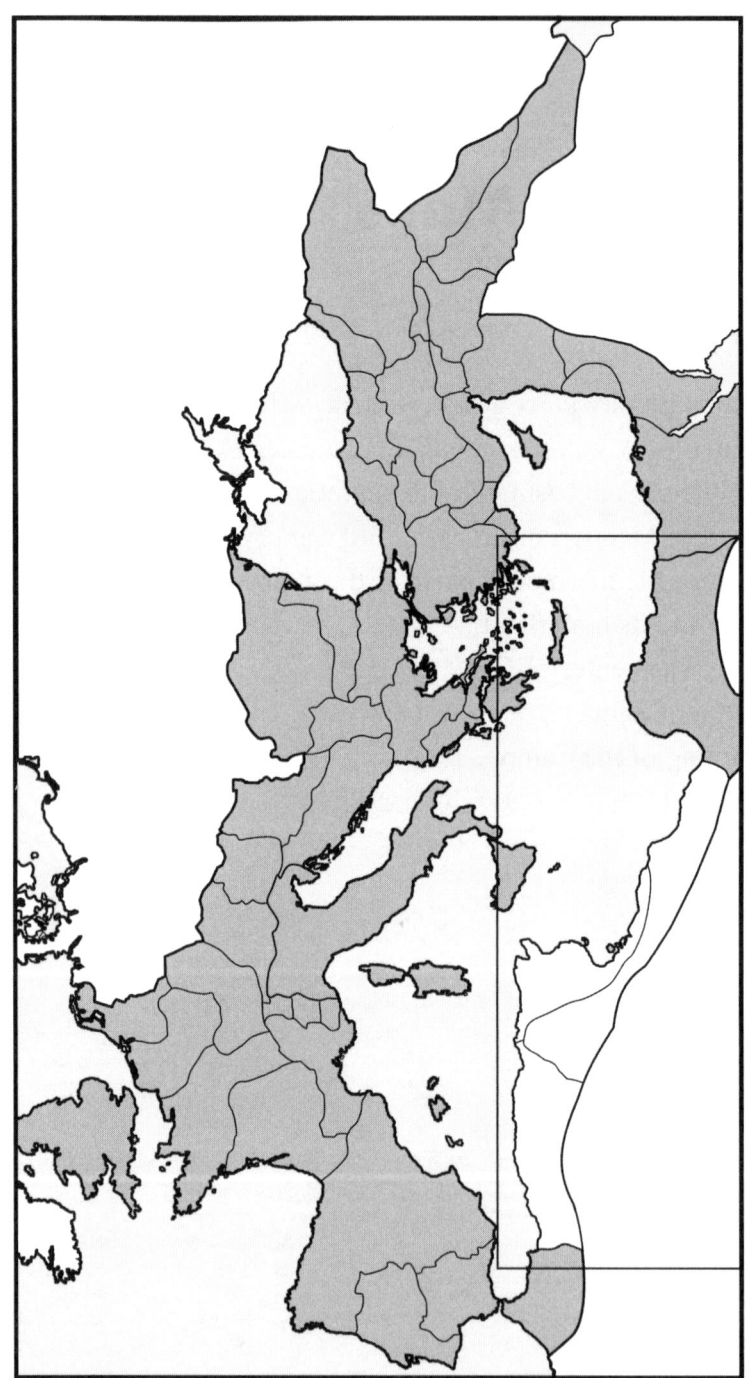

The Roman Empire at its greatest extent, with the area covered in this volume highlighted.

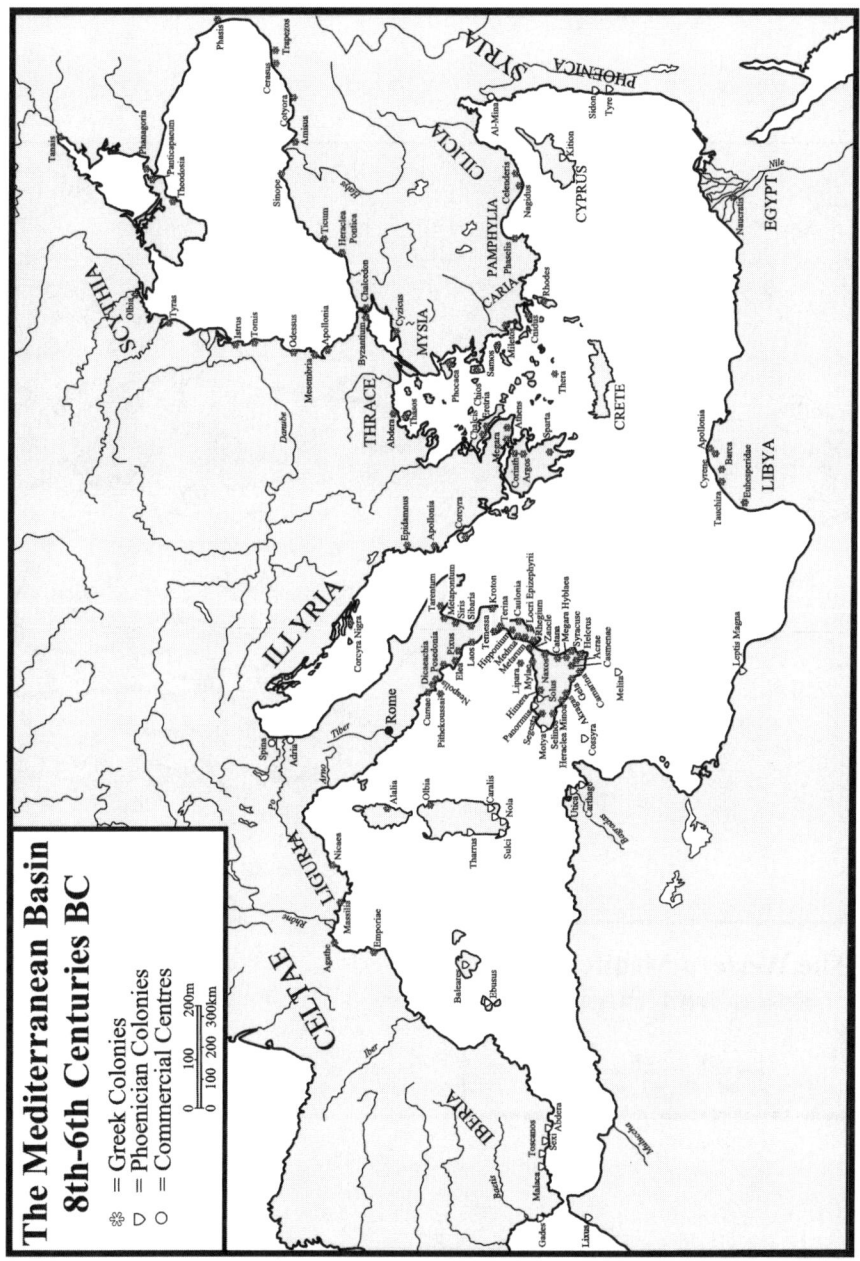

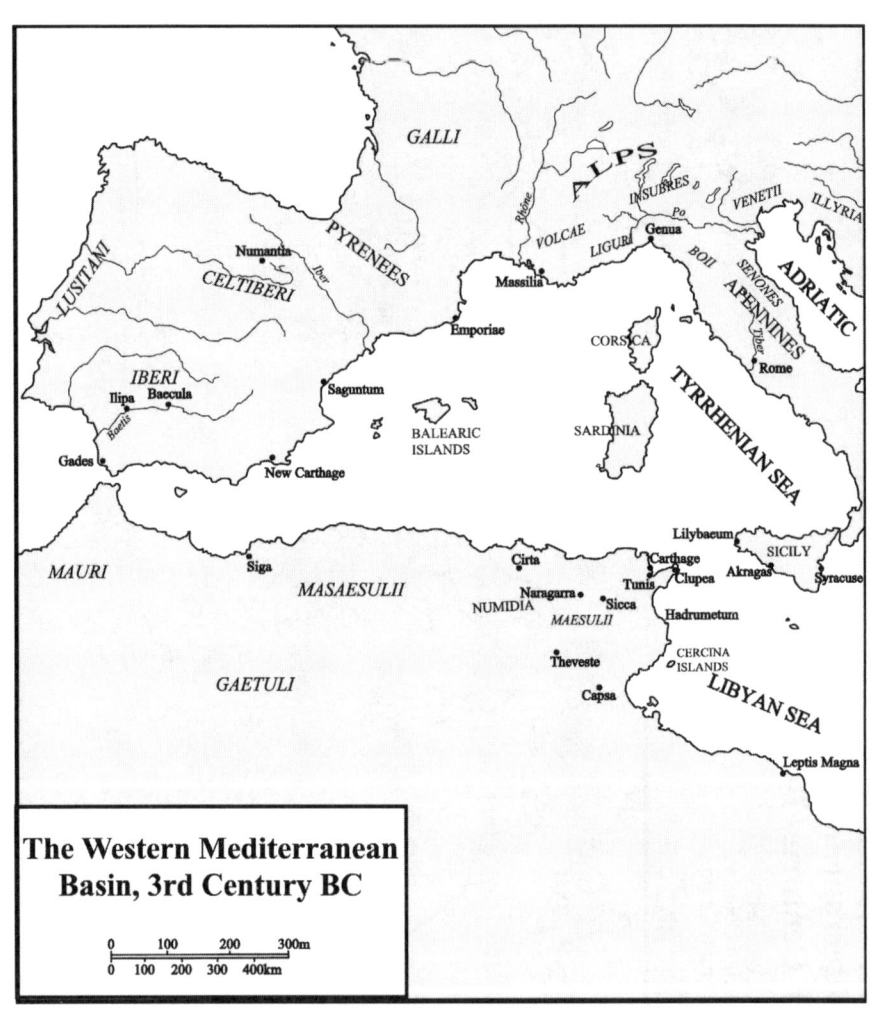

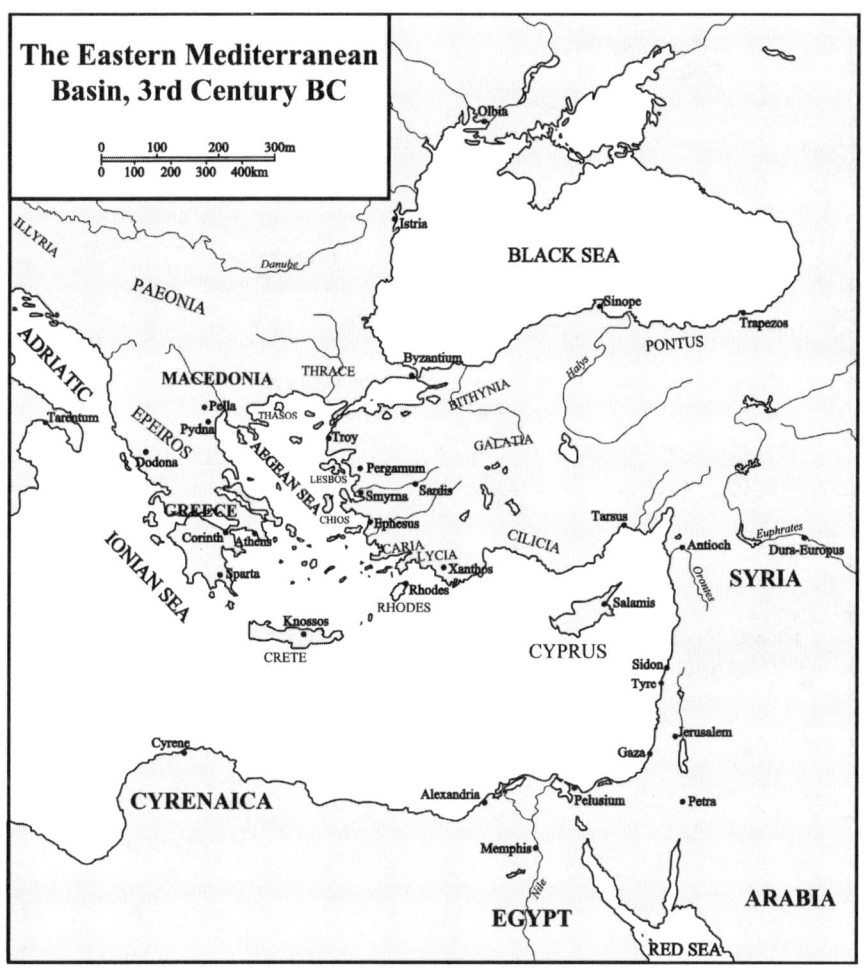

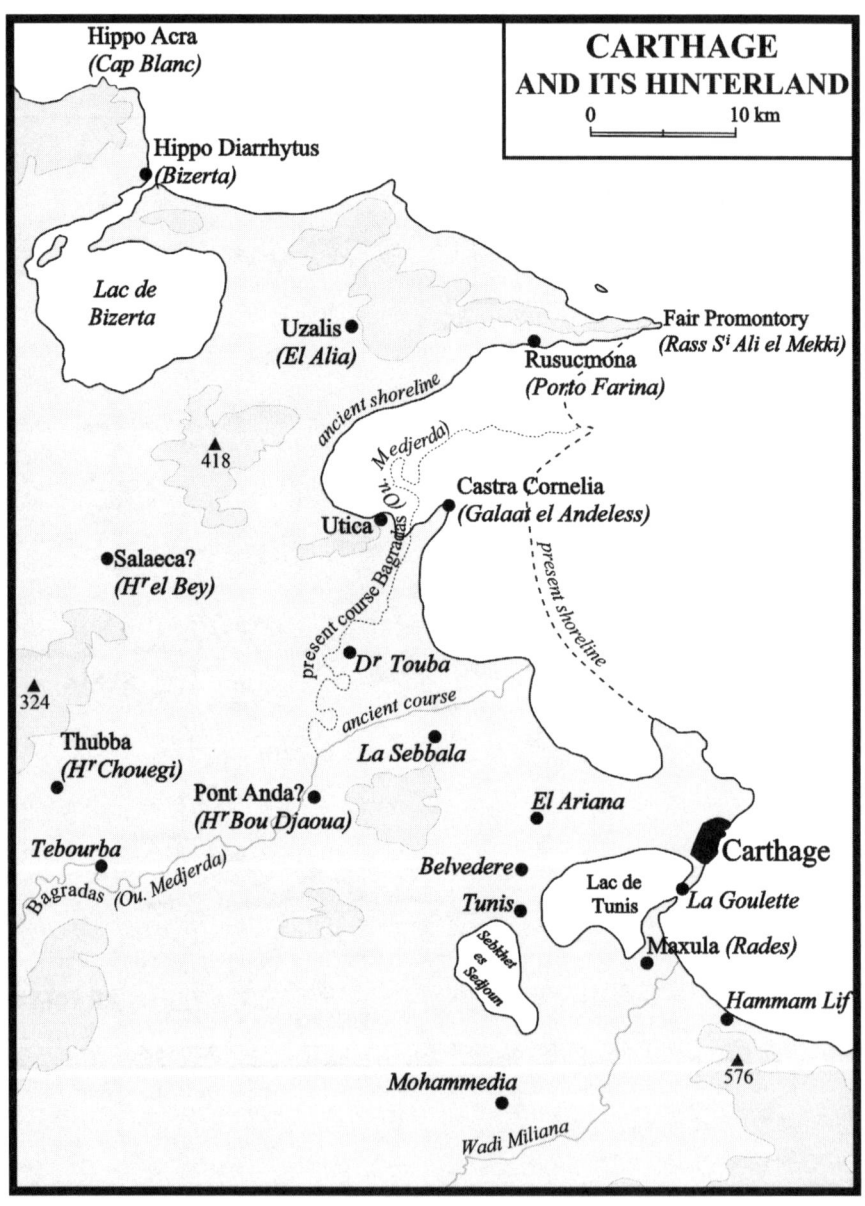

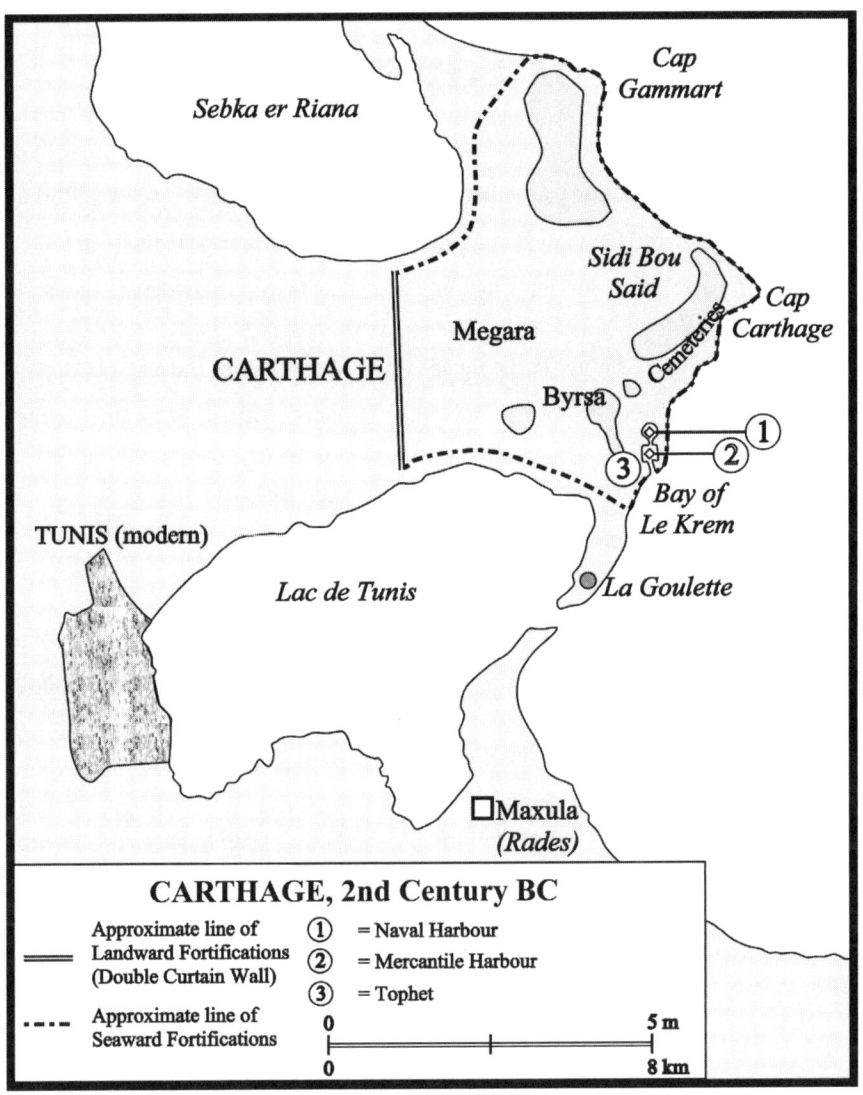

List of Illustrations

1. Marble head of Publius Cornelius Scipio Africanus (Rome, Museo Capitolini)
2. Marble statue of Hannibal Barca (Paris, musée du Louvre) (Esther Carré)
3. Limestone relief of Iberian warriors (Madrid, Museo Arquelogico Nacional) (Esther Carré)
4. 'Wounded Gaul', statue (Paris, musée du Louvre) (Esther Carré)
5. Bronze figurine of Numidian horseman (London, British Museum) (Esther Carré)
6. Greek mercenary spearman (painting by Graham Sumner)
7. Iberian *caetratus* (painting by Graham Sumner)
8. Carthaginian citizen spearman (painting by Graham Sumner)
9. Numidian warrior (painting by Graham Sumner)
10. Republican Roman *triarius*, recreated by Legio Prima Germanica (photo courtesy of Graham Sumner)
11. Military clerk on the Altar of Domitius Ahenobarbus (Paris, musée du Louvre) (Esther Carré)
12. Roman troops on the Altar of Domitius Ahenobarbus (Paris, musée du Louvre) (Esther Carré)
13. Mars as a Roman officer on the Altar of Domitius Ahenobarbus (Paris, musée du Louvre) (Esther Carré)

Prologue

ROME AND THE REST

Let us begin our story with an amusing anecdote. As the armies were deploying to commit themselves to the lottery of battle, it is commonly said that Antiochos of Syria turned to Hannibal Barca, the luckless but bewitching Carthaginian general who accompanied his entourage, to enquire whether his army, its ranks gleaming with silver and gold, its commanders grandly arrayed in their heavy jewels and rich silks, would be enough for the Romans. 'Indeed they will be more than enough', sneered Hannibal, 'even though the Romans are the greediest nation on earth'.[1]

If we were lucky enough to be able to ask the citizens of ancient Rome how they saw their empire, then almost certainly the view of the Augustan poet Virgil would probably cover the vast majority of current feeling: 'an empire with no limits'.[2] We, in our post-Cold War world, readily deplore the craving of conquest and the cruelty of conquerors. Imperialism, that ageless human concept of acquisitiveness, implies a conscious desire to take and possess, and if it is to carry weight in the historical balance, it must lead to some spectacular and abiding achievement. As westerners we tend to associate, by tradition, Rome with the superior aspects of Latin culture, namely the legacy still with us today in law, administration and language, while those of us who live in Europe, the Levant or North Africa have the added bonus of being surrounded by concrete reminders of its former grandeur. The Roman Empire at its zenith, and at its most confident (roughly, 27 BC to AD 235), covered vast tracts of three continents, Europe, Africa and Asia, encompassed countless cultures, languages and climates, and included nomads and farmers, tribesmen and urbanites, brigands and philosophers. Rome was anticipatory of a world composed of the most diverse elements and people, and its empire would be synonymous with that world at peace.

The idiomatic expression *pax romana* was borrowed from the elder Pliny, the learned Roman admiral who perished during the terrible eruption of Mount Vesuvius in the year AD 79. When he penned it, he was reflecting upon the flora 'now available to the botanist from all the corners of the world, thanks to the boundless majesty of Roman peace'.[3] So we read in Pliny that 'the cherry tree did not exist in Italy before the victory of Lucullus over Mithridates [70 BC]. He brought the first one from the Black Sea and in a hundred and twenty years it had crossed the Ocean and even reached Britannia'.[4] In Pliny's time, peach and apricot trees had just arrived in Italy, the former probably originating from China and the latter from the land we know now as Turkestan. Walnut and almond trees from the east had only recently arrived, as had the quince bush from Crete. Naturally all this talk of seeds, cuttings and grafts ignores the fact that empire had to be bought with the coin of human degradation: murder, brutality, starvation, dispossession.

Repugnant though this is, the *pax romana* is not to be sniffed at, more so if we consider the terrible plight of our own world today, where universal peace appears to remain a mere will o' the wisp. Conflict is as much a part of the contemporary world as ever, and we are all, either through actual experience or through mediated experience, the children of war. Though certainly not as 'happy and prosperous' as the supposed golden age of Edward Gibbon, the population of the Roman Empire, despite notable exceptions, was at least to enjoy relative quiet for two-and-a-half centuries.[5] This was something new, as yet to be repeated, to the human condition. Even so, there is something else. Empires are not acquired in a fit of absence of mind, but through a conscious policy of expansion.

In its broad outline, the manifest destiny of Rome was devastatingly simple. The mood of the time, if correctly reflected in the literature of the day, leans unmistakably toward irresistible expansion beyond the confines of the Italian peninsula on the grounds of mission, decreed fortune, and divine will. Rome's greatest orator, Cicero, gave it an air of the miraculous when he blustered 'that Romulus had from the outset the divine inspiration to make his city the seat of a mighty empire'.[6] Indeed, by the time of Augustus, the first emperor, it would be fashionable to call the rise of Rome prodigious. 'Go and tell the Romans that by heaven's will my Rome will be the capital of the world', Livy has Romulus, the first king, proclaim when he was becoming a god but the city he had founded was still little more than an insignificant palisaded hilltop overlooking a convenient crossing of the Tiber. 'Let them learn to be soldiers', he continues, 'let them know, and teach their children, that no power on earth can stand against Roman arms'.[7]

The immortal Romulus notwithstanding, in war Rome had no secret weapon and the basis of its world domination was forged from an indomitable blend of unlimited manpower, military skill and might, relentless aggression, doggedness in adversity and moral superiority, all of which was occasionally compounded with a large dose of self-deception and a long streak of cruelty. Rome believed its expansion had been sanctioned by the gods from the very beginning and that its wars had always been fought with a pitiless dedication to total victory.

In 29 BC, after Octavianus, the future Augustus, had made himself master of the known world by vanquishing Marcus Antonius and Cleopatra at Actium, Virgil finished his *Georgics*. Ostensibly a didactic poem on farming (in truth, few working farmers would have been readers of poetry) the *Georgics* is the great poem of united Italy. Others, including Varro in his contemporary and more serviceable prose manual, had praised the variety, fertility, self-sufficiency and temperate climate of Italy, and the elder Cato, who wrote the first agricultural treatise in Latin in the second century BC, had praised the sturdy qualities of its sons who were by turns farmers then soldiers.[8] Virgil's famous eulogy of Italy is the Augustan apogee in that it adds a new dimension, the association of this land with the greatness of Rome.[9] This virtuoso set piece ranges far beyond the workaday realm of agriculture and sometimes even of sober truth. Virgil, of course, was a poet and one for whom embellishment was no vice. Yet his allegory of a conscious and united Italy, where Romans are Italians and Italians are Romans, was to be an overture to the glorification of Augustus and his new regime, and an assertion of Rome's imperial destiny.

As the contemporary military engineer Vitruvius wrote, 'the truly perfect territory (*veros fines*), situated in the centre of the universe (*mundus*), and having on each side the entire extent of the world and its countries, is that which is occupied by the Roman people'. Therefore, Vitruvius concluded, 'it was the divine intelligence that set the city of the Roman people in a peerless and temperate country, in order that it might acquire the right to command the whole world'.[10] The belief that Romans enjoyed a privileged position in the ordered cosmos was echoed by Pliny when he picked up the theme of the role of the Italian peninsula and the Latin language:

> A land which is the nurseling and mother of all other lands, chosen by the divine might of the gods, to make heaven itself more glorious, to unite dispersed empires, to temper manners, to draw together in mutual comprehension by community of language the warring and uncouth tongues of so many nations, to give mankind *humanitas* and in a word to become throughout the world the single fatherland of all peoples.[11]

To us the notion of taking Roman dominion 'to the ends of the earth' is an egotistical view, to say the least of it, but to the Romans it was a neat way of justifying their acquisition of empire.[12] 'The Gods favour us', said Tacitus more tersely, while Virgil in the *Aeneid*, the new national epic on the origins and destiny of imperial Rome, made Iuppiter himself proclaim: 'On them [the Romans] I impose no limits of time or place. I have given them an empire that will know no end'.[13] Virgil's friend Horace, who too used his facile pen in the service of the new regime, was rather more particular in his choice of hyperbole when he claimed in his last Ode (13 BC) that 'the fame and majesty of our rule was spread to the rising of the sun from its western bed', and that 'neither those who drink deep Danubius (viz.Dacians) will break Iulian laws, nor the Getae, nor the Seres (viz.Chinese) or faithless Persae (viz.Parthians), nor those born by the River Tanaïs (viz.Scythians)'.[14] In the memoir composed by Augustus at the end of his long and eventful reign (27 BC - AD 14), and inscribed on public monuments all over the empire, he merely declared in the opening sentence that he had 'brought the world under the empire of the Roman people'.[15]

We can, of course, view all this as simply part of the hot air of Roman imperialism, which it was. But in earthly terms the *pax romana* would be an enormous human entity (enormous for the times, that is) spread over an area that was also enormous.[16] The civilized Romans, on whom it seems divine providence had bestowed earth's fairest portion, evidently marched steadily ahead with full belief in their right to create an eternal empire. Doubtless there was some conscious hypocrisy in all this, particularly as they anachronistically read this world view back into earlier times. Even Hannibal is made to call Rome the 'capital of the world'.[17] Yet it goes without saying that we are all, as were the Romans, swinish hypocrites under the cosy cloak that civilization fashions for us. The gap between civilized and barbaric is never as great as we like to think.

There was a very dark side to Rome's rise to world domination, and Gore Vidal, in one of his most brilliant of essays, throws a spotlight on its more disreputable doppelgänger. 'Suetonius', he says, 'in holding up a mirror to those Caesars of diverting legend, reflects not only them but ourselves: half-tempted creatures, whose great moral task it is to hold in balance the angel and the monster within - for we are both, and to ignore this duality is to invite disaster'.[18] Earlier in the same composition he hits the nail squarely on the head when he announces: 'Power for the sake of power. Conquest for the sake of conquest. Earthly dominion as an end in itself: no Utopian vison, no dissembling, no hypocrisy. I knock you down; now *I* am king of the castle'.[19] Of course we could politely point out that such luminance, elegantly written in the light of hindsight, should be given little weight. However, contemporary writers themselves were very well aware of the nature of the beast and their writings are filled with criticisms of war and empire. Even the ardently pro-Roman historian Flavius Josephus, a Jewish *protégé* of the emperor Vespasianus and reporting a supposed speech by the ardently pro-Roman Jewish prince Agrippa II, did not hesitate to equate Rome's outward march with pathological megalomania:

> And even the world is not big enough to satisfy them; the Euphrates is not far enough to the east, or the Danube to the north, or Libya and the desert beyond to the south, or Gades to the west; but beyond the Ocean they have sought a new world, carrying their arms as far as Britannia, that land of mystery.[20]

The Romans knew no limit or scruple. As Cicero tells us, 'the essential significance, surely, of those eulogistic words inscribed upon the monuments of our greatest generals, "he extended the boundaries of the empire", is that he had extended them by taking territory from someone else.'[21] And naturally such belligerent imperialism not only brought territories and taxes, but slaves and spoils too. Conquests were often awesomely bloody: a body count of 5,000 qualified a general for a triumph back in Rome, and was followed up by enslavement and pillage to defray the costs of the campaign, fill the yawning purse of the general, and give his threadbare soldiers something to take home into civilian life. Romans expected war to be profitable both in blood and plunder.

Prologue

Herein lies the rub, the working of empire and its double face, bringing as it does civilization and slavery. No matter how artful the patriotic histories and the heroic poems, there were inevitable tensions that could not be smoothed or wished away. Whatever Rome was able to take from its subject peoples, there was also a responsibility towards their welfare beyond the maintenance of the *pax romana*. Yet for the Romans 'peace gained by victories',[22] the physical process of pacification, and not peace itself, this was the function of empire. The nature and makeup of the Roman world view was not to be passive but to exert power, to conquer and dominate, 'to impose a settled pattern upon peace, to pardon the defeated and war down the proud', as Virgil has Anchises prophesy to his son Aeneas.[23] In short, Roman victories meant the forcing (viz. peacemaking), not maintenance (viz. peacekeeping), of Roman peace and order on others. The world had been not so much tempted into peace as battered into submission.

We moderns, burdened with our increased sensitivity to the iniquities of imperialism and unjust wars, find it hard to reconcile the positive aspects of Roman civilization with Roman cruelty. This was not however a mere aberration. What we see as the belligerence, brutality and bloodthirstiness of the Romans were fundamental to their culture and to their social system. The Romans knew very well that the ability to make war, which is what gives power to any state, does not function if it cannot be used, and therefore aggression was the fundamental rationale of their foreign policy. Moreover, the monopoly of military power was in the hands of a few, first the tightly knit oligarchy of the imperial Republic, then the emperor as an autocratic avatar of that oligarchy. So it follows that not only did Roman aristocrats make war, wars made Roman aristocrats. Throughout human history aristocracies have preserved for themselves power and wealth, and what else is deemed worth having. They too have had, to a greater or less degree, a strong military tradition, and for the fiercely competitive aristocrats of Rome warfare was gravy. It gave them a purpose, an opportunity to carry out what they had been trained to do since puerility, namely exercise their undoubted physical courage and tell other people what to do. It also made them priggish, patriarchal, brutal and, occasionally, psychopathic.

In the last resort, of course, the peace and order of the empire depended on the proletariat armed forces, which now had a permanent *raison d' être*. 'Legions, fleets, provinces, the whole system was interconnected', so Tacitus described the empire and its armed forces.[24] Thus a naked piece of imperialism could be seen as, depending on who (and where) the viewer (or the victim) was, either civic militarism (viz. defensive) or brute militarism (viz. offensive). The evidence strongly suggests that the Roman citizens, both rich and poor, thought primarily of the benefits that empire brought to Rome and were not ashamed to say so. In one of his last speeches (43 BC), Cicero reminds his fellow senators that their ancestors had gone to war not merely 'that they might be free but that they might rule'.[25] A Greek quip, again relayed by Cicero, might best describe the credible opinion at the capital's street level: 'Let them hate provided that they fear'.[26] Of bullies what shall we look for but bullying? Still, bullies and other repellent creatures can easily delude themselves that their wars and punitive expeditions are fought only when absolutely necessary, and then only for honourable humanitarian reasons or to punish the unjust, what the Romans traditionally regarded as acting in 'good faith', *fides*, and conducting campaigns according to the ideological rules of a 'just war', *bellum iustum*. Everything is so much easier when it is black and white, civilization against barbarism, us or them. But reality is never entirely black and white, naturally, because nothing occurs in a vacuum.

As we have just observed with Rome, such self-delusion is often reinforced by the belief that the imperialists are somehow a 'chosen' people destined to dominate the lesser races, that the use of organized violence by the military aristocracy was a legitimate activity in the cause of civilizing, and the army an agent in the divine plan. As Cicero tells the ordinary citizens in one of his early speeches (66 BC), Rome is a just conqueror, so much so that other peoples would rather be ruled by Romans than rule themselves.[27] Nor should it be overlooked that as the world 'went Roman' those 'effeminate' Greeks in Alexandria, 'long-haired' Gauls in Armorica, and 'reeking' Gaetulians in Africa now had something in common. As we would expect, all types of things still distinguished them one from another, language and customs to name but two, but they shared the condition that they were now subject to the domination of one single city. Rome was tolerant of the social and cultural 'pluralism' within its armed frontiers, as long as everyone paid their dues, showed due respect to its absolute authority, and revered its traditional gods. For the most part everyone was willing to play along with the Roman thing and nonchalantly identify themselves with the embracing imperial structure. Morally and ethically, Rome did not reach deeply into the private hearts of its subjects out in the provinces. That belonged to their local gods and exotic cults.

As a rule, civilized men do not readily move away from the centres of civilization: as Dr Samuel Johnson pronounced, a man who was tired of London was tired of life. Imperial capitals are invariably cities of consumers, of people who are civilized but not creative. In this regard Rome was no exception. It was also a marvellous Tower of Babel to which all roads led. By the age of emperors Rome began to see the arrival of a swelling stream of immigrants, mostly from different parts of the empire but also from beyond it. As resident aliens, Greeks, Gauls, Iberians and Africans soon contributed to the rich diversity of tongues, cults and customs of this huge parasitic city. Still, as is customary with multiracial empires, there was also a reactionary backlash to Rome's cosmopolitanism and cultural flexibility that readily found its Roman street tongue through the overt racism of a biting satirist vilifying the importation into his beloved city of alien culture and practice, especially those of the Hellenized east:

> I cannot, citizens, stomach a Greek Rome. Yet what faction of these dregs is truly Greek? For years now eastern Orontes has discharged into the Tiber its lingo and manners, its flutes, its outlandish harps with their transverse

strings, its native tambourines, and the whores pimped out round the racecourse.[28]

This is powerful stuff, but it does not do for us to forget that Juvenal was a satirist, and that satirists enjoy soaring to the dizzy heights of caustic invective. He needs checking against other evidence.

Juvenal's vehement dislike for the 'hungry Greeklings',[29] amongst other clever foreigners, had good literary antecedents. The elder Cato and the elder Pliny, self-appointed guardians of good old-fashioned Roman values, utterly detested them: in particular they were prejudiced against Greek doctors, whom they regarded as quacks and snake-oil sellers.[30] Nevertheless, in actual fact the Greeks, powerful and unconquerable as a cultural force, were very well integrated into Roman society. 'Conquered Greece took her uncultivated conqueror captive', as Horace had very nimbly said.[31] This paradox, of course, is what Juvenal finds particularly nettlesome, yet even those at the very pinnacle of Roman society held similar, if none so rancid, xenophobic attitudes: 'Those silly Greeklings all love a gymnasium, so it may be that they were too ambitious in their plans at Nicaea.'[32]

Such views say much about the Roman aristocratic mentality, yet there was at least one very learned gentleman who was willing to disrupt the existing pattern of society, to inject some mobility and dynamism into its fossilized, pyramidal structure.

Almost predictably, the sources portray the emperor Claudius (r. AD 41-54) as feeble-minded, engagingly dim, stammering, rambling, wholly under the thumb of his ambitious freedmen and his scheming wives. The alternative picture, which the sources say much to suggest that it may be equally valid as a description, is of a quiet, studious man, of considerable learning, with the ability to identify the problems facing the empire, and a gift for administration, if not the charisma for great leadership. Indeed, inscriptions and papyri from Claudius' reign give a more favourable impression of his personal contribution to the running of the empire than the literary tradition:

> Upon my word, I did wish to give him [Claudius] another hour or two, until he should make Roman citizens of the half dozen who are still outsiders. (He made up his mind you know, to see the whole world in the toga, Greeks, Gauls, Iberians and Britons, and all). But since it is your pleasure to leave a few foreigners for seed, and since you command me, so be it.[33]

The wearing of the toga was a distinctive right, under Augustus a duty, of the Roman citizen, and Seneca was plainly following the literary tradition of emphasizing the 'outlandish' appearance of the 'others', reinforcing their racial inferiority when compared with their 'civilized' conquerors.[34]

It goes without saying that this sarcasm from the pen of Seneca is blatant exaggeration, for out of the world population in AD 48 Claudius, in the role of censor, registered only 5,984,072 Roman citizens.[35] Yet it was Claudius, again as censor, who gave 'trousered, long-haired Gauls, chieftans from the area of Gaul conquered a century earlier by Caesar, the right to hold public office at Rome. What is more, one of the most striking initiatives was the Senate's decision to admit to membership a number of these Gaulish nobles. Tacitus tells us that the momentous decision followed Claudius' personal intervention in the senatorial debate, and all the available evidence strongly suggests that he was very much acting on his own initiative and not as a mouthpiece for others.[36] Although this farsighted policy led to integration and stability, Seneca, a typical product of his age in that he regarded his society as an immutable datum, obviously mocks the emperor (a reputed fool) for this.[37]

We can credit the progressive but eccentric Claudius with a concept of the unity of the empire, an empire in which the conquered, whatever their race, profited as much as the conquerors from the *pax romana*. However, bigotry and understanding are strange bedfellows at the best of times, and within the empire, despite the wisdom of men such as Claudius in taking the longer view, there was a permanent division between the conquered and their conquerors, the Romans and the rest. Racial intolerance is an insidious thread that runs throughout human history. In this respect the British Empire was no better (or worse) than that of Rome. Take, for instance, the plainspoken views of Cecil John Rhodes (1853-1902), the British imperialist and arch-capitalist who founded Rhodesia (Zimbabwe) with the mechanical help of the Maxim machine gun:

> Whites have clearly come out top... in the struggle for existence... Within the white race the English-speaking man has proved himself to be the most likely instrument of the Divine plan to spread Justice, Liberty, and Peace over the widest possible area of the planet. Therefore I shall devote the rest of my life to God's purpose and help him to make the world English.[38]

It is hardly surprising that this degree of racial superiority towards foreigners should give rise to an arrogance and a mismatch of pretension and reality. Later, as the Prime Minister and virtual dictator of the Cape Colony, the 'Colonial Colossus' speaks of his 'mission' to paint the map of the 'Dark Continent' pink, a British dominion of Africa from the Cape to Cairo.[39] Worldly empires naturally create a culture of pride and pomp, and foster the pernicious rhetoric of imperialistic transcendency.

The imperial poets Virgil and Kipling both supplied their readership with paeans of praise expounding the grandeur of imperial domains: Romans wanted the prestige of the *pax romana*, and Britons, looking at a world map that was one-fifth pink, could proudly boast that the sun never set on British shores. What interests us in this story are the ancient shores of the Mediterranean, especially the long African one. For the British, with their nautical imagination, the Middle Sea was not merely a segmented lake contained by three continents but the corridor to their far-flung empire, a watery highway from Gibraltar to Goa.[40] Similarly the Romans saw the *mare nostrum* as an organizing principle, albeit as landlubbers it was buckled firmly at the narrow passage of the Pillars of Hercules (Greek = Herakles), as the Straits of Gibraltar were then called, against outside intrusion. Naturally the Romans themselves did not just settle for the sun, the vine and the olive, the marginal province of Britannia is a testament alone to that fact.[41] Yet the warm pulse of this expanse of blue water and the fringe of provinces around its shores meant Mediterranean culture circulated well beyond its outer margins.

Of course dreams of a boundless empire are but dreams, the divine gift of celestial gods and court poets. In the early days of Rome's career, nothing seemed to single out for future greatness a puny riverine settlement that lay sleeping. Assume not, therefore, that this mighty empire came about by some automatic, let alone divine, process. In these obscure, slumberous times Rome was allied with the other Latin settlements in the neighbourhood, and the seasonal battles that preoccupied these Italic people were little more than parochial squabbles over cattle herds, water rights, and arable land. Rome did not happen suddenly, nor did it simply happen, and when it finally did happen, world dominion rested on its military arm, whose strength and length were definite. The Roman war machine, which relied on heavily-equipped infantry, was best suited for high-intensity warfare against a dense agricultural population with conquerable assets. It was less well suited for mobile warfare against lightly-equipped opponents. Rome would settle for what its army could handle and its agriculturists could exploit, and thus excluded the steppe, the forest, and the desert.[42]

Besides, for all its majesty and authority, the peace imposed by Rome would not live long into the third century AD. We see it, from the luxurious advantage of hindsight, as an extended respite from the gruesome norms of human behaviour. Admittedly world peace, universal laws, improved roads, new markets, urban growth, all these things and more besides contributed to a stability and prosperity unknown before the time of the Roman emperors. Yet though there was more wealth in the world, the impecunious, hovering between survival and starvation, received no more of it than they had received previously. Under the imperial Republic, the villain of our particular story, Rome had been ruled by an aristocratic plutocracy. This had disarmed the weary and cheated the unoffending poor by pressing swords in their hands, the cold-blooded assumption being that anyone who became a soldier became thereby once and for all one of the props of the ruling order. With the collapse of this political organization, Augustus would establish an autocracy that was backed ultimately by military force. Under both systems the poor, whose only worldly goods were their offspring, were reduced by hunger, social discrimination, illiteracy and the legal apparatus to the most wretched impotence. Under the new regime, however, where the ruler's relationship with his soldiers was of the foremost importance, there was the opportunity for a poor man to better his prospects by taking up a full-time career in the armed forces of his emperor.

Though two-and-a-half predominately peaceful centuries were a formidable achievement, the overall effect would be to pool up external pressures that one day would overflow. Hitherto independent tribes came together to form larger confederations. As the fable goes, the tiger was the lord in the jungle and the terror of lesser beasts, including the wolf. The wolf, himself a hunter, wearied of being hunted. He took to associating with other wolves, and then the wolves discovered the power of the pack, and took to hunting the tiger, with calamitous results to him. Some may think that Rome had been rotted by long peace and good times, but Iron Age man had little taste for order let alone domination by another. Peoples who have been free, and subject to no power, could not be reduced to order in an instant. Human nature is glacially slow to change, and it remains questionable whether even his post-atomic counterpart has the skill or the will to do better.

War, as the ancient Greeks teach us, seems innate to the human species, the 'father and king of all', as the philosopher Herakleitos of Ephesos asserted.[43] Unfortunately, we have to admit he was right. Let us take two straightforward examples: few national borders were determined by compassion and altruism; most people live on land that their forefathers snatched from others by force. War has been and is humanity's inseparable companion, and so new fashions and more advanced ideas, the benchmarks of human progress, do not include passive resistance:

> Had my high birth and rank been accompanied by moderation in my hour of success, I should have entered this city as a friend and not a prisoner. You would not have hesitated to accept me as an ally, a man of splendid ancestry, and bearing rule over many tribes. My present position is degrading to me, but glorious to you. I had horses, warriors and gold; if I was unwilling to lose them, what wonder is that? Does it follow that because you desire universal empire, one must accept universal slavery?[44]

This speech Tacitus puts into the mouth of the British prince Caratacus is typical of the historian (according to many the greatest of classical antiquity) echoing his constant theme concerning the destiny of Rome and the excesses committed in the name of Roman imperialism.[45] Was Rome's mission in the world, he asked, for universal peace and prosperity, or for plundering and enslaving its subject peoples?

Roman laws of war, as Tacitus surely knew, took for granted that conquered peoples surrendered their freedom and property to Rome. Seized and taken to Rome, where he was pardoned by our wise emperor Claudius, Caratacus asked a question of imperialism famous for its irony: 'You have so much; why do you covet *our* poor huts?'[46] Whatever Caratacus did or did not actually say, it was inevitable that 'barbarians' should stress Roman egoistic ambition and insatiable greed. All were familiar with rapacity at local level, tribe robbing tribe, as was their primordial way, but here was grand theft on a global scale. 'Globe grabbers' roars a Caledonian war leader to his gathered people. He continues his tirade: 'Plunder, murder and rapine, these things they misname empire: they create desolation and call it peace'[47] Written in the mode of tragic irony, Calgacus' speech against Rome is Tacitus' editorial on 'romanisation', that process whereby the lands conquered by the forces of Rome or settled by its citizens or agents were subject to a single rule of law. Modern empires have looked back on this process, which had the merit of being ambiguous, as a blessing, like their own ideals, and ascribed it to *la mission civilatrice*. For Tacitus, on the other hand, naked barbarism was not a monopoly of bare-limbed barbarians.

It is doubtful whether our two Britons really said these things, but their crisp appraisals of plundering Rome are highly plausible.[48] Still, Roman imperialism was concerned not with poor huts but rich fields. A pre-battle harangue of another Briton, none other than Queen Boudica of the Iceni, offers as much when she says of the legions facing her war host: 'They require shade and covering, they require bread and wine and olive oil, and if any of these things fail them, they perish'.[49] Perish they might, but not from a lack of these three staples. From an early stage, Rome had exported government and law but imported cargoes of food produced by the provinces to feed it citizens and soldiers. The first provinces of Sicily, Sardinia and Africa paid much of their taxes in cereal grain.

Shifting time and space, we now travel from the killing fields of Roman Britain to the rolling fields of Punic Africa. It is a time when Rome is a young commonwealth, feeling its feet and still a little unsteady. Others elsewhere were playing the great game of empires.

One of these players was Agathokles of Syracuse, one-time *condottiere* turned military tyrant. When his roughneck soldiers landed in Africa, they were amazed by the mild and highly-cultivated scenery of the Punic countryside. In his telling description of the event, Diodoros the Sicilian describes how it abounded with the tree crops for which North Africa became famous, such as grapes, figs, olives, almonds and pomegranates. He also mentions herds of cattle, flocks of sheep and numerous grazing horses, to which we can add an abundance of wheat and barley to complete his pastoral picture. The finely kept land of the northern coastal strip was certainly fat (much more so than now), the climate favourable (a lot cooler than it is today), and its bounty plentiful.[50] His summation says it all: 'In general there was a manifold prosperity in the region, since the leading Carthaginians had laid out their private estates and with their wealth had beautified them for their enjoyment'.[51] The message was loud and clear: here was a highly desirable land, a fragrant land dense with great fields and richly-bearing orchards, a thriving and comfortable land where every roughness had been softened away from the landscape. This was a land that deserved to be conquered. In all good time North Africa would serve as the breadbasket of Rome.[52]

If we are to believe in the poetical spells woven by Virgil, the singer of Rome's imperial destiny, the fates of Rome and Africa were inextricably linked from the earliest of times. According to his epic in praise of the emperor Augustus, the *Aeneid*, the Trojan hero Aeneas, fleeing from the fiery destruction of Troy, was fated, like his Greek contemporary Odysseus, to wander far and wide before finding a home. His travels took him to the shores of Africa where he was welcomed at Carthage by its young queen, Dido, who fell insanely in love with the fine-looking refugee and offered him permanent sanctuary and her feather bed. Iuppiter, however, had scheduled Aeneas as the father of the Roman race and the ancestor of Augustus, and ordered him to quit his dalliance with an alien queen and get on with the job in hand. Italy is his terminus: *hic amor, haec patria est*. He duly obeyed and Dido, deserted and heartbroken, committed suicide.

As she climbed onto the great pyre built from her nuptial bed and all the clothes and other objects that the 'pious Aeneas', had left behind, Dido launched her curse on him and all his descendants:

> Let there be no love between our peoples and no treaties. Arise from my dead bones, O my unknown avenger, and harry the race of Dardanus with fire and sword wherever they may settle, now and in the future, whenever our strength allows it. I pray that we may stand opposed, shore against shore, sea against sea and sword against sword. Let there be war between the nations and between their sons forever.[53]

Having prophesied the Punic Wars and Hannibal's invasion of Italy, she then fell upon the sword that Aeneas had given her as a gift. However paradoxical it may seem, civilizations have often been built on the back of waging war, and the problem of political morality, the problem of empire, which tormented Tacitus, has yet to be resolved. It seems that the future is to be interpreted with certainty only in the past.

Chronology

814 BC	Traditional date for foundation of Carthage from Tyre
753 BC	Traditional date for foundation of Rome by Romulus
574 BC	Tyre falls to Nebuchadnezzar of Babylon
535 BC	Carthaginian-Etruscan fleet engage Greeks off Alalia
509 BC	Traditional date for expulsion of Rome's last king
508 BC	First treaty between Carthage and Rome (according to Polybios)
496 BC	Latin League defeated by Romans at Lake Regillus
480 BC	Carthaginians defeated at Himera
474 BC	Etruscan fleet defeated off Cumae by Sicilian Greeks
409 BC	Carthaginians capture Selinous and Himera
406 BC	Carthaginians capture Akragas and Gela
405 BC	Carthaginians fail to take Syracuse (peace accord with Dionysios)
397 BC	Dionysios captures Motya
396 BC	Carthaginians retake Motya (foundation of Lilybaeum)
	Carthaginians capture and destroy Messana
	Carthaginians lay siege to Syracuse ('plague' destroys Carthaginian army)
392 BC	Armistice between Carthage and Syracuse
390 BC	Romans defeated at Allia
	Gauls sack Rome (387 BC according to Polybios)
348 BC	Second treaty between Carthage and Rome
344 BC	Timoleon of Corinth arrives in Sicily (revival of Greek Sicily)
343-341 BC	**First Samnite War: a war invented by Rome?**
341 BC	Timoleon defeats Carthaginians at Krimisos
340-338 BC	**Latin War: Rome versus its allies**
326-304 BC	**Second Samnite War: Romans face mountain warfare**
321 BC	Romans humiliated at Caudine Forks
316 BC	Agathokles takes power in Syracuse
311 BC	Agathokles defeated by Carthaginians in Sicily
310 BC	Agathokles lands in Africa
307 BC	Stalemate between Agathokles and Carthage
306 BC	Philinos' treaty between Carthage and Rome (disputed by Polybios)
298-290 BC	**Third Samnite War: old foes fight back**

295 BC   Romans defeat coalition of Samnites and Gauls at Sentinum
289 BC   Death of Agathokles
281 BC   Rome declares war on Taras
280-275 BC Pyrrhic War: Rome versus Pyrrhos of Epeiros
280 BC   Romans defeated at Herakleia
279 BC   Romans defeated at Asculum
278 BC   Pyrrhos sails to Sicily
275 BC   Pyrrhos defeated at Malventum (renamed Beneventum)
273 BC   Latin colonies at Cosa and Paestum
272 BC   Taras falls to Romans (end of pre-Roman Italy)
         Pyrrhos slain in Argos
270 BC   Romans recapture Rhegion
264-241 BC First Punic War: Rome takes the path to empire
264 BC   Roman alliance with Mamertini (consular army lands in Sicily)
263 BC   Hiero II of Syracuse becomes ally of Rome
262 BC   Romans lay siege to Akragas
261 BC   Akragas falls
         Carthaginian navy raids Italy
260 BC   Roman naval victory off Mylae
258 BC   Roman naval victory off Sulci
257 BC   Roman naval victory off Tyndaris
256 BC   Roman naval victory off Ecnomus
         Regulus lands in Africa (captures Tunis)
255 BC   Xanthippos defeats Regulus near Tunis (Regulus captured)
254 BC   Romans capture Panormus
250 BC   Romans lay siege to Lilybaeum
249 BC   Roman naval defeat off Drepana
247 BC   Hamilcar Barca lands in Sicily (seaborne raid on Bruttium)
         Birth of Hannibal Barca
246 BC   Hamilcar occupies Heirkte
244 BC   Hamilcar shifts to Eryx
241 BC   Roman naval victory off Aegates Islands
240-237 BC Libyan War: Carthage versus its mercenaries
238 BC   Rome annexes Sardinia (threatens Carthage with war)
237 BC   Hamilcar sent to Iberia
231 BC   Roman embassy to Hamilcar
229 BC   Death of Hamilcar (succeeded by Hasdrubal the Splendid)
229-228 BC First Illyrian War: Roman 'police action' against Queen Teuta
227 BC   Praetors raised to four (Sicily and Sardinia-Corsica made Roman provinces)
226 BC   Roman embassy to Hasdrubal (signing of Iber treaty)
225 BC   Romans defeat Gaulish invaders at Telamon

221 BC   Hasdrubal assassinated (Hannibal Barca acclaimed generalissimo)
219 BC   Second Illyrian War: Demetrios of Pharos knocked down
         Hannibal storms Saguntum
218-201 BC Second Punic War: Carthage strikes back
218 BC   Romans defeated at Ticinus and Trebbia
217 BC   Romans defeated at Lake Trasimene
216 BC   Romans defeated at Cannae
         Capua revolts
         Roman navy raids Africa
215 BC   Alliance of Carthage with Philip V of Macedon
         Hanno enters Kroton
         Roman navy raids Africa
214-205 BC First Macedonian War: Roman sideshow in Greece
214 BC   Defection of Syracuse
         Romans expel Carthaginians from Saguntum
213 BC   Hannibal enters Tarentum
         Romans besiege Syracuse
212 BC   Romans besiege Capua
211 BC   Hannibal marches on Rome (fails to prevent fall of Capua)
         Fall of Syracuse (Rome recovers Sicily)
         Cornelii Scipiones defeated and killed in Iberia
210 BC   Scipio appointed to Iberian command
         Hannibal levels Herdonea
         Roman navy raids Africa
209 BC   Tarentum recovered
         Twelve Latin colonies refuse to supply troops
         Scipio takes New Carthage
208 BC   Scipio defeats Hasdrubal Barca at Baecula (Hasdrubal leaves Iberia)
         Roman navy raids Africa (Carthaginian fleet defeated off Clupea)
207 BC   Hasdrubal crosses Alps (defeated and killed at Metaurus)
         Roman navy raids Africa (Carthaginian fleet defeat off Utica)
206 BC   Scipio's victory at Ilipa (end of Carthaginian resistance in Iberia)
         Masinissa defects to Rome
205 BC   Roman navy raids Africa
         Mago Barca lands in northern Italy
204 BC   Pact between Syphax and Carthage (marries Sophonisba)
         Scipio lands in Africa (begins siege of Utica)
         Masinissa joins Scipio
203 BC   Burning of winter camps near Utica
         Scipio's victory at Great Plains (Hannibal and Mago recalled)
         Capture of Syphax (bittersweet death of Sophonisba)
         Defeat of Mago (dies en route to Africa)

	Hannibal lands at Hadrumentum
202 BC	Hannibal marches to Zama (Scipio and Hannibal meet)
	Scipio's victory at Zama
201 BC	Carthage reduced to client status
	Triumph of Scipio (takes cognomen 'Africanus')

200-197 BC Second Macedonian War: Rome 'punishes' Philip V of Macedon

200 BC	Philip lays siege to Athens
198 BC	Philip retains Corinth
197 BC	Philip defeated at Kynoskephalai
	Praetors raised to six (Hispania Citerior and Ulterior made Roman provinces)
196 BC	Hannibal elected *sufete* (political and economic reforms in Carthage)
	Rome proclaims Greek freedom
195 BC	Hannibal's flight and exile
	Masinissa opens his raids on Carthaginian territory
194 BC	Romans evacuate Greece
	Hannibal in court of Antiochos III of Syria

192-189 BC Syrian War: Rome versus Antiochos

191 BC	Antiochos defeated at Thermopylai
190 BC	Seleukid fleet under Hannibal defeated by Rhodians
	Antiochos defeated at Magnesia by Sipylos
189 BC	Romans plunder Galatia
188 BC	Peace of Apamea (Asia Minor and Aegean divided between Pergamon and Rhodes)

186-183 BC Pergamon-Bithynia War: Hannibal's last fight

186 BC	Exile of Scipio Africanus
185 BC	Death of Scipio Africanus
183 BC	Suicide of Hannibal

181-179 BC First Celtiberian War

181 BC	Revolts in Sardinia and Corsica
176 BC	Final reduction of Sardinia
173 BC	Envoys sent to arbitrate between Carthage and Masinissa

172-168 BC Third Macedonian War: Rome versus Perseus of Macedon

168 BC	Perseus defeated at Pydna (end of Macedonian monarchy)
167 BC	Macedonia divided into four republics
	Romans plunder Epeiros (150,000 people enslaved)
	Polybios taken to Rome
163 BC	Final reduction of Corsica
157 BC	Birth of Marius

154-138 BC Lusitanian War: a long small war

153-151 BC Second Celtiberian War

151 BC	Carthage declares war on Masinissa

CHRONOLOGY

149-148 BC Fourth Macedonian War: rising of the pretender Andriskos
149-146 BC Third Punic War: *Delenda Carthago*
147-146 BC Achaean War: end of Greek independence
147 BC   Scipio Aemilianus takes command in Africa (tightens siege of Carthage)
         Macedonia made Roman province
146 BC   Destruction of Carthage (Africa made Roman province)
         Sack of Corinth
         Triumph of Scipio Aemilianus (awarded cognomen 'Africanus')
143-133 BC Third Celtiberian War: the fall of Numantia
137 BC   Roman force entrapped and surrenders to Numantines
135-132 BC First Sicilian Slave War: rising of the Slave-King Eunus
133 BC   Numantia falls to Scipio Aemilianus
         Asia Minor made Roman province
         Second triumph of Scipio Aemilianus (takes cognomen 'Numantinus')
129 BC   Death of Scipio Aemilianus (heart attack or poison?)
121 BC   Gallia Transalpina made Roman province
112-106 BC Iugurthine War: a 'dirty war' in Africa
112 BC   Fall of Cirta (murder of Adherbal)
111 BC   Campaign of Bestia (settlement with Iugurtha)
110 BC   Campaign of Spurius Albinus
         Campaign and capitulation of Aulus Albinus
109 BC   Metellus takes command in Africa
         Battle at the Muthul
         Siege of Zama Regia
108 BC   Romans capture Thala
         Romans occupy Cirta
107 BC   Marius takes command in Africa
         Romans capture Capsa
106 BC   Battle at the Muluccha
         Sulla arrives in Africa
105 BC   Bocchus' betrayal of Iugurtha
104 BC   Triumph of Marius
         Marius' army 'reforms'

CHAPTER 1

From emporium to empire

When Publius Cornelius Scipio Aemilianus, the Roman general who besieged and then burned Carthage, surveyed the wreckage of Rome's great enemy, he is said to have been moved to tears by the reflection that all nations, like men, were doomed to pass and that a time would come when Rome itself might be reduced to charred ruins.[1] Writing the history of nations is always about silencing voices. It involves drawing lines around people, excising connections between human communities and reading onto the untidy past the features of pure identities and immutable boundaries. The real life of peoples and cultures is usually cacophonous, occasionally choral, but seldom solo.

One of those still voices from the distant past is that of Carthage, the Semitic superpower that fought with Rome in a series of three epic wars (264-241, 218-201 and 149-146 BC), a titanic struggle that would lock the two cities into 'A Hundred Years War'. Probably the largest conflict of the ancient world, the Punic Wars, as history has named them, marked an important phase in the story of Rome and the rise of its world empire. Before the First Punic War, Rome was still a purely Italian power, not even in control of northern Italy; during the second Hannibal had destroyed its armies and overrun the Italian peninsula; after the last, its writ effectively ran from the Levant to Iberia and from the Alps to the Sahara. But what of Carthage?

Carthage, at the time of the first war with Rome, was the greatest power in the western Mediterranean. Its wealth was proverbial, with Polybios claiming that Carthage was the richest city in the Mediterranean world even when it fell in 146 BC, despite the fact that it had been deprived of its overseas territories after the second war.[2] Originally one of many landing sites and trading stations established by settlers and traders from Phoenicia, which broadly equated to that flat coastline overlooked by the mountains of Lebanon, Carthage had been founded even before Rome was only a huddle of huts and hovels squatting by the somnolent Tiber.[3] According to Timaios of Tauromenion the colonists pitched up sometime in 814 BC conveniently near the mouth of the River Bagradas (Oued Medjerda), having sailed directly either from the metropolis of Tyre, one of the leading mercantile cities of Phoenicia, or from the next-door colony of Utica.[4] The archaeological evidence is still short of this traditional foundation date, the earliest deposits found in the sanctuary of Tanit, the tutelary goddess of the city, belonging to 725 BC or thereabouts.⁵ Whatever the true date, Carthage was destined over time to take the place of Tyre at the head of the Phoenician world of the west, and to acquire sufficient power to become a rival on equal terms first with the Greeks and then with the Romans.

According to the Annals of Tyre, in the seventh year of the reign of Pygmalion (820-774 BC), his sister Elishat fled the city.⁶ Graeco-Roman authors (the most extensive version is told by Justin, who seems to depend on Timaios, while the essential outlines are confirmed by Flavius Josephus) later told of Elishat (Timaios' Elissa, Virgil's Dido) fleeing after her brother had her husband assassinated.⁷ The princess, heir to the throne together with her brother before the people elected the latter as sole sovereign, had married her maternal uncle, Acherbas (Virgil's Sychaeus), who was the high priest of Melqarth and fabulously wealthy.

With a band of loyal friends and her husband's riches, Elishat initially sailed to Cyprus, where the high priest of Astarte (Iuno in the Classical version) joined her, along with fourscore maidens destined for sacred prostitution.⁸ The voyagers finally landed on the site of the future Carthage. Granted as much land as an ox-hide could cover by the local Libyans, Elishat cut the hide into the thinnest of strips and laid them end to end so as to be able to claim far more ground than anticipated.⁹ Here we witness an early display of that deviousness that Romans considered a peculiarly Punic trait.¹⁰ This version of the foundation of Carthage, at least, satisfies the superficial inquirer, a version that for obvious reasons we cannot discount.

Apparently, the personal story of Elishat came to a tragic end. Justin tells us that the local king, Iarbas, fell in love with her and asked for her hand in marriage, the alternative being war. The doomed queen took her time, but eventually chose to immolate herself on a funeral pyre rather than marry the Libyan king, an act that protected her people and maintained faith with her dead husband. Her people, again according to Justin, elevated her to the rank of a deity, preserving her cult until the destruction of Carthage. The modified version made famous by Virgil, by grandly ignoring chronology, brought together Aeneas and Dido in a passionate love affair that ends tragically. Thence a later poetic elaboration, the love of Dido for Aeneas serves the purpose of emphasizing Carthage's strange and alien culture, its otherness. Still, the fiery relationship between Dido and Aeneas is one of the best-known love stories of antiquity, and countless writers, poets, painters, and composers have been inspired by it and its tragic end.¹¹

Whether or not the foundation myth contains a kernel of truth, and most myths actually do, the site itself was well chosen. It was naturally strong, situated as it was on what was normally a lee shore at the head of a promontory. On this promontory was a chain of sandstone hills, and it was these hills, running eastward and parallel to the Mediterranean coast, which provided the shelter from the prevailing north and west winds. The site's landward, western approaches consisted of the neck of the promontory, which overlooked a marine bay to the north and a small azure lagoon within a large natural harbour, the present Bay of Tunis, to the south. The presence of these shallow waters offered excellent anchorage and, in turn, their daytime evaporation gave the settlers life-giving salt flats.

The surrounding hinterland was fertile too, much of it being well watered by the Bagradas. A Carthaginian agronomist, a retired general by the name of Mago whose wide-ranging work on agriculture has reached us indirectly and in fragments, provides scores of methods for planting vines so as to protect them from excessive drought, for making fine wines, cultivating almond trees, grafting of fruit trees on to wild rootstocks, keeping pomegranates in clay for export, choosing the right sort of quality in breeds of oxen, and so on and so forth. Mago's agrarian ideal was the large estate worked in part by chattel slaves, procured either by piracy or through war, supplemented by free labour drawn from the Libyan peasantry, a model that was to very much influence the Romans.[12] When Mago lived is not certain, but in view of the already advanced agronomy of the late fourth century BC, he was from around that time if not before. At any rate, in all good time the combination of fertile land and scientific farming techniques was to bring Carthage a vast amount of agricultural wealth.[13]

The original foundation was probably what later became the Byrsa with its citadel, built on a rock outcrop that overlooked the celebrated double harbour.[14] The harbour quarter was soon built up into what became known as the Cothon, and Appian mentions buildings up to six storeys high arranged along three main streets that sloped up to the Byrsa from the agora. Diodoros refers to tall buildings in the neighbourhood of the agora too, adding a small detail regarding the narrow back streets hereabouts. As the city prospered it expanded north and west to form the suburb of Megara with, according to Appian again, grand houses surrounded by gardens and orchards, until the whole city covered, by the fifth century BC, an estimated area of some 37km in circumference.[15]

Excavations have revealed that the city was protected by enormous curtain walls, double on the landward side, the main one up to 40 cubits (17.8 metres) high by 22 cubits (9.8 metres) wide according to Diodoros, and studded with square, forward projecting, four-storey towers that, in Appian's estimation, were set at regular intervals of 60 metres. His statistics for the main wall virtually tally with those of Diodoros, 15 metres high by 10 metres wide 'without counting parapets and towers'. This was constructed as a casement wall with cisterns and magazines at basement level, stabling for 300 elephants at ground level, and above likewise for 4,000 horses and barracks for soldiers, 4,000 horse and 20,000 foot. Along its crenellated summit ran a wall-walk from which the defenders could discharge missiles and the like, while its projecting towers allowed them to enfilade assailants. Polybios corroborates these impressive landward defences, which had to be carried across the flat space of the 4.5 kilometre wide promontory neck. He, of course, had plenty of opportunity to see for himself the near-impregnable fortifications of Carthage when he was at Scipio Aemilianus' side during the final phases of the siege of the city. He mentions too that these high-lying double walls were shielded by an outer line, or *proteichisma*, consisting of a ditch and an earthwork topped with a timber palisade.[16] The three authors also agree in stating that the city, at least from the third century BC, was completely girded by walls. The existence of seawalls, again mentioned by the sources, has been borne out by excavations in the Magon quarter, which have turned up a line of powerful fortifications along the coast. Carthage would contain at the time of its destruction, so we are told by Livy, some 700,000 souls, though archaeology suggests a population density of no more than 100,000.[17] Nonetheless, this is still a dense population, which was clearly a reflection of the relatively advanced agriculture and surplus food supply that sustained the mercantile city.[18]

Culturally, the crowded, bustling new metropolis remained distinctively Phoenician in language and customs, the adoption of Greek and Libyan ideas not changing its essential nature.[19] It is clear that Carthage maintained a close link with the old metropolis across the sea throughout its history, annually sending to Tyre a seaborne delegation to sacrifice at the temple of Melqarth there, even after Carthage had grown in power and established colonies of its own.[20] The most typical image of the Phoenicians, which implied and exalted all the other gifts for which they were famous, was the one that showed them as indissolubly bound to the sea, undisputed masters of its lanes and secrets, both as expert and adventuresome explorers of the known world, and even beyond, and as effective and astute merchants. 'There came Phoenician men, famous seafarers', to use a single, lapidary line in Homer.[21]

Carthage was founded when the Assyrian Empire was at the pinnacle of its power and demanded huge quantities of raw materials to sustain itself, not least silver, which was now the main medium of exchange. According to Diodoros it was the far west, with its wealth of metals, which was the original objective of Phoenician expansion.[22] In fact, the Iberian peninsula represents the westernmost point of the Phoenician expansion in the Mediterranean, and although this was then the furthest known frontier, both Graeco-Roman authors and archaeological material show it to have been one of the first destinations chosen by the westbound Phoenician merchant venturers.[23] This means that we should not think in terms of an imperialistic progression in space, but rather as a mercantile network of ports-of-call established to service expeditions to the farthest destinations.

The ability to span the length of the Mediterranean appears to have come about because of the development of latitude sailing, which gave the Phoenician seamen, in their seafaring merchantmen with broad square sails and fat-bellied hulls, the confidence to probe open waters. Checking their position against the noonday sun or, at night, the Pole Star and the Ursa Minor constellation, which the ancient world called the 'Phoenician Star', the ships first cut across the Ionian Sea to Sicily. After coasting round Sicily, they set sail for the southern coast of Sardinia and from there to the Balearic Islands. The final leg took them to the southern coast of Iberia. Conveniently situated at the meeting place of the great western and eastern basins of the Mediterranean, the new colony provided a safe anchorage and supplies for

Phoenician merchant ships sailing east to west along the North African coast and for those making for Sicily and Sardinia too. So the early days of Carthage were spent in the usual manner of a Phoenician colony, namely serving the primary function of greasing the wheels of trade: purveying and conveying goods, in entrepreneurship (gold, copper, tin, and above all silver), and the occasional small affrays when the locals who surrounded it turned hostile.

Trade was more important to Carthage throughout its history than perhaps to any other ancient state. Initially most of it was conducted by barter with tribes in Africa and Iberia, where metals were obtained in return for wine, olive oil, cloth, ceramics and other commodities associated with civilized life. If Herodotos is to be believed, there was regular trade with the natives 'who live in a part of Libya beyond the Pillar of Herakles', on Carthaginian goods being exchanged for gold dust in a system which required each of the partners to lay out their wares on the shoreline and retreat.[24] Only when one partner felt that the offered goods displayed were fair exchange for what they had laid out would they take them.

Trade of this kind (silent trade, as it is called) clearly required the trust and honesty that would come only if both partners benefited and wanted the exchange to continue. The abiding principle was obviously equality and mutual benefit, with gain at the expense of another belonging to a different realm, to warfare and to raiding. An exchange based on mutual trust certainly contradicts the rather unflattering, or even downright villainous images of Carthaginian merchants as swindling thieves, petty shysters and profiteering pirates, which have been handed down by Graeco-Roman writers small and great. Being as they were in the opposite camp, it was only natural that they should put in a bad light, or sometimes openly disparage, their commercial competitors, not to mention the treatment reserved for their political and military rivals, who became the butts of every sort of scurrilous accusation.

If we were forced to place our complete faith in the judgements of these writers on the character of Carthaginian merchants and the epithets they cast at them, our brief journey back in time would certainly get off to a shaky start. To be sure, we could easily fall into the trap of demonizing the Carthaginians, accusing them of being well versed in the art of exploiting the natives (admittedly not a modern invention) by procuring gold on the cheap through profitable and unfair bargaining. But as Herodotos says in his lively piece on Carthaginian trade with the African locals, there was 'perfect honesty on both sides'.[25] Punic faith, to tell the precise truth, was distinctly as good as Greek or Roman faith, and we suspect that when Carthaginians acted this way, it was Punic fraud, but when the Greeks or Romans did, they were exhibiting Greek or Roman prudence. The black art of propaganda is not a modern invention either.[26]

Seeking new markets, voyages of exploration were undertaken beyond the Pillars of Hercules along the Atlantic coasts of Africa and Iberia, though there is nothing in the sources (or in the archaeology) to suggest that the Carthaginians, albeit giants of maritime navigation, were exploiting the tin mines of the islands known as the Cassiterides (British Isles). However, around the mid-sixth century BC the pattern changed. Initially Carthaginian imperialism rarely involved establishing state control, in a modern sense, over the outlying regions of the western Mediterranean. Rather, conquest was mainly about striking deals, paying off potential adversaries, and where possible turning competitors into clients. Under the guidance of one Malchus (*fl. c.* 580-550 BC), however, the city turned away from strict commercialism and began a systematic conquest of the surrounding region. Rome as yet was barely known.

Malchus is an enigmatic name: it means 'king' or 'chief' (*melek*) and thus may refer to an office rather than a person. In any case, Carthage's new career of expansion led to the subjugation of the indigenous North African peoples, called *Líbyes*, Libyans, by Polybios, *Afri*, Africans, by Livy, who inhabited the interior. At the same time, the smaller neighbouring Phoenician and Libyphoenician cities along the coast and up the Bagradas valley, of which the most important was Utica, were brought into its alliance. Livy describes the Libyphoenicians as people of mixed blood, half Punic and half Libyan, but this may be an over simplification.[27] In point of fact they could have been people of Phoenician race living in Libyan settlements, or simply native Libyans who had adopted Phoenician culture.[28] It seems probable that like the citizens of Carthaginian and Phoenician settlements, Libyphoenicians enjoyed a privileged position, Polybios implying they had the same laws as the Carthaginians while Diodoros notes they had the right to intermarry with Carthaginians.[29] But it also seems probable that the Libyphoenician cities were not always willing to accept the leadership of Carthage. The metropolis exacted dues on imports and exports, and there is evidence too that Libyphoenicians, unlike Carthaginian citizens, were liable for military service overseas.[30] Carthage also hammered out alliances with the various nomadic tribes (the people Polybios calls *Nómades*, Numidians, probably the ancestors of the present Berbers) of the deep interior (i.e. the more remote parts of Tunisia and Algeria), and these furnished auxiliaries for Carthage, in particular the cruel horsemen that, as we shall later discover, were to be the bane of many a Roman general.

The rule of Malchus and his successors marked a fundamental change in the attitudes of Carthaginian government, a change characterized by Carthaginian hegemony being ruthlessly established. The new African territory was based on a subdivision into districts (called 'lands' in Punic), which were put in the charge of officials appointed from the capital, while the new African subjects, we shall follow Polybios and call them 'Libyans', were treated as a conquered people, with few rights and heavy tithes.[31] They were also expected to furnish the fighting men that formed the bulk and backbone of Carthaginian armies. The cities meanwhile, though allowed to retain a titular independence as allies of Carthage, were forced to level their walls and surrender their foreign policy. Carthage therefore showed an indubitable capacity for coordination and control in the fields of tax collection and military organization. What it lacked was a unified grasp of the problems of empire and with it the ability to create a really homogeneous body of people, bound by the common conviction of being an integral part of a state that allowed some degree of political franchise. Unlike its future rival Rome, Carthage made no attempt to grant its citizenship to its Libyan subjects or Punic allies, the latter being treated as subject allies of course. This lack of corporate loyalty was to cost Carthage dear in the future, as a foreign invader could always find a certain amount of support from the local populace and the Phoenician and Libyphoenician cities, even if they wished, could offer little or no resistance.[32]

In the meantime, Carthage began to turn its attention overseas, and to establish what is best described as a grand maritime empire. As budding imperialists, the Carthaginians saw themselves as the rightful rulers of all the far-flung Phoenician settlements throughout the western Mediterranean, not only those strung out along the northern littoral of Africa but also those around southern Iberia and on the islands of Sardinia and Corsica. Our enigmatic Malchus, it is said, defeated the Greeks in Sicily and evidently subjugated the western part of the island, and then was defeated in turn in Sardinia. At this time Malchus was no tyrant but a removable magistrate, who in fact was deposed and banished for his failure, but he fought back and took Carthage, seizing the whole executive to himself. His rule lasted but a short time. Accused of tyranny he was put to death. Malchus was succeeded by another equally enigmatic character, Mago, who in turn was succeeded by his son Hasdrubal.[33]

As born seafarers and traders, the Carthaginians pursued a violent maritime policy to promote, protect and control trade, shipping and empire itself. Policy is not practice, of course, and so the instrument of this policy was to be a powerful navy, both to keep the seas safe from pirates and to discourage others from competing with Carthaginian merchants.[34] The state would provide protection for maritime trade and, in return, would receive a flow of revenue from increased trade and tariffs. It is about this time that we hear of the first established contact with Rome. A treaty (the first of three, in fact) was drawn up that effectually debarred Roman shipping from roaming the sea lanes to the west and established the western Mediterranean as a Carthaginian lake.[35]

From the mid-sixth century BC onwards, Carthage was an aggressive warfare state committed to the use of violence to maintain commercial predominance and territorial expansion. And so by the time of the first war with Rome it controlled the whole northern littoral of Africa from the silphium fields of Cyrenaica to the trackless blue waters of the Atlantic, partly through its own colonies, partly through having taken under its aegis other Phoenician colonies. Though numerous, these colonies were mostly quite small, surviving because the littoral zone was apparently otherwise sparsely inhabited. The eastern limit of the Carthaginian empire was at a place the Romans called Arae Philaenorum, Altars of the Philaeni (El Agheila, southwest of Benghazi), which marks the boundary between present-day Tripolitania and Cyrenaica in Libya. To the west, Carthaginian influence extended beyond the Pillars of Hercules and down the west coast of Africa at least as far as what is now Mogador in Morocco.[36] Beyond Africa, Carthage probably already controlled a few outposts in Iberia, which, like itself, had been originally founded by the Phoenicians, including Gadir (Cadiz) and Malaka (Malaga). In the Balearic Islands there were entrepôts on the southern coast of Ibiza, the best-known being Ebusus (Ibiza town), and there was a string of such settlements around the coast of Sardinia, including Caralis (Cagliari). In Corsica Alalia (Aleria), at least, was in Carthaginian hands, while the Lipari Islands were providing a safe anchorage for the navy. In Sicily, finally, Carthaginian power had been, albeit of a chequered quality, a feature for centuries.

Seafaring Carthage, now in the dawn of its career as a great naval and mercantile power, was a melting pot too, a down-to-earth, fast-moving civilization that attracted soldiers, sailors, journeymen, and other itinerants from far afield. Accepting many different cultures, it was by nature cosmopolitan. Yet at the same time it undoubtedly absorbed into its veins all kinds of African blood. With the passage of the years, the colonizing power was in turn colonized and something of a hybrid civilization developed that blended styles of life. The clear cultural line between Punic and native imagined by historian and archaeologist became extremely fuzzy indeed.

CHAPTER 2

Army and navy

It is a truism that a state's political organization and military system go hand-in-hand. Before we look at the army and navy of Carthage, therefore, it is worth considering the new Carthaginian constitution. A governor, responsible to the king of Tyre, ruled Carthage at first; whether by the seventh century BC it had its own king is far from clear. It is well known, as we have seen, that Carthage is linked, in the foundation myth of the city, to the figure of a royal princess, Elishat, yet Punic epigraphic sources always mention oligarchic-type magistracies as opposed to titles of a monarchical nature. In 574 BC, however, a most far-reaching single event took place when, after holding out for thirteen years, Tyre lost its independence to the new superpower in the Levant, the Babylonians led by Nebuchadnezzar (r. 586-573 BC). The Phoenician colonies were on their own, and out of the uncertainty Carthage soon emerged as the leader.

At any rate, by the end of the sixth century BC the Carthaginian constitution had become decidedly oligarchic in nature. Thanks to the curiosity of Aristotle, who very much admired it as a shining example of what he labels a 'mixed form of government', we know something of the governmental system of the city during the period of our study.[1] In point of fact, this was the only non-Greek political system treated by Aristotle in his treatise (around 336 BC) dealing with man as a political being and the nature of the state, the *Politics*. Interestingly, he knew of Rome too, but ignored that city. The stable government of Carthage was headed by at first one, later two annually elected chief magistrates called *sufetes* in Latin; Aristotle calls them 'kings'.[2] Aside from their judicial role, they presided over the ruling council, more of which below, convoked it and established the working agenda, and in this respect obviously resembled the consuls of Rome.

Nonetheless, unlike Rome, separately elected generals, invariably members of the ruling elite, held the military commands in Carthage. This separation of civil and military powers was extremely unusual, if not unique, in the ancient world, but probably arose out of the very nature of the Carthaginian army. A body of 104 men, chosen from among the councillors in office and referred to as 'the hundred' by Aristotle, scrutinized the actions of these generals, and a commander who failed in the field had to explain himself.[3] In fact Aristotle compares this much-feared, self-perpetuating body of blue bloods to the Spartan board of ephors, which, if the comparison is at all exact, implies it had a wide measure of control over all magistrates.[4] Anyway, if the commander's explanation was not satisfactory, the punishment was often crucifixion *pour encourager les autres*.[5] Conversely, a too-successful Carthaginian general might suffer the same slow agonizing death, simply because 'the hundred' feared he might use his success (and hired army) to overturn the constitution, just as the general Bomilcar attempted to do in 308 BC with the backing of 500 citizens and 1,000 mercenaries.[6] Yet this draconian treatment of their commanders was accompanied by a freedom of action while in command, which did give a Carthaginian general a chance to gain valuable experience, something not given to a Roman general. We also hear that Carthaginian generals were held in high esteem,[7] having 'the honour, too, of wearing as many armlets as they have served campaigns'.[8]

It was largely through 'the hundred' that the political elite was successful in preventing the rise of tyranny through generals manipulating the mercenary armies that served Carthage so well. While military service was obligatory for native subjects, it was not so for native-born Carthaginians, whose members were too small to support a large, regular citizen arm. Instead warlike mercenaries, down to the time of the second war with Rome, were hired from various western Mediterranean peoples and, ever increasingly, from the Celtic lands in the north. It was the enormous wealth deriving from trade and tribute that made it possible for Carthage to wage wars by proxy by employing others to fight on its behalf, a true privatization of warfare. By the third century BC Carthaginians no longer served in Carthaginian armies, except of course as senior officers and generals. The last recorded occasion citizen soldiers had served overseas had been when the victorious Greeks made a horrid slaughter of them on the banks of the Krimisos in Sicily (341 BC). But that is to anticipate.

Last, but by no means least, there was a powerful executive body, what Roman writers called 'the senate', while the Greeks used various terms, including *gerousia*, a council of elders.[9] It apparently had several hundred members, who probably held office for life, but whose method of appointment is uncertain. Nor is it clear what the relationship was between the 'senate' and 'the hundred', though it is usually assumed that the latter were members of the former. The powers of the citizens, however, were somewhat limited.[10] According to Aristotle, if the *sufetes* and the senate were in agreement, they could decide whether or not to bring a matter before the people, though Polybios records that the power of the popular assembly grew over times.[11]

Of course our knowledge of the civilization of Carthage derives mainly from Graeco-Roman writers, who usually make use of a terminology that is peculiar to Greek and Roman institutional framework, and from the results of modern archaeological investigation. Yet in the objectively positive words of Cicero: 'Carthage would not have held an empire for six hundred years had it not been governed with wisdom and statecraft'.[12] A fine tribute from a Roman at a time when the long and bitter struggle of the Punic Wars was not yet a dim and distant memory. Also, as we shall discover all in good time, some of the ancient world's finest soldiers came from the Punic family of Barca.

While the army of Carthage (more of which later) was generally of a mercenary character, its navy was very much a citizen affair, as was to be expected from such a maritime power. Unlike the army, which tended to be raised for any temporary crisis and disbanded when it was over, the navy of Carthage had a more permanent status with a pool of trained sailors to fight in its naval wars. The Carthaginian navy that reigned supreme in the western Mediterranean, therefore, was a highly skilled and professional force rich in knowledge of navigation and fighting at sea, which, by the time of the struggle with Rome, was built around the quinquireme as the standard fighting ship of the day.[13]

Ancient warships, which needed to move rapidly in any direction regardless of wind, depended mainly on muscle power. The quinquereme was so named not because it was propelled by five banks of oars but probably because the ratio of its oar-power to that of the classical trireme (which certainly did have three banks of oars) was 5:3. How many banks of oars a quinquereme had, and how many oarsmen manned each oar, is not known for certain. It is known from excavations of ship sheds at Carthage that a Carthaginian quinquereme was not much larger than an Athenian trireme, the practicable ultimate in the fast, ram-armed, oared warship (around 45m in overall length and less than 6m at the beam compared with around 37m in overall length and less than 4m at the beam) and thus similarly built for speed, long and narrow. It is therefore postulated that the quinquereme developed directly from the trireme.[14] Its crew, however, was much larger than that of a trireme (300 to 200) and it could carry many more marines: up to 120 crammed on a Roman quinquereme when fully manned for battle, and apparently 40 as a standard complement.[15] One suggestion is that there were three banks of oars like the trireme, but with two oarsmen to an oar at two of the three levels (i.e. arranged 2:2:1).[16] Since a trireme had a crew of 200 of which 170 were oarsmen, we would expect 270 of the 300 crew members of a quinquereme to be oarsmen. Thus, with an oar crew of 270 the quinquereme would have 81 oars a side.[17]

Such vessels were formidable in a sea fight, designed essentially to be highly manoeuvrable and capable of being driven by oars at high speeds for short spurts in battle, with the result that their sea-keeping qualities were not good. Lack of space in the hull for food and water, low freeboard, low cruising speed under oars, and limited sailing qualities lowered their range of operations. Hence naval engagements customarily took place near the coast, where ships could be handled in relatively calm water and there was some hope for the shipwrecked. Sails were used for fleets in transit, but when approaching the battle area the masts would be lowered and the ships rowed. There were only two methods of fighting, which placed contradictory demands on warship design. The first was manoeuvre and ramming. Theoretically, this called for the smallest possible ship built around the largest number of oarsmen. The Carthaginian navy with its minimum number of marines followed this naval doctrine. The other was boarding and battle. This called for a heavier ship able to carry the maximum number of marines, the naval doctrine adopted, as we shall presently see, by the unfledged Roman navy, which very much favoured an aquatic version of a land battle.

Whether boarding or ramming, oar-powered warships had to collide, and this tended to limit their tactical capabilities.[18] However, a numerically inferior fleet manned by good seamen should have had endless opportunities for the sort of hit-and-run tactics ably demonstrated by the legendary Carthaginian captain, Hannibal 'the Rhodian', during the First Punic War, of which more elsewhere.[19] For their class, Carthaginian quinqueremes tended to be light, swift and manoeuvrable, just as had been the triremes of the Athenians in the heyday of their naval skill, and Carthaginian oarsmen, like the Athenian oarsmen in the balmy days of their empire, were well practised in the intricate battle manoeuvres designed for ramming attacks on vulnerable sides and sterns, the *diekplous* and the *periplous*.[20] It is distinctly possible, as was the case in democratic Athens, that many of the poorer citizens of Carthage derived their livelihood from service as rowers in the large, busy imperial fleet. If this was so, then it may well have contributed to the city's political stability.

The famous naval installations at Carthage, namely the vast inner harbour as round as a cup, provided covered slipways, or ship sheds for around 220 warships and all the facilities for their maintenance. This military facility was a restricted area, walled off from the landward side, and its only seaward approach was through the outer mercantile harbour, whose narrow entrance could be quickly closed off by heavy iron chains if danger threatened.[21] In actual fact, both harbours were landlocked, artificially excavated basins. Modern, full-scale excavations at the naval harbour date its final form to the second century BC, during the years between the Second and Third Punic wars and before the destruction of the city by the Romans, although the evidence is not certain and it is possible that this was a period of rebuilding. Yet after the second war, Carthaginian naval strength was finally broken and Carthage was forbidden by a clause in the peace treaty with Rome to have a navy. Technically, therefore, the city had no need of a costly harbour to house and to furbish 200-plus ships of war. Nonetheless, the sheer scale of the naval installations is a clear reflection of the wealth of Carthage, and economically the Carthaginians do not seem to have suffered in the long run as a result of their territorial losses and war indemnities.

In the centre of the naval harbour was a round artificial island, the *Ilôt de l' Admirauté*, on which stood the admiral's headquarters, rising high above the surrounding facilities and fortifications and enabling him to keep a weather eye on the far horizon. Below the headquarters were thirty stone-built ship sheds. The archaeological evidence also reveals the slipways, mostly 5.9m wide and with a gradient of 1:10, built with rammed earth. In them socket holes placed at roughly 60cm intervals have been found, and these once held the upright timber staves that shipwrights employed to support the hulls of ships under construction or repair. A fighting ship was antiquity's most complicated piece of machinery, and artefacts recovered in the associated debris include copper nails for use in shipbuilding and terracotta moulds used in metal casting.[22]

Warships of this period were not 'Hearts of Oak'. For lightness and flexibility combined with strength, ship timber was mostly of softwoods such as pine and fir. Theophrastos, Aristotle's equally multi-talented successor, lists the three principal timbers for building ships as fir (*elatê*), pine (*peukê*), and cedar (*kedros*), the last having become more readily available from Syria as a result of Alexander's conquests.[23] Beforehand, in his trademark clinical tone, he had compared the fir and the pine:

> The latter is fleshier and has few fibres, while the former has many fibres and is not fleshy. That is why the pine is heavy and the fir light. Long ships [i.e. warships] are made of fir for the sake of lightness, whereas round ships [i.e. merchantmen] are made of pine because it resists decay.[24]

Elsewhere he says pine is second-best timber for warships because it is heavier.[25] The emphasis on lightness for ship timber is obviously a prime consideration in the overall design of a plank-built warship. However, one result of using softwoods was that its hull tended to soak up water like a sponge. Consequently, all warships, great and small, were manhandled out of the water as often as possible so as to dry and clean the hulls.

The hulls would not only become waterlogged and leaky, but they would also suffer from that scourge of wooden ships, the naval borer or shipworm, the maritime equivalent of a woodworm or deathwatch beetle.[26] Ancient shipwrights avoided using certain woods for the hull planking because they were thought to be susceptible to it, the larch particularly so according to the elder Pliny.[27] The hulls of stubbier, rounder merchantmen were as a rule protected by a drastic and expensive, but effective remedy, first by applying a layer of linen cloth soaked in pitch and then covering this with lead sheathing.[28] However, the additional weight of metal made lead sheathing highly undesirable for warships. Theophrastos remarks that the harm done to a ship's hull by the naval borer is impossible to repair.[29] Once hauled up in a ship shed, however, the caulking of worm-holes during the process of maintenance, and an application of pitch as a sealant, would have gone some way to remedying the effect of the naval borer provided the hull planks were not too much worm-eaten. Theophrastos explains the methods used to obtain pitch from fir, pine and cedar, and Pliny speaks too of pitch being produced from various trees and extracted by heat from pitch pine (*taeda*) for the protection of warships.[30]

Before we take our leave of the warship, a brief mention should be made of the *diekplous* and the *periplous*.

The *diekplous* was a battle manoeuvre involving single ships in line abeam, the standard battle formation, in which each helmsman would steer for a gap in the enemy line. He would then turn suddenly either to port or to starboard to ram an enemy ship in the side or row clean through the line, swing round and smash into the stern of an enemy ship. The top-deck would be lined with marines and missile-men at the ready, but their main role was mainly defensive. The primary weapon was the attacking ship's ram. Polybios, in his lively account of the sea battle off Drepana, describes it as such: 'To sail through the enemy's line and to appear from behind, while they were already fighting others [in front], which is a most effective naval manoeuvre'.[31] The Carthaginian quinqueremes executing this 'most effective naval manoeuvre' were well constructed, had experienced oarsmen and, even more important, the best helmsmen.

The *periplous* was either a variation involving outflanking the enemy line when there was plenty of sea room, or the final stage of the *diekplous*, when the manoeuvring vessel, having cut through the line, swung round to press home a ramming attack from the stern. Once the enemy formation had broken up, the *periplous* would have become the most important tactical option available to the helmsman. And so the *periplous* was a tactical manoeuvre that a single, skilfully handled vessel performed to make a ramming attack that did not involve a prow-to-prow contact. Even so, it required room for its execution, and timing was of the essence. It also called for high speed and, what is more important, smart-as-a-whip steering promptly supported by adept oarsmanship. It is interesting to note that Polybios finishes by saying that Roman quinqueremes were unable to perform these manoeuvres 'owing to weight of the vessels and their crews' lack of skill'.[32]

As far as the composition of Carthaginian armies is concerned, it is most probable that, at least at the outset, the core of an army was made up of citizen soldiers, backed up by levies from tributary allies and a handful of foreign mercenaries who over time became the main component. Carthaginian coinage came to be widely distributed throughout Sicily in the first instance, and later throughout North Africa and Sardinia, not only to check the economic power of the western Greeks but also to pay for those soldiers that were hired.

Citizen soldiers had been involved in the major events of the intermittent conflict against the Greeks of Sicily. A *corps d'élite*, which the Greeks described as a 'Sacred Band' (*hieròs lóchos*), was made up of solely of native-born Carthaginians (resident aliens in Carthage did not qualify) and was held back in reserve during battles, moving into action only when there was a possibility of defeat. According to Plutarch this noble band of picked citizens was magnificently decked out in ostentatious armour.[33] He talks too, of 10,000 Carthaginian foot soldiers bearing white shields who fought in the war against the Corinthian Timoleon. Here, we need to distinguish the citizens of Carthage itself from the Punic citizens of African and overseas cities. Diodoros, who in his history of his native Sicily is often at his best, says the Sacred Band itself consisted of 2,500 men, 'citizens who were distinguished for valour and reputation as well as for wealth', so that the remaining 7,500 'Carthaginians' were probably ordinary Punic citizens.[34] In this war the glittering Sacred Band was destroyed utterly, and after its second destruction three decades later, it appears no more in history.

Over the passage of time and according to the theatre of operations, Carthaginian armies became more and more heterogeneous as the deployment of Carthaginian citizens was gradually phased out in favour of subject levies and foreign mercenaries. We learn from Plutarch that Africa and Iberia were Carthage's great resource when it needed soldiers to fight its wars, raising most of its levies from areas under direct Carthaginian rule, such as North Africa, and hiring its mercenaries from places with which the Carthaginians had extensive trade links, such as the Balearic Islands or the Iberian peninsula.[35] So Thucydides, an experienced soldier, has his fellow Athenian general, Alcibiades, describe Iberian mercenaries as among the best fighting material of the kind to be had for hire in the western Mediterranean.[36] Even so, Carthage's recruiting officers sometimes went much farther afield, scooping up mercenaries from *outre-mer* regions that were noted for the warlike character of their peoples, such as Gaul or Campania, or where training and discipline formed the basis of military prowess, such as Etruria or Greece.

By the time Carthage was raising armies for its wars with the Greeks in Sicily they were principally made up of subject levies and foreign mercenaries. The great army of Hamilcar, son of Hanno, was recruited from Italy and Liguria, from Sardinia and Corsica, from Gaul and Iberia, as well as from the subject Libyans and Carthaginians themselves (480 BC), that of Hannibal, grandson of the aforementioned Hamilcar, had Carthaginians and Libyans too, stiffened by Campanian mercenaries that had formerly served Athens (409 BC). When Hannibal was preparing his return to Sicily in greater strength (406 BC), he sent his recruiting officers to Iberia and the Balearic Islands, and to Italy for more Campanians, who were highly prized. For his expedition Himilco, son of Hanno, hired mercenaries from Iberia (397 BC) while his successor, Mago (393 BC) commanded 'barbarians from Italy' as well as Libyans and Sardinians who were probably subject levies. In the war against the Corinthian Timoleon (341 BC), the Carthaginians used Iberians, Celts and Ligurians. For the large army mustered to fight the war against Agathokles of Syracuse (311 BC), Carthaginian recruiting officers hired mercenaries from Etruria and the Balearic Islands, while the general himself, yet another Hamilcar,[37] enrolled mercenaries in Sicily.[38] The last we surmise to be Greeks since the army was later divided before Syracuse into two divisions, 'one composed of the barbarians and one of the Greek auxiliaries'.[39]

In point of fact, after suffering a shocking defeat in the early summer of 341 BC, the Carthaginians fully realized the excellence of Greek armoured spearmen, or hoplites (*hoplítês*), as soldiers. The disaster in question was the massacre on the muddy margins of the Krimisos, less than 45km from Lilybaeum and on the Punic side of Sicily, where even the crack Sacred Band of Carthage was shattered and slaughtered by Timoleon's hoplite phalanx, the meat of which was made up of mercenaries.[40] Following the Krimisos the Carthaginians, in the words of Plutarch, 'had come to admire them [i.e. hoplites] as the best and most irresistible fighters to be found anywhere', and, according to Diodoros, it was after the battle that the

Carthaginians decided to place their reliance more upon foreign soldiery and, in particular, Greeks 'who, they thought, would answer the call in large numbers because of the high rate of pay and wealth of Carthage'.[41] At the time, of course, the other main competitor in the Greek mercenary market was the Great King of Persia.[42] For, like Persia, it was good, hard currency that allowed Carthage not only to hire mercenaries in large numbers, but also allowed it the liberty to hire the best on the market.[43] This, explains Diodoros, enabled the Carthaginians to win 'with their aid many and great wars'.[44]

Both Plutarch and Diodoros agree that it was the Krimisos débâcle, which motivated Carthage to look to Greece as a potential source of mercenaries. Both, too, report the city's utter shock over the fearful loss of so many of its brave citizens, Diodoros going so far to add that a decree was hurriedly passed, which curtailed the practice of sending overseas a body of citizen soldiers as Carthage had done to Sicily with fatal results.[45] Despite unexpected aid from the elements, Timoleon's victory was owed to the superior discipline and experience of the Greek mercenaries in his army. For, unlike bow-carrying Persia, Carthage had in its citizens soldiers whose primary function was to fight at close quarters in a well-drilled phalanx.

In their respective accounts of the battle, both Plutarch and Diodoros emphasize the fact that the citizens were well protected by corselets, helmets and large shields, and stelae (unpublished) from Punic Carthage are described as depicting similar soldiers in muscled cuirasses, conical helmets and round shields.[46] The conical-style helmet, usually in bronze, was a common pattern in the east, used by the armies of Assyria, Persia and so on, and an iron example was recovered from a second-century BC Numidian prince's tomb at el-Soumâa. Body armour in the form of stiff linen was worn too, since the traveller Pausanias saw three linen corselets at Olympia, describing them as 'the dedication of Gelon and the Syracusans after overpowering the Phoenicians (*Phoínikas*) either in a land or sea battle'.[47] Pausanias probably saw an inscription on the objects, which marked them as war spoils taken from the 'Phoenicians' (i.e. Carthaginians) by Gelon of Syracuse, perhaps at Himera (480 BC). Additionally, Diodoros says the citizen soldiers at Krimisos were armed with spears and, though we are uncertain of the spear's length in comparison to the long thrusting spear carried by a hoplite, Plutarch does mention that 'the struggle came to swords', which does suggest that a Carthaginian citizen was not inferior to a Greek hoplite.[48] For what it is worth, the above-mentioned stelae apparently show broad-bladed spears as long as their bearers are high, which makes the spear of a Carthaginian shorter than that of a Greek, the latter being fashioned out of ash wood and some 2-2.5 metres in length. In a sense the *dóru*, as the Greeks knew it, was their 'national' weapon. Others, such as the Etruscans and Romans borrowed it. But no other peoples used it with the confident ferocity of the Greeks.

It is therefore a matter of some significance that is was not until after the battle on the banks of the Krimisos that native-born Carthaginians would be held in reserve for home defence. In other words, from now on citizens were to be called to arms only in times of national emergency, as they were, along with the Sacred Band, to face the invasion force of Agathokles (310 BC), and again to deploy in the second line of Hannibal's army at Zama (202 BC).[49] Evidently Hannibal did not think much of the citizen soldiers who came out on this obligation, looking upon them as a cowardly lot, while in Polybios' considered judgement the Carthaginians made poor fighting material 'because they use armies of foreigners and mercenaries'.[50] Polybios is probably being rather too harsh here, for among the Carthaginians all the best men doubtless went to the navy, and the army, the Sacred Band aside, was the secondary service.

Returning to Agathokles' landing in Africa, it seems the Carthaginians, apart from those serving in the Sacred Band, who perished almost to a man, only put up a feeble resistance to the invader, and orders for reinforcements were sent to Carthage's general in Sicily, Hamilcar.[51] He shipped more than 5,000 men, and it is almost certain these were Greek mercenaries as we later hear of Greek cavalry in Africa, who were severely handled by Agathokles, and of 1,000 Greeks taken prisoner, of whom more than half were Syracusans, and presumably exiles from Syracuse.[52] Finally, many of Agathokles' soldiers, when he secretly sailed for home and abandoned them to their fate, made peace with Carthage and signed up to serve with the Carthaginian army.[53] For Carthage one of the key lessons of the Krimisos, though it is possibly more obvious to us in retrospect than it could have been to people at the time, was that it demonstrated the warlike superiority of the full-time hoplite mercenary over the part-time citizen soldier.

Jason of Pherai was no man to argue with; he had the backing of 6,000 hoplite mercenaries and he had personally trained this private army 'to the highest pitch of efficiency'.[54] The proof is in the pudding, as they say, for Jason now controlled his native land of Thessaly. Anyway, we shall pause for a moment and take note of our tyrant's views on the advantages of professionals over amateurs. Citizen armies, he is quick to point out, include men who are already past their prime and others who are still immature. On top of this, few citizens actually bother keeping themselves physically in shape.[55] The crux of Jason's argument is as simple as it is direct: mercenaries could be trained and then hardened through the experience of battle, they are in every sense of the word professionals. Indeed, experience, like a trade, was gained by an apprenticeship, and so professionalism was fostered because bands of mercenaries that had served together on a particular campaign, instead of dispersing at its conclusion, could hold together and move off to fight another campaign under another paymaster. The fundamental problem with citizen armies, as Jason fully appreciates, was they included soldiers who were likely to be inexperienced or ill-equipped both mentally and physically for battle, the central act of war. In brief, they were amateurs in the art of war.

Training and experience may have given the professional soldier total superiority over the armed amateur, but it also made him a social pariah. According to Polybios, the opposing generals at Cannae stood up and made lengthy pre-battle speeches before their respective armies. The theme adopted by the consul, Lucius Aemilius Paullus, was one of duty, the citizen soldier fighting not only for himself, but also for his fatherland, family and friends. Hannibal Barca, on the other hand, struck a different cord and harangued his hired soldiery not on patriotic duty, but on the wealth to be gained through victory.[56] Philosophically speaking, even if these two battle exhortations were rhetorical inventions of Polybios, what we witness here are two opposing extremes: the dutiful and honest citizen soldier versus the greedy and anarchic hireling. The truth, as usual, lies somewhere in between and, besides, if there were a thousand reasons for being a soldier, patriotism would come far down the list.

We would guess that these mercenary armies were singularly leaky, if we may use the term. Inspired by neither loyalty to a state nor devotion to a cause they were at the best held together by *esprit de corps*. However, though they were not a patriotic national army, but a motley, if not mongrel throng of mercenaries, treachery among the Noah's ark armies of Carthage was rare. One example from the First Punic War took place during the long-drawn-out siege of Lilybaeum, the most important Carthaginian base in Sicily, and involved one of those mercenary armies which were all that Carthage ever put in the field. According to Polybios, some of their senior officers, having talked things over, and convinced that the men would follow them, slipped out of the city at night to parley with the Roman commander. However, a Greek officer named Alexon, an Achaian, who had previously distinguished himself at the siege of Akragas, got wind of the treachery and informed the Carthaginian commander. Acting quickly, he assembled the remaining officers, and by means of lavish blandishments induced them to remain loyal to him. He then sent them to persuade their men to bide by their contracts. When the treacherous officers came up openly to the walls and endeavoured to persuade them to deliver up the city, they were driven off with a barrage of stones and missiles.[57]

The other example from this long weary war is the attempted betrayal of Eryx, the guerrilla base of Hamilcar Barca, to the Romans. The villains of this particular episode were a band of Gaulish mercenaries with an infamous career in robbery and treachery, which obviously fascinated our usually staid Polybios.[58] After having been driven out of their homeland by their compatriots, he says, these adventurers had been first employed by the Carthaginians as part of the garrison of Akragas, being then above 3,000 strong. This place they had pillaged as a result of a dispute over pay, perhaps early in the war, but presumably they had managed to break out with the rest of the mercenaries when the city fell to the Romans (261 BC).[59] Much later, as part of Hamilcar's command, around 1,000 of them tried to betray the town of Eryx, and when this ruse failed, deserted to the enemy, by whom they were put to guard the temple of Venus Erycina on the summit of the hill where the Romans maintained a watchful garrison (242 BC). Inevitably, they also plundered that, and as soon as the war with Carthage was over, the Romans banished them from the whole of Italy. Still numbering about 800, they were then hired by the good citizens of Phoinike in Epeiros, and naturally betrayed them, too, to the Illyrian raiders of the autocratic Queen Teuta (230 BC).[60] Meanwhile, the remaining 2,000, under their war chieftain, Autaritos, had returned to Africa and joined in the great mutiny of mercenaries (241 BC). Most of them were probably killed there in battle against their old commander, Hamilcar himself, though Autaritos escaped the destruction to be finally crucified with the other principal mutineers (237 BC).[61]

On the whole, the professional soldier was worth his salt until the First Punic War was over, and he would, by the time of the next one, supply the core of Carthaginian armies. Unlike a Roman army, therefore, a Carthaginian army was a heterogeneous assortment of races, and in the period of these two great wars we hear of Libyan levies, Numidians and Moors from the wild warrior tribes of the North African interior, Iberians, Celtiberians and Lustianians from the Iberian peninsula, deadeye shooters from the Balearic Islands, Celts or Gauls, Ligurians, Oscans, Etruscans and Greeks, a who's who of ethnic fighting techniques.[62] A Carthaginian army differed more from Hellenistic and Roman armies, based as they were around heavily equipped infantry either in a phalanx or a legion, than the latter two did from each other. Fighting with their native weapons, the mercenaries from the Balearic Islands were employed as skirmishers armed with slings, the accurate use of which the islanders were renowned for; their role was to open the hostilities, and then to irritate the enemy during the various stages of the battle.[63] The mercenaries from the Iberian peninsula, on the other hand, were armed with either the *falcata*, a curved single-bladed weapon much like a Gurkha *kukri*, or a straight-bladed, sharp-pointed sword from which the Roman *gladius* was probably derived, while those from Celtic lands wielded the long, blunt-pointed sword that was only effective in sweeping, slashing blows. The first were close-fighting warriors, the second adopted a much looser formation, yet both nonetheless carried spears and javelins. Meanwhile, the Greek and Etruscan fighting formation was the phalanx, a solid body of hoplites standing shoulder to shoulder with long spear and heavy shield.

As for the Libyan subjects, who already made up one quarter of Carthage's army in 310 BC and would be the foundation of the army Hannibal brought to Italy, some 12,000 of his 20,000 infantry being Libyans, we cannot be entirely sure about these.[64] Ultimately the official status of the Libyans was probably largely irrelevant, as their true loyalty was neither to their half-forgotten families nor fatherland nor to the distant paymaster that was Carthage, but rather to their comrades and to their commander.[65] All we can say for certain are that by Hannibal's day, at any rate, they were worse armed than Roman soldiers. Polybios says that Hannibal issued his Libyans with Roman war gear plundered from the booty of the Trebbia and Lake Trasimene, and Livy notes that thereafter they could easily have been mistaken for actual Romans.[66] But does this mean the Libyans re-equipped themselves only with Roman helmets, body armour, greaves and *scuta*, or did they take *pila* and *gladii* too? If the later, then we have to assume the Libyans were primarily trained, like Roman legionaries, as swordsmen, since it is unlikely that Hannibal would have risked retraining his best infantry in the course of a campaign.[67] Besides, extensive, uninterrupted training time was a luxury which the Libyans simply did not have.

Tentative evidence against their adoption of Roman weaponry comes from Plutarch, in a passage referring to a period after the assumption of Roman legionary equipment, when he says 'Carthaginians were not trained in throwing the javelin and carried only short spears for hand-to-hand fighting'.[68] In other words, just prior to contact with Roman legionaries, Carthaginian spearmen would have to endure a lethal hail of *pila* to which they had no response. However, we quickly notice that in this particular passage Plutarch makes reference only to the *pilum*, not to the *gladius*. Prior to Italy the Libyans had fought in Iberia under the Barca family for nigh on two decades, and it is possible that they had adopted a very efficient Iberian cut-and-thrust sword from which it is believed the Roman *gladius* developed.[69] This was a straight-bladed weapon with parallel edges and a tapered, sharp point. Hannibal's Libyans at Cannae were 'veteran troops of long training', says Frontinus, 'for as hardly anything but a trained army, responsive to every direction, can carry out this sort of tactics'.[70] He of course is referring to Hannibal's celebrated double envelopment.[71] In other words, whatever they were originally, namely subject levies or hired mercenaries, the Libyans had grown old in the service of the Barca family and were now professional soldiers serving in a private army.

One of the popular assumptions of modern European military history has been that national forces are superior in most respects to those composed of foreign mercenaries who, after all, are singularly indifferent about their nationality. Twentieth-century warfare democratized armies. The old pre-machine gun armies had been composed of volunteers (viz. patriotic soldiers) and mercenaries (viz. paid soldiers). After August 1914, Everyman went to war.[72] Henceforth the term 'mercenary' has acquired an unflattering connotation in most, if not all, European languages because it suggests someone incapable of elevated sentiments, such as loyalty to a cause, but who acts in his own interests.[73] Thus the mistaken belief that loyalty, and other such patriotic pretensions, gives the citizen army courage and determination that no mere mercenary army could hope to emulate.

We are not surprised, therefore, to find that it is almost an article of faith among western-style democracies to view mercenary armies as little more than dangerous congregations of footloose ruffians, foreign murderers even, with soldierly skills who could be faithful only to their greed. This is a prejudice that certainly goes as far back as the polemic writings of Isokrates, if not before.[74] Citizen armies, on the other hand, express national purpose and fight for national goals, which potentially make them more forceful and more flexible instruments in the hands of energetic and innovative commanders, less - in a word - mercenary. Nor are they likely to threaten the integrity of the state. Even so, constitutional governments, responding to the ideological dogma that their wars are waged in the name of a democratic civil society, have always been reluctant to send their own soldiers and often even to provide the cold, hard cash for low-level colonial ventures. In the case of France, for instance, its colonial officers were forced to recruit an army on the cheap in order to expand the boundaries of the empire and to garrison the lands already conquered. This meant creating an army specially tailored for *le tourisme*, as metropolitan army officers regarded colonial service, namely combinations of European mercenaries and indigenous levies. The existence of a separate 'two-army' tradition, however, is not unique to France: Britain, Belgium, Holland, Spain and Portugal have all used colonial and white mercenary armies in their imperial ventures outside of Europe.[75] Such armies were not only useful, but also, at times, utterly disposable.

As a prelude to his account of the Battle of Mantineia (207 BC), Polybios muses upon what he considers the fundamental differences in combat motivation for those mercenaries who serve for hire in a democracy, and those mercenaries who fight on behalf of a tyrant, the two ends of the political spectrum if you will. The crux of Polybios' argument is that a democracy, once it has destroyed those who conspire against it, will no longer need the services of its mercenaries.[76] As far as the ordinary rank-and-file mercenary was concerned, it was need and not greed that had forced him into his risk-ridden profession. From his standpoint, of course, serving a tyrant would seem preferable to defending a democracy. For the employers, on the other hand, the professional mercenary was a handy commodity that could provide unbiased support in the quest for power. There were occasions, however, when the mercenary was little more than a pawn on a political chessboard where mightier pieces struggled so as to dominate the game. As such, he was expendable.

The universal mercenary as a commodity is an obvious cat's-paw to secure a political goal of one form or another. Thus, in the ancient Mediterranean world, hired bands of mercenaries were readily available tools that monarchs, tyrants, plutocracies, and even democracies could seek and exploit in their quest for dominance. So no matter how objectionable the hired foreigner might be to the moralists, he could at least be trusted to serve as long as he was regularly paid. Besides, a mercenary was too busy to judge, and too hard-headed. He did not care for philosophy nor care for the quarrels of sovereigns or states; they will not fill his belly or stop a swinging sword. Anyway, as it always happens with fusty moralists, their opinions fell on deaf ears, and state governments, whatever their colour, continued to regard the hired foreigner's professional services a necessity during prolonged periods of conflict, the first two Punic wars being a notable example of this phenomenon where for Carthage, with its powerful navy in being, the ability to mobilize a mercenary army in a crisis was a clearly perceived necessity.

ELEPHANTS OF WAR

In war the elephant's major function was to terrify the opposition, fear being the beast's strongest weapon, and to wreak as much destruction as possible. They were used in two basic ways on the battlefield: as a screen against cavalry, horses, unless specially trained, disliking the sight, sound and smell of elephants; and to attack infantry, not least by offering a higher platform from which missiles could be launched. In these tactical roles the elephant was not conspicuously successful and its offensive promise never lived up to expectations. It was too vulnerable to missile weapons. It was also too slow, and well-trained infantry could successfully deal with them, and their tendency to run amok when panicked could wreak as much havoc among their friends as among their foes.

Certainly escorting infantry was deployed in elephant units. This was to try and prevent light-armed troops from getting too close to an elephant and hamstringing it. The *Mahavamsa*, a Buddhist chronicle from Tamraparni (later Ceylon, now Sri Lanka), has the war elephant burdened with no less than a dozen men, and an anonymous ancient commentator sensibly explains this as four riders and eight foot soldiers, 'two looking after each foot'. The weapons of the escort are described as bows, spears, javelins, axes, maces, clubs and swords, a pretty heavily-armed mob by the sound of it. Likewise, the *Mahâbhârata*, one of the founding epics of Indian culture, makes mention of seven riders, 'two held the goads, two were excellent archers, two fine swordsmen . . . while one held spear and flag'.[77] This, if not mere poetical fantasy, may easily derive from confusing escorting infantry with the crew onboard. In fact according to Megathenes, the Greek envoy sent by Seleukos of Syria to the Indian court of Chandragupta Maurya, an elephant 'carries three fighting men of whom two shoot from the side while one shoots from behind. There is a fourth man who carries in his hand the goad'.[78]

The pachyderm was first encountered in combat by the Macedonians at Gaugamela (331 BC), the third and final fray between Alexander the Great and Dareios III of Persia, and at the Hydaspes (326 BC), the bloody victory over Porus, elephants and all.[79] Alexander had well more than a hundred of them when he returned from India, but he died soon after and so it was left to his warring generals to incorporate these strange, imposing beasts into the military art of the period. These pugnacious gentlemen became inordinately fond of war elephants, developing large herds of them as part of a pre-industrial arms race. Elephants were imported from India, and the Seleukids of Syria had their own stud farm at Apamea on the Euphrates and bred them specifically for war, while their princely rivals, the Ptolemies of Egypt, founded a market town on the African side of the Red Sea called Ptolemais Theron, Ptolemais of the Beasts, to be the base for the hunters sent out to round up these valuable four-footed war machines.[80] In the quest for decisive victory against each other, between 321 BC and 217 BC elephants were used at least seven times in major battles between the Successors and, in a militaristic sense, the third century BC saw the rise and fall of the use of the elephant in the Mediterranean world.[81] Thus by the time of Hannibal, though the elephant was to reach the pinnacle of its fame when it crossed the snow-clad Alps, its heyday had come and gone.[82]

Anyway, after having witnessed Pyrrhos in action, the Carthaginians had added the elephant to their armoury, the forest elephant (*Loxodonta africana cyclotis*) to be precise, a breed that was still native along parts of North Africa, including, as Herodotos knew, on the coast of Mauretania.[83] It was systematically hunted out of existence there during the Roman period, the arenas being a vast consumer of wild animals, but was still to be seen until comparatively recently in the Gambia.[84] The African forest elephant was 2.15-2.45m tall at the shoulder, shorter in stature than the Indian elephant at up to 3.1m, and much smaller than the great bush elephant of present-day central Africa, not used in war, which can be up to 4m though 3.5m is the norm. In brief, the African bush elephant is larger than the Indian elephant (*Elephas maximus*), but the Indian is larger than the African forest elephant. Other differences between the subspecies include the African's more strongly segmented trunk, ending in two 'fingers' rather than one, and the line of its back is concave, whereas the Indian's is convex. The forest elephant also has ears with enormous flaps and rounded lobes, and little straight tusks. According to Polybios, a man who knew his elephants, at the Battle of Raphia near Gaza (217 BC) most of the Ptolemaic elephants 'shirked the fight, as African elephants are wont to do, because they cannot bear the smell and trumpeting of the Indian elephant. Furthermore, I believe that they are dismayed by the greater size and strength of the Indian elephants, with the result that they run away'.[85]

It is because of its small stature that the forest elephant did not carry the howdah as did the Indian elephants of Pyrrhos, but only their drivers: there is no real evidence as to whether they carried soldiers apart from the driver. It was the beast that was the weapon, though some would argue that Carthaginian (and Numidian) elephants were equipped with howdahs. But here I favour the arguments of Scullard, who has pointed out the lack of textual references to them.[86] We also have the occasional Punic silver coins from Hannibal's time depicting elephants with a driver only. This driver, who was probably brought especially from India in the early days, managed his charge, sitting astride its neck, armed only with a special hook.[87] Eventually, however, as part of their equipment they were provided with a mallet and sharp chisel with which to pole-axe their beasts, by a swift blow to the base of the skull, if they went into reverse and ran amok, as were the ten drivers of Hasdrubal Barca at the Metaurus (207 BC).[88] Obviously fielding elephants must have been something of a gamble, and this innovation was introduced by Hasdrubal himself to counter the chief danger of using them, yet some 300 elephants could be housed in the purpose-built stables within the thickness of the main landward wall of Carthage.[89] It is believed that the elephant superseded the chariot as a terror weapon in Carthaginian armies, four-horse chariots having been mobilized against Timoleon in Sicily when they exercised a disruptive effect on the Greek cavalry at the Krimisos (341 BC). They were mobilized once more to face Agathokles (310 BC), and thereafter they drop out of use.[90]

The Carthaginians probably used elephants for the first time at Akragas (262 BC), and the fact that they deployed them in the second line suggests they were somewhat unsure how best to use them.[91] Elephants were to play a large part in the defeat of Regulus' army in Africa (255 BC), when at Tunis Xanthippos, a general well versed in the Hellenistic art of war, used some hundred of them in a hell-for-leather charge to open the battle.[92] Probably his Carthaginian counterparts took good heed, and as a result elephants were greatly feared until Lucius Caecilius Metellus defeated a Punic army containing perhaps as many as 140 of them before Panormus (250 BC), this being the largest number known.[93] At the Trebbia (218 BC) Hannibal initially used his elephants to scare the Roman cavalry, but when they were driven off by the Roman *velites* he rallied his beasts and successfully launched them against Rome's Gallic allies.[94] At Zama (202 BC) he had eighty elephants, and he used them once again to open the battle with a rush attack, which mauled the *velites* but made little impression on the heavier legionaries.[95] None were used after Zama.

For their part, the Romans, though they fielded sixteen of the expensive monsters at Magnesia-by-Sipylos (190 BC), did not seem to bother with them much. Those, for instance, which Metellus had rounded up outside Panormus were shipped home to eventually be slaughtered before the spectators in the circus.[96] Thereafter the Caecilii Metelli adopted the elephant as a kind of family emblem, which was often used on coins issued by members of the family who became officials at the state mint.

CHAPTER 3

First contact

The Carthaginians had commercial interests in Etruria (low-cost iron and copper) and had combined with the Etruscans to challenge the Greeks of Massalia (Latin Massilia, modern Marseilles) in a naval engagement off Corsica in 535 BC, thereby preventing them from establishing themselves at Alalia (Aleria) on the east coast of the island.[1] This was also the end of the Greek dream of tapping into the Iberian copper and silver trade, with the river the Greeks knew as the Iber (Latin Iberus, modern Ebro) becoming the effective dividing line between Carthaginian and Greek (i.e. Massiliote) spheres. Archaeological excavations in a sanctuary at Pyrgi (Santa Severa), the port of the Etruscan city of Caere, have uncovered three gold plaques inscribed, two in Etruscan and one in Punic, with a dedication made to the Semitic mother-goddess Astarte and her Etruscan equivalent, Uni, by the ruler of Caere. They can be dated early in the fifth century BC.

This evidence gives us the context for the first of three treaties made between Rome and Carthage before the First Punic War. Dated, according to Polybios, to the beginning of the Republic and twenty-eight years before Xerxes' invasion of Greece (i.e. 508 BC), our Greek historian had difficulty reading this fascinating document on which he found the date because of its archaic Latin, which 'differs from the modern so much that it can only partially be made out'.[2] To the best of his understanding it said the Romans and their allies must not sail beyond the Fair Promontory unless forced to do so by storm or by enemies, and that they must follow certain regulations if they want to trade in Africa or Sardinia, though not with Carthaginian Sicily, where they enjoyed equal rights with others. The Carthaginians, for their part, agreed not to injure any Latin community or to establish a fort in Latin territory. Polybios tells us that the Fair Promontory, *Pulchri Promontorium* to the Romans, was on the African coast, lying 'immediately to the front of Carthage to the north', in other words the modern Cap Farina or Rass Sidi Ali el Mekki, the western horn flanking the Gulf of Tunis, the eastern one being Cap Bon or Rass Adder, the ancient Hermaia Promontory.[3]

Polybios says the treaty names praetors but neither a king nor two consuls, while the spheres of influence defined for both Carthage and Rome only fit this period (viz. the first years of the Republic) and Carthaginian interest in the area has been confirmed by the Pyrgi inscriptions. So the treaty of 508 BC was precisely drawn up to delimit the sphere of commercial activities of the Romans, who were excluded from trading along the African coast west of Carthage. More important, the actual conditions of the treaty give us a vivid glimpse into the way that the Carthaginians tried to exercise economic control in the western Mediterranean.

In 348 BC the Romans and their allies made a second treaty with Carthage and its allies, also reported but not dated by Polybios.[4] The terms of this treaty bound both sides not to harm the friends or allies of either, and again regulated the circumstances in which the Romans could trade in Carthaginian territory, but also adds southern Iberia to the original exclusion zone. The Romans are also prevented from marauding along the North African coast, implying those Phoenician cities such as Utica was now within the Carthaginian sphere, and if the Carthaginians capture any city in Latium, which is not subject to Rome, they may keep the captives and the booty, but must hand over the city. The advantage in the treaty again seems to lie with Carthage as the dominant power.

All this time the real enemies of the Carthaginians were the Greeks, and the real reason for this, as we shall soon discover, is not difficult to appreciate, namely the island of Sicily. A third and final treaty reported by Polybios was made at the time of the Pyrrhic War (280-275 BC) and 'before the Carthaginians had begun their war for Sicily'.[5] This probably places the signing of the treaty after Pyrrhos' two victories at Herakleia (280 BC) and Asculum (279 BC) when the Carthaginians must have feared that the 'elephant king' would cross to Sicily, as he would in the following year when he would almost drive them out of the island. In the treaty both sides confirmed their previous agreements, and added that if they should make an alliance against Pyrrhos each side shall provide help to the other, the Carthaginians especially by sea. The chief interest of the treaty, from our point of view, is the total lack of Roman naval forces it implies. This situation continued until the outbreak of the First Punic War.

So in 279 BC relations between Rome and Carthage (more friends than rivals) were reasonably good, albeit under a common threat. But following Pyrrhos' withdrawal from Italy after his defeat at Malventum (275 BC), the Romans planted two Latin colonies, Cosa and Paestum, on the west coast of the peninsula (273 BC). Was Rome afraid of Carthaginian seapower? To return to the third treaty, according to Justin, the Carthaginians despatched one Mago with 120 ships (Valerius Maximus says 130) to aid the Romans, but the Senate, while expressing their thanks, rejected the aid, whereupon Mago sailed away to negotiate with Pyrrhos.[6] This treaty between Carthage and Rome would thus appear to have been negotiated after these events; 'perhaps', as Lazenby says, 'after Pyrrhos had rejected some offer by Mago'.[7] It appears Mago had made his point. The 120 warships could be thrown into either scale.

North from Carthage, across 140km of water, lay the triangular-shaped island of Sicily, the key to the western Mediterranean as it commanded the narrow sea between the toe of Italy and the northernmost tip of the North African coast.

Initially, Carthage had not been strong enough nor even interested in acquiring the island, despite its good harbours and its fecundity. To quote Thucydides on the pre-Greek settlers of Sicily:

> There were also Phoenicians living all around Sicily. The Phoenicians occupied the headlands and small islands off the coast and used them as posts for trading with the Sicels. But when the Greeks began to come in by sea in great numbers, the Phoenicians abandoned most of their settlements and concentrated on the towns of Motya, Soleis, and Panormus, where they lived together in the neighbourhood of the Elymi, partly because they relied on their alliance with the Elymi, partly because from here the voyage from Sicily to Carthage is shortest.[8]

From his account, despite its brevity, we learn that the early Phoenician traders in Sicily were not forcibly driven to the western end of the island by an advancing tide of Greek colonists, as some scholars have held, but merely abandoned what were no more than trading stations. The value and accuracy of Thucydides' passage, in the light of archaeological discoveries, has become increasingly evident.[9]

However, sometime after 580 BC, Carthage was finally enticed into what would become troubled waters for it. As we have discussed elsewhere, the first Carthaginian army to land in Sicily was possibly under a general named Malchus. Anyway, whatever he did or did not achieve there, for the first hundred years Carthage was happy to maintain a low-key approach to Sicily, but the year 480 BC saw its first large-scale attempt at imperial expansion. Gelon, tyrant of Syracuse, was making moves to unite the island under his military leadership, and in doing so was menacing the Phoenician inhabitants of the south and west. Carthage responded, and despatched an expeditionary force under Hamilcar, son of Hanno, to meet this threat. In fact the Carthaginian armada was so formidable that contemporaries compared it with the host of Xerxes then being marshalled in the east. It was to suffer a similar fate. Hamilcar landed at the Punic city of Panormus (Palermo), only to be resoundingly defeated by Gelon near Himera on, it is said, the same day as the Persians were licked at Salamis.[10]

So great was the loss for Carthage at Himera (Hamilcar himself had died fighting), it seems to go into a decline over the next few decades.[11] The war was ended by this one blow. Carthage sued for peace, paid a large indemnity, and in the event, despite consistent rumours of invasions, left Sicily alone for seventy years. Meantime back home, the ruling Magonid dynasty was ousted from the executive and the aristocracy seized power. Relations with sub-Saharan Africa were strengthened, a region known for its gold-bearing rivers, and, most especially, Carthage fell back on the flat, fertile seaboard of North Africa, taking over a vast surrounding area for livestock-raising and fruit groves.[12]

In 409 BC, however, Carthage had recovered enough to intervene once more in Sicilian affairs. Under Hannibal, grandson of Hamilcar, a Carthaginian punitive force was successful in capturing Selinous (Selinunte) while the Greek relieving force was still at the stage of preparation. Next Hannibal broke into Himera, and having destroyed the city and slaughtered 3,000 Greek captives at the scene of his grandfather's death, took his army home to Carthage laden with much booty. The principal foe, Syracuse, was however still untouched, and three years later, a second Carthaginian expedition, again led by Hannibal, landed on the island to spread terror anew through the Greek cities. The Carthaginians, however, soon found themselves dogged by ill fortune. A 'plague' decimated their ranks, even killing Hannibal as his besieging army lay rotting below the walls of Akragas (Latin Agrigentum, modern Agrigento). Although his successor, Himilco, son of Hanno, succeeded in capturing both that wealthy city and Gela and defeating a Syracusan relief attempt, a return of the pestilence left his command so weakened that in 405 BC he signed a peace accord with Dionysios of Syracuse. The newly established tyrant was more than happy for the respite. Equally contented with the outcome, Himilco sailed back to Carthage with the survivors of his anaemic army.[13]

Seven years later Dionysios felt strong enough to renew hostilities with Carthage. The war was popular, and the Greeks began it with a massacre of all the Carthaginians and Phoenicians in their cities. Dionysios secured Greek Sicily and, the following year, marched on the Punic stronghold of Motya (Mozia). This well-walled offshore island fell with the help of a formidable array of siege machinery, including recently invented non-torsion catapults.[15] But this sparked off a new Carthaginian effort, in which Himilco not only retook Motya but also sacked Messina on the other side of the island and finally, after a decisive naval victory, drove Dionysios back to face a siege in Syracuse itself.[15] This expedition, however, also ended in a complete disease-ridden disaster and the loss of the entire army, which in turn sparked off a revolt by Carthage's African subjects.[16]

An agreed frontier was drawn up between the two spheres and an uneasy truce was to last over the next half century. But by now Sicily was an obsession. The astonishing seesaw continued when a third major attempt at its conquest was launched in 341 BC, and once again it ended in disaster and defeat. Yet despite this, the lack of unity amongst the Sicilian Greeks enabled Carthage to hold tight the extreme western end of the island. 'No land was more productive of tyrants than Sicily', wrote Justin, and it is generally agreed amongst modern commentators that the Sicilian tyrannies owed their outmoded existence at least in part to the need of a strong hand and central control against the Carthaginians.[17] Nonetheless, after the breakdown in the second generation of the tyranny established by Dionysios, the Corinthian Timoleon sought to purge the island of its larger-than-life warlords and their roughneck private armies, and revive the autonomy of the Greek city states. But though he was successful in beating the Carthaginians more decisively than they had been since Gelon's time, no long-term political stability was achieved for the war weary island. The liberty Timoleon offered was liberty in the old city-state style, and Greek Sicily had no longer the vitality to make use of it. Tyranny reappeared on the island.

In 311 BC Agathokles, whose dream was the complete unification of Sicily under thef aegis of Syracuse, attacked the last of these Punic possessions, but was heavily defeated and driven all the way back to Syracuse, most of the island falling into Carthaginian hands. In an act of sheer desperation, though others would argue this was true strategic insight, the tyrant loaded 14,000 troops, mercenaries mostly, onto 60 ships, slipped out of the harbour, and set course for Africa, hoping by this bold counterstroke to save the situation.[18] In this he was successful. Having literally burnt his boats, he defeated a Carthaginian army, conscripted in haste, which stood against him and thus was able to move at will through the fertile countryside and the undefended cities. Thence caught on the back foot, Carthage had to recall troops from Sicily to deal with the invader. However, Agathokles failed to take well-walled Carthage itself and eventually peace was made in 307 BC, which left the Carthaginians in control of most of western and southern Sicily.[19] Although Agathokles' daring African expedition failed, later it was to influence the Romans in the Punic wars.[20]

Carthage had one more foe to face before the curtain went up on the struggle with Rome. In 280 BC the Italian-Greek city of Taras (Latin Tarentum, modern Taranto), under threat from the Romans, had called in Pyrrhos of Epeiros, an outstanding mercenary warrior-king, to assist them.[21] His first bloody victory over Roman troops was near Taras' colony, Herakleia, after which he dashed northwards to Rome and sent his trusted diplomat Kineas to extend terms to the Senate. He offered to restore all prisoners and to end the war, if the Romans would make peace with Taras, grant autonomy to the Italian Greeks, and return all territory taken from the Samnites and Lucanians, Oscan peoples recently conquered by Rome. These terms would have severely limited the spread of Roman involvement in the south and have created a Tarentine supremacy there. He was refused bluntly and sent packing by the Senate, and he was said to have reported to his king that Rome was like a many-headed monster whose armies would keep on being replenished.[22] If this was true, then Kineas, erstwhile pupil of the great Athenian orator and democrat Demosthenes, was a shrewd judge of Roman manpower.

After this refusal Pyrrhos won a second bloody victory at Asculum, a ferocious two-day engagement, in which his elephants of war played a major role. Each one carried a tower, or howdah, strapped to its back as a fighting platform protecting two men armed with javelins. This is our first reliable reference to the howdah, and Pyrrhos may have invented it.[23] In any event, only when a heroic (or foolhardy) legionary hacked off the trunk of one elephant were the Romans said to have realized that 'the monsters were mortal'.[24] Nonetheless, they still terrified the enemy cavalry. Once again, the casualties on both sides were heavy. 'Another such victory', Pyrrhos is said to have remarked, 'and we shall be lost', whence our saying 'a Pyrrhic victory' for any success bought at too high a price.[25] As was becoming painfully clear, the Romans could afford such losses better than Pyrrhos could, as they had much of Italy from which to recruit, whereas the highly skilled professionals of Pyrrhos' Macedonian-style phalanx were irreplaceable.

In 278 BC Pyrrhos faced a choice: either to turn to Macedonia, where recent events gave him hope of the throne there, or else to Sicily, in keeping with his former marriage to a Syracusan princess, none other than the daughter of Agathokles, Lanassa.[26] While continuing to protect Taras, he chose to go south to Sicily where he now promised 'freedom' from the Carthaginians, who had high hopes of winning the whole of the island. For three years he showed no more commitment to real freedom than any true Hellenistic king and failed in his hopes. The plans of Carthage were indeed thwarted, the Carthaginians having been swept out from the island except for the one stronghold Lilybaeum (Marsala), but the autocratic Pyrrhos overstayed his welcome, and his Sicilian-Greek supporters, who were no keener to surrender their freedom to Pyrrhos than to Carthage, turned against him. On his return voyage to Italy he lost several of his precious elephants when he was soundly trounced by the Carthaginian navy, losing 70 out of his 110 ships, and he failed to win the third crucial encounter against the Romans at Malventum.[27] So Pyrrhos left a substantial garrison at Taras and sailed back across the Adriatic.

In the meantime the *status quo* in Sicily was restored, and the Carthaginians and Greeks were once again at each other's throats, oblivious to the world around. Pyrrhos' meteoric career there had prevented it from becoming a Carthaginian province, and on his departure he is said to have described the island as the 'future wrestling-ground for Rome and Carthage'.[28] At first, Rome and Carthage had reasserted their old alliances in the face of the new invader. But within a dozen years they would be locked in war, as Pyrrhos predicted. On and off, it was to last for more than six decades. As for Taras, its days of freedom were to be over. Three years after Malventum, in 272 BC, the Romans took control of troublesome Taras, allowing the garrison that Pyrrhos had left there to withdraw on honourable terms. Definitely crushed, its territory was confiscated and made *ager publicus*, state land. The plunder of Taras, according to the Hadrianic author and poet Florus, was enormous and its acquisition would be a turning point in the Republic's history:

> So rich a spoil was gathered from so many wealthy races that Rome could not contain the fruits of her victory. Scarcely ever did a fairer or more glorious triumph enter the city. Up to that time the only spoils that you could have seen were the cattle of the Volsci, the chariots of the Gauls, the broken arms of the Samnites; now if you looked at the captives they were Molossians, Thessalians, Macedonians [i.e. soldiers from Pyrrhos' army who had remained in Taras], Bruttians, Apulians and Lucanians [i.e. Italic peoples and Italian Greeks]; if you look upon the procession, you saw gold, purple, statues, pictures and all the luxury of Taras. But upon nothing did the Roman people look with greater pleasure than upon those huge beasts [i.e. Pyrrhos' elephants], which they had feared so much, with towers upon their backs, now following the horses [i.e. Roman citizen cavalry], which had vanquished them, with their heads bowed low, not wholly unconscious that they were prisoners.[29]

With the taking and sacking of Taras, continues the baroque Florus, 'all Italy enjoyed peace'.[30] Peace, however, would be short lived, as the Romans soon afterwards occupied Rhegion (Reggio di Calabria) on the straits of Messina, opposite Sicily. As fate would have it, the rival powers of Rome and Carthage were now face to face and about to cross swords.

THE ELEPHANT KING

The restless career of Pyrrhos of Epeiros epitomizes the age of Alexander's Successors. In spring 280 BC the king crossed into Italy and confronted the Romans for the first time with first-class professional soldiers who had been trained in the world-conquering tactics of Alexander the Great. He also brought another Hellenistic novelty: twenty war elephants.

But Pyrrhos was also a throwback; he was the last great rival of Homer's heroes. Like his cousin Alexander, he matched himself with Achilles, his assumed ancestor, and set off to fight a new Trojan War against the Romans of 'Trojan' descent.[31] The prince shone in the front line of battle in his ornamented armour and laurelled helmet. Yet he was no tinsel hero. He revelled in single combat and it is said that once, with a single swipe, he hacked a savage Mamertine mercenary in half.[32] But he was not just a heroic hooligan either. He was the most famous general of his day.[33] He wrote a treatise on tactics and a set of personal memoirs, and was later admired for his siegecraft and diplomacy.[34]

Nowadays, in the public imagination at least, it is Hannibal who is remembered as the celebrated user of pachyderms, probably first popularized as such when the embittered satirist Juvenal lampooned him as 'the one-eyed commander perched on his gigantic beast!'[35] As we shall discover later, this is something of a paradox, since elephants figured only in his earliest victories, the Tagus (220 BC) and the Trebbia (218 BC), and then, damagingly, at Zama (202 BC). In point of fact, Pyrrhos deployed them in far more settings, including the Italian peninsula, throughout his full and eventful career. In the west, he, not Hannibal, is the true 'Elephant King', and it is interesting to note that the Carthaginian genius classed Pyrrhos as second only to Alexander in his hierarchy of top-flight generals.[36] A similar sentiment was expressed by Antigonos Gonatas of Macedon, for when the king was asked who the best general of his day was, he replied, 'Pyrrhos, if he lives to be old enough'.[37] As Justin was to write later, 'all Greece in admiration of his name and amazed at his achievements against the Romans and the Carthaginians was awaiting his return'.[38] And return he did.

After Italy Pyrrhos ended up fighting first in Macedon, then in Sparta and Argos. In Macedon he replenished his elephants by a victory over Antigonos Gonatas, and then took them down to the Peloponnese. When Areus was chosen as king of Sparta, his uncle Kleonymos, who thought he had a better claim, went off to fight for Taras as a mercenary. Later, having seized Corcyra for himself, he signed on with the power most likely to help him to higher things, hence Pyrrhos' invasion of the Peloponnese during the spring of 272 BC,[39] but his attempt to place Kleonymos on the throne by force of arms failed. Later in the same year, while his stampeding elephants blocked the gates at Argos, he was knocked senseless by a roof-tile, apparently hurled from a housetop by the mother of an Argive he was trying to kill, and he toppled from his horse. In the confused street fighting, a soldier of Antigonos dragged him into a doorway and decapitated him. His head was brought to Antigonos, who was said to have rebuked its bearer, his son, and wept at the sight of the ashen visage. Pyrrhos' head and trunk were soon reunited and cremated with full honours.[40]

CHAPTER 4

Picking a fight

A fire that had been slowly smouldering for some time was kindled into flame in an unexpected manner. Following the death of Agathokles of Syracuse (289 BC), a band of his Campanian mercenaries found themselves discharged and without further employment. Instead of returning home, they decided to seize the Greek city of Messana (Messina), on the northeastern tip of Sicily within view of the toe of Italy, and to live as an independent community of brigands. This they did by slaughtering Messana's leading citizens and appropriating their wives and property.[1] Their position was further strengthened by a similar seizure of Rhegion, across the straits in Italy, by a force of Roman soldiers made up of Campanian 'citizens without the vote'.[2]

Going under the sobriquet of 'Mamertini' or 'sons of Mamers', the Oscan version of the pitiless war god Mars, the mercenaries-turned-brigands survived by harrying their small corner of Sicily, plundering the surrounding districts, Punic and Greek alike. Beaten but not exterminated by Pyrrhos, they were later defeated by Hiero II, the new king of Syracuse who, as a young general, had fought alongside the Olympian *condottiere*.[3] Thereupon, with their ill-gotten city now besieged by Syracusan forces, some of the Mamertini turned to the Carthaginians and offered to put themselves and Messana in their hands (265 BC). At the same time, however, another faction among them had sent envoys to Rome seeking protection as Campanians and so as 'a kindred people',[4] and they likewise proposed to surrender Messana. The acceptance of this appeal by the Senate was the spark that fired the train. The proximate cause of the First Punic War is thus clear, like the assassination at Sarajevo in June 1914, but it is not a circumstance.

If the fundamental cause of the First Punic War is not so clear, we do nonetheless have in Polybios' account some of the opinions that were supposed to have been aired in the Senate at the time. It seems in Polybios' view the overriding consideration in the minds of those senators who advocated acceptance of the appeal was fear, lest the island pass finally under Punic control and 'allow the Carthaginians as it were to build a bridge for crossing over to Italy'.[5] We have no means of knowing whether the Carthaginians had any intentions of interfering in Italy. Such information is lost to history. Nevertheless, Rome must have been sensitive about the attitude of Italian-Greek city states of the south with which it had so recently been at war, and there is the later annalistic tradition that a

Carthaginian fleet had sailed to the aid of Taras, which was still being held by Pyrrhos' captain general Milo, during the latter stages of the Roman siege.[6]

Thus Roman fears, though perhaps groundless, may have been quite genuine. It should also be noted that the acceptance of the Mamertini appeal did not mark any new departure in Roman foreign policy: it had long been characteristic of the Senate to accept such appeals, naturally, when it suited. The Carthaginians, for their part, could have avoided war had they been prepared to accept a *fait accompli* in Messana, but they must have calculated that if the Romans were allowed to interfere there, this might lead to further encroachment elsewhere in Sicily. At the same time, they had every reason to expect success: their navy could dominate the waters around Sicily and control of the island was ultimately bound to depend on seapower. It appears that the prime reason for the war was the mutual fear in both Rome and Carthage of the other's growing power, each believing their only long-term security lay in weakening the other's power before that power was big enough to pose a serious threat.[7] The potential for war became the reason for war, and once begun, it grew to such monstrous proportions that neither side was willing to back down.

Despite popular fantasy, fuelled by many popular books, it would be wrong of us to describe their first confrontation as an instance of big versus small, one between a gadfly (maritime Carthage) and an elephant (landlubber Rome). They were well-matched adversaries, capable in fact of coming to terms, as earlier treaties had shown. Polybios describes the First Punic War as 'the longest, most continuous and the greatest war of which we have knowledge', and the first round in the struggle between Rome and Carthage would rage for some twenty-three years, mainly fought out in the coastal waters of Sicily.[8] It was chiefly remarkable for the Roman achievement in not only building up a navy, but in winning all the naval engagements (Mylae 260 BC, Sulci 258 BC, Tyndaris 257 BC, Ecnomus 256 BC, Cape Hermaia 255 BC) save one (Drepana 249 BC), culminating in the decisive victory off the Aegates Islands (241 BC).[9] In fact this struggle at sea was the greatest naval war in antiquity, with fleets of more than 300 oared warships crewed by more than 100,000 sailors, and at the end of it Rome, a nation of alleged landlubbers, replaced Carthage as the most powerful maritime state in the western Mediterranean. This is a fact that is often forgotten, but partway explains Rome's eventual domination over all the lands of the Mediterranean basin.[10]

So the first war between Rome and Carthage was essentially a scramble for control of an island: Sicily. In 264 BC one of the two consuls for that year, Appius Claudius Caudex, was despatched by the Senate with an army across the straits into Sicily. This was the first country beyond the shores of Italy on which the Romans set foot, using ships borrowed from their *socii navales*, allies whose cities lay on the coast (especially those of the Italian Greeks) and were required to furnish ships, oarsmen and marines.[11] Having made a single, successful crossing at night, the consular army went on to defeat both the Carthaginian and Syracusan forces in a rapid series of sharp encounters.[12]

The following year Hiero of Syracuse dropped his alliance with Carthage and contracted one with Rome; from now until the end of the war the Greek king would provide Rome both men and supplies, and for the rest of his long life proved to be remarkably loyal. In any case, the immediate upshot of this new friendship with Hiero meant not only did the Romans no longer have to face two enemies at the same time, but they now had a secure foothold on the island. Alarmed, Carthage responded by hiring mercenaries, recruited mainly in Liguria, Gaul and Iberia, and focused its efforts around Akragas (Latin Agrigentum, modern Agrigento), a Greek city in southern Sicily and an important Carthaginian base.[13] Rome's countermove was to brutally sack the city, an action that quickly alienated many Sicilian communities.

According to Polybios, Roman policy was no longer one of just ensuring the security of the Mamertini in Messana, but one now geared to driving the Carthaginians entirely from the island.[14] By 261 BC Roman forces were winning the land war, but they were unable to take the strongly-fortified coastal cities by direct assault, many of which had sided with Carthage because of fear of the Carthaginian navy. These could only be forced into submission by starvation, but having no navy of their own prevented the Romans from blockading them by sea, even if the nature of ancient warships precluded a continuous sea blockade in the modern sense of naval power. In addition, Rome had been suffering from seaborne raids up and down the Italian coast and was unable to retaliate by doing likewise to the African coast.[15]

The almost impossible task of conquering an island without a proper war fleet was remedied by the construction of 100 quinqueremes and 20 triremes, all in the space of 60 days from cutting the timber; a Carthaginian vessel, which had run aground in the heat of battle, had been captured, whole and intact, at the beginning of the war and subsequently used as an indispensable model for the quinqueremes.[16] The discovery in a shallow stretch of water just north of Marsala of a Punic warship of the third century BC has told us, like the Romans before, a great deal about the carpentry and construction techniques used by the Carthaginians. The craft was entirely built of wooden components prefabricated separately and assembled later. This can be deduced from the presence of letters from the Punic alphabet on individual parts, and blueprints that must have been drawn for the shipwrights.[17] Though a ship's construction required expert calculations, it is assumed that its various component parts were mass produced separately with the aid of standard patterns, and were put together piece by piece at a second stage, after seasoning and according to need. Thus it was possible to assemble a large number of vessels at the same time, and make them seaworthy very quickly.

The Marsala wreck also tells us the nature of the timber used in warship construction, namely maple for the keel, oak for the ribs, and pine for the planking. But this has been dealt with elsewhere. The ship itself conforms to the eastern Mediterranean tradition of shipbuilding known as 'shell-first' or 'carvel'

35

construction. The hull itself is made up of keel, stem- and sternpost, frames, planks, gunwales, and beams. The longitudinal members are put together by use of mortise-and-tenon joints fixed by dowel-pins, brilliantly described by Homer in his quintessential sailor's story, the *Odyssey*, and covered by a stressed carvel-built shell of planks, namely edge-to-edge and not overlapping to give a smoother, faster hull.[18] The usual practice was to individually shape and fit the ribs inside the hull after it was completed: the reverse order of construction from that of a clinker-built boat.[19]

According to the remarkable story of Polybios, the Romans, having no previous experience of naval matters, then proceeded to train its greenhorn crews on dry land.[20] Naturally, the resulting ships were no-match for the more experienced Carthaginian navy; not only were the Roman crews untried, but their new ships were heavy in construction. Ever adaptable, the Romans decided to fit their quinqueremes with the *corvus*, 'crow', a mechanical gangplank that enabled enemy vessels to be boarded by lubberly legionaries serving as makeshift marines. This ingenious but simple device was clearly designed to enable the Romans, with their advantage in the weight of metal and of men, to turn a sea battle into a close imitation of a land battle and thus confront their adversaries with cold steel. This was their forte. Yet when we pause to consider, from the snug comfort of our armchairs, the class of warfare that lay before them, they, in fact, deserve our admiration for braving what was cooped-up fighting on an unknown element in a thing made of wood that might at any moment founder under foot.

Underneath the raised end of the gangplank was a heavy, pointed spike resembling a bird's beak, hence the device's nickname. The *corvus*, according to Polybios, who employs here the equivalent Greek noun *kórax*, was constructed as follows:

> On the prow stood a round pole four fathoms (7.3m) in height and three palms (25.4cm) in diameter. This pole had a pulley at the summit and round it was put a gangway made of cross planks attached by nails, four feet (1.2m) in width and six fathoms (10.9m) in length. In this gangplank was an oblong groove, and it went around the pole at a distance of two fathoms (3.7m) from its near end. The gangway also had a railing on each of its long sides as high as a man's knee [ie around 0.65m]. At its extremity was fastened an iron object like a pestle pointed at one end and with a ring at the other end, so that the whole looked like the machine for pounding grain. To this ring was attached a rope with which, when the ship charged an enemy, they raised the *corvi* by means of the pulley on the pole and let them down on the enemy's deck, sometimes from the prow and sometimes bringing them round when the ships collided broadsides.[21]

Some scholars have completely rejected Polybios' account of the *corvus*, mainly on the grounds that they would have made the ship top-heavy. These doubters have postulated that in reality the device was simply a form of a grapnel, as is suggested by some of the secondary sources.²² But Polybios' description is detailed, and there is no sound reason to question that the device he describes was practicable, especially so when we consider the viable working model of the *corvus* so ably constructed by Wallinga.²³

Following Polybios, therefore, we can presume that when released the *corvus* fell heavily onto the deck of an enemy vessel, the large spike embedding itself into its planking, locking the two vessels together. The oblong groove, which was cut about a third of the way along its length, allowed the gangplank to be swung around in a wide arc to fall ahead or either side of the ship's prow, depending on the direction of the approaching enemy. Once the gangplank was securely fixed in the other vessel, the Roman marines could swarm across, sweep through the doomed ship, and swamp its less numerous and less well-armed crew.

The new Roman fleet, under the *novus homo* Caius Duilius, set sail on the hunt and into the history books. And so it was that Duilius first deployed the *corvus* in the subsequent naval engagement off Mylae (Milazzo), on the north coast near Messana (260 BC). Here the Carthaginian fleet, overconfident in its seamanship and contemptuous of that of its adversary, was overcome in a blistering sea battle in which Duilius and his marines hammered the Carthaginians into submission with a loss of fifty vessels.²⁴ Duilius then sailed to the western end of Sicily where he landed his marines just in time to save Egesta (Latin Segesta), which was under siege and in the last stage of distress. At this point it would be worthwhile pausing for a brief moment and pondering a text in praise of Duilius' victory, which was inscribed on a monument erected in his honour and known as the *columna rostrata*:

> [Segest]ans[] he delivered [from blocka]de [all the Carthaginians and their gr]eatest magistrates in d[aylight after n]ine days fed from their camps, and Macel[a the town by force and s]torm he took. In the same mag[istracy good t]hings by sea as consul first (of all men) he d[id and forces(?) and f]leets of ships he first equipped and pre[pared] and with those ships the Punic fleets a[ll of them, and ve]ry great forces of Carthaginians, when [Hannibal] their dictator was present, he [defeated in ba]ttle on the high seas [and by fo]rce he [too]k ship[s] with their crews: one septir[eme] th[irty] [quinquere]mes and triremes [thirteen he sank(?)]. Gold taken 3,600 pieces [more details of the booty follow] [the first al]so he was naval booty on the people [to bestow and first of all] fre[ebo]rn Carthaginians to l[ead in triumph].²⁵

Fulsome in its use of boastful superlatives, the Duilius inscription superbly illustrates the fame that a victorious Roman commander could achieve in his own lifetime and, naturally, advertise posthumously. In an aristocratic society where personal glory counted for everything, enumeration was essential, just to make it clear how great your achievement has been. Thus, as can be seen in the most casual glance at the inscription, it boldly advertises the exact number of ships sunk, including the gargantuan *heptêrês* that Polybios says formerly belonged to Pyrrhos, and exact quantity of booty captured - objective proof that his victory was the best.[26] On top of this, Duilius had been the first in his family to gain the consulship, hence the appellation *novus homo*, 'new man', and the first in Rome to achieve victory on the high seas in a major naval engagement.

Rome was now a serious challenge at sea, and both sides displayed an outward confidence of victory. Fleets were commissioned and the expected showdown finally took place off Cape Ecnomus (Poggio San Angelo) on the south coast near Phintias (256 BC), 330 Roman quinqueremes under raised *corvi* sailed into action against 350 Carthaginian, the largest naval action to date.[27] Polybios claims the Romans packed 120 marines per ship, and the combination of sheer brute force and the *corvus* brought Rome a triumph. The price was the loss of twenty-four ships, while that for Carthage stood in the order of thirty plus ships wrecked and a further sixty-four taken as prizes.[28]

Encouraged by its triumph off Cape Ecnomus, Rome now took the important decision to mount a full-scale invasion of Africa, despatching the victorious 'fleet in being' under the two consuls Marcus Atilius Regulus and Lucius Manlius Vulso. Coming ashore near Aspis (Latin Clupea, modern Kelibia) without hindrance, the Carthaginians only having sufficient men in Africa to do no more than defend Carthage some 60km to the west, and the consuls soon forced the city to surrender. With winter fast approaching there was the looming logistic headache of feeding some 75,000 seamen, who outnumbered the soldiers of the fleet by threefold. Fresh orders from the Senate detailed one consul, Regulus, to remain in Africa with 15,000 foot and 500 horse, with a detachment of 40 ships to support them. This was probably a consular army, albeit below strength, since Polybios later mentions 'the first legion', which does suggest there was another one.[29] The lack of cavalry is best explained by the obvious difficulties involved in transporting horses by sea. Meantime, the other consul, Vulso, was to return to Rome with the bulk of the fleet, including all the transports.[30]

Early in 255 BC, having defeated the Carthaginians and occupied Tunis, Regulus was encamped within a few kilometres of Carthage, from where he dominated the surrounding countryside, the bounty of which provided his men with provisions in abundant quantities. Having partaken in the notable victory off Cape Ecnomus, landed successfully in the Carthaginian homeland, and pitched up outside their very capital, Regulus must have sensed glory lying within his grasp. All he needed to do was to push the already tottering Carthage.

Yet there was a rub. Carthage was still a formidable city to take by storm and time was pressing. In a society based on the pursuit of glory, as Rome clearly was, there is only a limited amount of glory to be had. Regulus' consular replacement could shortly be expected to arrive from Rome and thus snatch that precious glory. This would not do, so, according to Polybios, Regulus decided to negotiate with the Carthaginians, an offer which was gladly accepted. But with true Roman arrogance, he imposed too harsh conditions upon them.[31] The Carthaginians, therefore, decided to carry on with the war and sent recruiting agents to Greece.

There, says Polybios, 'a considerable number of soldiers' were employed and quickly shipped to Carthage. With them was 'a certain Spartan, a man who had been brought up in the Spartan discipline, and had had a fair amount of military experience'.[32] Xanthippos was a *condottieri*, and he was hired to reorganize and shake up the Carthaginian army.

In the late spring Xanthippos, who obviously excelled in his task, annihilated the Roman expeditionary force and Rome was compelled to send 350 ships so as to rescue the survivors of Regulus' shattered and starving army.[33] Off the African coast an engagement ensued, resulting in 114 Carthaginian vessels being captured. Returning home, however, the Roman fleet was overtaken by a terrific summer storm off Camarina and all but eighty vessels survived the tempest.[34] With this appalling reversal for Rome, Carthage bounced back.[35]

Stubborn as ever, as indeed they were, the Romans laid down another 220 quinqueremes, completing the task in three months, 'a thing', to use Polybios' words, 'difficult to believe'.[36] Yet, as he points out, the consuls of 254 BC were provided with 300 ships for an attack on Panormus, presumably the 220 new quinqueremes plus the eighty that survived the disaster off Camarina. Anyway, the combined army and navy operation was a complete success, Panormus quickly falling once its harbour was secured and its walls breached.[37]

During the campaign season of 253 BC the Romans crossed over to Africa with the aim of carrying the war right up to Carthage's doorstep once again. Unfortunately for Rome its fleet was all but lost when it became ignominiously stranded off the island of Meninx (Dejerba) on an ebb tide, the lubberly Romans saving themselves only by flinging overboard all their heavy gear, presumably including the *corvi*. But worse was to befall them. Limping homewards, they stopped off in Panormus, now in Roman hands, but instead of continuing along the north coast of Sicily, they rashly made a dash across the open sea for home and were caught in a storm; the losses totalled 150 ships together with their crews. Unsurprisingly, Rome now opted to concentrate its efforts on land.[38]

During the summer of 250 BC, Lucius Caecilius Metellus (*cos.* 251 BC) defeated the Carthaginian army attempting to retake Panormus. With this victory, the last set-piece land battle to be fought in Sicily during the war, Rome decided once again to take to the high seas; some 200 ships were hastily constructed and Sicily was occupied apart from the two Carthaginian strongholds of Lilybaeum (Marsala) and Drepana (Trapani), both situated on the westernmost tip of the island. Lilybaeum, the fulcrum of Punic military power, was subsequently besieged.

However, fifty warships under Hannibal, the son of the Hamilcar who had been one of the Carthaginian generals with Xanthippos at the victory over Regulus, sailed to the Aegates Islands and, having picked up a following wind, dashed into the harbour of Lilybaeum like some corsair on an afternoon foray. Here he disembarked substantial reinforcements and ample supplies, sailed out again unmolested by the blockading Roman fleet and proceeded to Drepana.[39] Thus the pattern was set, and another Carthaginian captain, the legendary Hannibal 'the Rhodian', frequently ran the blockade of Lilybaeum despite Roman efforts to prevent this, and despite the fact that the approach to its harbour was made doubly dangerous by the shoals.[40] Eventually his luck was to run out, the Romans having managed to take a Carthaginian quadrireme intact, which turned out to be one of the finest and fastest vessels that ever held oars. This they manned with a select crew and, packing on board a crack boarding party, the Romans overhauled and overwhelmed the slippery blockade-runner of 'the Rhodian'.[41]

Buoyed up by this success the Roman fleet now challenged the Carthaginians at sea. Publius Claudius Pulcher, one of the consuls for 249 BC, sailed against the Carthaginian naval base at Drepana, but was trounced when the commander there, Adherbal, trapped his fleet close inshore.[42] Amazingly, it was the only victory Carthage won on the high seas, yet this naval engagement ideally demonstrates the fact that the Carthaginians possessed the better quinquereme: lighter construction, therefore faster, and with better-trained crews who knew how to outclass and outmanoeuvre the heavy and clumsy Roman quinquereme. It is at this juncture that Polybios takes the opportunity to explain to his Greek readers the naval tactics employed by the Carthaginians: the *diekplous* ('sailing through') and the *periplous* ('sailing around'), the same naval tactics once employed by the imperial navy of democratic Athens.[43] If they had not done already, the calamitous result of Drepana demonstrated to the Romans that they had to abandon the *corvus*, particularly as it made their quinqueremes unseaworthy and sluggish, and this also partly explains their horrendous losses through storms.

Rome next sent ships to resupply its forces besieging Lilybaeum, and once again its lack of seamanship resulted in the complete loss of yet another fleet, this time shattered on the rocks off Cape Pachynon (Capo Passero), the southeastern tip of Sicily.[44] Once more Rome abandoned its naval effort for the time being, but continued its investment of Lilybaeum; eight years later when the war had finally limped to its finale, the city would still belong to the Carthaginians.

Yet Carthage failed to press home the obvious advantage it had gained by the destruction of the Roman fleet. At the very least we might have expected Carthage to ship troops over to Sicily to relieve the siege of Lilybaeum and begin the task of recovering the ground lost there. The other option afforded by its newly recovered seapower was to attack southern Italy, where Rome's grip was precarious. It is arguable that Carthage, unlike Rome, lacked the killer instinct. To Rome, wars ended when it dictated its terms to the vanquished: to Carthage, wars ended with a negotiated settlement, even Hannibal, as is told in the proper place, was later to think in much the same terms. The immediate problem for Carthage, however, was Africa. Ever since Regulus' landing and initial success there, unrest and discontentment simmered on the fringes of Carthaginian territory, which the savage reprisals immediately following Regulus' defeat will probably have done little or nothing to suppress.[45] But, as we have seen, this had not prevented the reinforcing of Lilybaeum with at least 10,000, if not 14,000 men.

There seems to have been a major shift in policy in Carthage. We know that at about this time the Carthaginian general Hanno 'the Great' conquered Hekatompylos (Latin Theveste, modern Tébessa on the Tunisian-Algerian frontier).[46] Since this lies at the furthest point Carthaginian conquest ever reached (it is some 160km southwest of Carthage) its subjugation was probably the culmination of some years of warfare, as Polybios hints when he says Hanno was 'accustomed to fighting with Numidians and Libyans'.[47] By 241 BC he was evidently the generalissimo in Africa, and judging by what Polybios says about his extortions from the Libyans, had been for some years.[48] It seems, therefore, it was felt by some Carthaginians, led perhaps by Hanno, that the war against Rome was as good as won, and that the time had come to consolidate and even extend their territory in Africa. One of the opponents of this African policy was almost certainly Hamilcar Barca. Everything we know about this man and his family, including his son Hannibal, and of Hanno's later opposition to them, would suggest this.[49] But if Hamilcar did push an aggressive strategy in Sicily, it would appear that he lost the argument.

It was in the year 247 BC that this venturesome and resourceful member of the Barca family entered the Sicilian arena. Not content to sit tight in Lilybaeum or Drepana, Hamilcar's intention was to take the offensive, but his resources were slim, limited basically to the existing garrisons within the two besieged cities. After raiding the Italian coast around Locri, he established a base on top of Mount Heirkte (Monte Castellaccio, 890m), an abrupt flat-topped hill 'lying near the sea between Eryx and Panormus'.[50] From this hulking sanctuary he maintained a low-key war, mounting guerrilla operations diversified with seaborne raids along the Italian coast, some of which took him as far as Cumae, in the hope of bringing the Italic peoples to revolt against the Romans.[51] Some three years later he would audaciously shift his base of operations to the nearby Eryx (Monte San Giuliano, 751m), just east of Drepana and, much like a sentinel, commanding the route from there to Panormus.[52] For a total of five years Hamilcar would remain a constant thorn in the side of the Romans.[53]

With both sides exhausted and almost spent, much like two punch-drunk boxers lurching around the ring, a stalemate had been reached. But Rome, with voluntary loans from private citizens, built 200 quinqueremes modelled on the captured blockade-runner of Hannibal the Rhodian.[54] The following year the consul Caius Lutatius Catulus positioned the newly commissioned ships off Sicily and, with no fleet in service outside of African waters, the Carthaginians were caught off their guard. Lutatius therefore took the harbour at Drepana and the anchorage ground near Lilybaeum, then spent the remainder of the campaigning season rigorously training his fleet for the inevitable clash that lay ahead.[55]

In early 241 BC the Carthaginians despatched a fleet, laden with supplies, its commander, yet another Hanno, ordered to join up with Hamilcar at Eryx. Here, having emptied his ships, he was to take on board as marines the best qualified mercenaries together with Hamilcar himself, 'and then', as Polybios says, 'engage the enemy'.⁵⁶ But Lutatius had other plans. Taking on board a picked force from the army, he stationed his fleet off the Aegates Islands, armed with the knowledge that the Carthaginians invariably approached Sicily this way. The following morning, despite choppy seas and the wind blowing against him, Lutatius formed for battle in single line abeam.⁵⁷ On sighting the Roman fleet, the Carthaginians, knowing they had to fight, lowered their sails and closed to engage.

There is some doubt about the validity of Polybios' account covering this crucial, final naval engagement, as he conveniently and very neatly states that just as 'the outfit of each force was just the reverse of what it had been at the Battle of Drepana, the result also was naturally the reverse for each'.⁵⁸ The Roman quinqueremes were of a superior design, their oarsmen highly trained, their marines the pick of the army, while their opponents' ships were heavily laden with stores, their crews poorly trained and hastily raised, and their marines new levies on their first voyage. The result, if we are to believe the usually honest Polybios, was a foregone conclusion. With no losses for the Romans, the Carthaginians lost fifty ships with a further seventy taken as prizes along with their crews.⁵⁹ Diodoros, however, though his figure of 117 ships for the overall losses is very similar, claims that only twenty were captured, and gives the Roman losses as eighty ships, thirty completely and fifty partially disabled.⁶⁰ If this is true, the sea fight was harder fought than Polybios implies. We may ask ourselves the one obvious question: was Polybios massaging the historical facts? Notwithstanding the problems of our principal source in this context, the Carthaginians decisively lost the battle and command of the sea rested firmly with Rome. Hanno got away to Carthage only to be nailed to the cross, while Hamilcar was left high and dry on Sicily and, therefore, was instructed by Carthage to negotiate the best terms he could with the Romans.⁶¹

The resulting peace treaty forced Carthage out of Sicily and it was also instructed not to make war on Hiero of Syracuse. Sicily effectively passed into Roman control; the western part of the island became the first Roman province overseas, while the eastern part remained under the rule of Hiero until his death (215 BC). In addition, Carthage had to surrender the islands, including the Aegates, between Sicily and Italy, and was condemned to pay over to Rome 3,200 Euboian talents of silver, 1,000 payable immediately, the balance over a period of ten years.⁶² It was a chastening blow, and the future of Carthage seemed reduced to that of a second-rate power. Polybios also adds that in the course of the war Rome lost about 700 quinqueremes and the Carthaginians about 500.⁶³ Despite this, however, Rome was now a fully-fledged naval power.

THE BATTLE OF TUNIS, 255 BC

Early in the year Regulus had defeated a Carthaginian army that had encamped on a hill, where their cavalry and elephants could not be properly deployed. Understandably, therefore, Xanthippos was loudly critical of the Carthaginian generals' performance to date and, accepting his criticisms, they agreed to listen to him. In particular, he pointed out that their long suit lay in cavalry and elephants would give them the advantage on level ground, which hitherto they had ignominiously avoided. As a graduate of the Hellenistic school of warfare, he doubtless knew the proper use of horse and elephant.

When Regulus marched across the flat Bagradas plain towards Carthage, Xanthippos confidently advanced to check him, leading an army of 12,000 infantry, 4,000 cavalry, and his ace in the hole, elephants close to 100 strong.[64] Precisely where the battle was fought is unknown, beyond Polybios' vague assertion that the Carthaginians were 'marching through the flat country'.[65] However, it is often referred to as the Battle of Tunis, since 'the town named Tunis' was the place he mentions as occupied by the Romans.[66] No matter, for whatever its true location, the battle was obviously going to be contested on ground of Xanthippos' own choosing.

Xanthippos deployed the Carthaginian citizens in the centre, with the bulk of his fellow Greek mercenaries on the right. The elephants were in a single line some way ahead of the Carthaginian phalanx, with cavalry and those mercenaries of a lightly-armed nature in front of the wings. In response Regulus split his few cavalry between his wings and, in the vain hope of halting the elephants, drew up his legionaries in unusual depth, 'many maniples deep', with the *velites* thrown out in front.[67] Normally a Roman legion deployed in three lines, *triplex acies*, the ten maniples of each side by side, but with gaps between them equal to a width of a maniple. The maniples of the second line covered the gaps between those of the first, and those of the third the gaps between those of the second. Before contact, the gaps of each line would be closed, probably by the rear century (*centuria posterior*) of each maniple moving up and deploying to the left of the front century (*centuria prior*).[68] The only hint from Polybios is that Regulus made the 'whole line shorter and deeper than before', perhaps by ordering the centuries of each maniple to remain one behind the other.[69] Whatever it was Regulus ordered with regards to his tactical subunits, Xanthippos must have smiled grimly when he surveyed the Roman order of battle.

Xanthippos, still smiling no doubt, opened the proceedings by ordering the elephants and cavalry to charge forward. Bravely, the Romans advanced to meet them, 'clashing their shields and spears together, as is their custom, and uttering their war cries' to stiffen their own resolve for the coming struggle.[70] The Carthaginian cavalry soon trounced their heavily outnumbered Roman counterparts, who vanished from the field to play no further part in the battle. However, the infantry on the left of the Roman battleline, avoiding the elephants, charged and broke the Greek mercenaries opposite them, pursuing them as far as the Carthaginian camp. Meanwhile, the charging elephants crashed into the remaining legionaries, who quickly discovered their deep formation only allowed them to be crushed underfoot more easily. To make matters grimmer for them, they were soon also assaulted on flank and rear by the returning cavalry. Those who managed to carve their way past the elephants were cut down by the waiting Carthaginian citizens, who, having until now mainly featured as 'extras', made great slaughter of them.[71]

Some 2,000 legionaries from the Roman left, who had hared after the mercenaries, got away and eventually made it to Aspis; Regulus and those who got away with him, probably his *entourage*, were shortly afterwards rounded up and taken to Carthage; the rest were slaughtered where they stood or hunted down by horsemen as they fled across the open plain. The Carthaginians lost 800 mercenaries, but no other casualties worth mentioning.[72] Carthage owed everything to the Spartan, and Polybios does not fail to give his fellow Greek his due, considering him a striking vindication of Euripides' sagacity that 'one wise counsel conquers many hands'.[73] In the very hour of his triumph Xanthippos disappears from the scene, quitting Carthaginian service, possibly for that of Egypt.[74] Much like Drepana at sea, Tunis was to prove Carthage's only victory in a land battle.

CHAPTER 5

Between the wars

In 241 BC the first epic struggle between Rome and Carthage came to an end. Carthage had evacuated Sicily, after some 500 years on parts of it, and was now forced to pay Rome a considerable war indemnity. Before long, its government would be plunged into a bloody and shameful debacle when Carthage's war-weary and penniless mercenary troops mutinied, believing, like many a frontline fighting man returning home to Germany after the 1918 Armistice, that they had received a 'stab in the back'.[1] Having been handed over to a general named Gesco and evacuated back to Africa in small staggered batches, Hamilcar Barca's veterans were left to rot on the streets of Carthage. Wisely, Gesco had reasoned that the authorities back home could pay the mercenaries their arrears as they landed and then pack them off to their own places of origin before the next batch arrived. Unwisely, the authorities chose to ignore these very sensible arrangements and refused to pay anyone until the whole army had collected in Carthage in the mistaken conviction that the mercenaries would let them off part of their arrears of pay. Anyway, after numerous disturbances in the city the 20,000 ill-disciplined but well-equipped mercenaries were shifted to Sicca (El Kef), the authorities even allowing them to take their baggage and their families.[2]

At Sicca, with nothing to do and with discipline sliding from bad to worse, the mercenaries, money-hungry and violent by nature, began to murmur and tot up what was due to them. When told by Hanno the Great, the man responsible for military affairs in Africa, that Carthage could not pay, those who talked of taking matters into their own hands gained the upper hand. Polybios makes the shrewd observation that the Carthaginian practice of hiring troops of various ethnic origins (in this case the military mosaic was made up of Iberians, Celtiberians, Gauls, Ligurians, Balearic islanders, Campanians, a good many Greeks and, of course, a great number of Libyans) though it made it difficult for them to combine, also had its disadvantages.[3] Since no Carthaginian could know all their languages and it was too laborious to address each group through a different interpreter, the only way to explain matters was through their own officers, and these frequently told them, either through misunderstanding or malice, something quite different. It also did not help that this great mixed army with its Babel of alien tongues had not served under Hanno, but under his political rival Hamilcar. Eventually, all 20,000 of them marched on Carthage, pitching camp at Tunis.[4] Their purpose, however, was not revolution but retribution.

'Such then was the origin and beginning of the war against the mercenaries', says Polybios, 'generally known as the Libyan War', clearly because, as he goes on to explain, 'nearly all the Libyans had agreed to join in the revolt against Carthage and willingly contributed troops and supplies'.[5] The Greek soldier-historian strongly emphasized the implications of a conflict between an organized state on the one hand and an anarchic barbarian mass of mixed race, owing respect to neither gods nor men, on the other. Polybios cites this as the perfect example of a 'truceless war' and stresses that the savagery and monstrous cruelty on both sides clearly appalled even contemporaries.[6] Ironically Carthage, which had always relied upon hired soldiery to one degree or another and was now reaping the consequences of such a dangerous policy, still had to enrol mercenaries so as to quash the mutiny.[7] Though it won in the end (237 BC), due mainly to the military skills and inflexible determination of Hamilcar, it was not before it had been brought to the brink of destruction, and Polybios unequivocally asserts that its citizens, who were compelled to take up arms in order to snuff out the mutiny, came near to losing their liberty and land.

The intimate details of the obscure campaigns of the mutiny do not concern us here, suffice to say the mutiny was the result of Carthaginian arrogance, insensitivity, careless mismanagement and gross stupidity, and Hamilcar preferred a war of mobility and small-scale action rather than full-blown battles. However, the wider repercussions do, and chiefly the effects on Carthaginian relations with Rome. It was during these internal troubles for Carthage that Rome intervened in the valuable Carthaginian dependency of Sardinia, despatching its armies to the island, and later also to Corsica.

Sardinia had not been included in the recent peace treaty as due to be ceded to Rome, but the pretext was that if the island had continued to be in Carthaginian possession, it would have been a perpetual menace to the western seaboard of Italy. The means was handed to Rome on a plate, for in 238 BC, the mercenaries stationed in Sardinia, no less disaffected towards Carthage than their brethren in Africa, invited the Romans to take over the island. At first Rome refused, and we would not be too cynical in thinking that the Senate hesitated because poaching was a game that two could play. However, the situation in Sardinia turned from bad to worse. Having killed their officers, the mutineers there had been joined by another force shipped over to deal with them, and had proceeded to systematically cleanse the island of all Carthaginians. The mutineers, now in forcible possession of Sardinia, fell out with the locals only to be driven out by them to Italy.[8] A second appeal was delivered, and Rome began to prepare an expeditionary force to sail to the island.

It was now that Rome acted as a swaggering bully set to run a blade through the vitals of any who opposed him. Indeed, Polybios pulls no punches when he says that the seizure of Sardinia was 'contrary to all justice'.[9] Earlier he had related to his Greek readership how Rome lifted Sardinia from Carthage and acquired what would effectively become its second overseas possession:

The mercenaries waged war on the Carthaginians for three years and four months, a war that far exceeded any I have heard of in savagery and lawlessness. At this moment the Romans received an appeal from the mutinous mercenaries on Sardinia, and decided to sail against the island. When the Carthaginians objected that dominion over the Sardinians belonged to them rather than to the Romans and that they were making preparations to hunt down those who had been responsible for the rebellion of the island, the Romans took this as an excuse and voted for war against the Carthaginians, claiming that their preparations were against themselves and not the Sardinians. The Carthaginians, who had just survived the war [against the mercenaries] I have described against all expectation, were in no state at the time to take up hostilities again against the Romans, and, yielding to events, not only abandoned Sardinia, but agreed to pay an additional 1,200 talents to the Romans to avoid undertaking a war at this time. And this is how all these things happened.[10]

The Roman occupation of Sardinia would cast a long shadow. While Roman arms were confined to Italy, the conquered became incorporated in some capacity into the Roman led confederation and acquired a share in the confederacy, subject to Rome but retaining a certain degree of autonomy, paying no tribute, but supplying men for the army. With Sardinia this all changed. The prolonged resistance of the warlike islanders required an almost continuous military presence, and this meant also the presence of a Roman magistrate with *imperium*: one or both consuls in 238 BC and from 235 BC to 231 BC. As a result, in 227 BC the number of praetors was raised from two to four, one, in future, being assigned to Sicily, the western part of the island being the spoils of the First Punic War, and one to Sardinia. Power may preserve that possession, which justice cannot ratify, and from now on, the *provincia* of these two praetors became not merely a 'sphere of duty', but a 'province' in the modern sense. Rome had its first extensions outside of Italy; its imperialism had truly begun.

THE THREE MUTINEERS

The ringleaders of the mercenary army were Spendios, a Campanian, a runaway slave and a deserter from the Romans whom he had perhaps served, because of his 'great physical strength and remarkable courage in war', by pulling an oar in their navy; a Libyan named Mathos; and a Gaulish gentleman whom we have already met, Autaritos the war chief of the 2,000 Gauls, a man who owed his influence to his excellent command of the Punic tongue, which many in the ranks of this polyglot, but long-serving army, seemed to understand.[11] At this point Carthage came temporarily to its senses and arranged for one of the generals who had served in Sicily to act as a mediator. It seems Hamilcar Barca was not acceptable to the mercenaries as they felt he had handed over his command too precipitously and thus, in a way, was responsible for their present fate. Gesco, on the other hand, having handled their departure from Sicily with due care and consideration, was acceptable. Gesco sailed to Africa and, after explaining the straitened circumstances of their employer, he then appealed to their loyalty and started to hand out the money he had brought with him. The majority of the mercenaries would probably have called it a day there and then.

But it was Mathos who bred sedition amongst his fellow Libyans, and once the sedition broke out, it was the Libyans who persisted in carrying the affair to a decision of arms, for the obvious reason that, should a compromise be effected, the other mercenaries might depart in safety to their homes, but their own homes and persons would be at the mercy of the wrath of the Carthaginians.[12] When they succeeded in preventing a reconciliation by way of a reign of terror, they had no difficulty in effecting a revolt of all the Libyan subject communities, who managed to put as many as 70,000 men into the field, though we have no real idea of their fighting value.[13] As well as their menfolk, these Libyan communities, in the cause of their freedom, willingly donated their money, which more than made up the sum owed to the mercenaries by Carthage.[14] In the meantime, poor honest Gesco and his cortege had been seized and clapped in irons. All hope of a compromise was at an end.

Now firmly in control, Mathos and Spendios divided the renegade army between them: while maintaining their entrenched camp at Tunis, Mathos mounted assaults on Utica and Hippo Acra, and Spendios blockaded Carthage. As for the tragedy of the bloody events that came after, these may be best summarized by way of a quick précis. Hanno's defeat at Utica; Hamilcar's recall and his victory over Spendios on the banks of the Macar (using his observation of a quirk of tide and wind to choose the time and place of fording an otherwise impassable obstacle); the false message sent to persuade the wavering mercenaries to fight on; their brutal butchering of Gesco and the other prisoners; tit-for-tat policy of no mercy; siege of Carthage; Hamilcar's ruse of luring the mercenaries into the defile of the Saw; their reduction to cannibalism and then starvation; dispatch of ten emissaries, among them Spendios and Autaritos, later to be crucified before Tunis, where Mathos and the remainder of the mercenaries were still holding out; the retaliatory crucifixion of the general Hannibal with thirty companions; and the final triumphal procession through the streets of Carthage, with Mathos suffering all kinds of horrendous torture at the hands of the jubilant people.

CHAPTER 6

Hannibal's revenge

Wars often have their origin and justification in earlier wars, and the very possibility of making wars stems from this archaic memory, from the awareness that it is an activity that has always existed. At the end of the First Punic War Carthage had lost Sicily, seapower and security. As we have seen, it was in this weakened condition that the once-proud Carthage would witness the unprincipled seizure by Rome of Sardinia and then be obliged to recognize the new state of affairs and forced to pay an added indemnity of 1,200 Euboian talents. After the loss of Sicily, Sardinia, woody and rich in warlike manpower, had acquired great significance in Carthaginian eyes, and so its loss weakened Carthage yet further, both militarily and economically. It goes without saying, and it is a smart lesson we should all mark, that a stinging iniquity imposed upon a defeated but resilient enemy bears the seeds of a further conflict.

It can be argued, therefore, that the Barca family (and Carthage) provoked the Second Punic War to reverse the decision of the first and its sordid aftermath and, by permanently weakening Rome, to make Carthage's western Mediterranean possessions safe. The activities of Hamilcar Barca and his successors in Iberia, whereby, building on the footholds Carthage already had in the mineral-rich peninsula, they created an empire based on the valley of the River Baetis (Guadalquivir) and the fertile territory of the Bastetani in what is now Murcia.[1] 'He subdued mighty and warlike nations and enriched all Africa with horses, arms, men and money', writes Nepos.[2] Iberia gave the Barca family and, depending on the view taken of the independence of their power, Carthage a formidable military force and the wealth to support it. Of course, with Nepos' assertion about the benefits to Africa out of mind, there was no such uncertainty amongst the rank and file of the army in Iberia. After Hasdrubal the Splendid was murdered in 221 BC, the soldiers, unanimously, acclaimed Hannibal Barca as their generalissimo in spite of his youth, 'owing to the shrewdness and courage he had evinced in their service'.[3] Here may be seen a reflection of the fact that the Carthaginian leadership in Iberia was a kind of personal absolutism vested in the Barca family (Hannibal married a local 'princess'), with a large degree of independence from the Carthaginian establishment in distant Carthage, which accepted the *fait accompli* of the army's choice.[4]

When the highly competent Polybios came to analyse the causes of the second war between Rome and Carthage, he was undoubtedly right to put first what he calls the 'wrath of Hamilcar', his anger at the end of the first war when he was forced to surrender despite remaining undefeated in Sicily.[5] Polybios later justifies his view that Hamilcar's bitter attitude contributed towards the outbreak of a war, which only began ten years after his death, by telling the celebrated tale of Hannibal's oath. The oath, sworn at the temple of Baal Shamaim, the 'Lord of the Heavens', to his father before their departure to Iberia in 237 BC, was to 'never to show goodwill to the Romans'.[6] At the time Hannibal was just 9 years old.

The story has inevitably been doubted, but Polybios says that Hannibal himself told it to Antiochos of Syria some forty years later when he was later serving the king, who was bogged down in a war with Rome, as a military advisor. The view that the Second Punic War was thus a war of revenge certainly gained widespread credence among the Romans, and revenge is part of war, as the Romans knew.[7] This was the war the Romans, who were in no doubt as to its instigator, often referred to as 'Hannibal's War'. Yet this notion of revenge is, perhaps, most dramatically expressed by Virgil when he has the Carthaginian queen Dido, heartbroken and furious at her desertion by Aeneas, curse him and his whole race and calls upon an 'unknown avenger, and harry the race of Dardanus with fire and sword wherever they may settle, now and in the future'.[8] She then fell on Aeneas' sword and killed herself. With such artistry did Virgil introduce Hannibal into his epic without naming him. Be that as it may, it would seem that all the leading officers swore the oath, not just Hannibal, and the oath they swore was not vengeance on Rome but a promise never to be 'a friend of Rome'. This is important phraseology: in those days the term 'a friend of Rome' implied a vassal of Rome, such as Hiero II of Syracuse.

It is true that neither Hamilcar himself, nor his immediate successor in Iberia, his son-in-law Hasdrubal the Splendid, made any overt move against Rome. The magnificent and charismatic Hasdrubal continued the policy of Hamilcar but with added flair, and largely increased the Punic influence in Iberia. In fact, Rome, probably after having been prodded by its Greek ally Massalia, eventually woke up to this new danger and in 226 BC signed the Iberus treaty with Hasdrubal, which defined spheres of influence in the Iberian peninsula by preventing the Carthaginians from crossing 'the Iber bearing arms'.[9] Naturally it could be argued that this treaty was practical recognition of Hasdrubal's supreme position in Punic Iberia, and implicit Roman acceptance of further Punic expansion across most of the peninsula, though in the view of our sole source on this matter, namely Polybios, it was the return of the Gaulish peril that prompted Rome to act so.[10] Yet we do not know how much Hamilcar and Hasdrubal influenced the young Hannibal, and it is his attitude that is important. Telling is his forthright attack upon Saguntum (219 BC), a town that he knew to be under Rome's protection less than two years after he succeeded to the supreme command of the Punic forces in Iberia.[11] Here Polybios uses the Greek word *pistis*, which corresponds (roughly) to the Latin *fides*, good faith; under traditional Roman policy, if a community handed itself over completely to Roman *fides* it entrusted itself to Rome absolutely, but without specific obligations (i.e. as most of Rome's allies had done).[12]

Located on the eastern extremity of a narrow, high rocky plateau reaching out to the coast - at the time Polybios was writing, it was a little over a kilometre from the sea: Saguntum (Sagunto) was an Iberian town, perhaps with some Greek admixture,[13] halfway between New Carthage (Cartagena) and the River Iberus.[14] Certainly before 220 BC Hannibal had left the town untouched so as not to provoke the Romans before he was ready.[15] Telling also is the bold and decisive way in which he matured his plans for the invasion of Italy (218 BC). Together, it at least suggests Hannibal was not too unwilling to have war with Rome. Alternatively, we can easily accuse the Romans of double-dealing as Saguntum lay far south of the Iberus. If the terms of the Iberus treaty prevented them from crossing the river under arms, as it did the Carthaginians, they could hardly come to the aid of Saguntum. Whatever, the Romans claimed that the alliance with this town overrode the treaty, and the Carthaginians claimed that the same agreement allowed them to attack Saguntum.[16]

As usual Polybios pulls no punches, for he has an unambiguous view that the Saguntum episode was a mere pretext. As he had earlier pointed out to his Greek readers, those Roman historians who have tried to identify the causes of the war between Rome and Carthage with the Carthaginian action in laying siege to Saguntum and the subsequent crossing of the Iberus have got it all wrong. And still to this day the juridical controversy over the responsibility of the war is discussed, fruitlessly for the most part, by many scholars. What Polybios does concede, however, is that 'these events might be described as the *beginnings* of the war'.[17] Thus our Greek soldier-historian has a clear view that the Saguntum episode was a mere pretext.[18] Following the fall of the town, the Senate sent a five-man embassy to Carthage demanding that the Carthaginians hand over Hannibal for punishment or else accept war. They could not speak Punic but one of them was competent in the other language of Carthage's *sufetes*, Greek. So, in a foreign tongue each side justified its case. Then Polybios says:

> The Roman ambassadors spoke no words in reply, but the senior member of the delegation pointed to the bosom of his toga and declared to the [Carthaginian] senate that in its folds he carried both peace and war, and that he would let fall from it whatever they instructed him to leave. The Carthaginian *sufete* answered that he should bring out whatever he thought best, and when the envoy replied that it would be war, many of the [Carthaginian] senators shouted at once, "We accept it!"[19]

It matters little whether the senior ambassador's histrionic gesture was real or apocryphal; a war that could decide the fate of the Mediterranean world had been accepted by Carthage whether it desired it or not. On the other hand, with war officially declared, Hannibal's long-term objective was fairly straightforward, namely to turn Italy, rather than Iberia, into the 'field of blood'.

From his father Hamilcar, he had learnt that is was inadvisable to be bogged down in a slogging match with Rome. If Polybios is to be believed, Rome and its confederate allies had a manpower resource of some 700,000 infantry and 70,000 cavalry.[20] No matter how many times Hannibal knocked out a Roman army, Rome could delve into its human reserves in Italy and another would stubbornly take its place. He, on the contrary, knew that he must save men, for in a war of attrition he would have no hope. Hannibal, knowing that over half of Rome's forces were furnished by its allies, deliberately set out to strangle this supply of manpower by claiming Italy would be freed from the Roman yoke. It is for this reason that he had to invade Italy, as distant rumours of Punic victories would not convince Rome's allies to switch sides.

The execution of the objective was, on the other hand, far from simple. Hannibal could invade Italy from the sea, a much faster and easier task than marching there by land. However, without bases in Sicily, even southern Italy was at the limit of operational range for a fleet of oared warships operating from Africa, and Carthaginian naval power in Iberia was not great. Carthaginian naval capability had in fact never been fully restored after the shattering defeats suffered in the first war, either in numbers or morale, therefore another stumbling block to the maritime option was Rome's superior naval strength, 220 quinqueremes to Carthage's 105; 50 of them stationed in Iberia.[21] And so, with Carthage outmatched, and perhaps outclassed, on the high seas, the risk of a seaborne invasion was too great a one for Hannibal to take. The next logical step, especially as he was based in Iberia, was to invade via Gaul, and thus Hannibal needed to march across the Alps.

Confident in its command of the sea, the Senate's plan for the conduct of the war was simple and direct. The two consuls for the year were to operate separately and offensively; one was to go to Iberia to face Hannibal across the Iberus, whilst the other was to go to Sicily to prepare an invasion of Africa.[22] Each would take with him the now-standard consular army of two legions, and two *alae* from the Latin and Italian allies, the *socii*; a further two legions, each under a praetor and supported by a Latin-Italian *ala*, would be stationed in Gallia Cisalpina, which was only half conquered and needed a garrison, but that was a local matter. The war would be fought aggressively and overseas.

To the utter surprise and consternation of the Romans, Hannibal crossed the Iberus and then proceeded to march over the Alps (his exact route is still a matter of fierce debate) during the late autumn of 218 BC.[23] He then proceeded to defeat one Roman army after another in a series of three brilliant victories: the Trebbia, Lake Trasimene, and Cannae.[24] All this should act as a salutary reminder to us that when embarking on a war no one knows exactly what is going to happen. As one of Euripides' characters remarks, 'whenever war comes to the vote of the people, no one reckons on his own death - that misfortune he thinks will happen to someone else'.[25] In the dog days of August 216 BC, we can reckon, no one on the streets of Rome anticipated the carrion-field of Cannae.

The immediate result of these Roman disasters was that practically all of southern Italy, excepting the Latin colonies and Greek cities, came over to Hannibal. Following the time-honoured practice of rushing to the aid of the victor, this was a series of political events that begun with the defection of Capua (216 BC), the capital of Campania and second only to Rome itself in size and prosperity, and would finish with the capitulation of Tarentum (212 BC), the third largest city of Italy.[26] Though Tarentum's citadel still remained in the hands of the small Roman garrison, possession of the city itself gave Hannibal access to a magnificent seaport.[27] The capitulation of Tarentum was immediately followed by that of three other Greek cities, namely Metapontion, Thourioi and Herakleia, and so the whole coastline of the instep of Italy passed into Carthaginian control.[28] Hannibal must have been fully convinced that he was now on the high road to success.

In the meantime the Carthaginian senate negotiated an alliance with Philip V of Macedon (215 BC), who hoped to recover Epeiros and seize Illyria, and the conflict spread into Sicily, where Syracuse broke its alliance with Rome and went over to Carthage (214 BC). This diplomatic coup was regarded as a real danger to Rome and the continued existence of its hegemony in Italy, as the Carthaginians could now use Sicily, which the Romans had so recently annexed, as a convenient stepping stone into the peninsula. Rome, therefore, rapidly mounted a major effort to recapture Syracuse, which, despite the fabulous mechanical and ballistic feats of the local genius Archimedes, was eventually achieved after treachery opened the gates to the Romans (212 BC).[29] This event, combined with the surrender of Capua (211 BC) despite Hannibal's march on Rome itself to divert the besiegers, is seen by many as the decisive turning point in the Second Punic War.

Of course it is all very well in hindsight to pinpoint a pivotal year when the course of events turned in favour of Rome. We must not forget that the year 211 BC saw the crushing defeat, by Hasdrubal Gisgo and the Barca brothers Hasdrubal and Mago, of the two Roman armies operating in Iberia; their commanders, Cnaeus Cornelius Scipio Calvus and Publius Cornelius Scipio, lost their lives to boot.[30] It was the greatest victory in the field for Carthage since Cannae, and Punic Iberia was once more secured. The two Cornelii Scipiones had stalwartly maintained the struggle in the peninsula for eight long years, and when Cicero later refers to the brothers as the 'thunderbolts of our empire' he presumably is thinking of their brief glory, followed by sudden extinction.[31] Though many senators were probably inclined to abandon Iberia, the Senate despatched a new commander to this distant theatre, the young Publius Cornelius Scipio, the son and nephew of the lately slain commanders, the future Scipio Africanus, who, after five years of hard fighting, would eventually drive the Carthaginians out of Iberia and invade Africa via Sicily.

In point of fact, contemporary opinion did not regard the war as going Rome's way after the carnage at Cannae. Reading Livy's grim portents and the discovery of coin hoards clearly support this. Even in 211 BC, with Syracuse already in Roman hands and Capua soon to follow suit, the two elder Cornelii Scipiones went to their doom and their armies perished wholesale. Two years later, utterly exhausted but not at all rebellious, twelve of the thirty Latin colonies, some of them very ancient, declared themselves incapable of providing further men and resources for the war effort, and so refused point blank to provide Rome with their annual contingents.[32] In 207 BC the sudden arrival of Hasdrubal Barca in northern Italy caused panic and despair in Rome; we can only speculate at what would have happened if the two Barca brothers had combined forces. Hasdrubal himself was certainly no second-rate general by any stretch of the imagination, and it is one of the fascinating though unprofitable 'what ifs' of history to speculate what would have happened if they had united, even more so as this is one of those 'what ifs' that grab our attention because the 'might have been' seemed so nearly realized. 'What if' scenarios in history are in a sense pointless, but they can be fun, and they can help us appreciate the significance of an outcome. Thus, by contemporary standards, it was not Syracuse or Capua that saw the decisive turning point in the war, but the Battle of the Metaurus.

And so the decisive year was 207 BC, the *annus mirabilis* when Hasdrubal suffered defeat, and death, on the meandering banks of the Metaurus in Umbria.[33] Having managed to extricate his treasure, his elephants and perhaps two-thirds of his army out of Iberia following the Scipionic drubbing he had received at Baecula (Bailén), Hasdrubal decided 'to march to Italy to share the fortunes of his brother Hannibal'.[34] Fortunately for Rome, however, its two consuls of that year, Marcus Livius Salinator and Caius Claudius Nero, joined forces and consequently crushed this audacious attempt to reach southern Italy. The first news that Hannibal received of the fate of his reinforcements was his brother's head, carefully preserved, thrown into his camp by the Romans.[35] 'Now, at last, I see the destiny of Carthage plain', Hannibal is said to have mourned.[36] According to Ovid, 'Hasdrubal fell by his own sword', and although Hasdrubal is not said to have committed suicide, it is quite clear that he deliberately sought death in battle when he realized that every last hope of victory had evaporated.[37] Having done all that a good general should, as Polybios emphasizes, Hasdrubal died bang in the thick of the fighting, sword in hand.[38]

This was the day that Ovid's fellow poet, the gentle Horace himself, describes as the first on which victory smiled at the Romans since the dreadful Hannibal had crashed through Italy like fire through a pine forest.[39] We can well imagine that when he gazed upon the head of his brother, his tower of hopes came clattering down about him. The entire character of the war had changed. Gradually forced down toward the southernmost tip of Italy, Hannibal was finally bottled up near Kroton and his Italian peregrinations came to an end. The sands of Hannibal's career in Italy were fast running out. In the autumn of 203 BC, having received a summons to return to Carthage, Hannibal, along with his youngest brother Mago, finally abandoned the peninsula. He had maintained himself in a hostile land for nearly sixteen years, during which time he continued to shower defeats on one consular army after another. In addition to the disasters already mentioned, as the years rolled by the armies of Tiberius Sempronius Gracchus (212 BC), Marcus Centenius Paenula (212 BC), Cnaeus Fulvius Centumalus Maximus (210 BC), and Marcus Claudius Marcellus (208 BC), went down like ninepins before Hannibal, and the Roman generals perished along with most of their men. He had won the battles, but like Pyrrhos before him, he could not win the war.

For Hannibal, however, there was one more Italian tragedy to be played out. Mago Barca, with the loss of Iberia, had sailed from Gadir to Liguria, collecting men and supplies from the Balearic Islands en route (206 BC). On reaching Genua (Genoa) the following summer, he landed with his mercenary army and marched westward (and therefore, away from his brother) and took the stronghold of Savo (Savona), where he stored his treasure. Some Ligurian tribes joined him and, incredible as it may seem, Carthage found it possible to send Mago, and not to Hannibal, a reinforcement of 7,000 men, 7 elephants, 25 ships, and money, with the preposterous directive to march on Rome and draw near to Hannibal. Never was there a worse example of too little, being sent too late, to the wrong location. Two Roman armies not only blocked the two routes by which Mago could ever hope to reach the south of Italy and his brother, but also prevented the Gaulish tribes from going to his aid. It was not until some two years had passed that he evidently felt strong enough to advance southwards. Nonetheless, on advancing into Gallia Cisalpina he was decisively defeated and himself seriously wounded in the thigh and had to be carried from the battlefield. The remnants of his army re-embarked, but Mago died at sea on the voyage back to Africa. Hannibal lost his last brother.

Hannibal had foreseen his own recall and taken steps to prepare for it. He embarked at Kroton, but Carthage had neglected to send him any transports to bring his army home. The upshot of this functionary negligence was that Hannibal had to slaughter his cavalry mounts, and their precious loss was to be crippling for Carthage in the next and last battle to be fought.[40]

Waiting for Hannibal was Scipio. After having demolished the Carthaginian empire in Iberia, the victorious general had returned to Rome and become consul (205 BC). When the Senate allocated provinces to the new consuls, Scipio received Sicily, the stepping-stone to Africa. This was a repetition of the situation in 218 BC, but in far more favourable conditions, and despite stiff opposition from certain powerful quarters holding up Regulus as a frightening object lesson, Scipio took the war into Africa. He was now impatient to measure his generalship against Hannibal. Still, with Scipio now operating in the Carthaginian homeland a peace treaty was tentatively agreed, but the negotiations were soon terminated and the final showdown between Hannibal and Scipio was played out at Zama (202 BC), as we shall see.[41]

The man who had most wanted the war with Rome now resolved to favour as the lesser of two evils the acceptance of a very hard peace. Though Carthage still had the strength of its formidable walls and position, and Hannibal's own military genius to direct it, it was nevertheless altogether exhausted in men, materiel and money. The mineral wealth of Iberia was lost, the fertile hinterland of Africa cut off, and access to the sea closed. And so Carthage became a 'friend of Rome', which meant it lost all its remaining overseas possessions and most of its African lands, was required to surrender all its elephants (and promised never to train any more, Livy adds) and reduce its once-proud navy to the purely symbolic number of ten triremes, as well as agreeing to a war indemnity of 10,000 Euboian talents of silver to be paid in fifty yearly instalments. The time span of fifty years was obviously intended to prolong the period of subjection and prevent the paying-off of the indemnity in advance. In addition to this millstone around its neck, Carthage was not to make war on anyone outside Africa, and on none in Africa without the prior approval of Rome. Thus defensive wars on African soil were not forbidden, but Livy's account forbids war to be carried on within Africa against a Roman ally.[42] If this second version of the clause is more reliable than that given by Polybios, the treaty was much harsher than he implied. This clause covered Carthaginian action, for example, against Masinissa. Moreover, another clause required that the Numidian king should recover from Carthage all lands and property once belonging to him and his ancestors. These two clauses, as we shall discover shortly, resulted in repeated provocations against Carthage, ticking timebombs that finally led to the Third Punic War.

ROME'S GREATEST ENEMY

The Carthaginians certainly have, in our eyes at least, the romantic glamour of the doomed. The Romans reduced their city to a heap of ashes and destroyed their culture at a time when republican Rome was the aggressive bully of the Mediterranean. Yet nothing is inevitable in history, and the Carthaginians put up far more resistance than any of the Hellenistic kingdoms, and came close, during the second in a series of three struggles, to destroying Roman power completely.

Their commander-in-chief during this titanic struggle was the cool, self-contained, locked-in hero Hannibal (247-183 BC), the eldest son of the charismatic general Hamilcar Barca (d. 229 BC), and, for my money at least, the greatest general of antiquity. Despite the notion that Hannibal supposedly rated himself as third after Alexander the Great and Pyrrhos of Epeiros, he was overly modest.[43] His victories were certainly more impressive than those of Pyrrhos were, and his strategic focus was clearer. Although Alexander achieved spectacular conquests, he did so using the superb Macedonian army created by his father, Philip II of Macedon, whereas Hannibal achieved his continuous run of successes with an ad hoc assemblage of polyglot mercenaries.

Hannibal, who was born shortly before or after his father's departure for Sicily (247 BC), probably never saw him until he returned to Carthage after the First Punic War was over (241 BC). Nevertheless, the absentee parent apparently ensured his son had a good education that included a strong Greek element. Later on Hannibal was to take Greek historians with him on his expedition, including the Spartan Sosylos, his former tutor who had taught him Greek, and the Sicilian

Silenos, though in what capacity he had taught the young Hannibal we do not know.⁴⁴ He then spent his youth in Iberia learning the trades of war and politics by his father's side and serving under Hasdrubal the Splendid, his brother-in-law, as his second-in-command-cum-cavalry-commander.⁴⁵

In Sicily Hamilcar had successfully maintained a struggle against the Roman forces in the northwestern corner of the island until the crowning Roman victory at sea left him no alternative but to open negotiations, the Carthaginian government having given him full powers to handle the situation. During this twilight period of the conflict, Hamilcar, whom Polybios considered the ablest commander on either side 'both in daring and in genius' and even the elder Cato held in the highest regard, displayed his talent in low-level raiding, skirmishing and ambushing.⁴⁶ He had the art, which he transmitted to his eldest son, of binding to himself the mercenary armies of the state by a close personal tie that was proof against all temptation.

It is of little surprise, therefore, that Hannibal had learnt his professionalism and confidence as a fighting soldier from his father, and there is more than a hint of Hamilcar, albeit on a grander scale, in his son's ability to maintain himself and his army in a foreign land for so many years. It is possible that he also inherited the plan for attacking Italy, just as Alexander inherited Philip's plan for invading Asia, for his father had once raided the southern Italian coast, 'devastating the territory of Locri and the Bruttii'.⁴⁷ It was his father who, because of his swiftness in war, was the first to be given the surname Barca, *bârâq*, the Semitic word for a lightning flash, and his brilliant progeny was to certainly honour the new family moniker. It was the Roman Florus who justly, and poetically, compared Hannibal and his army to a thunderbolt, which 'burst its way through the midst of the Alps and swooped down upon Italy from those snows of fabulous heights like a missile hurled from the skies'.⁴⁸ If Hannibal had learned his battle tactics from his father, as a strategist he was in a class all his own.

Modern commentators have been too quick to condemn Hannibal, criticizing his strategy for failing to comprehend the nature of the Roman-led confederation and to ensure that adequate reinforcements came either by sea from Africa or land from Iberia. Yet Hannibal himself could not be everywhere, and there is no doubt that this was the only way that Carthage could ever have defeated Rome. Whatever one's opinions, the audacity of the march from Iberia to Italy, crossing both the Pyrenees and the Alps, remains breathtaking, and we should not underestimate how near his strategy came to success. Hannibal's fifteen day march over the Alps in late October or early November 218 BC makes epic reading. Even in Livy's hostile narrative, the Carthaginian general emerges as its hero, rather like Satan in Milton's *Paradise Lost*, though in part this was done to justify the defeats Rome suffered at his hands. Hannibal had done the unexpected and was now poised to bring Rome to its knees.

Fighting his first battle on Italian soil along the Trebbia, a meandering tributary of the Po near Placentia (Piacenza), in bitter winter conditions, Hannibal had cleverly used seemingly flat open country to mask an ambuscade. The Romans, having emerged from their tents on empty stomachs and waded across the swollen Trebbia that snowy, solstice forenoon, lost two-thirds of their half-starved and rheumatic army before nightfall. It is said fortune is fond of crafty men, but she also smiles upon those who thoroughly prepare themselves for her gift of victory. That morning Hannibal had ordered his men to enjoy a hearty breakfast and to rub their bodies with olive oil around their camp fires.[49] The balance of fortune tipped in favour of the Punic invader.

Hannibal was a great exponent of ambush and Lake Trasimene, his next major engagement, was to be based on one giant snare. Marching along the northern shore of the lake, Hannibal very visibly pitched camp at the eastern end of the line of hills that ran parallel to, and overlooked, the lakeside. During the night he divided his troops into several columns and led them round behind the same hills, taking up positions parallel with the path the army had traversed earlier that day. Most, if not all, of the troops were positioned on the reverse slopes of the high ground, concealed from the enemy's view when the sun came up. As the first glimmerings of opalescent dawn dissolved the darkness, Caius Flaminius, the Roman consul, hurried his men with the expectation of closing with his quarry. The morning was misty, the line of hills mostly obscured by a clinging white veil, but it is possible that the straining eyes of Flaminius could just glimpse the Carthaginian camp at the far end of the narrow defile. While the consul sat upon his finely accoutred horse and dreamed of martial glory, those further down the pecking order shambled through the morning mist and dreamed mostly of more mundane things.

Doubtless Hannibal had counted on this early morning mist to rise over the lake and its miry margins, it was around the time of the summer solstice, and from the moment that the ambush was sprung his victory was certain. The Roman soldiers could see little, since the heavy mist still blanketed the defile and visibility was limited. Instead they heard outlandish war cries and the clash of weapons from many different directions simultaneously. In its world of mistaken shadows and magnified sounds, the mist-blinded consular army was soon thrown into utter confusion. 'In the chaos that reigned,' records Livy, 'not a soldier could recognize his own standard or knew his place in the ranks - indeed, they were almost too bemused to get proper control over their swords and shields, while to some their very armour and weapons proved not a defence but fatal encumbrance'.[50] By the time the sun was high enough to burn off the last wisps of mist, some 15,000 men had perished in battle, if that is what it can be called, and the consul himself had fallen heroically, dispatched by a Gaulish spear.

Hannibal, like his father before him, had been a soldier all his life, and by comparison the opposition were but babes in the wood. Not for the first or indeed the last time had an enemy underestimated his tactical brilliance, a brilliance that was to seem twisted and tricky to his less urbane opponents. Few commanders have been able to repeat Hannibal's feat of ambushing and effectively destroying an entire army. The carnage must have flooded the lakeside meadows with blood.

In truth Hannibal was a genius, not a general, and unsurprisingly his genius has seldom been questioned. It rested on a mixture of bluff and double bluff, and a truly remarkable ability to use all types of troops to their best advantage. His third battle, Cannae, remains a *chef d'oeuvre* to which generations of subsequent generals have aspired but never surpassed nor even equalled. However, perhaps the clearest light on Hannibal's character is shown by the fact that although he maintained his mercenary raggle-taggle permanently on active service in what was often hostile territory for almost sixteen unbroken years, he kept it 'free from sedition towards him or among themselves... the ability of their commander forced men so radically different to give ear to a single word of command and yield obedience to a single will'.[51] If this is how Polybios saw Hannibal, then his inspirational leadership and canny man-management must have been unsurpassed. As well as a great strategist he must also have been a great contriver, a practical expert who clearly knew how to compromise in order to accommodate the broad ethnic diversity of the assorted national and tribal contingents that constituted his mixed army of disinterested soldiers. As Colonel Ardent du Picq would later urge: 'A leader must combine resolute bravery and impetuosity with prudence and calmness, a difficult matter!'[52]

Some of the biographies and anecdotes that deal with those so-called great men of history should be viewed as romantic embellishments, anachronistic, or simply dubious. With Hannibal, as with any other signal historical figures, we should not depict the lives of millions being determined by the masterful will of a single actor. As the Greeks say, or used to say, like the chorus, one man may lead, but many play. Naturally, to do this, we have to sift the reality of Hannibal's life from the fable and fantasy, so removing him from the malleable domain of legend to the more resistant context of factual record. Take the Romans for instance, who tended to cast shadows on the Carthaginians by stressing their cruelty and perfidy and the like, and saw Hannibal as a fire-breathing warmonger indulging in a sadistic appetite for violence and revenge, a gun-for-hire approach that had some tendency towards that sort of barbaric adventure. Thus the lettered Seneca did not hesitate to relay one of those snippets that show the Carthaginian in the most odious light when, on the eve of battle, seeing a blood-filled ditch, Hannibal exclaimed 'Oh, what a lovely sight'.[53] The Romans could never forgive Hannibal for having put himself, like a single-minded adventurer, at the head of a fantastic barbarian rabble, leading it from one victory to another. Thus Hannibal, Rome's predestined enemy, was already metamorphosing into the ogre of fairy tale, a bogeyman for little Roman children and the stuff of nightmares, and the foundation of future legends were being laid. In the collective consciousness of nations exceptional figures are invariably despised.

CHAPTER 7

Zama, a lesson learnt

Roman strength lay in the set-piece battle, the decisive clash of opposing armies that settled the issue one way or another. In its crudest form, the two sides would deploy in close order, slowly advance, clash, and systematically set about butchering one another until one or the other could pay the butcher's bill no longer. And even success was dearly brought. Tellingly, Polybios saw the Romans as rather old-fashioned in their straightforward and open approach to warfare, commenting that as a race they tended to rely instinctively on 'brute force' (*bía*) when making war.[1] Nothing illustrates his criticism better than Cannae, when Roman tactics subordinated the other arms very much to the heavy infantry, who were to carry the heat and burden of that terrible day. Indeed, there was all the delirium of amateur soldiering in them that midsummer morning as they ponderously rolled forward at a moderate rate in open terrain, their ranks unusually packed into a close and solid mass, a veritable steamroller in motion. And on they tramped, moving ever forward in a courageous manner, but courage does not always win battles and it was not to do so in this case. Hannibal was about to demonstrate to the Romans that there was more to the art of war than mere brute force.

Being faced by a vastly larger army, Hannibal decided, in effect, to use the very strength of the enemy infantry to defeat it, deliberately inviting it to press home its attack on the centre of his line, much like the lion-tamer who vanishes into the maw of his own lion. His now-Roman-equipped Libyans would serve as the two jaws of the trap, the Gauls and Iberians as the bait. Finally, Hannibal took equal care with the deployment of his cavalry; it too would play an integral part in the entrapment of the Romans. All too often, swept up in the hot pursuit of routing opponents, victorious horse disappeared from the actual field of battle, leaving their foot to battle on alone. Hannibal anticipated his to do otherwise. And so, instead of distributing his cavalry equally between the wings, he would place more on the left against the river there. This virtually guaranteed a breakthrough against the numerically far-inferior Roman cavalry, and it would then be available for further manoeuvres on the battleground. The smaller body of cavalry on the open flank, away from the river, where the more numerous Latin-Italian cavalry was stationed, would be expected to hold them in play for as long as possible. Not only was this a beautifully thought out, audacious scheme, but it showed Hannibal's absolute confidence in the fighting abilities of all the contingents of his mixed army. And so it came to pass.

The Romans were naturally horrified when the news reached them of the defeat at Cannae and its scale. Of the two consuls, one had fled from the field, and the other lay rotting upon it, along with those of the preceding year. First reports made no mention of survivors, and the Senate was told that the entire army had been simply exterminated. On that day the Roman army, the largest ever fielded by the Republic, suffered the highest casualty totals in its history; on that day a citizen army, and the society that had created it, were introduced to the full terrors of annihilation. Not until fourteen years later, when Roman troops were in Africa, was Rome to exact its revenge for this absolute catastrophe. Having invaded Africa, the brilliant young Scipio turned the tables and Hannibal, the invader of Italy and for sixteen years the undefeated antagonist of Rome, was decisively defeated near the small town of Zama. No battle of the Second Punic War had a more definite outcome, and it effectively sealed the fate of Carthage. Without the resources or willpower to continue the struggle, it sued for peace and the war was over.

According to Livy the survivors of Cannae, after serving for several months in Campania, were transported to Sicily where they made up two legions, *legiones Cannenses*. Later reinforced by the fleet-of-foot survivors of the first Battle of Herdonea (212 BC), all these disgraced legionaries were not to be released from service and forbidden to return to Italy until the war was over.[2] Ironically, as Livy remarks, these penal-soldiers became the most experienced men in the entire Roman army, and Scipio saw fit to formally identify their seasoned units as *legiones V* and *VI* and make the pair the backbone of his African expeditionary army (204 BC). Livy adds that these were exceptionally strong legions, each of 6,200 legionaries but with the usual complement of citizen cavalry, and then, intriguingly says 'Scipio also chose Latin infantry and cavalry from the *Cannensis exercitus* to accompany him'.[3] Obviously what he calls the *Cannensis exercitus*, the army of Cannae, consisted of survivors, Roman and *socii*, of that slaughterhouse condemned to serve out the war with no prospect of discharge. Scipio, who had likely served with them at Cannae, knew that the day had not really been lost through any cowardice on their part.

The actual size of the invasion force Scipio finally took with him to Africa is difficult to say. Livy mentions three different totals given by unnamed sources, ranging from 10,000 foot and 2,200 horse, through 16,000 foot and 1,600 horse, to a maximum of 35,000 for both arms. Though Livy hesitates to opt for the largest figure, it is assumed here that the middle totals represent the number of infantry and cavalry furnished by the *socii*, while the maximum seems most probable for an expedition of this magnitude.[4]

On receiving orders from Carthage to return home, Hannibal, ever faithful to his country, duly abandoned Italy, taking with him those men who wished to leave; we have no record in the ancient sources of their number, but we suspect it does not seem to have been a very considerable force.[5] Hannibal landed in the neighbourhood of Hadrumentum (Sousse) 120km south of Carthage, and from here he marched his army to a place Polybios calls Zama, 'a town which lies about five days' march to the west [i.e. southwest] of Carthage'.[6] Of the two, three, if not four, places called Zama in the hinterland of ancient Tunisia, the one referred to here has been identified as the one that lay at present-day Seba Biar, some 13km east of Zanfour.[7] Between the two camps the opposing commanders met for their famous parley, each with an interpreter although both spoke Greek, and it was on the second day, at dawn, that the armies deployed for battle.[8] In keeping with his view of the importance of Zama in shaping the course of world history, Polybios says, with unaccustomed drama, that 'the Carthaginians were fighting for their very survival and the possession of Africa, the Romans for the empire and the sovereignty of the world'.[9]

On the day Hannibal probably commanded some 36,000 infantry, supported by 4,000 cavalry, half of them valuable Numidian horsemen, and 80 elephants.[10] Appian gives Scipio 23,000 Roman and Latin-Italian foot and 1,500 horse.[11] His infantry included those two penal legions, the *legiones Cannenses* now numbered as *legiones V* and *VI*. Masinissa, a Numidian prince of great ability who had once fought for Carthage, brought with him a force of 6,000 foot and 4,000 horse.[12] Hannibal was perhaps stronger in total, but weaker in cavalry.

Hannibal was in the unaccustomed position of having to rely on his infantry for the decision, and these he deployed in three lines, which was the standard formation for the Romans but unusual for the Carthaginians. The first line was composed of Ligurians, Gauls, Balearic slingers and some Moors, presumably lightly-armed warriors fighting with javelins, and appears to be the remnants of his brother's mercenaries brought back from Liguria. These were at any rate professionals and therefore troops of reasonable worth, and Polybios says there were 12,000 of them in this line.[13] The second line consisted of Punic, Libyphoenician and Libyan levies hastily raised for the defence of Africa, and probably therefore with little preliminary training or previous experience.[14] The third line, some distance behind the others and in reserve, consisted of Hannibal's own veterans, that is, the soldiers who had come with him from Italy.[15] Livy and Appian make these men Italians, predominantly Bruttians, but they clearly included all the survivors of his Italian army, even some Libyans and Iberians who had marched with him from Iberia and the Gauls who had joined him in Gallia Cisalpina.[16] Livy and Appian have blundered badly here because Polybios clearly says that Hannibal, in a pre-battle address, told these grizzled and lean men to remember above all the victories they had gained over the Romans at the Trebbia, Lake Trasimene and Cannae, and later Polybios emphasizes that they were 'the most warlike and the steadiest of his fighting troops'.[17] The cavalry was positioned on either wing, the Carthaginians (Punic, Libyphoenician) on the right and the Numidians on the left, with the elephants and skirmishers screening Mago's mercenaries.[18]

What would the military connoisseur have made of Hannibal's army and his state of affairs? For the first time in his career, the Carthaginian general was fighting on ground not of his choosing. Up to now Hannibal had always made the terrain fight for him, choosing his battlefields with great care and refusing battle until the ground suited him. Moreover, the sharp-eyed observer could hardly fail to notice that Hannibal was also fighting with inferiority in the mounted arm, which had always played a large and decisive part in all his victories.[19] What is more, not only was he rather deficient in this particular, but most of what he had was not much use.

Scipio had no such worries in this particular department. For it was during his campaign in Iberia that he had struck up a friendship with a most useful prince in Numidia, Masinissa, and now on African soil his brilliant horsemen would prove crucial allies. Scipio stationed Masinissa with his Numidian contingent on the right wing, and his friend and right-hand man, Caius Laelius, with the citizen and allied cavalry on the left wing. In the centre the Roman and Latin-Italian legionaries were drawn up in the standard *triplex acies*, except that the maniples of *hastati*, *principes* and *triarii*, instead of deployed chequer-wise, were placed one behind the other, leaving clear lanes to accommodate the elephants. All his *velites* were stationed in these lanes with orders to fall back in front of the beasts to the rear of the whole formation, or, if that proved difficult, to turn right and left between the lines, leaving the lanes clear for the elephants.[20]

In the event, a large proportion of the elephants, being young and untrained, were frightened out to the wings where they did more harm to their own side than to Scipio's, thereby helping his cavalry to sweep their counterparts from the field.[21] For Hannibal's elephants and cavalry the Battle of Zama was over.

It was now time for the main business to commence, and the opposing first lines, that is to say, the *hastati* and the mercenaries, clashed and set to. In Livy's patriotic account the Romans sweep all before them, but Polybios more soberly says that at first the mercenaries, who were professionals after all, prevailed through their 'courage and skill'.[22] Once the *hastati*, now probably reinforced by some of the *principes*, had eventually broken and scattered the second Carthaginian line, it too by all accounts having put up a desperate display of doggedness, Scipio redeployed his second and third lines on either wing of the first. If, as on previous occasions, Scipio planned to outflank the Carthaginian third line with his *principii* and *triarii*, this was not to be.

Tactical readjustments made, he then closed with Hannibal's veterans who were also probably now flanked by a substantial number of survivors from their first two lines as Polybios says the two forces were nearly equal in numbers. Up to this point of the battle, Scipio must have been acutely aware that Hannibal had never yet been defeated, but from the moment the citizen-allied cavalry and Numidian horse returned and fell on Hannibal's rear, his cause was lost.[23] The surviving mercenaries and levies turned and fled, Hannibal escaped with a scanty band of horsemen, but his hard-nosed veterans, largely armed and equipped in the Roman style, fought bitterly to the death, pitted against those very legionaries that they had disgraced at Cannae. The military connoisseur can use a little licence to fill in the final, tragic detail, enabling us to envisage not so much as one single man of them

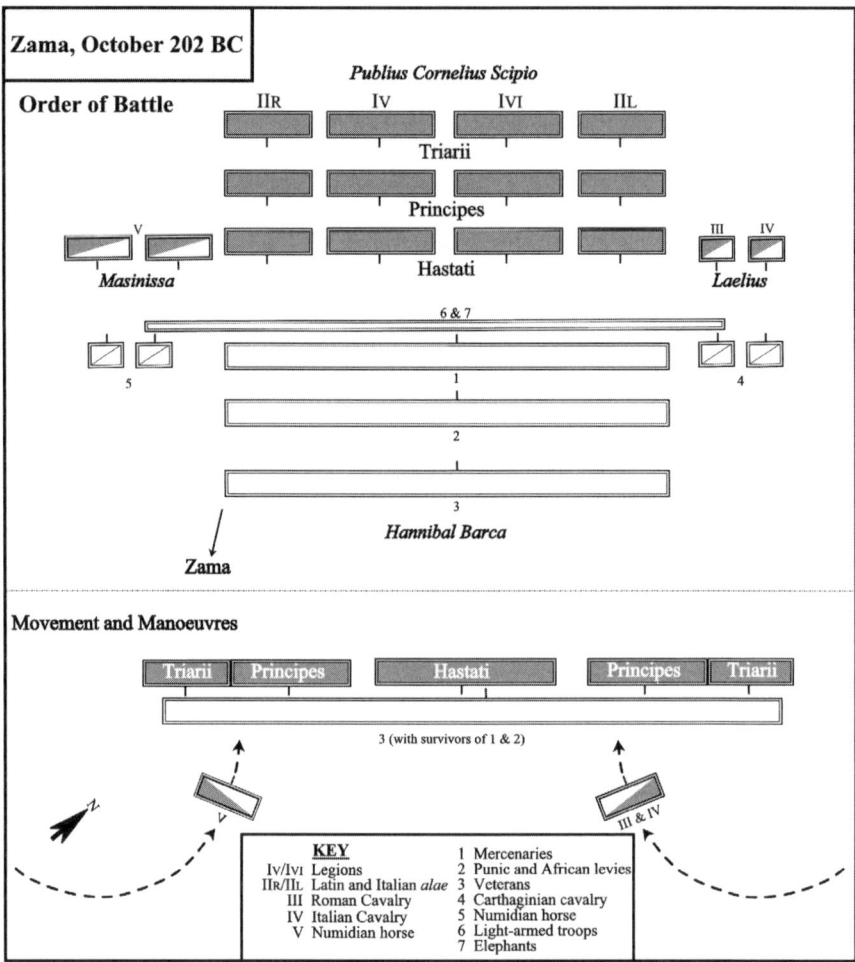

asked quarter, or threw down his arms, but every last one fought without holding back and defended himself to the finish.

Polybios concludes his account of the battle with the view that Hannibal had done all that a good general of long experience should had done, 'brave man as he was, he met another better', and left the tattered remains of his veterans to their self-elected doom.[24] It seems on the field of Zama, much like Napoleon on that of Waterloo, Hannibal could not avoid defeat. Unlike his brother Hasdrubal, who in similar circumstances had died with sword in hand, Hannibal took the longer view. Very probably he would have preferred to exit alongside his faithful veterans, but thought of Carthage first: alive, he could still hope to have some influence on events and continue to serve his country in peace as he had in war. The less charitable view is that he lost his nerve and abandoned the field of disaster in fear of being taken by his enemies and bundled off to Rome (the recent fate of the Numidian king, Syphax). True, he could have stayed in a glorious attempt to rally the survivors, but his army virtually ceased to exist: Polybios assesses the Carthaginian casualties as 20,000 dead and 20,000 prisoners, figures repeated by Livy but not by Appian, who gives 25,000 dead and only 8,500 prisoners. Whichever is correct it demonstrates the ferocity of the fighting and the completeness of Hannibal's defeat. As to the Roman losses, Polybios' of no more than 1,500 killed seems ridiculously low. Appian, however, assesses the Roman loss at 2,500 and that of Masinissa still more.[25]

The more we look at Zama, the more we can appreciate the real genius of Hannibal. Look at his third line, which was not only the best but very much the strongest of the three, and it becomes clear that Hannibal's order of battle represented not a plan of attack but an elaborate plan of defence, by which the Romans were to penetrate, and were expected to penetrate, a succession of screens. The first screen was the elephants, then the missiles (Balearic slingers, Moorish javelineers) with a stiffening of troops accustomed to mixing it at close quarters (Ligurians, Gauls), then close-order infantry (African levies), before they reached the third and final line, Hannibal's 'old guard', if you will, tough and intact. Moreover, this line was kept some way back so survivors from the first two lines had ground enough to rally on. When it came to the crunch, Hannibal did believe that his army, with its inexperienced levies and motley horse, could win. Hannibal's conscripts and cavalry were not brilliant, but they were not bad. Polybios' sober judgement on this particular matter says it all:

> He [Hannibal] had massed that large force of elephants and stationed them in front with the express purpose of throwing the enemy into confusion and breaking their ranks. He had also drawn up the mercenaries in front with the Carthaginians [i.e. the levies] behind them in the hope that the enemy would become physically exhausted, and their swords lose their edge through the sheer volume of the carnage before the final engagement took place. Besides this, by keeping the Carthaginians hemmed in on both sides he compelled them to stand fast and fight, so that in Homer's words, "Even those loth to fight should be forced to take part in the battle" [*Iliad* 4.300]. Meanwhile, he kept the most warlike and the steadiest of his fighting troops at some distance in the rear. He intended that they should watch the battle from a distance, leaving their strength and their spirit unimpaired until he could draw upon their martial qualities at the critical moment.[26]

In other words, Hannibal expected his veterans to deliver a *coup de grâce* to the badly damaged Romans. The failure of the plan was due entirely to Hannibal's weakness on the two wings, for Scipio by the rapid victory of his cavalry had time to take stock and reform for the final showdown with the 'old guard', which was soon surrounded by the victorious horsemen returning from their hunt. Indeed, the return of Scipio's cavalry was decisive, for until it came the issue was doubtful,

Polybios saying 'the contest for a long while hung in the balance until Masinissa and Laelius returned from the pursuit of the Carthaginian cavalry and arrived by a stroke of fortune at the critical moment'.[27]

Scipio was to adopt the cognomen 'Africanus' by virtue of his achievement, apparently the first Roman general to be known by a name derived from the scene of his victories.[28] This battle ended the Second Punic War, but Hannibal would continue to stalk like a gigantic shadow in the dimming light of recent events. He lived nineteen years after the battle at Zama, the last he had fought, the first he had lost. Rome never felt safe until his death.

THE MAN WHO BEAT HANNIBAL

The Carthaginians lost because Rome, with its huge reserves of high-quality manpower, refused to admit defeat even when it was down on its knees. Second, central Italy and its colonies did not revolt and the Gauls, as a nation, did not join Hannibal (or his brother Hasdrubal). Third, Carthage failed to gain the command of the sea and dissipated its war effort, and to no effect. Fourth, the Cornelii Scipiones confined Hasdrubal Barca to Iberia until 208 BC, and produced in the younger Publius Cornelius Scipio (consul in 205 BC and 194 BC), who would later celebrate a triumph and take the cognomen 'Africanus', a soldier whose tactical genius was at least an equal of Hannibal's.

Of course we have to remember the Cornelii Scipiones were one of the most influential of Roman families, and very much a law unto themselves. We only have to think of the way the future Scipio Africanus secured the command in Iberia, vacant after the deaths of his father and uncle (211 BC), despite being a private citizen, *privatus*, barely aged 25, and never having held any office higher than that of curule aedile.[29] The aedile was a middle-ranking magistrate without military duties, being solely responsible for maintaining roads and aqueducts, supervising traffic and markets, and organizing public games and festivals. It was an essential preliminary for those higher offices in Rome, the praetorship and the consulship. He had seen action aplenty, however, in the sharp cavalry skirmish on the banks of the Ticinus (218 BC) when, according to one tradition, he had singlehandedly saved his father's life.[30] Though there is no record of the part he played in the actual battle, he was also at Cannae (216 BC), where, from Livy's account, it seems he was among those who escaped across the Aufidus to the main Roman camp on the opposite bank. Then, rather than surrender, he was one of the unshaken 4,000 who managed to elude the prowling Carthaginian cavalry patrols and stagger into Canusium. There, in recognition of his leadership during this desperate time, Scipio was serving as military tribune with *legio II*, he was elected by the fugitives to be one of their two commanders.[31] Perhaps it was these deeds of derring-do in the face of defeatist machinations, which inspired the Roman people to invest him *imperium pro consule* to conduct the war in Iberia (210 BC).[32]

Scipio was an inspiring leader who could gain and keep the loyalty of his men.

His charismatic character and judicious diplomacy won him many allies, without whom Rome might have not won the war. Seeing the deficiencies of the rather static traditional Roman tactics, Scipio experimented with small tactical units that could operate with greater flexibility. His tactics were inspired by Hannibal's and needed good legionary officers as well as generalship to implement. He thus saw the value of capable subordinates who could proceed on their own initiative. Nonetheless, his realistic tactic appraisal remade the Roman army under his command into a force that made better use of its inherent strengths.

Scipio's strategy of striking at Carthaginian forces in Iberia, and letting the conquest of ground take care of itself, was brilliant, and was in complete contrast to that of his predecessors. But although he has been extravagantly praised for his strategy in invading Africa, this had been the Roman plan since 218 BC, and appears pedestrian in comparison with Hannibal's daring invasion of Italy and rapid succession of victories. To utter an impertinent truth, the strategy Scipio pursued in Africa was by no means original, for he was merely following in the footsteps of Agathokles and Regulus. It is easy for us to be critical, however, and Scipio's methods paid off in the end, particularly in drawing Hannibal inland away from his secure base by the sea, or the ravaging of the fertile and populous Bagradas valley with fire and sword, which probably forced Hannibal into battle before he was ready.

Both men were fine tacticians but Ilipa (206 BC), Scipio's most tactically sophisticated battle, appears cumbersome when compared with Cannae. Hannibal himself is supposed to have said that, if he had won Zama, he would have rated himself even better than Alexander the Great, Pyrrhos of Epeiros and all the rest, thereby deliberately flattering them both.[33] That is debatable, but few would agree with Suvorov (no doubt echoing Polybios, who is perhaps more generous than wise here) that Scipio was the better general, even though he won the battle, which in truth was little more than a traditional slogging match. It is always difficult to correctly assess the stature of a commander who was beaten in the end, and historians tend to assume that he is inevitably inferior to the commander who beat him, forgetting the circumstances that may have brought about that defeat. Much like Robert E. Lee, Hannibal was beaten, not by a better man, but by a better army. Great soldier as Scipio was, in almost every respect he falls short of the rank attained by Hannibal. Indeed, there was no one in that period who could match the Carthaginian's experience in war, the breadth of his strategic vision or tactical capabilities in all the configurations of land warfare.

CHAPTER 8

A military superpower

Like Livy after him, Polybios' special concern was with Rome. Unlike the moralizing Roman Livy, however, his prime object was to explain to horrified fellow Greeks 'by what means and under what kind of constitution the Romans in less than fifty-three years succeeded in subjecting the whole inhabited world to their sole government'.[1] Suffice to recall that for Polybios, Rome's victory at Zama was the turning point in its history.[2] Perhaps he is right. Of the fifty-three year period (220-167 BC) he covers in his near-contemporary account of the unification of the known world under the guidance and control of Rome, the Second Punic War dominates a third. When, in 211 BC, Hannibal had stood outside the gates of Rome, such a terrifying moment was not to be trumped until the Visigoth Alaric penetrated and pillaged the 'eternal city' in AD 410, a time, some would argue, when Rome's martial fury had long waned and the love of ease and luxury had well and truly taken over. It comes as no surprise, therefore, to learn that among its enemies Rome's chief *bête noire* was beyond question Hannibal, and the proverb '*Hannibal ad portas*' would retain its efficacy as a rallying cry for Romans in times of national crisis until the very end of the empire.[3] The crux is, before the war with Hannibal Rome was predominately an Italian power, but now its armies had marched through Gaul, Iberia, Sardinia, Corsica, Sicily, Africa, and Illyria. Rome's range and ambitions had been transformed.

After the crushingly one-sided success at Cannae, says Livy, Maharbal boasted to his victorious commander-in-chief that he, at the head of the cavalry, could ride to Rome where Hannibal should be 'dining, in triumph, on the Capitol within five days'. Hannibal, although he commends his cavalry commander's zeal, demurs. Maharbal retorts by saying that Hannibal knew how to win a fight, but did not know how use the victory. 'This day's delay,' Livy piously concludes, 'is generally believed to have been the salvation of the city and the empire'.[4]

With the hindsight we enjoy, which was already available to Livy, it would be easy for us to agree with him and find fault with Hannibal for not at once marching on Rome after Cannae and capturing the city by a *coup de main*. However, let us not judge him, as we are all too prone to judge, on insufficient knowledge, and see what his chances were. Rome was 480km away, a distance that would take at least three weeks to cover with the army marching at a forced rate of 20km a day, ample time for the Romans to organize the defence of the well-walled city.[5] Moreover,

Rome still had two legions sitting within the city itself, and a fleet stationed at Ostia, which raised a legion of marines after the appalling catastrophe of Cannae, while 8,000 able-bodied slaves were purchased and armed by the state.[6] It must also be remembered that the Roman army was a citizen force; the population of Rome could be armed from any available source and by this means defend the walls of their city.

In truth, throughout antiquity very few cities fell to a direct assault and, in the main, they were captured either through treachery or by conducting a long-drawn-out siege. The hazard of direct assault actually involved the besieger finding a way over, through or under the fortifications of the besieged, and so what the besieger often did was to shut the besieged off, and let disease, hunger or thirst, usually all three, do his work for him. As Philip II of Macedon once said, the best way to take a city is with asses heavily laden with gold.[7] Moreover, Hannibal may well have recalled what had happened to Pyrrhus some sixty years earlier when, having won a victory on the broad plains near Herakleia, he advanced to within 60km of Rome only to withdraw empty-handed. Anyway, having said all that, if Hannibal marched away from southern Italy he would have left an area that was offering him vital support in his war with Rome. No part of Hannibal's long-term strategy involved a march on Rome, and even in 211 BC when he came right up to its gates, he was tempting the Romans to lift their siege of Capua.[8]

There is the criticism amongst modern observers and military pundits that Hannibal was unable to capture the cities of southern Italy. This is valid only to a point. Hannibal was clearly attempting to win allies to his cause, and the indiscriminate sacking of cities (the fate of two, Nuceria and Acerrae) would hardly endear him to the Italic peoples.[9] It has also been said that Hannibal failed to capture cities because he lacked a siege train. A siege train was not the requirement of a successful general in ancient warfare, as only had to construct his siege machinery *in situ*.[10] Besides, Hannibal's idea of warfare was one of mobility, and he certainly did not envisage himself being strategically hampered through having to conduct lengthy sieges in southern Italy.

Yet another criticism levelled against Hannibal was his lack of understanding of the importance of seapower. This can be easily dismissed because he had certainly intended to rendezvous with the Carthaginian fleet at Pisae (Pisa) during the summer of 217 BC, but had missed the opportunity to do so as he was otherwise busy at Lake Trasimene, where he was demolishing the consular army of Caius Flaminius.[11] Hannibal also captured a number of seaports in southern Italy, the greatest being that of Tarentum, but the Carthaginian navy failed in supporting him throughout the war; the notable exception to this was its successful landing of 4,000 Numidian reinforcements (including 40 elephants) at Locri in 215 BC.[12]

The Second Punic War had revealed the latent power of Rome, that is, its hydra-like capacity to produce men. Most of Rome's previous wars had been fought with two consular armies each of two legions and their usual complement of Latin-

Italian *alae* and, as Polybios emphasizes, when eight legions were mobilized for the Cannae campaign this had never before been done.[13] But if Polybios is right in stating there were eight legions at Cannae, Rome had already mobilized a total of ten legions, since there were already two in Iberia, and by 211 BC there were to be twenty-five legions under arms in the different theatres of war, sixteen in Italy itself, which, taking the *alae* and the men serving at sea into consideration, represented something like 250,000 men.[14] As Kineas, the trusted diplomat of Pyrrhos, was said to have predicted, the many-headed monster could regenerate and struggle on.[15]

At the killing fields of Cannae Rome lost, according to Livy (for once his figures are less sweeping than those of Polybios), nearly 50,000 troops or, to put it more bluntly, its army had suffered some 80 per cent casualties.[16] The casualty rate suffered by Britain and its colonial allies on 1 July 1916, the date of the opening of the British offensive on the River Somme, does not compare with this shocking figure (19,240 killed, 35,493 wounded, 2,152 posted as missing and 585 captured). No other state in antiquity could have survived such a shattering defeat. At the time of the Gallic troubles, which flared up some seven years before Hannibal's arrival, Rome, according to Polybios, could mobilize 700,000 and 70,000 horse, whereas Hannibal invaded Italy with only 20,000 foot and 6,000 horse.[17] This inexhaustible supply of manpower is one primary reason as to why Rome ultimately defeated Hannibal, while another is the steadfastness of the Roman people. They were placed into dire situations that would have produced, at the very least, treachery in any other ancient state. Look at, for example, Rome's blunt refusal to ransom its prisoners after the humiliation of Cannae.[18] As the poet Ennius, who had reached manhood about this time, would write soon after in a memorable line: 'The victor is not victorious if the vanquished does not consider himself so'.[19]

Wars are the sum of battles, battles the tally of individual human beings killing and dying, and though the individual comforts himself with the belief that death might come to the next man, but not to him, concrete realities ultimately decide whether soldiers return home in safety after doing their butchery or were left in several inhuman chunks scattered messily over the battlefield. It could be argued therefore that the inexperience of Roman soldiers and the rigidity of Roman tactics were responsible for such an aggravated casualty rate, but we must not lose sight of the fact that the essential philosophy behind the manipular legion was that of winning a straightforward, mass engagement with the opposition. A quick, decisive clash with the enemy was desired, and in this role the manipular legion performed remarkably well.

After Cannae Hannibal would gather in a bushel the gold rings torn from the lifeless fingers of more than fourscore consuls, ex-consuls, praetors, aediles, quaestors, military tribunes, and scores of the equestrian order.[20] In other words, most of Rome's military leadership lay on the battlefield. So another disadvantage of course was the limited ability of Rome's aristocratic generals, but there is no real proof that the employment of grim professional soldiers in command would have improved matters. Hannibal's obvious skill as a general inflicted this catastrophic defeat on this militia army, yet the same type of army, when better led and with higher morale, beat him in turn at Zama. As Polybios rightly points out, 'the defeats they suffered had nothing to do with weapons or formations, but were brought about by Hannibal's cleverness and military genius'.[21]

Likewise, the inclusion of Latin and Italian allies, the *socii*, within the army of this period did not change the essential tactical doctrines behind it. Most if not all allied units, the *alae*, were disciplined, organized and equipped as legions and thus acted in a similar fashion. The Roman military system was precisely that, a system. Rome did not need brilliant generals and rarely produced them, it just needed to replicate and reproduce its legions, which it did on an almost industrial basis, though apparently at the phenomenal cost of 10 per cent of its entire male population.[22] War is not an intellectual activity but a brutally physical one, and the bloody reality is that all wars are won through fighting and most through attrition that is both moral and physical. By an ironic but saving paradox, Romans were at their very best only when in the most straitened circumstances: they knew that all wars with Rome would have a long run because Rome never gave up.

As well as having a relentless attitude to warfare, Rome also had a solid core of support amongst its closest dependencies, the Latin communities, despite a bout of war-weariness at Rome's endless calls on their manpower, and even those dozen that had refused to supply manpower never opted to side with Hannibal. With northern and central Italy refusing to back Hannibal, his long-term strategy was not going to be a success. In fact he overestimated the spirit of rebellion against Rome, and here he was perhaps fifty years too late, and to many Italic peoples there was more reason to identify with, rather than against, Rome. The evidence from negotiations between those who did defect (mainly Samnites, once fierce enemies of Rome) and Hannibal shows that what they really wanted was autonomy and the chance to determine their own fate. Defection to Hannibal, who was after all an outsider, was changing one master for another, or so many feared.

The Senate's overall handling of the war was first class; not to be confused with the tactical handling of Rome's forces in the field. When Hannibal, for instance, arrived in northern Italy, an army was being readied for Iberia. The consul in charge, Publius Cornelius Scipio senior, sent the army on and remained himself in Italy, picking up local forces to oppose Hannibal. In this fashion the Senate, which ratified Scipio's decision, kept a presence within the Iberian peninsula, a presence that was to last throughout the war regardless of any horrendous disasters in Italy. Likewise, when Carthage signed the treaty with Philip V of Macedon, the Senate simply checkmated its designs by despatching a fleet to the Adriatic to prevent any Macedonian aid reaching Hannibal in Italy.

By stark contrast, Carthage lacked such a body as the Roman Senate to direct its war aims. The Carthaginian generals tended to act on their own, as was customary, with only the threat of crucifixion for failure limiting their horizons. Carthage sent more than 78,000 troops to outlying areas of its empire during the war, and only 4,000 to Hannibal in Italy. This was in part because of appreciable political opposition. Moreover the Carthaginian senate deemed the protection of its territories in Iberia more important than the war in Italy. Seapower was also sadly neglected, the Roman navy commanding the seas throughout the conflict. In 212 BC, for example, the Carthaginian admiral Bomilcar, apparently married to the eldest daughter of Hamilcar Barca, attempted to relieve Syracuse but Marcellus, despite his numerical inferiority in ships, opposed him and the admiral with that scuttled off to Tarentum. Without the command of the sea, Syracuse was lost and any attempt by the Carthaginians at controlling Sicily doomed.

As we have already alluded to, it is almost certain that Hannibal did not envisage a final triumph amongst the smoking ruins of a sacked and gutted Rome. At the Trebbia and at Lake Trasimene Polybios clearly shows him courteously releasing his Latin and Italian prisoners-of-war without ransom money having been demanded of them, sending them home with the message that he had come to emancipate Italy from the yoke of Rome and to hand back the territories it had stolen.[23] Livy also has Hannibal continuing this policy after Cannae, adding that Hannibal addressed his Roman prisoners and stressed that he was not fighting to destroy them, but 'for honour and hegemony.'[24] Though he may have sworn eternal hatred of them, Hannibal was not planning to exterminate the Romans. Two facts support this hypothesis. First, Hannibal, after Cannae, attempted to open negotiations with Rome. Indeed, he had expected the Romans to send the overtures for peace, it being the obvious thing to do because if they fought on, he would defeat them again, and meanwhile more and more of their allies would be deserting them. Second, an article in the sworn treaty between Philip of Macedon and Carthage shows Rome being stripped of its allies but allowed to exist as a Latin state of little consequence and held in check by those who had just had their autonomy restored to them.[25] Hannibal's aim was to disrupt Rome's confederacy and thereby drag it battered and shrunken to the negotiating table, where it would be then stripped of any remaining allies and burdened with a crippling war indemnity. With Rome reduced to the status of a second-rate power, Carthage would have been able to regain Sicily, Sardinia and its other lost territories, as well as having a free hand in mineral-rich Iberia. Everything that Hannibal did was subject to this principle, and undertaken with this objective, using military means only as an instrument, albeit a very powerful one, to achieve.

CHAPTER 9

Hannibal's retreat

There is no reliable evidence that Rome demanded Hannibal's surrender in 201 BC; this would come later. Returned to civilian life, Hannibal now had the opportunity to employ his great powers of statesmanship, no longer masked by his prestigious soldierly skills. There was plenty of scope for it, in his politically bankrupt and physically exhausted country.

One of his first tasks, after his appointment as one of the two *sufetes*, was to have an investigation made of the resources left to Carthage. The situation in fact was far better than could be expected. The city was on the road to recovery with regards to its commercial prosperity, but before long a scandal broke out. The first instalment of the war indemnity due to Rome under the terms of the peace treaty was paid in 199 BC, but the silver was found to be of such poor quality that Carthage had to make up the deficiency by borrowing money in Rome.[1] In looking into the scandal, Hannibal soon found himself up against 'the hundred'. He obtained a major revision of the constitution, and 'the hundred' was subject to annual elections with the proviso that no man should hold office for two consecutive years. By eradicating administrative corruption and functionary embezzlement, and collecting arrears of unpaid taxes, Hannibal showed how the heavy war indemnity could be paid without an increase in public taxation.[2] Government putrescence and peculation were of course scarcely novel in Carthage, but his far-reaching reforms, which also embraced commerce and agriculture, were so successful that by 191 BC Carthage could offer to pay off the whole of the outstanding debt, forty years' instalments, in a lump sum (viz. 8,000 talents), while also supplying the Roman army currently at war in the eastern Mediterranean with large quantities of grain. The offer, either for reasons of spite or arrogance, was disdainfully declined.[3]

Hannibal had another, and trickier, situation with which to deal. When his brother's army left Liguria, a Carthaginian officer with the name of Hamilcar stayed behind and placed himself at the head of a number of malcontent Ligurian and Gaulish tribes. The Latin colonies of Placentia and Cremona were attacked. Rome naturally complained to Carthage, demanding a recall and surrender of this freebooter, whose activities were a clear breach of the peace treaty. Suspicion, naturally, was laid on Hannibal of having taken some dastard part in these guerrilla operations in Gallia Cisalpina, but the senate in Carthage replied that it had no power to do anything beyond exiling this Hamilcar and confiscating his property.

Meantime, in the aftermath of Hannibal's defeat, the Romans had turned their attention towards the east. Ostensibly in response to appeals from tiny but independent powers of Pergamon and Rhodes, Rome decided to intervene in Greece before Philip V of Macedon (r. 221-179 BC) and Antiochos III of Syria (r. 223-187 BC) had a chance to upset the balance of power in the east. This is an example of Rome's increasing propensity to regard other people's business as its own, viewing events in regions bordering on its sphere of influence as events upon which it was entitled, at the very least, to voice an opinion. The possession of irresistible power tends to lead to such arrogance. Of course, Rome had never forgiven Philip for his alliance with Hannibal, but Antiochos was a very different kettle of fish.

One of the greatest Hellenistic monarchs who, in conscious imitation of Alexander, bore the epithet 'the Great', Antiochos earned this title attempting to reconstitute the kingdom by bringing back into the fold the former outlying possessions. He thus managed to reassert the power of the Seleukid dynasty briefly in the upper satrapies and Anatolia (Asia Minor to the Romans), which effectively made him ruler of the eastern world from the Indus to the Aegean, but then inadvisably challenged Rome for control of Greece in 194 BC. Concerned first and foremost with maintaining in their entirety the territorial possessions he had inherited from his forefathers, having just retrieved them, what Antiochos wanted was for Rome to mind its own business and leave him free to do as he wished on his side of the Hellespont. It was not to be. Towards the end of 190 BC Rome, backed by Pergamon and Rhodes, won the final battle over Antiochos on the level plain of Magnesia-by-Sipylos in Lydia, driving that magnificent and ambitious king back across the Taurus Mountains and out of Anatolia.[4]

It was suspected in Rome that Hannibal had been in touch with Antiochos. This would of course have been another breach of the peace treaty by which Carthage was bound not to partake in any hostilities without Rome's acquiescence, especially not when they appeared to be directed against Rome itself. Rome had another reason to be furious with Hannibal, for his skill in reorganizing the finances of Carthage had made the Roman plans miscarry; they had hoped that the war indemnity would cripple Carthage, and they were disappointed. Despite the reasonable objections of Scipio Africanus, who had been censor in 199 BC and *princeps senatus* in 198 BC, a commission was sent to Carthage in 195 BC, the very year Marcus Porcius Cato, the elder Cato as he is known to history, was consul, alleging that Hannibal was aiding an enemy of Rome. In the senatorial debate, where Scipio Africanus brought his full weight to bear against those he saw lending a favourable ear to what he viewed as a baseless accusation, 'considering that it consorted ill with the dignity of the Roman people to associate themselves with the animosities of Hannibal's accusers, to add the support of official backing to the factions at Carthage'.[5] Noble words, forsooth, which fell on deaf ears.

Be that as it may, at this very moment Hannibal's position in Carthage was insecure. For not only had he made implacable enemies of all those functionaries whose peculations and perks he had stopped, but his year of office as *sufete* had now expired. And so, with his keen sense of appreciation that the Roman commissioners could not fail to demand his surrender, and the probability that the Carthaginian senate would comply, he withdrew from their grasp by a series of characteristic tricks. Pretending to be going for a short ride with two trusted companions (Sosylos and Silenos?), he rode through the night, hell for leather, to his seaside estate near Thapsus, which was more than 150km as the crow flies. His treasure had already been embarked on a fully outfitted and crewed ship, and he sailed for Cercina (Kerkennah), an island just off the coast. There he was recognized by the crews of some Phoenician merchantmen, which was unwelcome to him as the news of his presence there could not fail to reach Carthage. In order to forestall them, Hannibal suggested to the ships' captains that they should dine with him on shore and bring their sails and yards with them to provide shelter from the midsummer sun, which they did, taking care to leave his own vessel fully rigged. What they did not realize was that by doing so, they had delayed the time of their departure next day.

Naturally, Hannibal showed a clean pair of heels during the night while the revellers slept off their drink. Back in Carthage the Roman commissioners were naturally furious, and Hannibal's enemies in the Carthaginian senate placated them by formally declaring him to be an outlaw, confiscating his property (such as he had left behind him), and razing his property to the ground.[6] So was Hannibal honoured in his own country.

Hannibal sailed away to Antiochos, who must have been an attractive host to him because he was soon to be engaged in fighting the Romans. By accusing him of plotting war with Antiochos, his enemies in Carthage and, in Rome, the senators determined on his downfall, had propelled him into the king's arms. Hannibal caught up with the busy king in Ephesos, and there, it is said, explained to him his grandiose plan for opposing Rome.[7] If we are to believe Livy, it involved entrusting to Hannibal an army of 10,000 foot and 1,000 horse and a fleet of 100 warships, with which he would first sail to Africa to win over Carthage, and then on to Italy to raise war there against the Romans. At the same time Antiochos was to lead his main army into Greece, where he would take up a strong position to paralyse Rome's efforts.[8] It seems the Romans got wind of Hannibal's war plan, and the combination of artful agents and covetous courtiers scuppered his chances to carry the upcoming war into Rome's backyard.[9] As we have noted, Antiochos was eventually defeated at Magnesia, and Rome predictably demanded the surrender of their most implacable foe. When Hannibal had resumed the struggle against the Romans, the exile, in their eyes, had become a rebel. Semantics aside, it was too late anyway. For Hannibal had already embarked his treasure on a ship and sailed away again, this time for Crete.[10]

Though Crete had remained aloof from all the fighting in the eastern Mediterranean, Hannibal now ran the danger that the proverbially covetous Cretans knew how great the sum of money was that he had brought with him. He countered this by filling a number of large narrow-necked jars with lead and covering this with a shallow layer of gold and silver pieces at the top. These heavy jars he deposited in a local temple, where the Cretans jealously mounted guard over them, without troubling Hannibal. His real fortune he stuffed inside a pair of humdrum bronze statues, which he left carelessly lying around his garden, so that when he wanted to leave he was able to take his treasure with him without the Cretans suspecting it.[11]

This story, of course, can be taken for what it is worth. Nevertheless, Hannibal lived quite comfortably on the island of Crete, but being one not fain to take life calmly as it comes, he was not likely to want to live there for too long. We next find him offering his services to Prusias I of Bithynia (r. 228-181 BC), who, from about 186 BC to 183 BC, was at war with his neighbour, Eumenes II of Pergamon (r. 197-158 BC), an ally of Rome who had fought at the Battle of Magnesia. This local spat gave Hannibal one last opportunity for showing his military genius. Prusias was defeated on land and transferred hostilities to the sea. Outnumbered in ships, Hannibal advised the king's marines to gather venomous snakes, stuff them in earthenware pots, and catapult them onto the enemy's ships. The sailors of Pergamon began by jeering at such ridiculous tactics of fighting with pots instead of swords. But when these pots crashed on board the Pergamene ships, which were soon crawling with snakes, the laugh was on the other side of their faces and, as Trogus Pompeius relates, 'they yielded the victory'.[12]

There followed yet another demand for the surrender of Hannibal, whom the Romans pursued, as Plutarch says, 'like a bird that had grown too old to fly and had lost its tail feathers'.[13] He was then 64 years old. Hannibal headed off his captors by taking poison, and in his final agony, or so said Livy, he cried out: 'Let us free the Roman people from their long-standing anxiety, seeing that they find it tedious to wait for an old man's death'.[14] Thus perished Hannibal of unhappy memory. The year was 183 BC, and the Romans breathed freely for the first time since that day, some thirty-five years back, when Hannibal crossed the Alps, elephants and all. There was no room for forgiveness in the hearts of the Roman nation; they had been too frightened for that. There are some things which can never be forgiven, let alone forgotten.

CHAPTER 10

The final act

Carthage had scrupulously followed the terms of the peace treaty of 201 BC, which included the paying off of the massive war indemnity in the fifty year period as prescribed then by Rome. Yet its rapid recovery (together with Hannibal's dealings with the Syrian king, Antiochos) made the Romans apprehensive, and rekindled their bitter hatred and desire for vengeance. During this half century of uneasy peace with Rome, Carthage's Numidian neighbour, Masinissa, who, after going over to the Romans during the closing stages of the Second Punic War, had been awarded the kingdom he now ruled, tirelessly badgered Carthage.[1]

Even though Carthage offered, and gave, the Romans assistance in their imperial ventures, the Senate in Rome regularly countenanced Masinissa's annoying encroachments upon its remaining dominions in North Africa. The pro-Roman Numidian king was determined to turn Numidia into a modern state (of this more shall be said later) and in the course of doing so to expand his boundaries at the expense of Carthage. As a 'true and loyal friend', the king knew very well that in any dispute the Senate would always back him. In fact on seven separate occasions Carthage was forced to appeal to Rome for redress against Numidia, and though on some of these occasions the Senate did act to restrain its client king, on none of them was he forced to disgorge his ill-gotten gains. To Carthage, Masinissa seemed like a felonious bad hat on the make, a daylight robber given to the impertinent singeing of Carthaginian beards. The Carthaginians therefore began to build up military forces, but for defence against the Numidian king and not for a war with Rome. All the same, a more truculent Carthage emerged, which led to the reiterated demand of the elder Cato that the city must be destroyed.[2] And so it was, after the Third Punic War. But that is to anticipate.

A fresh dispute arose in 153 BC and the Senate responded by despatching an embassy to Africa, headed by Cato, in order to arbitrate. Masinissa was willing for Rome to settle the issue, but Carthage obviously declared there was no need. Naturally this aroused the Senate's suspicions, especially as Cato, veteran of the war with Hannibal, had seen signs of Carthage's military build up.[3] From the time of his return to Rome, Cato argued for war, which led to a long-running dispute between him and those who opposed war, the Cornelii Scipiones faction led by Publius Cornelius Scipio Nasica. A senator of considerable weight who had already been consul twice (162 BC, 155 BC), Scipio Nasica saw all this as an unjustified act of aggression by Rome, but Cato was impressed by the Carthaginian revival and saw the latest quarrel with Masinissa as just the start of an impending war with Rome. Plutarch continues the story by relating how Cato brought back a fresh fig from Carthage, robustly declaring in the Senate that he had only picked the fruit three days before.[4] Many scholars have taken this anecdote as positive proof of Rome's jealousy of Carthage's economic revival, and the call for death which he repeated henceforth in the Senate merely jealous greed voicing itself. However, the message was loud and clear; Cato was only demonstrating to his fellow members of the Senate how close he thought the potential military threat was. Clever was Cato in the art of making the white look black.

Notwithstanding Cato's blatant manipulation of his fellow senators' fears, Scipio Nasica put forward two arguments. First, Rome should make no rash move without justification, in other words war required a *iusta causa*. Second, *hostilis*, that is the natural fear of a strong rival, was a salutary right by which the nobility kept ready and prepared for war. Without Carthage, in other words, Rome would have no worthy opponent and, as a consequence, the nobility would slowly slide into a moral decline.[5] In matter of fact this is the celebrated argument put forward by writers of the Principate such as Livy and Tacitus, the year 146 BC and all that is seen as the pivotal date when the rot in Rome set in.[6]

Like a dripping tap, Cato steadily wore down his opponents. Moreover, the Carthaginians finally played right into the Senate's hands by attacking Masinissa and war was duly declared amid the raucous cries of *Punica fides*, the stock charge of Punic ill faith. The words of Cato had become the policy of the Senate. According to Polybios, the Romans 'had long ago made up their minds to act thus, but they were looking for a suitable opportunity and a pretext that would appeal to foreign nations'.[7] Legalistic pretext seized, the tragic end result would be the utter destruction of the hated city by Scipio Africanus' adopted grandson and Polybios' close friend, Publius Cornelius Scipio Aemilianus who, 'with tears in his eyes', would carry out the brutal wishes of the Senate to root out Carthage like some old fig tree.[8] A new Roman province, the sixth, would rise from the ashes of a once-proud metropolis: that of Africa.[9]

It was back in 151 BC when a Carthaginian army under a hitherto-unknown Hasdrubal invaded Numidia, but was soundly beaten, and after being besieged in its camp was virtually wiped out through starvation and disease. Only Hasdrubal and a handful of survivors managed to escape back to Carthage, the remainder being butchered as soon as they laid down their arms to surrender. The attempt to check Masinissa's encroachments had thus proved abortive; it had merely established the ambitious king in more territory and had roused the anger of Rome. Indeed, that clear breach of the peace terms (Carthage was not allowed to go to war without Rome's permission), as well as Cato's acerbic oratory in the Senate, convinced the Roman government military action was necessary.

In the summer of 149 BC Rome despatched a fleet and army (probably a double-consular one) to Carthage under Manius Manilius and Lucius Marcius Censorinus. When the two consuls landed on the African shore at Utica (which surrendered without a fight) they were at once met by a Carthaginian delegation begging for peace at any price. The Carthaginians were promptly told that peace could be had, but that Carthage first must give up 300 noble hostages and hand over all arms of any kind within the city. Since resistance seemed futile, Carthage agreed. The hostages were punctually given up, and apparently some 200,000 panoplies were turned over to the Romans, as well as 2,000 catapults, and a huge quantity of weapons and ammunition.[10] Then with Carthage, as they thought, completely helpless, the consuls delivered the final blow: the citizens must quit the city. Carthage was to be utterly destroyed, but the inhabitants could build a new dwelling place wherever they liked, provided it was no less than 10 Roman miles (14.8km) from the sea.

Not for the first time, however, Rome had overplayed its hand. When the news reached the city, the people resorted to that age-old habit of peoples faced with an obstinate government: rebellion. When the populace erupted into violence, those who had counselled peace and complied with Rome's harsh terms were lynched on the streets by an angry mob. This aggressive response by the citizens of Carthage is a classic case of how people are beaten only when they understand they have lost, and the government was now forced into attempting the defence of the city. Thus empowered, and despite the earlier surrender of war gear, the citizens went to work with such good effect that they started turning out new swords, spears, shields, and catapults at a prodigious rate. The women of the city willingly cut the tresses of their hair to serve as torsion springs for the new catapults. Within an incredibly short time Carthage was put in a state of defence and messengers sent into the hinterland to raise a relief force. Hasdrubal, who had managed to escape from certain crucifixion after his Numidian fiasco, was pardoned and soon took command of a field army of around 20,000 troops near Nepheris (Bou-Beker), some 30km southeast of Carthage.

Nevertheless, the Romans hardly anticipated any serious resistance, fully expecting to cross the walls and kill, and they were quite unprepared for the fanatical fury with which the city was defended. Not only was the expeditionary force poorly led and badly trained, it also lacked siege engines, and all direct assaults against the landward walls were beaten back with bloody loss before the armed militia that had sprouted from the streets of Carthage. Flabbergasted, the Romans withdrew to lick their wounds and settle down to a prolonged siege. Not content to watch events, the defenders made constant damaging sallies, and the Romans were also faced with a new enemy, as disease decimated their ranks in the insalubrious surroundings of the lagoon. Meanwhile, a foray across the lagoon to secure timber ran into serious opposition from Hasdrubal's cavalry, under the very able command of one Himilco Phameas, but ultimately sufficient wood was gathered to construct two battering rams. These were brought up near a stretch of the fortifications near the lagoon, considered weaker here, and manned by one team supplied by the army and the other by the navy. Despite the competitive rivalry between the two services, spurred on by their respective officers, and two breaches being made, the defenders drove back all the assaulting parties. Worse still, under cover of darkness, a raiding party went out and managed to set fire to both of the Roman engines. As the summer heat intensified, the Roman camp was relocated away from the lagoon to the southern end of the city where the troops would benefit from the fresh sea breezes. Roman ships anchored there to provision the army, but they were almost completely destroyed by Carthaginian fire ships. The year drew to a close and Carthage remained unconquered.[11]

The following year, only one of the new consuls went out to Africa. This was Lucius Calpurnius Piso, who brought with him Lucius Hostilius Mancinus to command the fleet. Six years earlier Piso had tasted defeat in Iberia, while Mancinus does not appear to have been any more gifted. In fact the pair made no progress, handling affairs with gross incompetence, and being saved from complete disaster only by the skilful efforts of Publius Cornelius Scipio Aemilianus, who was serving as military tribune with *legio IIII*.[12] Rather than press the siege it was decided to attack the stronghold near Nepheris, where Hasdrubal's field army was ensconced. In a council of war Scipio Aemilianus advised against this operation but was overruled. When the Romans were on the verge of defeat at the hands of the Punic cavalry commander, Himilco Phameas, Scipio Aemilianus' timely arrival with reinforcements covered the Roman retreat. He then played a key diplomatic role. Masinissa's offer of assistance early in the siege had been brusquely rebuffed; now the Romans needed all the help they could get.

The king invited Scipio Aemilianus, as the grandson of his illustrious patron, Scipio Africanus, to join the Roman delegation visiting him. When they arrived, they found him dead (he was well into his eighties) and his three surviving legitimate sons awaiting Scipio Aemilianus, who was charged with choosing the successor. He chose all three: one to rule in the palace, one as minister of foreign affairs, one as minister of justice, each according to his talents. Scipio Aemilianus brought Gulussa, the most warlike of the three and the minister of foreign affairs, with him back to the Roman camp, along with a large cavalry force.

The arrival of Numidian reinforcements had a profound effect on Himilco Phameas, who perhaps sensed a change in the winds and defected to the Romans in exchange for a free pardon.[13] Scipio Aemilianus, however, returned to Rome to seek office and was there nominated and elected consul by the people on account of his military record, though he was under the legal age and had not held the praetorship (he had intended to stand as a candidate for the more junior post of curule aedile). All opposition was swept aside and, as at the election of his adoptive grandfather, the constitution had to give way to the will of the people. It seemed the right thing to do, especially as his military record stood out in high relief against the recent military defeats, and intervention by one of the tribunes of the

THE FINAL ACT

people then ensured that Scipio Aemilianus, rather than his colleague, was given Africa as his province.[14]

With his return to Africa in the spring of 147 BC the whole aspect of affairs would be dramatically changed. Upon his arrival Scipio Aemilianus set about raising the morale and efficiency of the soldiers, expelling the swarm of prostitutes and traders and focussing the army on its task. He also ensued that from now on the soldiers were properly provisioned. In the meantime, Hasdrubal was recalled to take charge of the city's defences, leaving one Diogenes (probably a Greek *condottiere*) in charge of the field army. Scipio Aemilianus pressed the siege with vigour, and an attack on the Megara quarter met with early success, but withdrew under pressure. Hasdrubal responded by concentrating his forces in the Byrsa, then for good measure tortured and mutilated his Roman prisoners on the walls. This was intended to stiffen the defenders' resolve, but instead motivated the besiegers. Scipio Aemilianus spent the rest of the summer building a contravallation to isolate Carthage from landward approaches: a series of palisaded ditches with sharpened stakes at the bottom, an earthwork facing the city with regularly spaced watchtowers, and a four-storey tower in the centre to serve as an observation post. These siegeworks dominated the peninsula and made access to the city from the landward side out of the question.

Scipio Aemilianus next began attempts to block off Carthage's seaward supplies. From its southern extremity the mercantile harbour was connected to the sea by a channel some 21m wide, and he began by building a mole running across its mouth. Concealed from sight behind the encircling harbour walls, the Carthaginians responded by cutting a new outlet to the sea due east from their naval harbour. They also secretly began constructing from scratch fifty triremes out of whatever material they could lay their hands on.[15] When both fleet and outlet were complete they sailed out, but inexplicably did not attack the unmanned Roman ships. When they finally mounted an assault on the third day, the Romans were ready and drove them back. Unfortunately a bottleneck in the new outlet kept many Carthaginian ships exposed without, and the Roman ships hammered them. Scipio Aemilianus then assaulted the outer quay protecting the mercantile harbour, bringing in catapults and rams. This move suffered a setback when a night attack by the defenders destroyed most of them, but Scipio Aemilianus patiently rebuilt them and threw up defences too. Persevering with his attacks, Scipio Aemilianus eventually secured the harbour walls and took possession of the newly constructed harbour entrance. He spent the remainder of the year capturing what cities still remained loyal to Carthage, and defeated the field army near Nepheris. By the end of the year Carthage was entirely cut off from the outside world. This provoked an offer to negotiate from Hasdrubal, but he would not concede to Scipio Aemilianus' demand that the city be razed. The final agony of Carthage was at hand.

In the spring of 146 BC Scipio Aemilianus gave the orders for the final assault. By now, the shortage of food had taken its toll in the city, and when the Romans launched a savage and slaughterous assault from the harbour area, where they had established themselves the previous autumn, a stretch of the city wall fell after brief resistance. Thence he advanced without difficulty to the agora, while the defenders fled to the Byrsa, and here the last desperate, half-starved remnant held out. Tall houses along narrow lanes proved to be individual strongholds, and the fighting was house-to-house, floor-to-floor, room-to-room, hand-to-hand for six days.[16] The account given by Appian, which gives a graphic description of the bitter fighting, was probably taken from Polybios, whose own eyewitness record has been largely lost:

> The streets leading from the agora to the Byrsa were flanked by houses of six storeys from which the defenders poured a shower of missiles onto the Romans; when the attackers got inside the buildings the struggle continued on the roofs and on the planks covering the empty spaces; many were hurled to the ground or onto weapons of those fighting in the streets. Scipio ordered all the sector to be fired and the ruins cleared away to give a better passage to his troops, and as this was done there fell with the walls the bodies of those who had hidden in the upper storey and been burned to death, and others who were still alive, wounded and badly burnt. Scipio had sections of men ready to keep the streets clear for rapid movement of his men, and dead or living were thrown together in pits, and it often happens that those who were not yet dead were crushed by the cavalry horses as they passed, not deliberately but in the heat of the battle.[17]

Meanwhile the city below burnt and resounded to the shouts of the victors as they glutted themselves hideously upon the fruits of victory, looting, pillaging, and wiping out men, women, children, and even dogs indiscriminately. The blood lust of the Romans was such that they were still pulling victims out of the debris and butchering them as they cried in vain for quarter, hours after the streets had been won. Maybe they were just extremely brutal men. More likely they had been badly scared by the vicious street fighting, nerve-racking even for those trained in urban combat, and this was the only way to quench their fears. On the seventh day the citadel surrendered and supposedly 50,000 men and women, accompanied by their children and elderly parents, came forth to slavery.[18]

Expecting short shrift if taken alive, 900 deserters from the Roman army made a final stand in the enclosure surrounding the temple of Eshmun.[19] Crowning the summit of the Byrsa, it was reputed to be the most beautiful temple in the city, and, as their numbers gradually shrank, it was in the building itself, then on the roof, the renegades fought before finally immolating themselves in the temple's blazing ruins. Here also the (unnamed) wife of Hasdrubal, with her two children, joined those who, unlike her husband, refused to give in and chose fire and death rather than captivity and slavery.[20] The epic cycle was complete: a woman had presided over the birth of the city, and a woman witnessed its demise. For ten more days the fires of Carthage raged. The elder Pliny speaks of the 'pitch-covered roofs' of the tall many-storeyed houses, and therein lies the explanation for this terrible fire.[21]

Finally, the ruins were systematically razed, a plough was symbolically drawn over the site and the salt of sterility scattered over its smoking remains, and a solemn curse was pronounced against its future rebirth, lesson and punishment from the proud conqueror. With this arcane rite the three exhausting wars between Rome and Carthage had ended in the extermination of one of the two cities. A terrible ending, which illustrates that the fight for survival, far from being just a concept, and often a metaphor, is in many cases a real and violent fact. Carthage was beyond destroyed; it was void as though it had never been.

A Greek in Rome

It is often said that the historian of antiquity soon has all his or her cards on the table, and the best card, sometimes the only one, is a reasonably well-informed Greek who wrote a narrative history of Roman expansion in our period of study, Polybios son of Lykortas (c. 200-118 BC). Sadly for us, his *Histories* has not survived the ravages of time, only the first five of forty books survive intact, the remainder being cobbled together from shorter and longer fragments, so his coverage is at times patchy. Yet for us the account of the three-part struggle between Rome and Carthage is of inestimable value. Not least in that a contemporary writes the detailed description, himself a former cavalry commander, *hipparchos*, in the Achaian League, who had seen the Roman army in action against his fellow-countrymen during the Third Macedonian War (172-168 BC) and had perhaps observed its levying and training during his internment in Rome (167-150 BC). Polybios wrote as a Greek, in Greek, and mainly (though not exclusively) for Greeks.

As a historian Polybios is almost unequalled not only because of his constant search for the causes of the events he critically describes, but also because of his own personal experiences.[22] Not only was he fated to serve in the Achaian League, his father having spent the greater part of his life in its service, but his early interest in the profession of arms is demonstrated by the fact that he was chosen to carry the urn containing the ashes of Philopoimen, the last great soldier of Greece in decline, at his state funeral (182 BC).[23] Stuck between Macedonian militarism and Roman imperialism, the Greeks at the time were living through very difficult times, especially those like Polybios and his father who had responsibilities in their homeland. The defeat of Perseus at Pydna (168 BC) and the collapse of Macedonian power resulted in a terrible purge in Achaia. A thousand hostages were deported to Italy, Polybios among them. He was fortunate enough, as he himself recounts,[24] to attract the attention of the young Publius Cornelius Scipio Aemilianus, grandson of the Lucius Aemilius Paullus killed at Cannae and grandson by adoption of Publius Cornelius Scipio Africanus victor at Zama.[25] Scipio Aemilianus had first seen service as a teenager at Pydna.

Polybios was no less passionate about geography. In this way he visited the theatres of operations that he describes and, as he himself tells us, he questioned veterans who had taken part in Hannibal's long march to Italy, and to have followed the same route over the Alps sixty-odd years after the event in order to satisfy himself about its details.[26] Polybios witnessed the sieges of Carthage (149-146 BC) and Numantia (134-133 BC) at the side of his chief patron, Scipio Aemilianus.[27] This Greek soldier and politician in fact became the young Roman's friend and advisor, almost his mentor. Exiled as he was, and in his convictions a sturdy Greek, Polybios became in his sympathies a great admirer of Rome, and, perhaps for that reason, of Rome's great rival. Yet his authorship was the product of his personal character, and was little modified by patronage.

As a man of action turned historian, Polybios felt the necessity of firsthand evidence wherever it was obtainable, and spared no pains to obtain it. Now convention decreed that a defender would normally only be permitted to surrender on terms if it did so before the first battering ram touched the wall, otherwise the city would be subject to a sack and its surviving inhabitants sold into slavery. It was the way a victorious besieger usually collected its reward, and the price the vanquished defender generally paid for resistance. Thus the main thing that enters a soldier's mind when gets into a city is the desire to loot, and most will go off in search of spoil. Having seized Akragas (261 BC), for instance, Polybios says the Romans comprehensively sacked the city, selling its Greek inhabitants, 25,000 according to Diodoros, into slavery.[28] He actually tells us that he had witnessed the aftermath of a Roman sack of a city, in all likelihood when he had accompanied Scipio Aemilianus on campaign in Africa or Iberia, and had seen the dismembered bodies of men and even animals lying in the streets. Polybios believed that such atrocities were intended to inspire terror, both to overawe the population and prevent further resistance, but also to deter other cities from opposing a Roman army.[29] The Roman disembowelment of a city was brutal even by the standards of the day, which assumed general massacre of men and rape of women.

Polybios was a man of great intelligence, largely free from the inveterate disease of national prejudices, and who was anxious to take the broader view. In this respect he was keen to demonstrate that he had not become involved in the partisan interpretations of events between Carthage and Rome, and makes an explicit declaration of impartiality in describing these events and of objectivity with regard to the images of the contenders. He exposes the limitations of their respective sources, Philinos of Akragas and Quintus Fabius Pictor, who seem to him 'to have been much in the case of lovers; for owing to his convictions and constant partiality Philinos will have it the Carthaginians in every case acted wisely, well, and bravely, and the Romans otherwise, whilst Fabius takes the precisely opposite view'.[30] Thus the image of the Carthaginians that emerges from the narrative of Polybios does not seem to be distorted by factious hostility or the hatred born of prejudice. So, for instance, we find ample testimony to the courage and skill of Carthaginian seamen.[31]

But the point of view of Polybios, and his determination to adopt a position as objective as possible towards the Carthaginians, is best exemplified by the picture he has given us of the man who was in a sense their symbol, Hannibal.[32] Take this

Polybian anecdote, for example. In one council of war the question of logistics during the approaching march to Italy via the Alps was raised once again, and one of Hannibal's senior officers, Hannibal's unrelated namesake, nicknamed Monomachos, suggested that the problem could be eased by training the men to survive off human flesh. Hannibal appreciated the practical value of cannibalism but could not bring himself to consider it. That there was much injustice and brutality there can be little doubt, for that is how soldiers behave in a conquered land, but Polybios recognized that the reputation for ferocious cruelty, which the Romans attached to Hannibal, may in reality have been due to his having been confused for Hannibal Monomachos.[33] Here we can pinpoint the trait of *inhumana crudelitas*, enthusiastically sketched by Livy as one of the chief components in his moral portrait of Hannibal.[34] Of course, as a good Roman, Livy had no liking for Hannibal.

On the whole Polybios is a remarkably sober historian, so much so that this inclines his readers to trust him. He calls his writing *pragmatikê historia*, pragmatic history, based on written evidence, his own knowledge of events, the evidence of eyewitnesses, and so on.[35] His own experiences as a soldier fighting Rome had led him to reflect in later life on the phenomenon of Roman expansion. For him, the triumph of Rome was somehow decreed by destiny, the result of a kind of law of nature. So instead of opposing it, it would be much more sensible to come on board and join the conquerors.

Polybios, had no doubts that the Romans of his own and earlier times wanted to grow from a village by the Tiber to a world empire. And so when the Gauls withdrew from Rome in 390 BC, Polybios tells us, the Romans 'began from that time to enlarge their territory, and in the years that followed they waged a succession of wars against their neighbours'.[36] After the conquest of the Latins, they went on to defeat the Etruscans, Gauls, and Samnites, and so when the Tarentines invited the intervention of Pyrrhos of Epeiros, Polybios continues, 'they now for the first time made war upon the rest of Italy, not as if its inhabitants were foreigners, but as if the country were already rightfully theirs'.[37] Belief too can be a form of imperialism. In any case, in Roman eyes, the Greeks were no good at war. So much for the Greeks, whom the Romans regarded as people who talked too much and were too clever by half. They were double-tongued too.[38]

For two years after the tragic events at Corinth, the once-great Greek city-state that suffered in the same year the same fate as Carthage, Polybios acted as an intermediary between the conquerors and the conquered. His services to Greece were widely recognized, and statues were erected in his honour in Megalopolis, his hometown, and in Mantineia, Tegea, Olympia and elsewhere. The peripatetic Pausanias saw one of them and quoted the inscription on its plinth: 'Greece would never have come to grief, had she obeyed Polybios in all things, and having come to grief, she found succour through him alone'.[39] A man of action to the last, he met his death at 82 years old by an accidental fall from his horse as he was returning home from the countryside.[40]

CHAPTER 11

The horse lords

The Numidians (Greek *Nomádes*, Latin *Numidae*) were akin to the Berbers, the fair-skinned people who occupied large areas of the Maghreb before the Arab invasion of North Africa in the period AD 642 to AD 711.[1] Originally nomadic herdsmen and hunters subsisting in small clans, the Numidians sometimes practised a mix of simple agriculture and transhumant pastoralism. Those on the coast came under the influence of Carthage, which enabled them to live in larger more sophisticated societies, and it is known that the princes of Numidia were allies of the Carthaginians at one time or another, and presumably their famed horsemen were, in theory at least, confederates rather than mercenaries. We know that in the war with the renegade mercenaries the Carthaginians were greatly helped by a friendly Numidian prince, Naravas, who offered to defect with his followers, and eventually fought for them with his troop of about 2,000 horsemen. He was rewarded by marriage to the third daughter of a man he much admired, none other than the daredevil commander of Eryx, Hamilcar Barca.[2]

By the time of the Second Punic War their small clans, consisting of several agnatic kinship groups, had coalesced into two main tribal confederacies. One was the Masaesulii, under their king, Syphax, with his capital at Siga (Takembrit, Algeria) with a second one at Cirta (Constantine, Algeria), whose extensive kingdom, the more westerly of the two, occupied over two-thirds of present-day Algeria. The other was the Maesulii, under their kings, first Gaia and then his son Masinissa (r. 201-148 BC), whose much-smaller kingdom contained the inner mountains and plains of what is now Tunisia, with its principal town of Thugga (Dougga). There were also many minor tribes with their own chieftains and domains.[3] The elder Pliny says in his day some 463 Numidian tribes gave allegiance to Rome.[4]

As we might guess, these indigenous princes had not remained passive spectators of the struggle between Carthage and Rome. They had sided with one or the other, alternating their loyalties. Gaia had supplied Carthage with native contingents, which had been sent to Iberia under Masinissa, who was to fight alongside the Carthaginians from 212 BC and play a far-from-negligible role in the defeat of the elder Cornelii Scipiones. In particular, Numidian horsemen were formidable and well respected by the Carthaginians, but tribalism and disunion made them difficult allies politically. Their earlier relationship to Carthage resembled that of a protectorate, far removed from an alliance of independent states. To reinforce their influence, the Carthaginians had planted a number of fortresses on Numidian territory, including Sicca (El Kef, formerly La Kef, Tunisia), a town we are already familiar with from the war against the mercenaries. But generally Carthage, following the time-honoured tradition of using tribe against tribe, maintained its authority by diplomatic manoeuvring, playing off local tribal and kingdom rivalry.

Masinissa had led a somewhat chequered career, and towards the end of the war with Hannibal he would do Rome the signal service of deserting his ally, Carthage. After the crushing defeat the Carthaginians suffered at Ilipa (206 BC), the prince, sensing a change in the wind, had escaped to Gadir from where he made his way back to Africa. On returning home he found that his father Gaia, who had ruled as a feudatory of Syphax, had died and the succession was caught up in a nasty little civil war, in which Masinissa's uncle (who had inherited the throne) and cousin were cut down at the hands of a brigand, Mazaetullus, who then placed on the throne a boy, Lacumazes, while he himself retained the power as guardian. The cunning brigand then married the old king's widow, who was the daughter of Hannibal's third sister, the one who had married Naravas, and by that means sought to ingratiate himself with Carthage.

In the mean time, finding that his claims were being ignored, Masinissa promptly raised an army, overthrew the puppet king and took possession of the kingdom, only to be driven out by Syphax, who was egged on by Hasdrubal Gisco, the latter rightly suspecting that Masinissa had thrown his lot in with Rome. A landless king, Masinissa sought refuge in the mountains of his homeland and survived by raiding the adjoining Carthaginian lands. Syphax sent a posse to hunt Masinissa down, and the latter barely escaped with his life, hiding in a cave, nursing his wounds, with only two companions. Livy has an exciting tale to tell here, whereby Masinissa was hunted down by an officer named Bucar, who finally drove him into a gully from which he escaped with only fifty horsemen. The little band was eventually cornered and its desperate members picked off in a running fight, only Masinissa, himself wounded, and four others getting away. In the hot pursuit that followed two were drowned in a raging torrent into which Bucar dared not venture. To save face, Bucar reported to Syphax with the news of the fugitive's demise. Of course, as soon as his wounds were sufficiently healed, Masinissa miraculously returned to seek his inheritance, announced his identity, and was immediately joined by supporters who constituted a new army with which he provoked Syphax, once again, to civil war. Between Cirta and Hippo Regius (Annaba, formerly Bône, Algeria) a savage battle was fought in which Syphax won a complete victory. Masinissa just managed to escape with sixty horsemen to the shores in the Emporia region (Latin Syrtis Minor, modern Gulf of Gabès, Tunisia) where he remained in hiding, and he was still at large when Publius Cornelius Scipio landed in Africa.[5]

When Scipio was winding down the war in Iberia and making his preparations for its inevitable sequel, a war in Africa, he had not only entered in negotiations with Masinissa but with Syphax too, the king thinking that Rome would aid him to free himself of Carthage's yoke.[6] It appears that Syphax was of the wait-and-see nature, because as early as 213 BC the elder Cornelii Scipiones had sent envoys from Iberia charged with concluding a treaty of friendship. Three years later, it was Syphax's turn to send an embassy to Rome to assure the Senate that it had no trustier ally than himself, and Rome responded with gifts of a toga and purple tunic, an ivory curule chair and a golden goblet weighting no less than 5 Roman pounds.[7]

Carthage, knowing of these dealings with Scipio, sent Hasdrubal Gisgo to Syphax in order to win back the Numidian king. The Carthaginian general succeeded in doing so by marrying Syphax to his daughter Sophonisba, as famous for her beauty as for her intelligence and culture.[8] To strengthen this bond before his passion had time to cool, Hasdrubal urged and Sophonisba persuaded Syphax to send envoys to Scipio warning him not to cross over to Africa and carry on the war there. His reasons were that he, Syphax, was now tied to Carthage by marriage and by treaty. Rome might fight Carthage outside of Africa, but if it invaded Africa, Syphax would be obliged to take sides.[9] Whether or not we choose to believe that Syphax was enslaved by Sophonisba, we may well imagine that the wily king, though flattered by the attention of Rome, was not anxious to have Carthage on his back, as its intact presence in Africa was still something to be feared. Moreover, he had become its immediate neighbour since, profiting from Masinissa's difficulties with regard to the succession, he had annexed the kingdom of the Maesulii on Carthage's western flank.

In the spring of 204 BC Scipio set sail from Lilybaeum and stepped ashore with his invasion force near Utica at the Fair Promontory, today the Rass Sidi Ali el Mekki, Tunisia. In order to have use of a seaport he moved to besiege Utica. Carthage was in a fix as it had no proper army to hand, and anxiously awaited a band of Celtiberian mercenaries from Iberia.[10] Masinissa, having survived his many adventures and escapes, had joined Scipio with 200 of his loyal horsemen, all the more readily, if we are to believe Diodoros, as he had been Syphax's rival for the hand of Sophonisba, and, as Livy unkindly remarks, 'Numidians surpass all other barbarian peoples in the violence of their appetites'.[11] Hasdrubal, however, quickly raised an army, together with his son-in-law Syphax, although only a rabble of poor quality. Nonetheless, Hasdrubal marched towards Scipio, who raised the siege of Utica and established a fortified camp on a sea-girt peninsula just 3km to the east of the city, the *castra Cornelia*, the name by which the site would still be known in Caesar's day, who would say that is was a particularly suitable place for a camp.[12]

His first year's campaigning in Africa had been cautious and not too successful, and Scipio, entrenched and hunkered down on his promontory, was besieged in

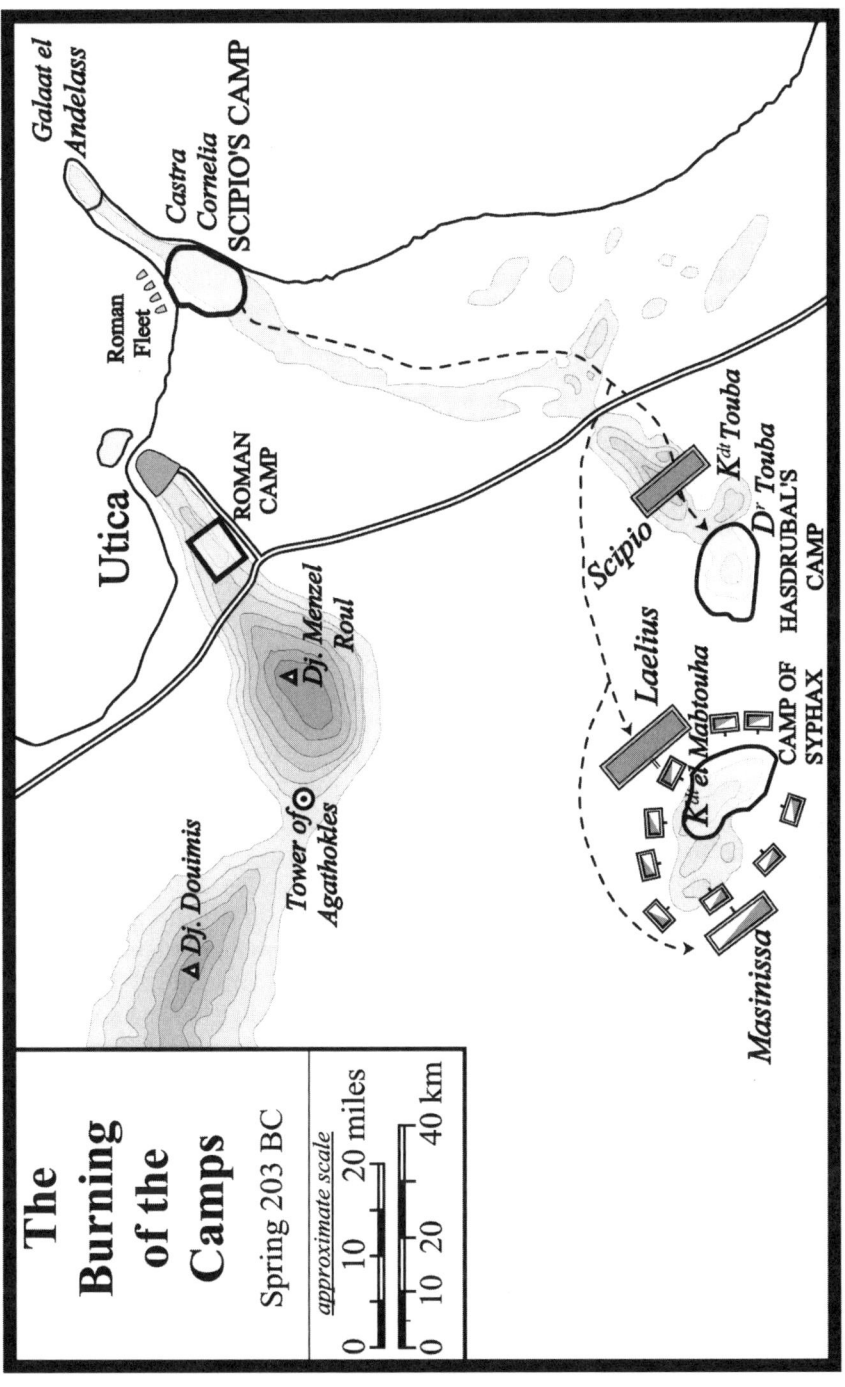

turn by the two armies of Hasdrubal and Syphax, who were encamped about a dozen or so kilometres away. So over the winter months Scipio used his time acquiring intelligence about the opposition. Pretending to open negotiations for peace, though he had no authority from the Senate to do so, he sent out envoys accompanied by experienced centurions disguised as servants, who soon snooped out every secret in the Carthaginian and Numidian camps. They found discipline lax and both camps badly guarded.

Throwing off all semblance of negotiations, in the spring Scipio sent a small body of troops towards Utica equipped with a siege train. The ploy was to make the Carthaginians believe that he was about to reopen the siege. It worked, for the collective attentions of Hasdrubal and Syphax were fully occupied when Scipio made his night attack on their respective camps. Syphax's men were asleep in their huts of reeds and foliage, the famous *mapalia*, and these Masinissa and Laelius torched.[13] Syphax's men, believing that the fire was an accident, were either incinerated in their huts, trampled to death in the rush to escape the flames, or cut down as they tried to escape the camp. Meanwhile, Hasdrubal's men in the other camp, also thinking the fire was accidental, rushed out, some to assist their allies, some to simply goggle in growing alarm. Scipio then fell upon those who had come out, killing some and driving the other back into the camp, to which he immediately set fire, with horrifying results as their huts, made of wood and branches, went up in flames too. In this way the combined forces of Hasdrubal and Syphax perished, though the two leaders themselves managed to get away.[14]

Amazingly, Hasdrubal and Syphax then set about and succeeded in raising another ragtag army, in which the only reliable fighters were the Celtiberians, who had been recruited in central Iberia from one of the toughest of the peninsula's many warlike tribes. With this army, in the spring of 203 BC, they confronted Scipio at the Great Plains.[15]

In the spring Scipio had marched with something like 20,000 men in light marching order to the Great Plains where, if Polybios is to be believed, an army of 30,000 Carthaginians, Numidians and Celtiberian troops had gathered.[22] For two days the two sides skirmished, no doubt taking the measure of each other, discovering as much as they could about their respective strengths and weaknesses. On the third day, Hasdrubal Gisgo and Syphax deployed their combined forces, placing the Numidian horse on the left wing, the Carthaginian cavalry on the right, and the 4,000 Celtiberians in the centre along with the Numidian foot levies. Following the usual Roman practice, Scipio deployed his legions and *alae* in *triplex acies*, with the Roman and Latin-Italian cavalry, under Laelius, facing Syphax's Numidians on his right wing, and Masinissa's Numidians facing the Carthaginian cavalry on the left.

At the first charge the battle passed irredeemably out of Carthaginian hands, as both cavalry wings gave way, soon to be followed by the Numidian foot, so exposing the flanks of the Celtiberians in the centre. Though Polybios says no more than that these fierce warriors were then 'swiftly surrounded by the *principes* and *triarii*', it would seem that Scipio replayed the tactics he had successfully employed at Ilipa.[23] If this was indeed the case, he would have held the Celtiberians frontally, though this time probably engaging them directly with the *hastati*, and then extended his fighting line, by bringing up the second and third lines, so that it could be wheeled in from the flanks to outflank their exposed flanks. Such an option was available to Scipio because of the tactical independence of the Roman system of the *triplex acies*. It is possible, though no means certain, that Scipio's envelopment was completed by the victorious cavalry. The Celtiberians died where they stood, fighting stubbornly to the finish. Polybios points out that their gallant last stand enabled Hasdrubal and Syphax to escape the field.[24] Anyway, the consequences of this defeat were immediately apparent to the senate in Carthage, and the decision was taken to recall Hannibal and Mago from Italy.

Posthaste, after this latest fiasco, Hasdrubal and Syphax escaped a second time, the Carthaginian general taking refuge in Carthage and the Numidian king in Cirta. As for scraping together another army, the highly-prized Celtiberians lay dead and the hastily-recruited Numidian peasants had probably run for their homes to help with the crops.

Entrusting the blockade of Utica to the fleet, Scipio's next move was to march with the greater part of his army against Carthage, laying waste to the country as he went. In a state of near panic, the Carthaginian senate dispatched a delegation to Hannibal, armed with orders for his recall from Italy without further ado. In the meantime, a flying column under Masinissa and Laelius had pursued the fleeing Syphax into Numidia. Masinissa's own tribesmen at once rallied to him, but Syphax, acceding to the entreaties of his wife, was able to raise yet another army and turn at bay. In the ensuing action, however, his raw army was again utterly routed and he himself thrown from his badly wounded horse and taken prisoner. Cirta and Sophonisba fell into the hands of the Romans.

Cirta had been the eastern capital of Masinissa's bitter rival Syphax, and Masinissa was now installed there as the king of all Numidia. Consequently, he was to furnish much needed cavalry to Scipio at the Battle of Zama, which meant the Romans faced Hannibal with more cavalry than he, horsemen that had often fought for Carthage.[16] No doubt the prince had gauged the Romans, more tenacious than the Carthaginians, would prevail, and when this happened he was rewarded, as he had doubtless hoped, with a good slice of Carthaginian territory, namely those towns and lands that he had lightsomely appropriated during the closing stages of the war.

The one thing Masinissa did not get, however, was the beautiful Sophonisba. Apparently, though this amatory interlude has been much doubted, upon her capture she presented herself before Masinissa, imploring him to save her from the only possible fate the Romans could have in store for her.[17] Buckling under to her irresistible charms, Masinissa fell head over heels in love, promised to grant her request, and married her that same day so that she should be recognized as the consort of a Numidian king, and not be a prisoner of the Romans to adorn Scipio's forthcoming triumph.[18] Critics tend to interpret the presence of women in the historical narrative as mere literary devices or cyphers, inserted at strategic places to titillate or to carry the story forward. Nevertheless, it is refreshing to be reminded of the one great truth that often escapes the (male) academic historian: half of the population are women.

Anyway, Scipio saw things rather differently. Having congratulated Masinissa on his military prowess, he then castigated him for his inability to resist the temptations of sensuality. Syphax was a prisoner of Rome, and Sophonisba, who was Syphax's wife, was likewise a prisoner and must be sent to Rome. Having pledged not to hand her over to the Romans, yet unable to renounce his friendship with Scipio, Masinissa ordered a trusted servant to mix a cup of poison and take it to Sophonisba, with the injunction to remember her father was Hasdrubal Gisgo, a general of Carthage. Sophonisba took the hint and drained the cup.[19] Her father's fate, however, is less certain. Though Hasdrubal escaped crucifixion in spite of being sentenced to death, it seems that he took his own life in 202 BC, driven so by his fellow citizens' hostility. At all events he disappears from the record. As for her lawful husband, he was bundled off to Italy in chains. Here the former all-powerful Numidian king languished and died in prison at the resort town of Tibur (Tivoli) before Scipio's triumph, thus sparing him being reduced to total degradation.[20]

So, Syphax passes from history too. Not so Masinissa. Having sacrificed Sophonisba for reasons of state, the following day the ephemeral husband was paraded before the soldiers of Rome and hailed as a king. Scipio then presented him with the insignia, including an ivory sceptre: in Latin, *scipio*. It was to be a dawn of a brave, albeit rather brief, new era for Numidia.

Under Masinissa nomadism was largely abandoned, at least in the more placid eastern part of the kingdom, for mixed agriculture and urban life developed, while Punic was unhesitatingly adopted as the language of the ruling élite, coins minted using the Semitic language and characters, and the worship of Baal Hammon became popular alongside indigenous cults.[21] In many ways Numidia had been transformed into a kingdom of a large number of settled farming communities ruled by a bilingual, bicultural court. Under the superficial structure of the Numidian state, however, tribal social systems remained strong and skilled horsemen still abounded. This was particularly so in those communities situated in distant, wild and desert-like lands, with their worn, hardy, ill-clad people who relied on herding and hunting to survive and, therefore, were constantly fighting and foraying.

Wealth could be hoarded in several ways. Coins, silver naturally, were by Masinissa's day widely used, but many among those tribes in the more remote regions, where the nomadic lifestyle of the horse warrior still prevailed, the number of one's cattle still provided the simplest and most readily recognizable means of displaying wealth and status. Cattle, providing milk, meat and hide, were the measuring stick of worth; in that respect, and only in that sense, cattle were currency. Little wonder, therefore, that cattle rustling was endemic, as much a part of the pastoral scene as the spring sowing or autumn reaping. Raising cattle meant generously, if unwittingly, handing hostages to fortune. There is little that human predators can do to arable farming except destroy crops, an unprofitable proceeding for all concerned. Cattle, on the other hand, can be rustled with reasonable facility and become an asset to the rustler. Indeed, cattle were not only a measure of wealth, but also provided material evidence of a man's prestige. The successful warrior could build up a large herd by raiding and penetrating deep into a neighbour's territory and ranging widely, and driving off his cattle and horses, as well as taking precious salt.

Worse could come in the form of a sudden raid on a settlement, plundering it, destroying its meagre crops, and herding the inhabitants into slavery. Pressing the point even further, we know that a brisk foray into an out-of-the-way settlement is hardly to be counted as one of the greatest events in the history of warfare, involving as it probably did a handful of Numidian horsemen who rushed into the village, launched their javelins, slashed around a bit and then rushed out again. But it was all very real for the occupants of the village. The first they learned of the arrival of a hostile band of horsemen was probably a cloud of dust, followed by the dull thud of hooves, followed by a rain of javelins. Life at the top of Numidian society may have changed for the better, but at the bottom of the pile it was very much a case of same old same.

CHAPTER 12

Mobile warfare

At the outset, it should be stressed that the Numidian lifestyle was by no means one of peace and tranquillity. Intertribal conflicts flared; raids, ambushes, and theft were commonplace occurrences and hunger and disease constant companions in lean years. Whereas raiding was a matter of taking the enemy's property, war meant taking his life. In the latter, tribal troops followed their own chieftains, but it was terribly difficult for Numidian chieftains and princes to hold a large force together in the field for more than a few weeks. Used to mounting raids of short duration, raiding parties were small, for concealment was a prime consideration, and could be raised quickly, but the need to remain in the field for a protracted period was alien to them. After battle these 'armies' had the disquieting habit of melting away with the spoils, particularly at sowing or harvesting time. After all, the Numidian warrior was a hunter and a provider too; war was only one facet of his life.

Though the best warriors were horsemen, especially those from the arid steppe areas of the Sahara were the nomadic cattle-rearing life still prevailed, the bulk of Numidian armies were composed of barefoot tribesmen with legs strong from the peripatetic life. Their weaponry was generally light, with javelins and bucklers much more common than spears or swords,[1] though better-equipped (or wealthier) warriors could carry a sword, mostly taken from (or given by) the Romans.[2] With helmets or body armour being virtually nonexistent, for battle warriors usually wore minimal clothing, consisting of a baggy tunic, probably of undyed wool, and very little else. Livy speaks of Numidian 'horsemen without armour [viz. unshielded], and without weapons [viz. sidearms], apart from the javelins they carried', Polybios also speaks of javelins, whereas Herodotos speaks of North African shields made of 'ostrich skin' and Strabo of rawhide, and what we can imagine here is a small, round, boss-less, hide shield, which was slightly convex with a narrow rim.[3] All in all, the impression to be gained from the literary evidence confirms that it is highly unlikely that all Numidians were equipped in an identical manner.

For really close work, when their store of javelins should have been exhausted, and delivering the *coup de grâce* to one's fallen enemy, the favoured weapon was the dagger. Generally, the blade of this shock weapon was short and double-edged, and was designed primarily for stabbing, rather than slashing, to penetrate deep into the body of an opponent, though only creating a narrow wound. Of course, a dagger was also useful for those more mundane chores in the field, such as skinning and butchering game, and was commonly regarded as a utilitarian tool as well as a personal weapon. The earliest daggers are made from a single sheet of flat metal, whilst later examples are made with a clearly defined mid-ridge to the blade, which gives additional strength. Handles were of organic materials, such as wood, bone or ivory, and scabbards of wood or leather were used to protect the blades when not in use. These early examples are small enough to be carried tucked into the belt of the warriors' tunic. Otherwise, they could be carried on a band around the arm. The arm dagger is a weapon habitually worn by peoples of Saharan and Sudanic Africa, amongst them the Tuareg, a branch of the Berber race. The style here is to keep it in a sheath attached to the inner side of the left forearm by a loop, the sheath and loop usually of leather but sometimes of metal, such as decoratively engraved brass. The blade points to the elbow and the flat hilt rests against the inside of the wrist, from which position it can be quickly drawn with the right hand.[4]

Their confrontations with the mail-coated soldiers of Rome who finally destroyed their independent existence occupied only six or seven decades, and was not typical of the Numidian experience. True, the most powerful kings of Numidia, such as Syphax and Iugurtha, also raised élite units of slaves, freedmen and mercenaries paid through taxation. These infantry formations were based upon the Roman model, with some of the best-equipped troops in the world, and even abided Roman training and discipline. Little is known of their origins, though those levied by Iugurtha included Thracians and Ligurians, and Sallust specifically talks of deserters fighting for the king, in other words Roman and/or Italian legionaries.[5]

Ordinarily, in the more limited primitive encounters that characterized small-scale warfare between tribes and smaller groups, the two sides encamped opposite one another for several days. A local decision, however, was produced speedily. Either the attacker was repulsed and allowed to withdraw, or he broke through the defender's formation, killed those still inclined to offer active resistance, pursued the flying remnants for a kilometre or so slaughtering the hindmost freely, picked up anything of value, and returned triumphant to his camp. Victory in the scientific sense was rarely exploited: limited operations were undertaken to achieve limited objectives. In this way, for instance, hunting grounds were not won through pitched battles, but through constant harassment.

The greatest tool, and the focal point for all warfare in their society, was the horse. Often ignored, and frequently abused, it was the horse that offered the Numidian the obvious advantages of speed, mobility, and freedom of targeting. As he was unarmoured, and it was never his intention to arm himself to fight pitched battles but rather for the dash of hit-and-run tactics, his defence lay in his horse too. This is not to say that the Numidian was lacking in courage. Being lighter-armed and equipped, he was able to move with greater speed and agility than his opponents. If things were going well, he would stand his ground, but if any time the foe began to gain an advantage then he would fade from the scene, prepared to take up the fight again when the advantage should lay with him.

Though obviously he was one with his mount, it seems more likely that the Numidian horseman rode bareback, rather than upon the four-horned rigid saddle employed by contemporary Celtic and Roman cavalry. His only tack was a simple neck strap of leather or rope and he guided his mount with voice and legs. One thing the Graeco-Roman sources do have in common, however, is praise for the Numidians' mastery of their desert horses, so much so that these sources make much of Numidian 'bareback horsemen', who rode 'without bridles'.[6] They also appear as such on the later Trajan's Column in Rome, and the unique 'Rastafarian' hairstyle of these horse warriors may be artistic licence and not necessarily dependent on autopsy, an instance, if you will, of 'Burnt Cork Zulus'.

The Numidians seem to have been frequent victims of negative stereotyping, a veritable carnival sideshow of human oddities viewed from a distance. For though their power of endurance were often remarked upon,[7] their greatest accomplishment, as Polybios will have us believe, was self-preservation, for if beaten in battle they had a habit of fleeing for up to three days.[8] Livy, on the other hand, scorns them as untrustworthy, undisciplined, hot-tempered, and with more violent appetites than any other so-called barbarians.[9] Aelian, while praising their ability to endure fatigue, denigrates the care that Numidians gave their horses, saying 'they neither rub them down, roll them, clean their hooves, comb manes, plait forelocks, nor wash them when tired, but when dismounted turn them loose to graze'.[10] Lazy or not, turning a horse loose to graze immediately after a tough ride is the best treatment he can have and often prevents muscle and limb ailments. Numidian horses appear to have been small, hardy animals.[11] Livy depicts both horses and riders as 'tiny and lean' in a passage that praises Numidian horsemanship but ridicules their appearance.[12] Strabo comments on the size and speed of African horses in general, and they are prominent in the chariot-racing inscriptions at Rome.[13]

The use of big, barley-fed horses made Roman cavalry dependent on supply lines, especially when grass was scarce. However, the Numidians' grass-fed animals were incapable of sustained winter use, which did not hamper the Roman animals, provided supplies of grains were available of course. Even when stripped down to bare essentials, carrying limited rations and fodder, as Metellus was to do when he marched on Thala, a train of pack mules was still an essential requirement.[14] The Athenian *condottiere*, Xenophon, an expert horseman himself, emphasizes the importance of sufficient fodder for horses so that they would be able to perform as well as required, 'since horses unfit for their work can neither overtake nor escape'.[15] A horse in its natural habitat, living on grass, would eat most of the time. As a grazing animal the horse requires food in small amounts frequently, thus it is better to feed a stabled horse about three or four times a day rather than only once or twice. Grass alone, even when supplemented by hay in the winter months, is not sufficient for stabled horses (e.g. Roman cavalry mounts)

(*Left*) Marble head of Publius Cornelius Scipio Africanus (Rome, Musei Capitolini, inv. MC 562). Scipio has been hailed as 'greater than Napoleon', but many would rightly disagree with this cocksure judgement. As a general Scipio blended personal magnetism with careful planning based on good use of intelligence and attention to training. He was not afraid to use innovatory tactics too, often based on the element of surprise. His tactics were obviously inspired by those of Hannibal, and required good legionary officers as well as generalship to implement. Despite his success, however, Scipio would end his life in exile. (*Nic Fields*)

(*Right*) Marble statue of Hannibal (Paris, musée du Louvre, inv. MR 2093) by Sébastien Slodtz and François Girardon (1704). We know next to nothing about the personal appearance of the man who is perhaps the most famous of all the enemies of Rome, aside from the fact that he became blind in one eye. Here he is portrayed counting gold rings. Apparently after his brilliant victory at Cannae, Hannibal gathered in a bushel the rings torn from the lifeless fingers of more than fourscore consuls, ex-consuls, praetors, aediles, quaestors, military tribunes, and scores of the equestrian order. In other words, most of Rome's military leadership and social élite lay on the battlefield. (*Esther Carré*)

3. (*Right*) Limestone relief (Madrid, Museo Arqueológico Nacional, inv. 38424) from Osuna, Seville, depicting two Iberian warriors. Each wears a short linen or woollen tunic, usually (sun bleached?) white with crimson (mixture of indigo and madder) borders, bears a flat, oval body shield, much like the Italic *scutum*, hence the Latin name *scutarus*, and wields a short, but deadly sword, the *falcata*. Like the Greek *kopis* from which it was derived, the *falcata* had a single-edged, curved blade (35–55cm long) that widened towards the point, thereby increasing the kinetic energy of a blow. (*Esther Carré*)

4. (*Bottom left*) 'Wounded Gaul' (Paris, musée du Louvre, inv. MR 133), Roman copy of an earlier Greek bronze. In the *omnium gatherum* that was his army, it would seem that Hannibal used his Celtic allies (mainly Gauls from northern Italy) as 'cannon fodder', suffering the casualties and receiving few rewards. Yet this wild, warlike race fought in an undisciplined throng, rushing and swinging long swords, and it would be altogether wrong to think that Hannibal rode to victory over the backs of his fallen 'barbarian' friends. Gauls normally fought stripped to the waist in just trousers, usually of plaid and tied at the ankles, though they might retain their *sagum*, the traditional Celtic cloak. (*Esther Carré*)

5. (*Bottom right*) Bronze equestrian figurine (London, British Museum) of a Numidian horseman. Riding without either bridle or saddlecloth almost from infancy, Numidians rode small, swift horses that appeared scrawny and neglected but were capable of enduring where fleshier mounts could not. These horse warriors, lightly equipped and exceedingly mobile, were brilliant skirmishers, and on campaign were ideal for foraging, reconnaissance, raiding, and ambush. Under a first-class general, such as Hamilcar or Hannibal, Numidians made excellent irregular horse. Of course, under the slippery Iugurtha, they were to cause the Roman invaders no end of bother. (*Esther Carré*)

This reconstruction depicts [on]e of Xanthippos' Greek [m]ercenaries on the morning of [Tu]nis. He peacefully stands, [fe]et slightly astride, leaning on [hi]s spear with his spear arm, [an]d holding with his other [ha]nd a morsel of hard bread [up]on which he is chewing. By [hi]s feet lays his helmet, which [is] of the 'Phrygian' pattern. The [pr]incipal tool of our [me]rcenary's trade is a long [th]rusting spear, the *dóru*. [Fa]shioned out of polished ash [wo]od and averaging 2–2.5m in [le]ngth, his *dóru* is equipped [wi]th an iron spearhead and [bro]nze butt-spike. As well as [ac]ting as a counterweight to the [sp]earhead, the butt-spike [all]ows the spear to be planted [in] the ground when not in use, [or] to fight with if his spear [sn]aps in the mêlée. He also [pa]cks a sword, the *kopis*, a [he]avy, one-edged blade [de]signed for slashing with an [ov]erhand stroke. The cutting [ed]ge is on the inside like a [Gu]rkha *kukri*, while the broad [ba]ck of the blade curves [for]ward in such a way to [w]eight the weapon towards [the] tip. (© *Graham Sumner*)

7. In this reconstruction we show a fully equipped *caetratus* (pl. *caetrati*), so named by our Graeco-Roman sources for the small round buckler, the *caetra*, he bears. Our warrior is wearing a short woollen tunic, white (sun bleached?) with crimson (mixture of indigo and madder) borders, and wielding a short, but deadly sword, the *falcata*, a curved single-bladed weapon derived from the Greek *kopis*. The *caetra* was made of wood, anything from 30–60cm in diameter, with metal fittings and ornaments on the face, and a large metal boss protecting a stout metal handgrip on the inside. Slung on a long carrying strap when not in use, while in battle its lightness allowed the warrior not only to parry enemy blows, but to punch with the boss or chop with the rim of the *caetra* too. (© *Graham Sumner*)

. Despite being a fresh-faced tyro, our young citizen in this reconstruction has equipped himself well. The great advantage of the linen corselet (Greek *nothôrax*) was its comfort, as it is more flexible and much cooler than bronze under an African sun. To complete his body protection, he wears a 'Phrygian' helmet, so-named because its shape resembled the 'Phrygian bonnet' worn during antiquity and borrowed during the French Revolution. This style commonly had a fairly substantial brim to provide some protection to the upper face, and long pointed cheek-pieces extending below the chin to provide some protection to the throat. These were usually plain, but could occasionally extend to cover the whole face, only leaving apertures for the eyes and mouth and frequently decorated with embossed facial hair. Once again our young citizen has spared no expense as the cheek-pieces of his helmet are superbly embossed with stylized curls to represent a luxuriant beard and moustache.

(© *Graham Sumner*)

9. Though a peasant conscript, nature at least had designed our Numidian for a javelineer. As this reconstruction shows, he is light, athletic and lissome, with a good length of arm. He is armed with the chief missile of all north African peoples, namely the broad-bladed javelin. Javelins could be equipped with a finger loop, a thin leather thong that provided leverage and acted like a sling to propel the javelin, and as it was launched the thong unwound, having the same effect as the rifling inside a rifle barrel: it spun the javelin, ensuring a steadier flight. The other personal weapon of our Numidian is the arm dagger, which is housed in a leather sheath attached to the inner side of his left forearm by a leather loop. For quick extraction with the right hand the flat wooden hilt rests against the inside of his left wrist. His hardy pony, able to thrive on the meagrest grazing, affords him unrivalled mobility in raiding and battle. (© *Graham Sumner*)

10. (*Left*) A member of the Tarragona-based reenactment group *LEGIO PRIMA GERMANICA* equipped as a veteran citizen-soldier, a *triarius*, from the time of the war with Hannibal. He wears a superbly reconstructed mail shirt. Combining strength with flexibility, the Celtic innovation of mail consisted of a matrix of alternatively riveted and simple iron rings, each being linked through its four neighbours. With this complicated construction, the force of a sword blow was spread over a wide enough area for the wearer to be no more than bruised. (*Graham Sumner*)

11. (*Bottom*) Roman annalistic tradition has the penultimate king of Rome, Servilius Tullius (r. *c.*579 to *c.*534 BC) introduce a major reform of its socio-political and military organization. His first consideration was the creation of a citizen army, and the most important point was to induce the citizens to adequately arm themselves for the defence of the state. So a census of all adult male citizens recorded the value of their property and divided them accordingly into five classes. A clerk on the Altar of Domitius Ahenobarbus (Paris, musée du Louvre, inv. Ma 975) records names, either as a census or as part of the levying, *legio*, of citizen-soldiers. (*Esther Carré*)

12. (*Above*) Two legionaries and an *equites* on the Altar of Domitius Ahenobarbus (Paris, musée du Louvre, inv. Ma 975) equipped with the arms and armour of the last two centuries of the Republic. They wear iron mail shirts, thigh-length with shoulder doubling for extra protection against downward sword strokes. The belt around the waist would transfer some of the shirt's weight (*c*.15kg) from the shoulders to the hips. While the foot soldiers wear Etrusco-Corinthian helmets, the horseman sports a plumed Boiotian helmet, a popular style with Graeco-Roman cavalry of the period as it provided unimpaired vision and hearing. (*Esther Carré*)

13. (*Right*) Mars, god of war, on the Altar of Domitius Ahenobarbus (Paris, musée du Louvre, inv. Ma 975) dressed in the uniform of a senior officer, most probably that of a *tribunus militum*, military tribune. Looking more Greek than Roman, he wears a short muscled cuirass equipped with two rows of fringed *pteruges*, which was necessary for those who rode a horse, greaves, and a crested Etrusco-Corinthian helmet. Developed from the Corinthian-type, this pattern commonly preserved the eyeholes for decoration. He also has a circular shield, a spear, and a sword, which he wears on the left side. The knotted sash around his waist probably denotes his rank. (*Esther Carré*)

since it will not keep them in hard condition. To achieve this, extra food, usually hard fodder in the form of cereals, must be given.

The quantity of fodder necessary to sustain each managed horse depends upon its size and amount of work it has to perform. The ratio of cereals to hay can be varied, provided the horse always receives adequate food-value to sustain the amount of work it is doing. Modern horses are generally fed more hay and less cereal when they are not working. When in work, on the other hand, horses require less roughage, so the quantities of hay can be reduced, but require more protein so the cereal ration is accordingly increased.[16] Oats, barley and maize are the most commonly used modern cereals, but barley is fattening, and usually slightly less barley or maize is given compared to oats. Modern barley has approximately 11 per cent protein, as do oats and maize, but varieties grown today differ very much from ancient ones and, in the main, have far less nutritional content than ancient strains.[17]

As ancient grains would have given much better nutrition than the modern feedstuffs, a smaller quantity could be fed and still achieve good results. At the turn of the twentieth century, British army cavalry horses were given a daily forage ration of 5.4kg of hay, 4.5kg of oats and 3.6kg of straw, divided into three or four feeds. In addition, chaff was mixed with feeds, and bran mash, sometimes with linseed cake, was given once a week.[18] In AD 187 a Roman cavalry unit stationed at Coptos, Egypt, received 20,000 *artabai* of barley as the year's supply for its mounts.[19] Using this evidence, Davies estimates that a single Roman cavalry unit (i.e. an *ala quingenaria*), which usually mustered 560 horses in this period, would eat its way through 625 tons of barley in a year.[20]

Varro, Columella and the elder Pliny all mention a mixed crop of barley, vetch and legumes, called *farrago*, Varro adding that it is good for purging horses at the beginning of spring, which is also the beginning of the campaigning season for the military. However, the evidence for cereal rations issued to the cavalry is not abundant.[21] Polybios confirms the men were issued with wheat and the horses were fed on a ration that was about 1kg dry weight of barley a day,[22] though the latter could be used as punishment rations for the men too.[23] Papyri from Doura-Europos confirm that barley still formed the basis of the cereal ration for the cavalry horses of the Principate, while papyri from Egypt show them receiving regular supplies of hay.[24] In truth barley is not very suitable for horses as it is apt to induce short-windedness and sweating until digestive tolerance is achieved, but it is universal in recorded antiquity until the adoption of the northern fodder-grain oats in early medieval Europe.

The hay and green fodder mentioned most often and favourably in Roman agricultural literature is what we know as lucerne or alfalfa. The Romans called it *medica* as it originated from the lush Median plain where the famed Nisaean horses were raised.[25] Good grass hays have a protein content ranging from 7-10 per cent, whereas lucerne cut at the optimum time has almost double that.[26] Columella enumerates all its splendid qualities, ending with the statement that the yield from one *iugerum* (0.25 ha) of it provides enough to feed three horses for a year.[27]

By comparison, the Numidian keepers of horses did not stable them or give them special food and, therefore, had no incentive to breed a horse unfit for its environment. Generally, desert breeds can feed on virtually any quality of pasturage, fending for themselves in the very severe conditions of a desert environment. Coping well and gaining sustenance in a poorer country would give critical advantage to horse warriors on extended raids, as their mounts would not require the cartage of fodder but were simply let loose at the end of a day's riding to fend for themselves on the available vegetation. Such horses offered a definite advantage to anyone intent on a quick raid over any distance at any time of the year. The Numidians thus had a mount that was not only universally resilient but also low maintenance, and these qualities were not lost on the Romans.

It was under Masinissa that Numidian horsemen became the prime military resource of the state, and by the early second century BC Numidian mercenaries were being employed, especially in Iberia, as Roman auxiliaries. According to Strabo the kings were 'much occupied with the breeding of horses thus 100,000 foals in a year have been counted with a census'.[28] True, these horses were of a hardy though 'ungroomed' breed, but what must be remembered is that here the Graeco-Roman authors, Aelian, Strabo et cetera, are subconsciously comparing the pasture-fed horse of the Numidians with the stall-fed horse of the Romans. It was very graceful and fast. It was surefooted and strong. It was far better at climbing, jumping and swimming than Roman horses, and the main equine characteristics looked for being a flat back for ease of riding and the long slender neck of a good jumper.

The Numidians were strong in the use of horses, and horses were an advantage in a fast-moving, swirling clash. On the other hand, their enemy, the Romans, were strong in the use of heavy infantry, and heavy infantry were an advantage in a slow-paced, slogging match. In this each of them naturally relied upon their strengths. Initially the Numidians faced the Romans in open battle, but soon resorted to the art of ambushing the enemy in terrain of their own choosing. After all, the ground of their own country was their ally and they had an instinctive ability in the use of cover. As we can well appreciate, this meant the Roman army was forced to fight a form of irregular warfare at which it did not excel, for which its soldiers were untrained and its equipment unsuited. The Numidian aim was not to wage set-piece battles and win big victories, but to nibble at the pedestrian Roman, taunt and harass him in such a way that he could neither eat nor sleep in peace, to give him no respite, to wear him out physically and mentally, and finally to annihilate him.

The Romans were strangers in a strange land. As Napoleon would later write, of all the obstacles to impede an army, 'the most difficult to overcome is the desert'.[29] Whereas rich, fertile regions offer to the invader a thousand necessary supplies, while in barren or desert regions huts and straw are about the only resources. Roman commands, so long accustomed to the relative comforts of the Iberian and Balkan peninsulas, would almost perish in the arid wastes of Numidia, whereas the Numidians were extremely effective on terrain that was intrinsically hostile to any form of wheeled transport. Indeed, their uncanny speed and mobility were enormously enhanced by the minimal supply lines required. Perhaps four or five days' provisions in the shape of cereal stuffed inside gunny sacks, and a herd of cattle proportional to the distance to be traversed accompanied each native army. The Numidians faced annihilation by superior arms if they challenged Roman supremacy, but elusively mobile they could strike viciously and recoil swiftly, using their ancient skills to evade pursuit.

Numidian horsemen were what we moderns would recognize as light irregular horse, excellent for skirmishing, harassing, terrifying by their unearthly war whoops and their unbridled gallop. Instability incarnate, they were unable to hold their own against steady, bridled horse, that is to say, the spear- and sword-carrying cavalry favoured by the Romans. Yet they were men who had been on their mounts since childhood, who could launch javelins with deadly accuracy at a gallop, and slash and hack away with daggers at close quarters as easily mounted as on foot. They were but a swarm of desert flies that always plagues and kills at the least mistake; elusive and perfect for a long pursuit and the massacre of the vanquished to whom the Numidians gave neither respite nor quarter. With the Numidian, war remained a matter of agility and cunning, and in the actual moment of violence their battleline was right on the heels of the enemy. Hunting was his principal pastime and the pursuit of game taught him the pursuit of man.[30] The mature and seasoned hunter was as keen, cunning and hardy as the prey he sought, and he knew the peculiarities of nature. The Numidians, savage but skilful horsemen, inspired a veritable terror by the incessant alarms they caused. They fatigued without fighting and slaughtered by stealth.

As an ideal warrior society, whatever that may be, the Numidians simply do not come up to scratch. A military nation and a warlike nation are not necessarily the same. The Romans were warlike from organization and instinct, and many of their mawkish accounts of the Numidians fit the conventional racially-biased characterization of barbarians as argumentative, stupid, volatile and with little intelligence, except animal cunning. They lie, break their oaths and, in battle, they are cacophonic and prefer ambush and long-distance fighting to the good old, honest hand-to-hand combat for which Rome's armoured and disciplined soldiers were specially trained. It is said that real bravery is that inspired by devotion to duty, yet the bravery sprung from hot blood pleased the wild desert nomad more. He understood it, and it appealed to his vanity; it was the characteristic of his nature. But such bravery was fleeting; it failed him at times when he sensed the ripples of hesitation through the masses around him. By comparison the Romans were not mighty men, but men of tough discipline and hardheaded stubbornness.

The Battle of the Great Plains has already been touched upon, and it was here that the Numidians on the Carthaginian side broke at first contact. The reason for such a poor showing when hard-pressed lies in the fact that Syphax's men were recently recruited peasants, sketchily trained and conspicuously erratic, with little or no experience as horsemen.[31] The means to attain a disciplined, effective fighting force are quite simple (at least on paper): organize properly, train extensively, and motivate thoroughly. Thus repetitive training furnishes the means for co-ordinated, articulated movement on the battlefield, whereas disorder dooms one's battle tactics and turns the conflict into an utter shambles. A small, well-disciplined force can usually overcome a numerically superior one if the latter lacks cohesion and direction. The legionary might be individually less impressive as a fighting man, but his dogged, plodding legions did not dwindle and drift apart as warriors became bored, tired, disheartened, or worried about their crops, herds and families. The legionary was a tool, in theory, and usually in practice, of a single overall command with a unified plan of campaign.

Caesar's legate in Africa, Caius Scribonius Curio, would lead his small army to disaster in a waterless wasteland against the Numidians. Curio with two legions and 500 cavalry, partly worn out by campaigning, pursued a Numidian force of 3,000 horsemen and 10,000 foot levies across a dust-filled barren plain. True to form, the Numidians swirled like smoke around Curio, shooting and yelling and avoiding contact until his troops were exhausted, then, when he tried to retreat, cut him off from the safety of high ground and destroyed his army at leisure by smothering it with missiles. Disdaining to flee, Curio paid the price for his impetuosity, dying alongside his breathless men, who, it was said, perished packed so tightly around him that their corpses were left standing like sheaves of corn in a field. According to Appian, 'Curio's head was cut off and brought to Iuba'.[32] Ironically, the previous year, as a tribune of the people, Curio had proposed a bill making the king's territory a Roman province.[33]

A year or so later, Caesar's legionaries were to experience the same frustrating tactics that had led to Curio's catastrophic defeat. According to the unidentified historian of the *Bellum Africum*, perhaps a serving Caesarian tribune, the 'enemy troops were Numidians and light-armed infantry, endowed with remarkable quickness and used to fighting alongside the horsemen and keeping pace with them as they advanced or retreated'.[34] Battles are damn dangerous affairs and foot-soldiers, even to this day, are heavily dependent on agility and foot speed for both their survival and aggressiveness. Yet the legionary, like all professional foot-soldiers before his day and after, was grossly overloaded with kit. Often, in the heaviest hours, when the legionaries were drowsily advancing over the plains weighed down by war gear, a great line of dust would suddenly arise on the horizon; hordes of centaur-like Numidians would appear, and out of a cloud full of terrifying flashing eyes a hail of missiles would rain down. Thus during the Thapsus operation, so our anonymous author tells us, Caesar issued 'instructions that three hundred men out of each legion should be in light order', so that they might co-operate with the cavalry and thus match the enemy horsemen with their supporting light-armed infantry.[35] Since the dawn of warfare, 'civilized' armies bogged down in foreign lands have tended to ape the tactics of the 'uncivilized' locals, an affectation declaring both supremacy and respect, possibly, an expediency seeking both victory and conquest, certainly. So it was with Caesar (though not Curio) in Africa.

HORSE SENSE

As we know, Numidian horsemen preferred to fight in a loose formation, continually harassing their quarry with deadly barrages of missiles and avoiding hand-to-hand combat, which made them difficult opponents to handle on the battlefield. They would also take every opportunity to enhance their terrifying image, attacking with much disorderly movement while making savage noises. But what of the opposition, the steady, bridled cavalry favoured by the Romans?

Generally, as cavalry was unsuitable to holding ground because of its tendency to advance and retreat rapidly, the tactical principles were: the use of cavalry for flank attacks and encirclement; the placing of a force in reserve; the deployment of a combat line that could maintain contact, readiness to counterattack, flexibility in the face of unexpected enemy manoeuvres. As Napoleon succinctly puts it, 'charges of cavalry are equally useful at the beginning, the middle, and the end of a battle'.[36] When the army deployed for battle it was the infantry who were expected to form up in the centre to fight the main action and deliver the crushing blow. However, the success of the cavalry in protecting the flanks and defeating the enemy cavalry could decide the outcome.

Walls of galloping horseflesh rushing like battering-rams to smash the enemy lines with so-called shock attacks, this is an image more suited to the Hollywood screen fantasy or the pages of historical fiction. In encounters at full tilt, men and mounts would be mashed, a matter of mutual extermination, and neither men nor mounts wished such an encounter. More often than not, one or the other side would panic and dissolve. Colonel Ardant du Picq, the French military theorist, now takes up the story:

> And if ever they met, the encounter was so weakened by the hands of the men, the rearing of the horses, the swinging of heads, that is was a face to face stop. Some blows were exchanged with the sword or the lance, but the equilibrium was too unstable, mutual support too uncertain for real sword play. Man felt himself too isolated. The moral pressure was too strong.[37]

The shock at suicidal speed is a myth, the reasoning of our shrewd infantry colonel being that so-called shock in battle is in actual fact moral or psychological rather than physical. Always before the encounter, the weaker runs away, if there is not a face to face check. These hurricanes of horsemen would halt face to face, abreast, to fight man to man; or each passes the other, thrusting with spear or sword. But as each was trying to strike the other, he thought of keeping out of harm's way himself.

As horses refuse to collide into an oncoming line of horsemen, encounters between opposing cavalry forces would have been very fluid, fast-moving affairs.

When combats occurred, it was because either the two lines had opened their files, allowing them to gallop through each other's formation, or they had halted just before contact, at which point individuals would walk their mounts forward to get within weapon's reach of the enemy.

Similarly, the offensive use of cavalry against infantry was far less common than the defensive use. Cavalry were not normally expected to charge well-ordered infantry, as the results would have been mutually catastrophic to the opposing front ranks. Besides a horse, especially one being ridden, will not in normal circumstances collide with a solid object if it can stop or go around it. As Keegan rightly stresses, 'a horse, in the normal course of events, will not gallop at an obstacle it cannot jump or see a way through, and it cannot jump or see a way through a solid line of men... for the 'shock' which cavalry seek to inflict is really moral, not physical in character'.[38] In other words, cavalry cannot charge into an infantry formation and shatter it by brute force, but rather cause the formation to flinch or flee before the point of contact is made. Cavalry, therefore, would employ typical skirmishing tactics, that is, riding up, shooting, wheeling away, and then rallying ready to try again.

The object of shooting at an enemy infantry unit was to weaken it, so that it would be unable to stand up to a mounted charge. Having said all that, it is difficult to hit a stationary target, let alone a moving one, when the shooter is shooting from a moving horse. Thus, whilst the speed of his mount made a firing horseman a difficult target hit, its irregular motion made his own aim uncertain. Thus, as Napoleon says, 'it is the business of the cavalry to follow up the victory, and to prevent the enemy from rallying'.[39] Hence when the battle had been won, the cavalry naturally came to the fore, pursuing and harrying the broken foe.

CHAPTER 13

Iugurtha's gamble

The long-lived Masinissa was succeeded upon his death in 148 BC by his three sons Mastanabal, Gulussa and Micipsa. It should come as little surprise to find that the first two soon disappeared from the scene, leaving the last brother as the sole ruler of the kingdom. Mastanabal, however, had a son by a concubine who, because of his mother's low status, remained a commoner.[1] Nonetheless, he seems to have grown up with all conventionally desired princely traits: an outstanding physique, good looks, intelligence, bravery, skill-at-arms and an all-round athlete. And he was popular with the people too. The illegitimate boy was Iugurtha.

All of this presented Micipsa with some difficulties. He himself had two sons, Adherbal and Hiempsal, who he naturally wished to see succeed him. He had, however, raised Iugurtha in his royal menage with the two younger boys, making little distinction between their status. Sallust, writing years later and with the benefit of hindsight, suggests that Iugurtha's princely qualities began to trouble the king, who saw the young man as a threat to his own beloved offspring, particularly in view of his popularity. Yet it was this popularity with the masses, continues Sallust, which protected him from his uncle, who feared rebellion if he discreetly disposed of the young man. Sallust again takes up the story, telling us that Micipsa hit upon the idea of making Iugurtha the commander of a Numidian contingent he was about to send to Iberia. Once there, the contingent would serve alongside the Roman forces under Publius Cornelius Scipio Aemilianus (the destroyer of Carthage) during what would turn out to be the closing stages of the Third Celtiberian War (143-133 BC). Overseas, and out of the public eye, there would always be a chance that the impetuous young man, who seems to have found an outlet for his personal frustrations in battlefield aggression, would be killed in action.

The habitually reckless, gallant Iugurtha not only survived but served with individualistic distinction (as did a fellow officer, one Caius Marius). It was indeed during the siege of Numantia (134-133 BC) that he was to earn Scipio Aemilianus' approval by his soldierly qualities, but it also encouraged a Roman belief that their most dangerous opponents were men whom they themselves had taught how to fight. This deep-rooted attitude of racial superiority, coupled with a deficiency in practical application where Numidians were concerned, reveals a Roman disregard for Numidian fighting potential, a pretermission that would come back to haunt the

Romans. For the time being, though, Iugurtha was to learn in Iberia the venality of many of the Romans. Flamboyant, ambitious and unscrupulous, Iugurtha became involved, or so says Sallust, with other less savoury Romans, men who saw opportunities as cronies of Iugurtha if he ever became master of Numidia. These men, Sallust continues, pointed out to Iugurtha that he was already preeminent in Numidia, while 'at Rome money could buy anything'.[2] Now all this was probably largely anti-senatorial carping on the part of a historian who himself fell foul of the Senate and engaged in the ever-popular Roman historical pose of denigrating the current age as one of lost virtue. However, it is certainly true that Iugurtha's later conduct was extremely egregious.

With the destruction of Numantia, Iugurtha was mustered out. He returned home with his reputation greatly enhanced through his successful military service. On top of this, he had operated as part of the Roman army itself, and he had gained a very good understanding of the Roman character. He had even mastered Latin. He was altogether more fit to rule than his younger cousins and certainly more than willing to take the kingdom from them when the time came.

And so it was, after the death of Micipsa in 118 BC, Iugurtha put to death first one then the other of his less aggressive cousins, Hiempsal and Adherbal, and made himself master of Numidia (r. 112-106 BC). The old king had in fact adopted Iugurtha and put him on a level with his own sons three years before his death, his intention being to bequeath his realm to the three men in common, an extremely bad idea in any case, particularly in a kingdom which, despite its veneer of urbanism, was still very much tribal in its makeup.[3] Anyway, a senatorial commission from Rome, headed by the notorious Lucius Opimius (*cos.* 121 BC), of hated memory for his part in achieving the murder of Caius Gracchus, had been sent to settle Numidian affairs after the murder of Hiempsal, Numidia having been divided into two warring camps. Sallust implies the delegation fell under the spell of Iugurtha, yet the outcome was to be a division of the kingdom between him and Adherbal. Whether cash actually changed hands, and the theme of venality of senators is a commonplace, the Senate as a whole could see little more in Numidia's situation than a sanguinary and squalid succession struggle, hence the compromise.

Notwithstanding this, three years later Iugurtha began raiding Adherbal's half of the kingdom, which bordered on the province of Africa (viz. the former territory of Carthage and roughly coextensive with modern Tunisia), 'taking many prisoners as well as cattle and other plunder'.[4] The hope was to provoke Adherbal into counterattacks and thus provide Iugurtha with a suitable excuse for making open war upon him. But Adherbal would not be provoked. He put his faith in Roman power and sent envoys to Rome. He also sent envoys to remonstrate with his cousin, but to no effect. Iugurtha took this parleying as a sign of weakness and began war in earnest. With little or no option, Adherbal raised forces and met Iugurtha outside his royal capital, the hilltop fortress of Cirta. The two armies approached each other but as it was late in the day did not engage. During the small hours of the following morning, however, while it was still fairly dark, Iugurtha attacked Adherbal's camp and routed his sleepy army completely. Adherbal escaped in the confusion with a small mounted force and fled to Cirta, where he was saved from capture by resident Italians, traders (*negotiatores Italici*) to be exact. They obstructed the pursuit from the walls, probably with missile weapons, and had it not been for this, 'a single day would have seen the beginning and the end of the war between the two kings'.[5]

Iugurtha thus settled into a siege and assaulted the fortress, which squatted upon a ravine-girt promontory, with mantlet, tower and ram.[6] This approach showed his army was more technologically sophisticated than might be expected from an out-of-the-way desert kingdom. Nonetheless, the siege was to drag on for some five months, during which time a pantomime of negotiations were conducted between Iugurtha and Rome, the king blatantly ignoring instructions from two Roman missions to disarm. Eventually, fearing for their own safety, the Italians defending Cirta prevailed upon Adherbal to surrender his capital on the terms that he would be spared and that the Senate would then sort the mess out. Adherbal was rightly dubious, but submitted to the Italians' pressure. Adherbal's assessment of the situation was more astute than that of the Italians. Upon surrender, Iugurtha tortured Adherbal to death and slaughtered all Italians that were found bearing arms. With their massacre Rome declared war.[7]

In spite of Iugurtha's lavish use of bribery (according to Sallust – how fair this accusation is we cannot say, but it is probably exaggerated), the Senate decided to crush him.[8] After two unsuccessful attempts (111-110 BC), it despatched the quixotic but capable Quintus Caecilius Metellus against him. The Caecilii Metelli were the most prominent family in Rome at this time (six consulates in fifteen years), having risen past the Cornelli Scipiones, who had held this position since the war with Hannibal. On his arrival in Africa, Metellus had to knock the army into proper shape; the troops were in poor condition after the command of the two Postumii Albini, who had allowed the campaigning army to rot and decay.[9] They had abandoned military routine to spend weeks in ill-disciplined idleness, not bothering to fortify or lay out their camp as per regulations, and shifting it only when forced to by lack of locally available forage or because the stench of their own waste became unbearable. Soldiers and camp followers marauded and plundered at will. This was the army in Africa when Metellus assumed command in the summer of 109 BC.

Metellus' response was a traditional one, namely to put the men back under the tight, all-embracing discipline that the Roman army was famed for. Traders, sutlers and other unscrupulous parasites were expelled, and soldiers forbidden to buy food; many had been in the habit of selling their rations of grain to purchase ready-baked civilian bread rather than eating the coarse camp bread they had to prepare and cook themselves, which was often a recipe for gastronomic disaster. Ordinary ranks were barred from keeping their own servants or pack animals. Metellus ordered gruelling daily drills to reintroduce the men swiftly to the intricacies of military life, as well as to improve battle skill and endurance. From now on the army broke camp every morning, and marched fully equipped to a new position where it constructed a marching camp as if in hostile territory. 'By these methods he was able to prevent breaches of discipline, and without having to inflict many punishments he soon restored the army's morale'.[10]

Obviously no martinet, Metellus understood that when a commander leads his soldiers into battle, they must follow without hesitation. He works hard to earn this loyalty by knowing and caring for his men. He is what we would call a good commander. With natural inquisitiveness about how people function, the good commander connects to his soldiers in an intimate and personal way. Loyalty above all is based on appreciation. It develops when people appreciate what they are involved in and when appreciation is expressed for them. The good commander earns the loyalty of the soldiers by first genuinely expressing loyalty to them in even the smallest gestures. He does not miss the opportunity to win someone's trust and never gives up on anyone. In this way he creates a unified entity where before was an assembly of individuals and gains an army that follows him through extreme conditions and conflict. Metellus was of this stamp.

When the commander does not command, the army cannot obey. All becomes confusion. Yet united in profound kinship with their commander, the soldiers respond with uncompromising loyalty. They will obey every order. They will accompany him far and wide, into grave danger, into death. When soldiers face death, the structures of military life become irrelevant. At the same time, creating certainty and fostering commitment are paramount because when the good commander exudes confidence and his commands and orders are clear and simple, when doubts have no chance to arise, the men will be confident and assured in their actions. Enthusiastic, unquestioned commitment will dispel doubt, carry men through battle and rob the enemy of his spirit, thus causing fear, consternation and confusion in his ranks. Orders must never be issued lightly, nor should they be rescinded; otherwise, they lose their power and impact. The fearsomeness of a commander in the midst of battle depends on the acceptance and execution of his orders and this execution depends on the fear, respect, and willing allegiance of the men. In particular, their respect is hard to win and could be snatched away in a single moment of cowardice or indecision. 'You should know that while success wins for commanders the goodwill of their men,' the Caesarian legate Curio explains to his war council, 'failure earns their hatred'.[11] Clearly, the most extensive efforts must be taken to preserve this interrelationship because once a crack such as doubt appears, the collapse of authority is imminent. Paradoxically, a man is not born a commander. He must become one through experience.

But back to Metellus. Invading Numidia, he occupied Vaga (Beja, Tunisia). Marching southwestwards, he soon had to fight a major battle.[12] The site of this confused whirling fight was beside the Muthul (Oued Mellag), a tributary on the right bank of the Bagradas, not far to the north of Sicca, which city then came over to the Romans.[13]

The Battle of the Muthul River, 109 BC

Having left a small detachment in Vaga to guard a supply dump he had established there and to protect its resident Italians,[14] Metellus pulled out. In the meantime, Iugurtha assembled his forces, horsemen of course, foot levies and elephants. The latter, forty-four in number, along with part of the infantry, he placed under his old friend Bomilcar. He then got his troops ahead of the Roman column and decided to fight among the barren hills near the Muthul River. The king placed his troops in a thin line along the top of a hill overlooking the route he knew the column would pass along. He hid his men as best he could among the scrub trees on the hill and concealed his banners and flags so as not to advertise his whereabouts. He then waited for the moment of ambush.

Descending from a height, the Roman column was slowly uncoiling and heading towards the Muthul when Metellus spotted the ambush against the browns, greys and greens of the landscape. He immediately halted the column and turned to face the nearby scrubby hill now bristling with glistening, war-caparisoned warriors, thereby putting his army into battle formation. He bolstered the right wing, which was closest to the hostiles above, with three more lines of maniples and distributed archers and slingers between them. He then divided his cavalry and set them on the wings. Iugurtha did not attack at once, probably he had to rethink his tactics and reorder his men accordingly, and Metellus, concerned that his men might be worn down by thirst, sent one of his two legates, Publius Rutilius Rufus,[15] with a body of horse and some lightly-equipped cohorts down into the plain to establish a camp besides the Muthul.[16] As this detachment passed below the Numidians, Bomilcar proceeded after it with his infantry and elephants.

Then, with quiet steadiness, the Roman army faced left and became a column once more. With Metellus and cavalry acting as vanguard, and his other legate, Caius Marius, and more cavalry acting as rearguard, the army descended slowly but surely into the plain below. As the rear of the column reached level ground, Iugurtha sent some 2,000 men to occupy the route through which they had passed, apparently with the intention to trap them in the plain, which, excluding the herders subsisting along the Muthul, was deserted owing to the lack of water.

Iugurtha then began to attack the column's flanks with his horsemen, which dashed hither and thither casting javelins. When pursued they simply melted away, fleeing in all directions and trying to cut off any isolated Roman cavalrymen they could find. Sallust says that these shoot-and-scoot assaults disordered all the ranks, which suggests the column was caught off-guard before it could properly deploy into battle formation. Nonetheless, there was a good deal of hot fighting at close quarters, and a final successful charge by, as Sallust makes plain, 'four legionary cohorts' towards some of the Numidian infantry that had pulled back upon high ground put an end to the engagement in this quarter.[17] Most of these Numidians slipped silently away into the surrounding bush, and only their dead and badly wounded were left with the Romans.

In the meantime, Rutilius and his command had found a suitable camping site, had marked out a camp and begun to entrench, when a great cloud of dust appeared before them. The Romans guessed at first that it was merely dust that had been carried up by the wind, the plain was broken country covered with thick scrub, and it was difficult to see that it was really a sign of the approaching enemy. There was no sense of urgency yet. The Romans continued with their labour. But when they saw the dust cloud was not dispersing but getting nearer, they grabbed their arms and, pouncing upon the Numidians, the rest was quickly over. To return to Sallust's account, 'The Numidians stood their ground only as long as they thought they could rely on the elephants for protection'.[18] They took to their heels, however, when the Romans slaughtered all but four of the beasts, which had got themselves entangled in branches of trees. The sudden African fall of night meant that the cavalry of the divided Roman force met in the dark. Luckily they recognized each other, which thus enabled the fagged column to reach the camp. All told, Metellus had just managed to win a confused and hard-fought and expensive victory.

Apart from the forty-four elephants, Sallust gives no figures for either side.[19] In fact, the historian eschews any estimate of numbers (along with chronology) in the *Bellum Iugurthine* War, even on the Roman side. Metellus presumably had a standard consular army of two *legiones* and two *alae*, say some 20,000 men. It may have been smaller; he must have left troops to garrison various points, such as Vaga, and also to protect the province of Africa, but then he had brought some additional manpower with him when he took up his command, so 20,000 men seems a good guess. As for Iugurtha, it is impossible to say.

Iugurtha got away, and thereafter Metellus, wary of heavy losses in pitched battles against an unencumbered and highly mobile enemy, would settle down to a piecemeal conquest. Nonetheless, Metellus would fail to bring the war to a conclusion; the problem was physically capturing Iugurtha. Metellus, therefore, resorted to bribery coupled with a policy of reducing the urban communities in Numidia so as to deprive Iugurtha logistically. As we shall see, Marius was to employ the same strategy against Iugurtha, thus we should be wary of criticism of Metellus' conduct in Africa. That said, there was a senatorial tradition glorifying Metellus, asserting that he had broken the back of Iugurtha's resistance when for reasons of (unjust) home politics he was replaced by Marius.[20]

THE COMING OF MARIUS

After the battle, Metellus went on into the richest part of Numidia, taking and torching many settlements. The final episode of the campaign was a vain attempt to capture Zama Regia and, Iugurtha having put together another army, a fierce battle in the vicinity.[21] Then Metellus retreated, taking up winter quarters in the province of Africa, but near its border with Numidia.[22] The Senate, meantime, prorogued his command.[23]

The winter saw the sudden loss (through treachery) and swift recapture (through trickery) of Vaga. Then followed Metellus' intrigue with Iugurtha's old confidant Bomilcar. This was an attempt to put Iugurtha out of the way. It failed.[24] After that Metellus took the field again.[25] There was a battle in which Iugurtha was defeated. The king thereupon retired into the desert and took asylum at Thala (not identified), where his children and much of his treasure were stashed. Undaunted, Metellus marched across the sun-parched waste to Thala and captured the place, but Iugurtha slipped away with his children and most of his treasure and fled into the country of the Gaetulians. After a time he induced Bocchus, the king of Mauretania and his father-in-law, to intervene and lend a hand. Things gathered apace, and the two kings appeared in force near Cirta, which had come into Roman possession.[26] Negotiations followed and warfare lapsed. Metellus meanwhile had received news from Rome not only that Marius, his erstwhile legate, had been elected to the consulship, but that Numidia had been assigned to him.[27]

So far in the campaigns of 109 BC and 108 BC Metellus had repeatedly defeated his enemy (he was to gain the cognomen 'Numidicus' for his efforts) but had found it impossible to bring Iugurtha to heel, who remained at large in the dusty, snake infested land. Metellus had learnt to adapt his tactics to find and fight an elusive cunning foe, but Iugurtha, who was sufficiently wise not to mass his peasant levies for battle in open country, would only skirmish with the Roman forces or fight them on his own terms. With the eye of a hawk and the stealth of a wolf, he had the kind of bravery - the most effective kind - that derived from playing only when one is assured of victory. With their emphasis on fitness and fleetness, the Numidians had three societal diversions, and of Iugurtha it was said 'he took part in the national pursuits of riding, javelin throwing and competed with other young men in running', and 'also devoted much time to hunting'.[28] Of prime importance would be the ability to ride and fight well. Worked on until they became proficient in all, these athletic pursuits undoubtedly steeled the Numidians for the style of war they preferred. Armed with a handful of javelins, the Numidian horseman was the master of skirmish-type warfare, depending on baffling their opponents by their almost hallucinatory speed and bird-like agility, alternating between headlong flight and snapping-at-the-heel pursuit.[29] Like Syphax and Masinissa before him, Iugurtha would combine the military skills he had learned while fighting under the Romans with the classical Numidian use of irregular cavalry and slippery guerrilla tactics.[30]

Like many dynamic rulers, the wily Iugurtha appears to have been a heady blend of contradictions, at once conscientious and cutthroat, capricious and careful, cruel and compassionate. Of course, this may be a case of history being construed by the victors, but Iugurtha does seem to have been the stuff of a dark fairytale. Sallust sees the constant failure to overcome the Numidian king was in part due to Roman incompetence, with a deeper reason down to the corruption of the Roman aristocracy, an accusation we shall examine in more depth later. Somewhat naively perhaps, Sallust also represents Iugurtha both as the 'noble savage', immune against the corruption of Roman civilization, and as the 'ignoble barbarian', a paradigm of 'Punic' perfidy. Of those who doubted the danger of Iugurtha, Sallust saw that their attitude could only be accounted for by the sort of toleration a man extends to his pet wolf who, living in the house like a dog, only eats his neighbours' sheep and occasionally their children too. It is easy to assert with 20:20 historical hindsight that Iugurtha was of such nature.

Next Marius in 107 BC. Despite being bitter, Metellus accepted the change in command. In fact, Marius did not bring with him any fresh ideas on how to conduct or even win a war conducted in country favouring the enemy, but he did, on the other hand, realize that the anti-insurgent war against Iugurtha required more troops on the ground. Rome, however, was suffering a long-standing manpower shortage, and its army had yet to become the formidable empire commuter in hobnailed sandals that was well used to victory over 'barbarian' enemies in Europe and elsewhere. But Marius took a bold step and opened the ranks to all who wished to volunteer, including the *capite censi* or 'head count', those citizens listed in the census simply as numbers because they lacked significant property. And so volunteers from the *proletarii* flocked to join the legions, 'imagining that they would make a fortune out of the spoils',[31] and the Senate, despite assuming that he would raise the soldiers by means of the usual selection process based on the census, the *dilectus*, raised no protest. It was a simple step, revolutionary only in that Marius created, without realizing it, a new type of client army, bound to its commander as its patron because, as Plutarch lets on, 'contrary to law and custom he enrolled in his army poor men with no property qualifications'.[32]

Bred lean and resilient in the vicissitudes of survival at subsistence level, most of the men recruited undoubtedly were members of the rural population; they were considered to be better material than their urban counterparts, at best a rough undernourished lot. The desire for a life free of routine drudgery, the chance of adventure into the unknown and adrenalin-fuelled excitement all played their part, but want was the prime cause for their abandonment of civilian life. Only too grateful to have escaped the filth and fickleness of civilian life, on their demobilization at the end of a campaign they naturally looked to their general for rewards, namely a grant of land.

With that Marius, as consul in 102 BC, had to propose a land bill, which was passed for him by the unscrupulous and brilliant tribune of the people, Lucius Appuleius Saturninus. It is a common argument that from now on the armies of Rome looked to their aristocratic generals and not the oligarchic Senate, the oft-quoted example being that when Lucius Cornelius Sulla, the future dictator, got his legions to march on Rome in 88 BC. This view, however, is too pessimistic as not all soldiers would follow their general. It is probably true that throughout Rome's history soldiers exhibited more loyalty towards a charismatic and competent commander. Therefore, what we really witness with Marius is not a change in the attitude of the soldiers but a change in the attitude of the generals. Let us, for instance, take Scipio Africanus. If he had held revolutionary ideas, he could have easily marched on Rome at the head of his victorious army after Zama. Similarly, if we return to Sulla, his soldiers did not follow him come what may as he had to convince them that he had right on his side. According to Appian, when envoys met Sulla on the road and asked him why he was marching on Rome, he replied, 'to free it from the tyrants'.[33] Tyranny, alongside monarchy, being an anathema to all proper Romans.

Anyway, this is another story, so let us return to Marius. He was by nature a soldier, much in his later life would show it, and he had begun his long military career as a cavalry officer, serving with distinction under Scipio Aemilianus at Numantia. Marius (much like Iugurtha) had enhanced his reputation there when he killed an enemy warrior in single combat, and in full view of his general. For a man of relatively humble origins it must have looked as if the future belonged to him. And so, some twenty-six years later, the new consul took command in Africa and began his campaign.

His army was obviously an interesting mixture of veterans and novice soldiers. Much of the army was now experienced, having been put under discipline by Metellus and led by him with constant, if moderate, success, and they had been hardened to soldiering under an African sun. This was not the case with Marius' poor volunteers. Lacking the same stamina and steadfastness as those who had already faced the Numidians, he knew he had to break them into the African war slowly. Accordingly he exposed his soldiers, war-worn and greenhorns alike, to small fights until they were confident of themselves and the new and old hands grew easy with each other. After these preliminary preparations and opening operations, which involved largely fluid short-lived skirmishes, a spirit of teamwork henceforth prevailed among his soldiers. He was ready for a new effort against Iugurtha, who he was able to defeat in an engagement near Cirta.[34]

However, finding that it is not so easy to end the war (with half the forces) as he had claimed, events now took an ugly turn with Marius adopting a policy of plunder and terrorism, burning fields, villages and towns and massacring the civilian population.[35] After which, Marius conceived and planned a daring venture, a long march to surpass his predecessor's exploit at Thala and to continue to spread terror of the Roman arms deep in the very heart of the hostile Numidian country. His goal was Capsa (Gafsa, Tunisia). Achieving a complete surprise, Marius captured the place, burnt it, massacred the adult males, sold the rest into slavery, and divided the booty among his soldiers.[36] The destruction was complete. Sallust himself calls the treatment of Capsa a 'violation of the usages of war', but feebly excuses it as necessary since 'the place was important to Iugurtha and hard for the Romans to reach'.[37] This act of calculated cruelty certainly intimidated the Numidians into evacuating many settlements, and those few that foolishly resisted were captured by assault and razed to the ground.

The expedition to Capsa belongs late in the summer of 107 BC. Sallust is for once explicit.[38] But then we find Marius and his army assaulting a fortress of

Iugurtha perched upon a precipitous rock not far from the River Muluccha (Moulouya). Sallust describes (here and in two other places) this river as the boundary dividing the realms of Iugurtha and of Bocchus, which means that Marius is now far to the west of Cirta (about 800km as the crow flies) and not far from what is now Melilla in Spanish Morocco.[39] However that may be, and it suggests an efficient commissariat and an endless ability to march, it was here that he came ever so close to losing the war. The long, hot march to the Muluccha was an act of folly, which only fortune corrected.[40] It is curious to note that whilst Sallust sees Marius as the living embodiment of the just qualities most precious to him, he does hint that it was Marius' quaestor, the patrician Sulla, who saved the day, the fortress being captured and with it the largest treasury of Iugurtha.[41]

We next see Marius in retreat: even Sallust's hero was fallible. He had to fight two engagements towards the end of his march, the first 'more like a fight with bandits than a proper battle',[42] and the second a sharp encounter near Cirta, the goal of his march.[43] Here we should point out that Marius turned out to be an able commander who, though lacking the brilliance of his nephew Caesar, understood the basic requirements for a good army were training, discipline and leadership. More a common soldier than an aristocratic general, it was in Africa that he 'won the affection of the soldiers by showing he could live as hard as they did and endure as much'.[44] As a tactician Marius relied mainly on surprise and always showed a reluctance to engage in a traditional, set-piece fight. He preferred to determine the time and place and would not be hurried.

The following winter and spring were a time of long parleys, the upshot being the eloquent Sulla befriending Bocchus and skilfully playing on the king's ambitions and fears. What followed was Sulla's spectacular desert crossing, culminating in Iugurtha's betrayal and capture (105 BC). This bit of family treachery, proving that popular saying 'it requires an Indian to catch an Indian', thus terminated a conflict full of betrayals, skirmishes and sieges. Sulla had the incident engraved on his signet ring, thus provoking Marius' jealousy.[45] Nevertheless, Marius was the hero of the hour. He triumphed on 1 January 104 BC, entering on the same day his second consulship, and Iugurtha was publicly executed.[46] In antiquity as today, tyrants tend to slip on the blood they have shed. The war with Iugurtha had been a rather pointless, dirty affair, a campaign of annihilation, obliteration and destruction. Yet it had made Marius' reputation and begun Sulla's career.[47] Worse than that, it saw Marius and Sulla fall out over who was responsible for the successful conclusion to the hostilities, an acrimonious quarrel that was to cast a long sanguinary shadow on Rome.

The Senate, however, did not annexe Numidia, giving instead half of its territory to Bocchus, as a reward of his treachery, and half to Gauda, the weak-minded half-brother of Iugurtha.[48] This should not be seen as evidence of the Senate's pacifism but of its sound military and political sense. As Harris points out, there was no particular Roman reluctance to annex territory in this period, quite the contrary in fact, but it seems that Numidia was 'an exceptionally unattractive prospect as a province'.⁴⁹ In other words, the Senate, seeing only a wasteland good for very little except subsistence farming and grazing, but would have to be defended nonetheless, refused to annex it (there may be a lesson here for us today). Subsequently two Mauretanian kingdoms emerge, separated by the Muluccha,⁽⁵⁰⁾ and at the time of Caesar's campaign in Africa, eastern Mauretania was ruled by a second Bocchus, who, along with the Campanian *condottiere*, Publius Sittius, invaded Numidia (now markedly reduced in size) and captured Cirta (46 BC).⁽⁵¹⁾

CHAPTER 14

Sallust on Iugurtha

The *Bellum Iugurthinum*, the second of Sallust's historical monographs, explores the intertwined themes of Rome's dirty war in Africa and the concomitant political upheavals in Rome (118-105 BC). The monograph appears to be built up around the character and vicissitudes of one person, the Numidian prince: manic energy and criminal ambition, ending all so miserably. Yet the *Bellum Iugurthinum* is more than a biography. It is a narration of an international war that impinges on the internal politics of Rome, with dire and distant repercussions. Before we finish with Numidian affairs, therefore, we must examine the opinion of Sallust (Caius Sallustius Crispus, b. 86 BC) that failure in the war against Iugurtha in Africa was primarily down to corruption in Rome.

It was commonplace among Roman historians to contrast the vitality of early Rome with the degenerate, self-destructive Rome of their own age. In the preface to his *Bellum Catilinae*, his first historical monograph, Sallust has much to say of the contrast between the virtuous Romans of yore and the depravity of their successors. No doubt he exaggerates it, like other sermonizers on similar themes. Yet for Sallust, the decisive turning point in Rome's fortunes was the final destruction of its arch-rival, Carthage and the consequent removal of what Sallust gloomily labels 'fear of the enemy'.[1] This was the pessimism that domestic tranquillity depended on the fear of a strong external threat, that is to say, the Romans, nobility and people alike, would remain united in self-defence and their civil affairs would remain peaceful as a result. The alternative was obvious; the citizens would turn their energies to unrestrained and violently destructive rivalries among themselves.[2] The idea that loyalty to Rome in the face of a foreign enemy takes precedence over domestic rivalries recurs prominently throughout the first pentad of Livy's magisterial work.[3] We should note too that external pressures stimulated military skills, organizational abilities, and tactical thought simultaneously. It kept the Romans on their mettle.

The political geography of North Africa at the end of Micipsa's reign was essentially quadripartite. In 146 BC, at the end of the third war with Carthage, Rome had annexed Carthage's territories, creating *provincia Africa*, the province of Africa, with its capital at Utica. This left to the Numidian king much of the land his father, Masinissa, had appropriated from the Carthaginians as well as his own kingdom. To the west was found the kingdom of the Moor Bocchus. Moors (Greek

Maurousiai, Latin *Mauri*) had served with Hannibal in Italy, both horse and foot, and as a race they inhabited the most westerly part of North Africa, what the Romans knew as Mauretania and we recognize as Morocco today.[4] Though their eastern frontier was bounded by the River Muluccha (Moulouya), they had been remote and independent of Carthage; we know of an alliance in the fourth century BC and again around 150 BC.[5] Ethnically speaking they were of the same racial stock as the Numidians, and Polybios evidently regarded these ancestral cousins as one and the same. In fact, during the Second Punic War the Moorish tribes formed a confederacy under a king called Baga, and appear not to have had any formal relationship with Carthage at this time.[6] As we well know, the Moors deployed in Hannibal's first line at Zama were mercenaries, having been initially recruited by his brother Mago.[7] Moorish foot levies appear to have been lightly armed, as indicated by the statement of Livy that in 216 BC Hiero of Syracuse sent a force of foreign archers and slingers, 1,000 strong, to serve for Rome so as to aid the Romans against the threat posed by Hannibal's missile troops, notably the slingers from the Balearic Islands and the Moorish javelineers.[8]

The fourth and final part of our African jigsaw consisted of a long band along the pre-desert, on and south to the Atlas Mountains. Here, in what was a rugged hostile territory of climate extremes, the Gaetulians (Latin *Gaetuli*) eked out a contented if challenging existence, a cluster of tribes who lay outside the two kingdoms of Numidia and Mauretania and resisted any attempts to tax or control them.[9] The Gaetulians, like the Moors, were of the same racial stock as the Numidians, and the elder Pliny, obviously simplifying matters, says there were three tribes: the Autoteles in the west, the Baniurae in the east, and the Nesimi in the desert south of the Atlas Mountains.[10] Our first reference to them comes from Livy, who talks of Hannibal sending an advance party of Gaetulian horsemen under an officer named Isalcas to Casilinum in 216 BC.[11] Later references to them suggest Gaetulian horsemen, like their Numidian cousins, lacked bridles.[12] It is assumed they were armed and fought in the same fashion too, which would explain why Polybios, for instance, never mentions them. In a barbed comment, Sallust describes them as savage nomads, living on grass and raw flesh.[13]

In 116 BC, after the murder of Hiempsal, Adherbal came before the Senate to plea his case. Iugurtha, meantime, acted through the agency of envoys. There followed a senatorial debate in which Sallust says the flatterers of Iugurtha, apparently bribed, and the majority of the house praised him and derided Adherbal. Ten senatorial envoys next went to Numidia and divided the kingdom. Before following Sallust too closely here, so jumping to indiscreet conclusions, we may wish to pause a while and consider the following relevant points:

- As these upheavals are occurring on the border of the province of Africa this issue is a matter for the Senate.
- The Senate, therefore, must investigate, and this is what it does.

- The outcome of the investigation is perfectly logical, and there was no room for flagrant bribery in the settlement.

The settlement was achieved, according to Sallust, through Iugurtha winning over the senatorial commission. Stories of senatorial corruption, dreadful in truth and much exaggerated in the telling, had been circulating for some time. But was this in fact the case? To answer this, let us look at the following key points:

- For Sallust to make sense the division of Numidia should be in favour of Iugurtha: 'the more fertile and more thickly populated part' - but this is Roman propaganda as Adherbal receives the major cities and ports of the kingdom, including Cirta.

- In truth, Iugurtha's share is much less valuable in terms of real-estate and, besides, he is shoved over to the west towards Mauretania. This implies Rome sees him as a troublemaker, and thus establishes him furthest from the province of Africa. In effect, Adherbal's territory is to act as a buffer state.

- There was no reason for Rome to directly intervene in Numidia, and for this reason the Senate achieves a workable settlement through diplomacy. The sensible course seems to be to leave the princes to stew in their own juice.

In 112 BC Iugurtha invaded Adherbal's territory and the Senate responds by despatching two delegations. Sallust claims that both these delegations were 'soft' on Iugurtha, and his explanation is simple: bribery.[14] That, of course, suits Sallust's purpose. Again, however, let us look at the facts behind the larger issues facing the Senate at the time:

- With regard to his claim that the delegates are young and inexperienced, we should appreciate that such men are invariably the sons of senators, many of whom are gaining valuable political experience for the first time.

- Marcus Aemilius Scaurus (*cos.* 115 BC), the *princeps senates* 'chief of the Senate' or what we would call the Father of the House, who advocates going to war on behalf of Adherbal, is in the minority.[15] However, the supporters of Iugurtha, for whatever motive, prevent it. Interestingly, for Cicero, Scaurus is the paramount statesman and master of civic wisdom, never named except for praise, but Sallust has much to say of pretence and inconsistency in politics, and seems to have disliked Scaurus, as he evidently disliked Cicero, because he was prepared to change his policies and adapt himself to circumstances.[16] As Sallust sees him, Scaurus was cunning and unscrupulous, making sure he was never associated with a losing cause. Surely, the willingness to compromise is essential to successful statesmanship.

- A Roman expeditionary army in Macedonia, under Caius Porcius Cato (*cos.* 114 BC), has just been whipped by the Thracian Sordisci, and thus Rome could hardly get itself embroiled in another ground war. Indeed, Rome has to face a grave emergency on the northern frontiers provoked by the recent migrations of the Cimbri and Teutones, a Roman consul having crossed the Julian Alps only to be routed by the Cimbri (113 BC). So the Numidian situation was the least of the Senate's cares, and some senators probably would have liked to have ignored the problems of Numidia in the hope that they would solve themselves.

Dynastic squabbles of this nature had never been uncommon amongst the Numidians, and as we well know it was just such a quarrel that had first prompted Masinissa to see aid from Scipio. However, with the slaughter of Italian traders at Cirta the Senate has no option but to accept the *fait accompli* and so take direct action against Iugurtha. Not only had this African massacre knocked away the prop on which the peace of Numidia rested, but also, as the tendrils of empire, it must have confirmed for all the Italians (and Romans) in Africa that they depended on the credibility of Rome's reach to intervene. With that one of the consuls for 111 BC, Lucius Calpurnius Bestia, has Numidia allotted as his province (i.e. area of military operation) and after a single campaign drags Iugurtha to the peace table. Sallust, again, smells graft and degeneracy: Bestia had energy, a keen intelligence and skill in warfare, but all these noble qualities of his were hampered by his greed for profit.[17] That, for Sallust at least, is sufficient to condemn Bestia. But let us consider the following points before we do the same:

- Bestia could have clobbered Iugurtha in a short sharp campaign, or so say the armchair strategists. Sallust, to his credit, knew Africa and knew warfare.

- Bestia's objective, however, is to placate Iugurtha while Rome deals with the Sordisci who had invaded Macedonia, and it is hard to dissent from the Senate's determination to try and deal with this particular threat. 'War', remarked James Wolfe, before storming the heights of Abraham, 'is an option of difficulties', and the Senate certainly has its fair share of troubles to choose from.

- The articles of the surrender, whereby Iugurtha accepts *in fidem populi Romani se dare* (*deditio*), makes perfect sense. As a consequence, the king surrenders thirty war elephants, a good deal of cattle and horses, and some silver.

Of course, from the standpoint of Bestia, it was better to bring the Numidian campaign to a profitable conclusion while he remained in office, in spite of Iugurtha's continued freedom. The Senate, seeing no reason to fight Iugurtha to the death, seem to have acquiesced. Pandemonium breaks loose, however, when a tribune-designate and a dogged enemy of the ruling oligarchy, Caius Memmius, turns the war into a political issue and thus uses it as a weapon with which to attack the Senate. Given the fact that the 'villain' was still at large, somebody must be fixed for the blame. So, assuming we are in the business of making moral judgements of this kind, who are we going to point the finger at?

- All the men currently at the top are those who had opposed the Gracchi brothers and were involved in the cruel repression of their reforms and supporters.
- Memmius, whether or not there was corruption, sees a small chink in the armour of the Senate.
- Iugurtha gets his elephants back.

In 109 BC a tribune of the people, Caius Mamilius Limetanus, proposes to the *concilium plebis* that a court of inquiry, the *quaestio Mamiliana*, should be set up in order to investigate various kinds of corrupt practices in relation to Numidian affairs. In consequence, Sallust, a careful contriver, concerns himself with those senators who had either 'accepted presents of money' from Iugurtha or made terms with him.[18] Undoubtedly much to the discomfiture of the Senate, five prominent men, four of consular rank and one holder of the priesthood, were subsequently convicted thereby paying the penalty for what they had done (or not done) in Numidia.[19] It was not a happy time to be a senator, especially if you happened to be one of the following:

- Lucius Opimius (*cos.* 121 BC), as an archenemy of the Gracchi, is a prime target; as Sallust tells us, he was the leader of the commission that divided Numidia between Iugurtha and Adherbal.
- Lucius Calpurnius Bestia (*cos.* 111 BC), as a tribune of the people back in 120 BC, had proposed that Publius Popilius Laenas (*cos.* 132 BC) be recalled from exile - he had tried the supporters of Tiberius Gracchus and was subsequently exiled by Caius Gracchus.
- Unfortunately, we do not know the connection of the Gracchi with the other three convicted men named by Cicero, viz. Caius Porcius Cato (*cos.* 114 BC), Spurius Postumius Albinus (*cos.* 110 BC), and Caius Sulpicius Galba, a patrician and holder of a priesthood.

One senator who did escape the witch hunt was Scaurus. Obviously sensing how the wind was blowing, he took the appropriate steps and got himself appointed as the one of the three members of the court of inquiry.[20] Anyway, whether or not the tribune's purpose was well meaning, the intention behind it was the classic conjurer's misdirection. As the magisterial Syme puts it, 'It is strange that Sallust now neglected this signal act of justice and revenge'.[21] Strange, it may be, but Sallust saw, albeit with a more than slightly jaundiced eye, the Iugurthine War as marking a fundamental phase in the decline of the senatorial oligarchy and the organization of the attack upon it.[22] As has been indicated, this attack is first mounted by the tribune Memmius, and then maintained by the tribune Mamilius with the setting up of his *quaestio*. Indeed, to be fair to Sallust, we should appreciate that the main source for his *Bellum Iugurthinum* were the forensic speeches from the judicial examinations of those five nobles. Sallust, therefore, did not provide the gloss himself. Leastways, to illustrate his notion concerning the decline of the senatorial oligarchy, Sallust's large issue, we can mention one example from the pages of his African monograph.

In 118 BC, as we well know, the dying Micipsa had bequeathed his kingdom to his two legitimate sons, Hiempsal and Adherbal, and, going on an earlier recommendation of Scipio Aemilianus, to the illegitimate son of his younger brother, Iugurtha. Iugurtha had another cousin, Massiva, a son of Gulussa, who had fled to Rome after the fall of Cirta and murder of Adherbal. This prince had fallen in with Spurius Postumius Albinus, one of the consuls for 110 BC, who had drawn Numidia as his province. Spurius Albinus, 'eager', as Sallust says, 'to conduct a war', persuaded Massiva, who, after all, was a grandson of Masinissa, to claim Iugurtha's throne from the Senate.[23] When he took office Spurius Albinus would replace Bestia in command of the army in Africa and if he could place Massiva on the Numidian throne, he would practically have a client running the kingdom. It must have seemed a very sweet proposition. Iugurtha was duly alarmed at the possibility so he turned to the usual Iugurthine solution: murder. With characteristic rashness, he ordered his confidant, Bomilcar, to hire out Massiva's murder. It was to be done secretly, if possible, but any case it was to be done, and done quickly. The wishes of the unscrupulous prince were duly obeyed and Massiva was duly liquidated. The murder itself, however, was bungled in that one of the assassins was caught and persuaded to confess all. The war was renewed.

The ignominious surrender of the consul's brother, Aulus Postumius Albinus, whom he had left in command while he returned to Rome to hold the elections, was inevitably repudiated by the Senate.[24] And thereby hangs a miserable tale. The brother had indulged himself in a rather rash foray, his objective Suthul (not identified), the city where Iugurtha kept his treasury. He found the city on heights above a plain turned into a lake by the winter rains. Nonetheless, he set about reducing the place. Meantime, Iugurtha turned to the most useful tool in his armoury: trickery. And so the Roman was lured into a trap by the Numidian, and with his army in a desperate situation, he was forced to capitulate. Iugurtha was ready to let him go after Aulus Albinus and his men passed under the yoke and agreed to quit Numidia within ten days. The very symbol of defeat, the yoke was a frame made from two spears stuck in the ground with a third one lashed across horizontally at a height that compelled the soldiers of Rome, who were disarmed and clad only in a tunic, to crouch down underneath. The alternative was simple: 'starvation or the sword'.[25] To be trounced by a pack of 'naked unqualified savages' made this humiliation all the greater.

It is enough for us to point out that imputations of bribery, gladly taken up by

Sallust, do not have to be invoked to explain Aulus Albinus' incompetent and catastrophic behaviour.[26] The general was just that, incompetent and, possibly, greedy. The folly of Aulus Albinus abolished all hopes of an accommodation between Iugurtha and Rome: the knavish king was to be taken dead or alive. Hence Metellus and Marius were to devote efforts not so much to the conquest of territory as to the pursuit of an individual.

EPILOGUE

Rome alone

The most decisive year in Roman history: which year most deserves this description? If a date had to be set for this event, then the year of the destruction of Carthage, 146 BC, would be as good a one as any. But was the year 146 BC really as pivotal as all that? Virgil's *Aeneid* contains pre-echoes of the death of Carthage. We sense the dramatic irony as Aeneas describes in such detail the building of Carthage – '*Their* walls are already rising!' he cries enviously.[1] We, the passive readers, know that his descendants were to destroy them.

These tragic events in Africa certainly mark a turning point in Roman imperialism and political affairs. In less than a century, with the acquisition of six extra-Italian provinces, Rome had gained control of the entire Mediterranean basin. It had also become the greatest of imperial powers. This was also recognized by the ancient writers, although they analyse it rather differently. The Greek Polybios records the divergent opinions in Greece about the treatment of Macedon and Carthage:

> There were some that approved the action of the Romans, saying that they had taken wise and statesmanlike measures in defence of their empire... Others took the opposite view, saying that far from maintaining the principles by which they had won their supremacy, they were little by little deserting it for a lust of dominion. For at first they had made war with every nation until they were victorious and until their adversaries had confessed that they must obey them and execute their orders. But now they had struck the first note of their new policy by their treatment of Perseus, in utterly exterminating the kingdom of Macedon, and they had now completely revealed it by their decision concerning Carthage. For the Carthaginians had been guilty of no immediate offence to Rome, but the Romans treated them with irremediable severity, although they had accepted all their conditions and consented to obey all their orders.[2]

Polybios himself follows a traditional Greek view that is clearly presented in Herodotos' treatment of the Persians, and can be found in Plato and Aristotle too - that power inevitably corrupts.[3] Polybios links this theory to the general rule that constitutions tend to decay once they are free from external threats. Indeed, the Greek idea that warfare is good for the citizen body was known to aristocratic

Romans, many of whom feared foreign contact was not only putting an intolerable strain upon their political, social and economic institutions, but rotting the moral fibre of Rome too. Around 40 BC the Roman historian Sallust took the same viewpoint as Polybios, except he believed the decline began with the destruction of Carthage rather than the liquidation of Macedon. Before 146 BC, Rome had enjoyed domestic harmony but, after the removal of Carthage, fell into civil strife:

> Before the destruction of Carthage, the Roman people and Senate managed the affairs of the state between themselves in a peaceful and restrained fashion, and there was no struggle for glory or domination between citizens: fear of the enemy kept the citizen body in good ways of behaving [*metus hostilis in bonis artibus civitatem retinebat*]. But when that fear left their minds, those things that go with success, self-indulgence and pride, replaced it. So it happened that the quiet that they had longed for in times of trouble became, once they had got it, only too harsh and bitter. For the nobility began to turn their privilege and the common people their liberty into licence, everyone trying to take and drag a snatch for himself. Thus all things were divided into two factions, and the business of the nation, which was in the midst of all this, was torn asunder. But the nobles were stronger, being a clique, while the forcefulness of the common people, dissolved and dispersed through a large number of people, was less powerful. Decisions about warfare and about domestic matters were left at the beck and call of the few, and the same people controlled the treasury, the provinces, the magistracies, the glories and the triumphs. The populace was afflicted by military service and by poverty; the generals shared the spoils of war with a few. In the meantime the parents and children of the soldiers, if any had a more powerful neighbour, were driven from their homes. So greed and power ran riot without check or limit and polluted and devastated everything, and held nothing to be of worth, nothing to be sacred, until they had plunged to the depths of their own destruction. As soon as men could be found from among the nobility who preferred true glory to power unjustly gained, then the state began to be convulsed and civil strife began to rise, as though the earth were being torn apart. For after Tiberius and Caius Gracchus, whose forebears had added so greatly to the state in the Punic and other wars, began to champion the liberty of the common people and expose the crimes of the few, the nobility, wounded and shaken by this, tried to prevent the work of the Gracchi, first by means of the allies and the Latins and then through the equestrian order, who had been separated from the common people by hope of association with the nobles. And they cut down first Tiberius, and then Caius, coming a few years after him, and one a tribune and the other a triumvir for the establishment of colonies, and with him, M. Fulvius Flaccus.[4]

Epilogue

Sallust, who instead of a chronological record gives a continuous story, endeavours to explain in his two historical monographs the causes of political events and the motives of men's actions. In moralizing about the degeneracy of the recent past, albeit in a rather terse and dramatic style,[5] Sallust has put forward a convincing case that fear was essential for national well-being.[6] With the destruction of Carthage at the end of the Third Punic War, Rome had removed the last rival 'superpower' in the Mediterranean and was thus left without reason to fear, much like the United States of America with the breakup of the Soviet Union at the end of the so-called capitalist-communist Cold War. Once again the world is dominated by the military power of one state. Fear has been and is the dominant emotion in war fighting, and should be for war preparation too. As Florus ruefully puts it, 'the imminent threat of our Carthaginian foes kept alive the ancient discipline'.[7]

APPENDIX 1

Roman politics

In most (perhaps all) city states in the Graeco-Roman worlds (and Rome to begin with can be described as a city-state), there were three primary elements in the body politic: the assembly of citizens, the council, and the magistrates. The powers that constitutions gave to each of these three elements determined whether a state could be described as a democracy, an oligarchy, or as something else in between. If a lot of power was given to the citizens' assembly (e.g. to debate and vote on legislation, to elect magistrates, and to uphold justice) then the state would be described as a democracy, as in fifth-century BC Athens, which gave power to the people, *demos*. If most power lay with the council and magistrates, then it would be an oligarchy (from the Greek: 'rule by the few').

The form of government adopted by the Romans after the end of the monarchy was, by these criteria, definitely oligarchic. Real power lay with the magistrates supported by the council, with powers remaining to the people being minimal. Furthermore, like all classical city states, Rome was devoted to the principle of amateur leadership, as rotation in office was essential to its notion of citizenship, coupled with the belief that a Roman aristocrat could handle anything in war or peace.

Under the Republic, Rome was ruled by pairs of annual magistrates called consuls, who were invested with authority, *imperium*, for one year only. Lesser magistrates were also annual and in pairs, an expedient to allow them to veto each other and thereby prevent the concentration of power in one man's hands (cf. monarchy or tyranny). This principal of collegiality was basic to the Roman constitution. A council of 300, the Senate, advised the consuls.

In the days of the early Republic there was no fixed order or set ages for holding magistracies. However, from the later third century BC onwards a legal career structure developed. Known as the *cursus honorum* (from the Latin: 'the course of honours'), the rungs of office that ambitious aristocratic young Romans climbed on their way to political power, this socio-political construction was constitutionally formalized by a law of 180 BC, the *lex Villia annalis* of Lucius Villius. For our purposes, the ladder of public advancement can be best summarized as follows:

APPENDIX 1

1. EARLY YEARS

From the age of 17 a young aristocrat commenced his military service, perhaps first as a junior cavalry officer followed by a spell as a military tribune; he could also undertake some legal work, perhaps a minor post such as a circuit judge or supervisor for street cleaning; thence by gradually building up his curriculum vitae, a hopeful young man was exposed to the public eye.

2. QUAESTORSHIP

A minimum of ten years' military service was a necessary qualification for the quaestorship. (From the Latin: *quaestor*: 'investigator' and reflects the pre-Republican origins of this magistracy.)

Power: without *imperium* but did hold *potestas*, the legal sanction to allow discharge of duties.

Duties: aided consuls and provincial governors, especially with financial matters; controlled the state treasury, *aerarium Saturni*, which was not only a store for public money but also for copies of statutes and other state documents.

Number: originally two, but more created as the complexity of running a world empire increased, to eventually number twenty under Sulla. Two of them served in Rome (*quaestores urbani*) and were responsible for the *aerarium Saturni*; one accompanied each holder of *imperium* to his province to act as financial officer; attached to a consular army, a quaestor was responsible for the military chest and had to see to the collection and listing of booty, the selling of captives, etc.; others performed administrative functions in Italy, one being in charge, for instance, of the grain supply coming to Rome from Ostia.

3. AEDILESHIP

It was necessary to have served as a quaestor before becoming an aedile.

Power: without *imperium* but did hold *potestas* greater than that of quaestor.

Duties: maintained roads and water supply; supervised traffic and markets; organized public games and festivals.

Number: four, consisting of two plebeian aediles elected in the *concilium plebis*, and two curule, that is, patrician aediles elected in the *comitia tributa* and representing the whole people.

Privileges: *ius imaginum*, the right to display wax death masks of famous ancestors in the atrium of the house; curule aediles could use the curule seat, *sella curialis*, a special folding chair made of ivory.

4. TRIBUNATE

After the quaestorship, a plebeian could be elected a tribune of the people (sometimes written as tribune of the plebs).

Power: without *imperium* but did hold *potestas* greater than that of quaestor; had power of *intercessio* (veto over decisions of the Senate or any magistrate, however senior) and *ius auxilii* (right to help), thereby able to prevent arbitrary (and aristocratic) attacks on the plebeians; could summon the *concilium plebis* and there pass resolutions called *plebiscita*.

Duties: to look after the interests of the people; to protect their lives and property; to be always accessible to the people (but we should note they were normally young senators at the early stage of their *cursus honorum*).

Number: ten.

Privileges: tribunes were not magistrates, and the tribunate was technically outside the *cursus honorum*; but they were protected by a religious taboo against any attacks (*sacrosanctitas*), that is to say, they were considered sacrosanct, *sacer*, which made them inviolate and anyone injuring or killing a tribune could be killed with impunity. Potentially, the powers of this office were considerable.

5. Praetorship

The minimum age for the praetorship was 39, and a man also had to have been aedile before becoming a praetor.

Power: held *imperium* (sovereign power in war and peace); the holder of *imperium* could compel obedience except from someone with greater *imperium*; power of life and death in battle, which was symbolized by an axe (*securis*) enclosed in a tied bundle of rods (*fasces*) carried by the lictors, their bodyguard attendants, who walked in front; in peace only *fasces* carried by their lictors, while *intercessio* and *provocatio* (right of appeal against arbitrary treatment by a magistrate) limited *imperium*.

Duties: running civil and criminal courts; could summon assemblies and propose legislation if the consuls were busy (or dead); governing smaller provinces; leading armies (technically, of one Roman *legio* and one Latin-Italian *ala* only); had right to consult the gods (*auspicium*) through the auspices (*auspicia*). The antiquarian Messalla, writing in the late Republic, appropriately describes them as 'colleagues of the consuls'.[1]

Number: originally one, then two (242 BC), later four, two of which normally administering the extra-Italian provinces of Sicily and Sardinia (227 BC), then six (196 BC), and eventually Sulla would make the total up to eight, the senior being the urban praetor (*praetor urbanus*) who was responsible for the administration of justice in cases between Roman citizens.

Privileges: accompanied by six lictors; could use a curule seat; worthy of a triumph (200 BC onwards).

6. Consulship

From 150 BC, or thereabouts, 42 years of age was the minimum age for the consulship.

Power: *imperium* superior to everyone else except a dictator.

Duties: summon and chair the Senate and assemblies in peace; propose bills (*rogationes*) to create legislation; had right of *auspicium*; see to the common good of the Republic; lead armies in times of war (technically, each commanded a consular army of just two Roman *legiones* and two Latin-Italian *alae*). 'In the elections for consuls', Cicero said in a speech when he was consul, 'it is generals that are chosen, not legal experts'.[2]

Number: two

Privileges: accompanied by twelve lictors; could use a curule seat; wear purple-fringed *toga praetexta*; worthy of a triumph; gave their name to the year.

7. CENSORSHIP

After having held the consulship, one could be elected a censor, a magistrate who was normally appointed once every five years.

Power: without *imperium* but did hold *potestas* greater than that of aedile.

Duties: no military duties, the primary job being, as the title implies, is to conduct the five-yearly census, which gave information on property and wealth and thus determined military obligations, tax obligations and corresponding political rights; revising the list of the Senate to include ex-magistrates of previous five years; control of public morals (could place a mark of disgrace against anyone and expel members of the senatorial or equestrian orders for conduct unbecoming; supervise state lands (*ager publicus*) and let public contracts; had right of *auspicium*.

Number: two.

Privileges: use a curule seat; wear *toga praetexta*.

8. DICTATORSHIP

The dictatorship, by its very nature, was an irregular office, and often the duties were quite trivial, though the appointment was a high honour. Thus when no consul had been elected, an *interrex* would normally be appointed, for five days at a time, until the elections had been held. However, in times of a dire emergency the consuls themselves could appoint a dictator (full title: *dictator rei gerundae causa*, 'dictator for the purpose of carrying on the business of the state') with the other magistrates acting as his subordinates.

Power: held double-consular *imperium*.

Duties: running all military and domestic affairs in time of crisis; office lasted six months; assisted by a *magister equitum*, master of horse.

Number: one.

Privileges: accompanied by twenty-four lictors and *fasces* always included the *securis*, even within Rome.

As we can now appreciate, these magistracies were of differing importance, and an ambitious Roman aristocrat had to seek them in ascending order (quaestorship, aedileship, praetorship, consulship, censorship). There had to be a gap of at least a year between magistracies, so that a magistrate could be called to account after his term of office.

Candidates for public office rarely stood for election on the basis of particular policies, instead relying on their reputation for ability. It was system that heavily favoured a small clique of wealthy aristocratic families who were skilled at promoting the virtues and successes of former generations and implying as much or more could be expected from younger members of the family. Thus the government of Rome was to a large extent in the hands the *nobiles*, which consisted of men who had held the consulship or were descendants of consuls. It was difficult for men outside this charmed circle to win their way to office: those who succeeded were called *novi homines*, new men (e.g. Marius, Cicero). With only two posts for the consulship per annum, competition for this high honour was fierce, especially since a mixture of law and tradition prevented anyone attaining this rank before his early forties, and was supposed to prevent it being held twice within ten years. In reality, it was unusual for a man to hold the consulship more than once, and highly exceptional more than twice.

Sometimes, however, it was found desirable to keep a man in office for a longer period, especially in wartime, when it might be disastrous to supercede an efficient commander at the end of one year. So as early as 326 BC, the device was adopted of prolonging commands (*prorogare imperium*) for a year, or even longer. In point of fact, it was the *imperium*, and not the magistracy, that was prolonged: a man was invested with the powers of a consul or praetor without holding the office, and so was called a proconsul or propraetor. This sensible practice met a further need: in a large-scale conflict fought in many theatres, as where the first two Punic wars, Rome might not have enough higher magistrates to command the various armies, so the custom was adopted of prolonging the *imperium* of a magistrate beyond the annual limit of his magistracy, or even conferring *imperium* on a private citizen, *privatus cum imperio*, as on Scipio in 210 BC for the Iberian campaign.

However, as stressed before, the fundamental principle of Roman government was that no one individual should hold supreme power and that all power should be of a limited duration, normally a year of office. This was intended to prevent the emergence of a tyrant or king. Therefore there were two consuls in each year, whose power was absolutely equal. Only rarely was this canon abandoned for a short time and the extraordinary expedient taken of appointing a dictator with supreme authority to direct the state. The dictator held office for six months and had not a colleague but a junior assistant, the *magister equitum*. When the office of dictator had been created in an earlier period, it was considered important that he should fight on foot with the warriors of the phalanx, the yeoman-farmers who were the heart of the military system of the early Republic. So the dictator was prohibited from riding a horse, leaving his deputy to command the cavalry. Such a restriction was no longer appropriate for the task of commanding the much larger and more sophisticated armies of the middle Republic. Despite this however, with the Romans being obsessed with the culture and traditions of their ancestors, *mos maiorum*, a newly appointed dictator still had to gain special permission from the Senate to ride a horse.

To Romans in general fresh innovations were a simple return to the past, with new ideas being rediscovered for use again. In a sense this helps to explain why the Romans padded their traditional history with these innovations. For example, the warlike Romulus was attributed with establishing the trappings of a magistrate (robes, chair, etc.) and the pious and peaceful Numa Pompilius with those of religion and forming the office of the Vestal Virgins. There are no concrete reasons to disbelieve the existence of the early kings of Rome and by tradition a monarch was surrounded by a group of elder-advisors. These advisors were drawn from the heads of the leading families, *patres*, and thereby constituted the Senate.

The word Senate is connected with the Latin for old man, *senex*, and it reflects the fact that senators were appointed for life, and that many of them were aged by the standards of the ancient world. The Senate existed already under the monarchy, although we know very little about it at the time. Under the kings and for much of the Republic it consisted of about 300 members. A broad purple strip, *latus clavus*, on their togas distinguished its members. In the early Republic it probably did not have any effective functions, but its importance increased enormously during the time of the Samnite Wars when it acquired greater authority.

Festus, a Roman grammarian writing in the late second century AD but quoting an earlier grammarian of the time of Augustus, defines the Senate thus:

> There was a time when it was considered disgraceful for senators to be passed over, because, just as kings by themselves used to choose men who would serve them as public advisers, so under the Republic the consuls used to choose for themselves their closest friends from among the patricians and then from among the plebeians. This practice continued until the law of the tribune Ovinus put an end to it. Ovinus' law [*lex Ovinia*] bound the censors by oath to enrol in the Senate the best men from all ranks. The enforcement of this law had the consequence that senators who were passed over and thus lost their place were held in dishonour.[3]

The *lex Ovinia* had been passed sometime between 339 BC and 318 BC. Theoretically, the Senate had no constitutional powers.[4] Its decrees, passed on a majority vote, were not law but merely advisory.[5] It functioned, therefore, as a *concilium* or advisory council, advising the magistrates. It discussed a whole gamut of political and religious business, but came to be particularly important in foreign affairs. It met only when summoned by a consul or tribune of the plebs, often in a temple (the first meeting of the year was in the Temple of Iuppiter on the Capitol). When it debated, the presiding consul would invite speakers to express their opinions in order of their personal standing. Consequently, lower status members might never speak. After some debate the consul might invite members to express proposal in the form of a *sententia*. There might be several of these. The house then divided, the members moving across the floor to stand by the proposer whose *sententia* they approved. If there was a majority, that *sententia* became a *Senatus consultum*. Or, to put it more simply, the Senate was a body made up of anybody who was anybody in Rome.

Though the republican machinery of government was not democratic in any proper sense of that term, there were three main assemblies where the Roman people expressed its collective. The *comitia centuriata*, 'assembly of centuries', voted to declare war or accept a peace treaty, elected consuls, praetors, censors, and curule aediles, the senior magistrates of Rome, and tried capital cases. The *comitia tributa*, 'tribal assembly', elected most of the junior magistrates and could pass legislation. The *concilium plebis*, 'gathering of plebeians', was very similar, but excluded members of the numerically smaller patrician order. There was another assembly, the *comitia curiata*, 'assembly of wards', but by the middle Republic this organ was a mere rubber stamp where the thirty wards, *curiae*, were represented by lictors. And so by the time of Augustus it was said by the poet Ovid that most Romans did not know which *curia* they belonged to. It should be understood that these assemblies did not debate issues and were summoned only when required to vote for or against a proposal.

The 'timocratic principle', the common idea whereby the property-owning classes lived in a 'stakeholder' society, where political rights are defined by military obligations, which in turn spring from the need to defend property; property itself gives the financial means to engage in that defence. Those who have property, and thus a stake and a role in the defence of society are considered more likely to take sensible decisions about how the state is run. The richer you are, the truer this becomes, and conversely, having nothing to lose will make you irresponsible. Anyway, the three assemblies can be summarized as follows:

1. *COMITIA CENTURIATA*

This assembly operates on a 'timocratic principle', and Edward Gibbon describes it well: 'In the purer ages of the commonwealth, the use of arms was reserved for those ranks of citizens who had a country to love, a property to defend, and some share in enacting those laws, which it was their interest, as well as a duty, to maintain'.[6] The 'timocratic principle' meant that only those who could afford arms could vote; so the *comitia centuriata* was an assembly of property owners, and thus of soldiers. The *comitia centuriata* transformed from the people voting under arms to a main assembly, where voting groups were still called centuries (*centuriae*: originally a military unit of 100 men), though now much larger. As a former military institution the *comitia centuriata* met mainly on the *campus Martius*, Field of Mars, an open area outside the city. Here we should note that it was forbidden to carry arms inside the city because of the (obsessive) fear of armed tyranny, and even provincial governors must lay aside military *imperium* if they cross the *pomoerium*, the sacred boundary of the city. The one exception to this rule was for triumphs, which are in essence religious festivals.

APPENDIX 1

Servius Tullius, the penultimate king, had instituted the *comitia centuriata* originally. A constitutional reform later known still as the 'Servian system' divided the centuries up between classes (*classes*) based on landed wealth. This probably happened in 406 BC, and seems to be related to introduction of military pay (*stipendium*) and taxation (*tributum*). The censors registered Romans in classes, and this registration formed the basis of tax assessment, military obligations and political rights. Thus, the 'Servian system' had 193 centuries; some were for younger men (*iuniores*), and others were for older men (*seniores*). More important was the subdivision of these five classes into centuries, *centuriae*: in each class half the centuries were made up of the elder men (*seniores*, those from age 47 to 60), and half of younger men (*iuniores*, those from age 17 to 46). The centuries in each class were unequal in number, as the state naturally drew more heavily upon the well-equipped wealthier men than on those lower down the property ladder. Thus class I contained eighty *centuriae*; classes II, III and IV twenty each; and class V thirty. Below them were five *centuriae* of unarmed men, four of artisans and one of *proletarii*, whose property was too little to justify enrolment in class V. Known as *capite censi*, 'counted by heads', these men were simply counted and had no military obligations, no political rights and were not taxed. In other words poverty, curiously perhaps to us moderns, freed men from conscription. At the other extreme were those who served on horseback, the sons of the well-to-do making up eighteen *centuriae*, which took precedence over the *centuriae* of the other five classes.

The *comitia centuriata* voted from the top down with decisions reached by a simple majority of ninety-seven centuries. Thus, if the top classes were pretty much agreeing about a particular candidate (i.e. for magisterial post with *imperium*) a decision might be reached with just the votes of the *equites* and class I (i.e. ninety-eight centuries). This often happened, and showed how the conservative timocratic values of Rome weighted the exercise of political rights in favour of the rich. In about 241 BC the 'Servian system' was reformed, at a time when the number of tribes was increased from thirty-three to thirty-five (see below). The five classes were retained, but the 193 centuries were rearranged. Class I was reduced from eighty to seventy, two to a tribe, one of seniors and one of juniors (thirty-five in each). The other, now redundant, ten centuries of class I were redistributed among some or all of the other four, although the method of redistribution remains uncertain. The century which voted first, *praerogativa*, and generally had considerable influence on those that followed, was chosen by lot from class I; then the *equites* and the five classes voted in order until a majority of the centuries' votes was obtained. As before the *capite censi* remained outside the system. Under this system a majority could be reached with the votes of the class II, whereas hitherto the *equites* and class I had had a clear majority. This represented a minor democratization of the process compared to the original 'Servian system'.

2. COMITIA TRIBUTA

Perhaps from the time of Servius Tullius new 'regional' tribes were instituted, probably to speed up military organization and recruitment. Originally there had been four tribes covering the area of the city, later these were the 'urban' tribes (often mostly freedmen and city plebs) but with Rome's gradual conquest of the Italian peninsula the *ager Romanus*, Roman land, expanded and 'rural' tribes were subsequently added. By the beginning of the First Punic War, in 264 BC, there were thirty-three tribes (four urban, twenty-nine rural), with two more rural tribes being added by its end in 241 BC, but they were the last.

Every Roman, rich or poor, belonged to a tribe, denoting where he lived or at least where his family came from. A man's tribe stayed the same, unless he was demoted (into an urban tribe) by the censors, or took over a better tribe as a result of a prosecution (i.e. taking the guilty party's tribe). The *comitia tributa* voted by tribes, in order determined by lot. As soon as a candidate (i.e. for magisterial post with *potestas*) has a majority of the tribes (i.e., eighteen) he is declared elected. The next candidate to pass the majority is next elected and so on. More than one go might be necessary. As for passing legislation, this was done on a simple majority in the tribes, for or against. When this assembly elected magistrates, it met on the *campus Martius*. For voting on legislation, the venue was the *Comitium* in the *forum Romanum*.

3. CONCILIUM PLEBIS

The plebs, originally all who were not patricians, formed a 'state within a state' in the fifth century BC to put pressure on the patrician aristocracy. Through this institution they elected their own officers (tribunes of the people and plebeian aediles). Its resolutions were called *plebiscita*, 'decrees of the plebs'. The *lex Hortensia* of 287 BC enacted that all *plebiscita* should be legally binding and equivalent to *leges* passed in the *comitia*. This law marked the formal end of the 'Struggle of the Orders', which had effectively been lost to the patricians with *leges Liciniae Sextiae* in 367 BC, which effectively opened the consulship to plebeians. The *concilium plebis* votes, in elections and legislation, by tribes, but only plebeians are eligible. Procedure and place as per *comitia tributa*.

Although the number of Roman citizens steadily increased, and by the third century BC many lived long distances from Rome, the political life of the state was still entirely conducted in the city. Only when physically present in Rome might a citizen vote or stand for office. Nevertheless, as stressed before, in these assemblies the People could only vote for or against a proposal, and there was no opportunity, unlike in the Senate, for debate or for a citizen to present a counter proposal. In all three the opinion of the wealthier citizens tended to predominate. This was especially so in the *comitia centuriata*, where the voting system, even after its 'democratization', was based upon archaic military organization. The more prosperous citizens voted first and had fewer members in each century, in the same way that they had once provided the cavalry and the most heavily armed infantry, who had the most prominent role in wartime.

Lest we forget the *equites* and class I combined fell not far short of a majority out of the 193 centuries composing the assembly. It is also important to remember that popular support, most of all in the consular elections, always meant that a man had the favour of the bulk of the prosperous citizens at Rome and not simply the poor. Even the ten tribunes of the people, who had originally been created to defend the plebeians against aristocratic and especially patrician oppression, by this time were normally young senators at an early phase in their career.

As a final, yet important point, candidates for political office were not elected for membership of a political party (for such things did not exist), and only rarely for espousing a particular policy. A man was elected on the basis of his former achievements or those of his family. The Romans believed very strongly that characteristics and ability were passed on from one generation to the next. If a man's father or grandfather had won the consulship and led Roman armies to victory in battle, then there was every reason to believe that he would prove equally competent. The noble families took care to advertise the achievements of former generations, and those men who achieved high office were the kind of nobles who flourished on long lineages, brave deeds, broad acres and patronage.

APPENDIX 2

Roman army

By the time Rome was no longer the hilltop village on the bank of the Tiber, Roman warfare had become an adaptation of Greek warfare and the hoplite ideology of the decisive battle. Yet when Rome was no longer the humble city of the seven hills, but plundering Rome at the time of Hannibal, the army had assumed the more familiar form of the manipular legion. In both these instances, the model is that of the disciplined infantry formation in a set piece battle, first with the rigid phalanx and then with the more flexible legion, but both with an excellence in, and a preference for, the head-to-head encounter that seeks to destroy the enemy. In this decisive clash of opposing armies, which tended to settle the issue one way or another, the Roman legion usually performed very well, returning any blows vigorously and viciously. The Roman citizen soldier, like his Greek counterpart, excelled at close quarter combat, but his legion could be manoeuvred more readily than the phalanx. In contrast to the one solid block of the Greeks, the legion was now divided into several small blocks, with spaces between them. The Romans, in other words, gave the phalanx 'joints' in order to secure flexibility, and what is more, each soldier had twice as much elbow room for individual action, which, as we shall discover, involved swordplay.[1]

We have two accounts of the manipular legion's organization. First, the Roman historian Livy, writing more than three centuries after the event, describes the legion of the mid-fourth century BC. Second, the Greek historian Polybios, living and writing in Rome at the time, describes the legion of the mid-second century BC. The transition between the Livian and Polybian legion is somewhat obscure, but for the sake of brevity and clarity, we shall just concern ourselves with the Polybian legion. Indeed, for the actual organization of the Republican legion *terra firma* is reached only with Polybios himself, who breaks off his narrative of the Second Punic War at the nadir of Rome's fortunes, following the three defeats of the Trebbia, Lake Trasimene, and Cannae, and turns to an extended digression on the Roman constitution and the Roman army.[2]

POLYBIAN LEGION

In our chosen period of study, the Roman army was based on the principle of personal service by the citizens defending their state. It was not yet a professional army. The term *legio*, 'levy', obviously referred to the entire citizen force raised by

Rome in any one year, but by at least the fourth century BC it had come to denote the most significant subdivision of the army. Then, as Rome's territory and population increased, it was found necessary to levy two consular armies, each of two legions, *legiones*. Yet accompanying each Roman legion were soldiers provided by Rome's Latin and Italian allies, the *socii*.[3] Their principal unit was known as the *ala*, wing, which deployed the same number of infantry as the Roman legion. By the time of Hannibal, if not before, in a standard consular army the two Roman *legiones* would form the centre with two Latin-Italian *alae* deployed on their flanks. They were known as the '*ala* of the left' and the '*ala* of the right', a positioning obviously reflecting the term *ala*, wing.[4]

All citizens between 17 and 46 years of age who satisfied the property criteria, namely those who owned property above the value of 11,000 *asses*, were required by the Senate to attend a selection process, the *dilectus*, on the Capitol. Although Polybios' passage is slightly defective here, citizens were liable for sixteen years' service as a legionary, *miles*, or ten for a horseman, *eques*.[5] These figures represent the maximum that a man could be called upon to serve. In the second century BC, for instance, a man was normally expected to serve up to six years in a continuous posting, after which he expected to be released from his military oath. Thereafter he was liable for enlistment, as an *evocatus*, up to the maximum of sixteen campaigns or years. Some men might serve for a single year at a time, and be obliged to come forward again at the next *dilectus*, until their full six-year period was completed.

At the *dilectus*, height and age arranged the citizens into some semblance of soldierly order. They were then brought forward four at a time to be selected for service in one of the four consular legions being raised that year. The junior military tribunes of each legion took it in turns to have first choice, thus ensuring an even distribution of experience and quality throughout the four units. They then ordered the soldiers to take a formal oath. Though the exact text of the oath is not given by Polybios, he does say a soldier swore 'he would obey his officers and carry out their commands to the best of his ability'.[6] To speed up the process the oath was sworn in full by one man, and each of the rest swore that he would do the same as the first, perhaps using the phrase *idem in me*, 'the same for me'. They were given a date and muster point, and then dismissed to their homes.

The standard complement of the Polybian legion was 4,200 foot and 300 horse, in theory if not practice, and consisted of five elements: the heavy infantry *hastati*, *principes*, and *triarii*, the light infantry *velites* (*grosphomachoi* in Polybios' Greek), and the cavalry *equites*, each equipped differently and having specific places in the legion's tactical formation.[7] Its principal strength was the thirty maniples of its heavy infantry, the *velites* and *equites* acting in support of these. Its organization allowed it only one standard formation, the *triplex acies* with three successive, relatively shallow lines of ten maniples each, these fighting units supporting each other to apply maximum pressure on an enemy to the front.

Hence, the legion was divided horizontally into three lines, and vertically into maniples (*manipuli*), with the first line containing 1,200 *hastati* in ten maniples of 120, the second line 1,200 *principes* organized in the same way, and the third line of 600 *triarii* also in ten maniples. The *hastati* ('spearmen') were men in the flower of youth, the *principes* ('chief men') in the prime of manhood, and the *triarii* ('third-rank men') the oldest and more mature men.[8] Of the 4,200 legionaries in a legion, while 3,000 served as heavy infantry, the remaining 1,200 men, the youngest and poorest, were serving as light infantry. Known as *velites* or 'cloak-wearers', that is to say, they lacked any form of body armour, they were divided for administrative purpose among the heavy infantry of the maniples, each maniple being allocated the same number of *velites*.[9] Finally, accompanying the legionaries were 300 fellow citizens on horseback.

POLYBIAN LEGIONARY

The Romans attached a great deal of importance to training, and it is this that largely explains the formidable success of their army. 'And what can I say about the training of legions?' is the rhetorical question aired by Cicero. 'Put an equally brave, but untrained soldier in the front line and he will look like a woman'.[10] The basic aim of this training was to give the legions superiority over the 'barbarian' in battle, and even as late as the fourth century AD, Vegetius attributed 'the conquest of the world by the Roman people' to their training methods, camp discipline, and military skills.[11] Having said all that, the Romans took great pride in their ability to learn from their enemies too, copying weaponry (and tactics) from successive opponents and often improving upon them. This was one of their strong points and, as Polybios rightly says, 'no people are more willing to adopt new customs and to emulate what they see is better done by others'.[12]

The *hastati* and *principes* carried the Italic oval, semi-cylindrical body shield, conventionally known as the *scutum*, the famous Iberian cut-and-thrust sword (*gladius Hispaniensis*), and two sorts of *pila*, heavy and light. The *triarii* were similarly equipped, except they carried a long thrusting spear (*hasta*) instead of the *pilum*.[13] This 2m weapon survived from the era when the Roman army was a hoplite militia.[14] The *hasta* was perhaps obsolete in Polybios' day, though probably still in use during the Gallic *tumultus* of 223 BC, when they are, for the only time, mentioned in action, while the annalistic tradition does not notice it at all.[15] The close-quarter, battering power of the legion was thus provided by the legionary wielding *pilum* and *gladius*, and the combination of *pilum* shower and blade-work rendered the Roman army so deadly.

In the Livian legion there is no reference to the *pilum*, which, if Livy's account is accepted, may not yet have been introduced. The earliest reference to the *pilum* belongs to 293 BC during the Third Samnite War, though the earliest authentic use of this weapon may belong to 251 BC.[16] The *pilum*, therefore, was probably adopted from Iberian mercenaries fighting for Carthage in the First Punic War.

Polybios distinguishes two types of *pilum* (*hyssos* in his Greek), 'thick' and 'thin', saying each man had both types.[17] Surviving examples from Numantia (near Burgos, Spain), the site of a Roman siege (134-133 BC), confirm two basics types of construction. Both have a small pyramid-shaped point at the end of a narrow soft-iron shank, fitted to a wooden shaft some 1.4m in length. One type has the shank socketed, while the other has a wide flat iron tang riveted to a thickened section of the wooden shaft. The last type is probably Polybios' 'thick' *pilum*, referring to the broad joint of iron and wood. This broad section can be either square or round in section, and is strengthened by a small iron ferrule. The iron shank varies in length, with many examples averaging around 70cm.

All of the weapon's weight was concentrated behind the small pyramidal tip, giving it great penetrative power. The length of the iron shank gave it the reach to punch through an enemy's shield and still go on to wound his body, but even if it failed to do so and merely stuck in the shield it was very difficult to pull free and might force the man to discard his weighted-down shield and fight unprotected. A useful side effect of this 'armour piercing' weapon was that the narrow shank would often bend on impact, ensuring that the enemy would not throw it back. The maximum range of the *pilum* was some 30m, but its effective range something like half that. Throwing a *pilum* at close range would have improved both accuracy and armour penetration.

A later lexicographer, possibly following Polybios' lost account of the Iberian war, says the *gladius Hispaniensis* was adopted from the Iberians (or Celtiberians) at the time of the war with Hannibal, but it is possible that this weapon, along with *pilum*, was adopted from Iberian mercenaries serving Carthage during the First Punic War.[18] It was certainly in use by 197 BC, when Livy describes the Macedonians' shock at the terrible wounds it inflicted.[19] The Iberians used a relatively short, but deadly sword. This was either the *falcata*, an elegant curved single-bladed weapon derived from the Greek *kopis*, most common in the south and southeast of Iberia, or the cut-and-thrust sword, straight bladed weapon from which the *gladius* was derived.[20] The earliest Roman specimens date to the turn of the first century BC ('Mainz' type), but a fourth century BC sword of similar shape has been found in Spain at the cemetery of Los Cogotes (Avila), as is an earlier Iberian example from Atienza some 100km northeast of Madrid. The Roman blade could be as much as 64 to 69cm in length and 4.8 to 6cm wide and waisted in the centre. It was a fine piece of 'blister steel' with a triangular point between 9.6 and 20cm long and honed down razor-sharp edges and was designed to puncture armour. It had a comfortable bone handgrip grooved to fit the fingers, and a large spherical pommel, usually of wood or ivory, to help with counterbalance. Extant examples weigh between 1.2 and 1.6kg. The story of the *gladius* is an object lesson in the Roman way of taking the best of what others have learned and making it their own.

The legionary also carried a dagger, *pugio*. The dagger, a short, edged, stabbing weapon, was the ultimate weapon of last resort. However, it was probably more often employed in the day-to-day tasks of living on campaign. Like the *gladius*, the Roman dagger was borrowed from the Iberians and then developed.

Polybios says all soldiers wore a bronze pectoral, a span (223mm square), to protect the heart and chest, although those who could afford it would wear instead an iron mail shirt (*lorica hamata*).[21] He also adds that a bronze helmet was worn, without describing it, but the Attic, Montefortino, and Etrusco-Corinthian styles were all popular in Italy at this time and were probably all used, as they certainly all were by later Roman troops. He does say helmets were crested with a circlet of feathers and three upright black or crimson feathers a cubit (444mm) tall, so exaggerating the wearer's height.[22] Interestingly, Polybios clearly refers to only one greave being worn, and Arrian, writing more or less three centuries later, confirms this, saying the ancient Romans used to wear one greave only, on the leading leg, the left.[23] No doubt many of those who could afford it would actually have a pair of bronze greaves covering their legs from ankle to knee.

To complete his defensive equipment, each soldier carried the *scutum*, an Italic body shield probably derived from the Samnites.[24] Polybios describes the *scutum* in detail, and his account is confirmed by the remarkable discovery in 1900 of a shield of this type at Kasr-el-Harit in the Fayûm, Egypt.[25] It is midway between a rectangle and an oval in shape, and is 1.28m in length and 63.5cm in width with a slight concavity. It is constructed from three layers of birch laths, each layer laid at right angles to the next, and originally covered with lamb's wool felt. This was likely fitted damp in one piece, which, when dry, had shrunk and strengthened the whole artefact. The shield board is thicker in the centre and flexible at the edges, making it very resilient to blows, and the top and bottom edges may have been reinforced with bronze or iron edging to prevent splitting. Nailed to the front and running vertically from top to bottom is a wooden spine (*spina*). Good protection came at a price, for the *scutum* was heavy, around 10kg, and in battle its entire weight was borne by the left arm as the soldier held the horizontal handgrip behind the bronze or iron boss (*umbo*), which reinforced the central spine of the shield.

Finally, lest we forget, these short-term citizen soldiers provided their own equipment and therefore we should expect considerably more variation in clothing, armour and weapons than the legionaries of the later professional legions. There is no good reason to believe, for instance, that they wore tunics of the same hue or that shields were adorned with unit insignia. In fact, Polybios makes no mention of shield decoration, despite his detailed description of legionary equipment down to the colour of their plumes. This seems to be supported by sculptural evidence, such as the Aemilius Paullus monument or the Altar of Domitius Ahenobarbus, which show *scuta* left plain.

LIGHT INFANTRY

The *velites* were armed with a sword, the *gladius Hispaniensis* according to Livy, and a bundle of javelins, with long thin iron heads a span in length, which bent at the first impact.²⁶ For protection they wore a helmet without a crest and carried a round shield (*parma*) but wore no armour. In order to be distinguished from a distance, some *velites* would cover their plain helmets with a wolf's skin or something similar.²⁷ As for the number of javelins carried, Polybios does not specify. Livy, on the other hand, says *velites* had seven javelins apiece, whilst the second-century BC Roman satirist Lucilius has them carrying five each.²⁸

CAVALRY

Each legion had a small cavalry force of 300 organized in ten *turmae* of thirty troopers each.²⁹ The military tribunes appointed three *decuriones* to each *turma*, of whom the senior commanded with the rank of *praefectus*. Each *decurio* chose an *optio* as his second-in-command and rear-rank officer.³⁰ This organization suggests that the *turma* was divided into three files of ten, each led by a *decurio* ('leader of ten') and closed by an *optio*. These files were obviously not independent tactical subunits, for the *turma* was evidently intended to operate as a single entity, as indicated by the seniority of one *decurio* over his two colleagues.

The cavalry or *equites* formed the most prestigious element of the legion, and were recruited from the wealthiest citizens able to afford a horse and its trappings.³¹ By our period these included the top eighteen centuries (*centuriae*) of the voting assembly, the *comitia centuriata*, who were rated *equites equo publico*, the equestrian élite, obliging the state to provide them with the cost of a remount should their horse be killed on active service. Cato was later to boast that his grandfather had five horses killed under him in battle and subsequently replaced by the state.³² Being young aristocrats, the *equites* were enthusiastic and brave, but better at making a headlong charge on the battlefield than patrolling or scouting. This was a reflection of the lack of a real cavalry tradition in Rome, as well as the fact that the *equites* included the sons of many senators, eager to make a name for courage and so help their future political careers. Before being eligible for political office in Rome a man had to have served for ten campaigns with the army.

The allied cavalry force was generally two or three times larger than that of the citizens. These horsemen were organized in *turmae* probably the same strength as the Roman, and were presumably also from the wealthiest strata of society. This is certainly suggested by Livy's references to 300 young men of the noblest Campanian families serving in Sicily, and to the young noblemen from Tarentum who served at the battles of Lake Trasimene and Cannae.³³ The cavalry were commanded, at least from the second century BC, by Roman *praefecti equitum*, presumably with local *decuriones* and *optiones* at *turma* level. Like their citizen counterparts, as well as having a higher social status, allied horsemen were much better paid than those serving as foot soldiers.³⁴

Polybios discusses the changes in the Roman cavalry in some detail, emphasizing that the *equites* were now armed in 'the Greek fashion', namely bronze helmet, stiff linen corselet, strong circular shield, long spear, complete with a butt-spike, and sword, but he observes that formerly (perhaps up to the Pyrrhic War) they had lacked body armour and had carried only a short spear and a small ox-hide shield, which was too light for adequate protection at close quarters and tended to rot in the rain.[35] Polybios actually compares its shape to a type of round-bossed cake, namely those that are commonly used in sacrifices. This earlier shield may be the type shown on the Tarentine 'horsemen' coins of the early fourth century BC, with a flat rim and convex centre. For what it is worth, Livy mentions 'little round cavalry shields' in use as early as 499 BC, but this may be anachronistic.[36]

Intriguingly the sword now carried by the *equites* appears to have been the *gladius Hispaniensis*, for when Livy describes the horror felt by Macedonian troops on seeing the hideous wounds inflicted upon their comrades, the perpetrators were Roman cavalrymen. If true, then the *gladius* used by the *equites* may well have been a little longer than that of the infantry. Livy refers to 'arms torn away, shoulders and all, heads separated from bodies with the necks completely severed, and stomachs ripped open'.[37]

Contrary to popular belief, the lack of stirrups was not a major handicap to ancient horsemen, especially those 'born in the saddle' like the Numidians. Moreover, Roman cavalry of the time were perhaps already using the Celtic four-horned saddle, which provides an admirably firm seat.[38] When a rider's weight was lowered onto this type of saddle the four tall horns (*cornicule*) closed around and gripped his thighs, but they did not inhibit free movement to the same extent as a modern pommel and cantle designed for rider comfort and safety. This was especially important to spear- and sword-carrying cavalry favoured by the Romans, whose drill called for some almost acrobatic changes of position. In an age that did not have the stirrup, the adoption of the four-horned saddle, as experimental work has shown, allowed the horseman to effectively launch a missile while skirmishing, or confidently use both hands to wield his shield and spear (or sword) in a whirling mêlée.[39] The main function of its wooden frame was to protect the horse's spine from shock during a charge, and its design transferred the rider's weight to the animal's flanks. The saddle was secured with breast strap, haunch straps and breeching, and a girth that passed through a woollen saddlecloth under which a smaller cloth of fur may have been placed to give the horse greater protection from chafing.

BATTLE TACTICS

Polybios does not offer his readers an account of the legion in battle, but there are a number of combat descriptions both in his own work and that of Livy. However, very few accounts describe tactics in detail; a contemporary Roman (or Greek) audience would take much for granted. Even so, the legion would usually approach the enemy in its standard battle formation, the *triplex acies*, which was based around the triple line of *hastati, principes,* and *triarii,* with the *velites* forming a light screen in front. As we know, each of these three lines consisted of ten maniples. When deployed, each maniple may have been separated from its lateral neighbour by the width of its own frontage (approximately 18m), though this is still a matter of some debate. Livy tells us that the maniples were 'a small distance apart', which does not really help us a great deal.[40] Moreover, the maniples of *hastati, principes* and *triarii* were staggered, with the more seasoned *principes* covering the gaps of the *hastati* in front, and likewise the veteran *triarii* covering those of the *princeps*. This battle formation is conveniently called by modern commentators the *quincunx,* from the five dots on a dice cube.[41]

Battle would be opened by the *velites* who attempted to disorganize and unsettle enemy formations with a hail of javelins. This done, they retired through the gaps in the maniples of the *hastati* and made their way to the rear. The maniples of the *hastati* now reformed to close the gaps, either by each maniple extending its frontage, thus giving individuals more room in which to handle their weapons, or, if the maniple was drawn up two centuries deep, the *centurio posterior* would move his *centuria* to the left and forward, thus running out and forming up alongside the *centuria* of the *centurio prior* in the line itself.[42]

The *hastati* would discharge their *pila,* throwing first their light and then their heavyweight *pila,* some 15m, the effective range of a *pilum,* from the enemy. The term *hastati,* spearmen, should be taken to mean armed with throwing spears, namely *pila,* instead of thrusting ones. This is after all the sense it bears out in our earliest surviving example of it, in Ennius' line *hastati spargunt hasti,* '*hastati* who hurl *hasti*', and their name probably reflects a time when they alone used *pila*.[43] If the *pila* did not actually hit the enemy, they would often become embedded in their shields, their barbed points making them difficult to withdraw. Handicapped by a *pilum* the shield became useless. Additionally, the thin metal shaft bent or buckled on impact thus preventing the weapon being thrown back.

During the confusion caused by this hail of *pila,* which could be devastating, the *hastati* drew their swords and, said Polybios, 'charged the enemy yelling their war cry and clashing their weapons against their shields as is their custom'.[44] He also says the Romans formed up in a much looser formation than other heavy infantry, adding this was necessary to use the sword and for the soldier to defend himself all round with his shield.[45] This implies the legionary was essentially an individual fighter, a swordsman. Yet Cato, who served during the Second Punic War as an *eques* and a quaestor, always maintained that a soldier's bearing, confidence and the ferociousness of his war cry were more important than his actual skill with a blade.[46]

In his brief description of the *gladius Hispaniensis,* Polybios evidently says the sword (*iberikós* in his Greek) was 'worn high on the right thigh' so as to be clear of the legs (a vertically-held scabbard would normally be impractical for walking let alone for fighting) adding that it was an excellent weapon 'for thrusting, and both of its edges cut effectually, as the blade is very strong and firm'.[47] The wearing of the sword on the right side goes back to the Iberians, and before them, to the Celts. The sword was the weapon of the high status warrior, and to carry one was to display a symbol of rank and prestige. It was probably for cultural reasons alone, therefore, that the Celts carried the long slashing sword on the right side. Usually a sword was worn on the left, the side covered by the shield, which meant the weapon was hidden from view.

If, at this early date, the legionary already carried his sword on the right-hand side suspended by a sword (waist) belt, it would not be for any cultural reason. As opposed to a scabbard-slide, the four-ring suspension system on his scabbard enabled the legionary to draw his weapon quickly with the right hand, an asset in close-quarter combat. In view of its relatively short blade, inverting the hand to grasp the hilt and pushing the pommel forward drew the *gladius* with ease. With its sharp point and four-ring suspension arrangement, the Delos sword, firmly dated to 69 BC, shows all the characteristics of the *gladius* described a century earlier by Polybios. Another such example is the Mouriès sword, found in a tomb in association with a group of pottery and metal artefacts, notably a bronze washing-kit with an Italic jug and *patera*. This assembly can be dated to around the turn of the first century BC.[48]

Polybios, in an excursion dedicated to the comparison between Roman and Macedonian military equipment and tactical formations, says the following:

> According to the Roman methods of fighting each man makes his movements individually: not only does he defend his body with his long shield, constantly moving it to meet a threatened blow, but he uses his sword both for cutting and for thrusting.[49]

What we are witnessing here is the intelligent use, by a swordsman, of the sword. It appears, therefore, that the tactical doctrine commonly associated with the Roman legion of the Principate was already in place during Polybios' day. We know from the archaeological record that the *gladius* of the Principate ('Pompeii' type) was an amazingly light and well-balanced weapon that was capable of making blindingly fast attacks, and was suitable for both cuts and thrusts. However, Tacitus (b. *c*. AD 56) and Vegetius (*fl. c.* AD 385) lay great stress on the *gladius* being employed by the legionary for thrusting rather than slashing. As Vegetius rightly says, 'a slash-cut, whatever its force, seldom kills', and thus a thrust was certainly more likely to deliver the fatal wound.[50] Having thrown the *pilum* and charged into contact, the standard drill for the legionary of the Principate was to punch the enemy in the face with the shield-boss and then jab him in the belly with the razor-sharp point of the sword.[51]

In his near-contemporary account of the Battle of Telamon (225 BC), Polybios tells us that 'Roman shields were far better designed for defence, and so were their swords for attack, since the Gallic sword can only be used for cutting and not for thrusting'.[52] Soon after, when he covers the Gallic *tumultus* of 223 BC, it is disclosed that legionaries 'made no attempt to slash and used only the thrust, kept their swords straight and relied on their sharp points inflicting one wound after another on the breast or the face'.[53] In a much later passage he hints that they were trained to take the first whirling blow of the Celtic slashing sword on the rim of the *scutum*, which was suitably bound with iron.[54] The principal weakness of a wooden shield was that it could be split in two with a well-aimed sword blow, leaving a soldier virtually defenceless.

The use of the thrust also meant the legionary kept most of his torso well covered, and thus protected, by his *scutum*. The latter, having absorbed the attack of his antagonist, was now punched into the face of the opponent as the legionary stepped forward to jab with his *gladius*. Much like the riot-shield of a modern policeman, the *scutum* was used both defensively and offensively to defects blows and hammer into the opponent's shield or body to create openings. As he stood with his left foot forward, a legionary could get much of his body weight behind this punch. Added to this was the considerable weight of the *scutum* itself.

Ideally, the *hastati* fought the main enemy line to a standstill, but if they were rebuffed, or lost momentum, the *principes* advanced into the combat zone and the process was repeated. Hand-to-hand fighting was physically strenuous and emotionally draining, and the skill of a Roman commander lay in committing his second and third lines at the right time. Obviously the survivors of the *hastati* and the *principes* now reinforced the *triarii* if it came down to a final trial of strength. The phrase *inde rem ad triarios redisse*, 'the last resource is in the *triarii*', passed into the Latin tongue as a description of a desperate situation.[55] Victory would eventually go to the side that endured the stress of staying so close to the enemy for the longest and was still able to urge enough of its men forward to renew the fighting. It was the inherent flexibility of the manipular system that made the legion a formidable battlefield opponent. In Polybios' measured analysis:

> The order of battle used by the Roman army is very difficult to break through, since it allows every man to fight both individually and collectively; the effect is to offer a formation that can present a front in any direction, since the maniples that are nearest to the point where danger threatens wheels in order to meet it. The arms they carry both give protection and also instil great confidence into the men, because of the size of the shields and the strength of the swords, which can withstand repeated blows. All these factors make the Romans formidable antagonists in battle and very hard to overcome.[56]

Hellenistic armies, for instance, preferred to deepen their phalanx rather than form troops into a second line, and made little use of reserves, as the commander's role was usually to charge at the head of his cavalry in the manner of Alexander the Great. The deepening of the pike-armed phalanx gave it so much stamina in the mêlée, but even the men in the rear ranks were affected by stress and exhaustion of prolonged combat. The Roman system, on the other hand, allowed fresh men to be fed into the fighting line, renewing its impetus and leading a surge forward, which might well have been enough to break a wearying enemy.

In battle, physical endurance is of the utmost importance and all soldiers in close contact with danger become emotionally if not physically exhausted as the battle proceeds. When writing of ancient warfare, Colonel Ardent du Picq notes the great value of the Roman system was that it kept only those units that were necessary at the point of combat and the rest 'outside the immediate sphere of moral tension'.[57] The legion, organized into separate battle lines, was able to hold one-half to two-thirds of its men outside the danger zone (the zone of demoralization) in which the remaining half or third was engaged. Obviously the skill of a Roman commander lay not in sharing the dangers with his men but in committing his second and third lines at the right moments. Left too late then the fighting line might buckle and break. Too soon and the value of adding fresh soldiers to the mêlée might be wasted.

Notes

PROLOGUE

1. E.g. Hoyos (2003), p.203. However, it appears that Hannibal was not present at Magnesia-by-Sipylos, the battle in question, Grainger (2002), p. 320. Indeed, our ancient sources are extremely silent on any part played by him on that day, where his presence could hardly have gone unnoticed, unless we opt to believe that he was as passive and discrete as Fabrice del Dongo on the field of Waterloo. Anyway, it appears this particular Hannibalic anecdote was jotted down by one Aulus Gellius (*Noctes Atticae* 5.5), a learned Roman gentleman who was ever fond of collecting anecdotes but, unfortunately for us moderns, he did not give their origins.
2. In Latin: *imperium sine fine*, Virgil, *Aeneid* 1.279.
3. In Latin: *immensa Romanae pacis maiestate*, Pliny, *Historia Naturalis* 27.1.3.
4. Ibid. 15.30.102. Cultivated around Kerasous on the southern shores of the Black Sea, tradition has it that this former Greek colony gave its name to the word that many peoples would adopt for the tree's red, tart fruit: Latin *cerasus*, Turkish *kiraz*, French *cerise*, English cherry.
5. Edward Gibbon, *The History of the Decline and Fall of the Roman Empire* (Penguin Abridged Edition), ch. III, p.83.
6. Cicero, *de re publica* 2.10, cf. *Philippics* 6.19.
7. Livy, 1.16.7.
8. Varro, *On Agriculture* 1.2.3-7, Cato, *On Agriculture* preface 4.
9. Virgil, *Georgics* 2.136-76.
10. Vitruvius, *de architectura* 6.1.10,11.
11. Pliny, *Historia Naturalis* 3.5.39.
12. In Latin: *ultimos terrarum fines*, e.g. Livy 38.60.5. Of course there was another great empire of the world at this time, the Han dynasty of China (206 BC - AD 220). By the end of the second century BC, the Han had included within their empire part of Vietnam in the south, part of Korea in the northeast, and in the northwest a strip of land just above the line of the Himalayas, which would soon make possible the movement of the precious caravans along the Silk Road. Between these two giants sat Parthia of the Arsacid dynasty (247 BC - AD 224), which by the early first century BC stretched from the Euphrates to the Indus. It is evident that the Romans considered the Parthian state as a worthy imperial rival, but neither side trusted the other: the Parthians remember the double-dealing of Pompey (66 BC), and the Romans remembered the standards lost at Carrhae (53 BC). And so the tug of war between the two rivals continued off and on until they worked out a *modus vivendi* with the Romano-Parthian border stabilized on the banks of the Euphrates. Still, Parthia was often able to project its political power beyond this boundary and into the Roman province of Syria. So conflict was always a threat and though Rome mounted six major campaigns between 53 BC and AD 217, Parthia was never conquered. Anyway, the first caravan to travel along the string of oases right through to Parthia left China in 106 BC, and from then onwards the development of the Silk Road was rapid. By the time of Caesar the Romans had established a silk market in the *vicus Tuscus* in Rome.

Roman Conquests: Notes

13. Tacitus, *Germania* 33.1, Virgil, *Aeneid* 1.278-9 West, cf. 286-90, 3.714-18, 6.791-800, 7.601-15.
14. Horace, *Odes* 4.15.14-16, 21-24.
15. *Res Gestae Divi Augusti* preface.
16. The empire statistics in the second century AD are conventionally estimated at 46,000,000 souls who inhabited an area of nearly 5,000,000 km^2. Subsequently numbers started to decline, so that by the end of the next century the population has dropped to 39,000,000. See McEvedy (2002), p.108.
17. In Latin: *caput orbis terrarum*, Livy, 21.30.14.
18. G. Vidal, 'Robert Graves and the Twelve Caesars', in *Rocking the Boat* (1962), p.214.
19. Ibid. 213.
20. Agrippa II, in Josephus, *Bellum Iudaiacum* 2.363.
21. Cicero, *de re publica* 3.24.
22. In Latin: *parta victoriis pax*, *Res Gestae Divi Augusti* 13.
23. Virgil, *Aeneid* 6.852-3 West.
24. Tacitus, *Annales* 1.9.
25. In Latin: *non modo ut liberi essent, sed etiam ut imperarent*, Cicero, *Philippics* 8.4.12.
26. In Latin: *oderint dum metuant*, ibid. 1.14.
27. Cicero, *pro lege Manilia* 14.41, cf. 2.6.
28. Umbricius, in Juvenal, *Satires* 3.60-5 Green. The Orontes (Nahr el-Asi) was the largest river in ancient Syria; it rose in the hills near Damascus and flowed northwards by Epiphania and Apamea, turning sharply southwest by Antioch to the Mediterranean Sea. The name Umbricius is Etruscan, and much has been written about this (in every sense) shadowy character (Umbricius, *umbra*): real person or fictional *alter ego*? Most scholarship has leaned towards an Umbricius who was probably real, though not, as formerly suggested, the official soothsayer, *haruspex*, mentioned by the elder Pliny (*Historia Naturalis* 10.6.19), Tacitus (*Historiae* 1.27.1), and Plutarch (*Galba* 24.2).
29. In Latin: *Graeculi*, Juvenal, *Satires* 3.77 Green.
30. From the second century BC onwards, the ideal of *mos maiorum*: 'customs of our ancestors', became a statement of the key virtues of the Roman citizen, which included valour (*virtus*), prestige (*gloria*), greatness of spirit (*magnitudo animi*), praiseworthiness (*dignitas*), authority (*auctoritas*), seriousness (*gravitas*), standing (*honos*), and nobility (*nobilitas*). The literati of Rome, it seems, were keen to reconstruct the glories of a semi-mythical past, those good old days of uncorrupted simplicity, the tug of heroic nostalgia set against the harsh realities of the present. See Lind (1979), p.28-41.
31. In Latin: *Graecia capta ferum victorem cepit*, Horace, *Epistulae* 2.1.156. This clever play on words is frequently found in the speeches and writings of the elder Cato (e.g. Livy 33.4.3).
32. Trajan to the younger Pliny, in Pliny, *Epistulae* 10.40.2.
33. Clotho to Mercury, in Seneca *Apocolocyntosis* 3.3 Rouse. The English title of this wicked satire is *Pumpkinification of the Divine Claudius*. Clotho is one of the Moirae or Three Fates who determine the destiny of mortals, her sisters being Lachesis and Atropos. They were the daughters of the supreme god Zeus (Roman = Iuppiter) and the goddess Themis, the personification of orderliness. Usually portrayed as three forbidding old spinsters, Clotho (the Spinner) spun the web of life of humans, Lachesis (the Apportioner) decided how long each human was to live, and Atropos (the Inevitable) cut the thread of life when someone's time had come.
34. Virgil, *Aeneid* 1.282 (right), Suetonius, *Divus Augustus* 40.5 (duty).
35. Tacitus, *Annales* 11.25.8. This total, like the figure of 4,937,000 recorded by Augustus in AD 14 (*Res Gestae Divi Augusti* 8.4), probably includes all citizens, their spouses and children; at the last census held under the Republic, that of 70 BC, only 910,000 citizens were registered. Nonetheless, if we assume that a million of them were males of military age, a 15 per cent call-up would be sufficient to sustain the army's twenty-five legions (there had been twenty-eight before the Varian disaster of AD 9).
36. Lyon Tablet, *CIL* 13.1668 col. 2. This bronze tablet from Lyon, discovered in November 1528, immortalizes a *verbatim* copy of the speech the emperor made before his fellow senators in AD 48.

The speech, an argument in favour of enlarging the Senate by opening its hallowed portals to foreigners', is also recorded by Tacitus (*Annales* 11.24), who does not reproduce it exactly or faithfully but brings out the main points. As a point of interest, Claudius himself was born at Lugdunum, present-day Lyon, capital of the province of Gallia Lugdunensis and main focus for the cult of the deified emperors in Gaul. Occupying the portion of Europe that now forms France and parts of Belgium and Germany, Gaul was divided into three provinces know as the Three Gauls: Gallia Aquitania in the west, Gallia Lugdunensis to the north and east, and Gallia Belgica in the northeast. There was also a further Gallic province in the south, Gallia Narbonensis, which had come under permanent Roman control in the second century BC. Roman Gaul was, *tout ensemble*, an important agricultural region, producing grain and wine, and with perhaps thrice the population of Italy it supplied valuable manpower for the army. The last benefit was especially important for an imperial power, and by the time of Vespasianus nearly 40 per cent of the legionaries serving on the Rhine frontier would be from Gallia Narbonensis (Forni, 1953).

37. Seneca was typical in this reactionary attitude, and it is no accident that the words in both Greek and Latin for 'make a revolution' (Greek: *neoterísein*, Latin: *res novare*) simply mean 'innovate', 'do something new'. Indeed, the term *novus* implied disturbances in the normal cycles of civic life, thence the disparaging tag *novus homo*, new man, for a senator without consular ancestors in the male line, like Marius, Cicero or indeed Augustus.

38. C.J. Rhodes, November 1893. Remarkable as it may seem, his 'English-speaking man' included the American too. Like his good friend Rudyard Kipling, Rhodes continued to hope that the United States of America would re-federate with the British Empire and rule the world.

39. In the 10 December 1892 edition of *Punch*, Rhodes is shown in a visual pun as the Colossus of Rhodes, one of seven wonders of the ancient world. He measures with the telegraph line the mileage from Cape Town (at his right boot) to Cairo (at his left boot) illustrating his 'Cape to Cairo' concept for British dominion of Africa.

40. In 1922, the year Alexander Graham Bell passed away, about 458,000,000 people, one-quarter of the human race, lived under the Union Jack in a geophysical conglomerate of nearly 34,000,000 km^2. The big difference, of course, was that Rome took centuries to crumble, while for the British Empire it was almost overnight.

41. Cf. Kipling's picturesque verse line 'Dominion over palm and pine' in 'Recessional' (1.4), composed on the occasion of Queen Victoria's Diamond Jubilee in 1897. Born in British India, Rudyard Kipling (1865-1936) travelled all over the British Empire and came to think of himself as its bard, thence 'White Man's Burden' and other songs of empire. He is recognised as an incomparable, if controversial, interpreter of how empire was experienced. In 1907 he was awarded the Nobel Prize in Literature, making him the first English language writer to receive this prestigious prize and, to date, its youngest recipient. Later in life he came to be recognized (by George Orwell, at least) as a 'sedentary apostle of violence' ('An American Critic', *Observer*, 10 May 1942) and many saw prejudice and militarism in his works. And yet Orwell, an Anglo-Indian himself, could still balance his regret at Kipling's 'jingo imperialist' tendencies with an awareness of the profound effect his work had on Orwell's boyhood. In a strange sideways glint ('Rudyard Kipling', *Horizon*, February 1942), he argues that Kipling's 'Recessional' is an denunciation of British (and German) power politics, and indeed the poem, while expressing obvious pride in the British Empire, does find fault with jingoism. From opposite ends of the political spectrum, Orwell (internationalist) and Kipling (imperialist) were true prophets of globalism in the sense they both had the universal eye for the whole picture.

42. Strabo, the geographer from Amaseia (Amasya) near the southern shore of the Black Sea, wrote the finest work we possess on the political geography of the Roman Empire. In a passage (4.5.3) concerning distant Britannia, he explains why it was useless to conquer lands with poor resources, that is to say, keeping them would soon outstrip any economic benefits. Strabo was writing in the age of Augustus and of course we are faced with the ironic fact that the Claudian invasion of AD 43, and the campaigns that followed, meant the Romans nevertheless occupied a large chunk of the island.

Roman Conquests: Notes

43. Herakleitos fr. 44.
44. Carataeus, in Tacitus, *Annales* 12.36.
45. Carataeus is probably better know as Shakespeare's Caractacus, the pugnacious son of Cymbeline.
46. Cassius Dio 61.33.3.
47. Calgacus, in Tacitus, *Agricola* 30.4, 5.
48. Speeches before battle were a fact of ancient life and a convention of ancient historiography. However, the good ancient writers (e.g. Herodotos, Thucydides, Sallust, Tacitus) were also students of humankind, and so employed these dramatic speeches as a vehicle of interpreting the story they were relating, to make a point for their readers, not to display their own rhetorical skill.
49. Cassius Dio 62.5.5.
50. E.g. in what is now western Libya, Roman olive presses are found 80km south of the present-day limit of olive cultivation (Barker-Jones, 1980-1981).
51. Diodoros, 20.8.4.
52. E.g. in the civil war of AD 69, Vespasianus planned first to seize Africa so as to cut off the grain supply of Rome (Tacitus, *Historiae* 3.48.3, cf. 8.2). By this date the province of Africa supplied at least two-thirds of Italy's grain imports, the other third coming from Egypt.
53. Dido, in Virgil, *Aeneid* 4.625-9 West.

Chapter 1

1. There are three versions of Scipio Aemilianus' reflections at Carthage: Polybios 38.21.1; Appian, *Bellum Punicum* 132 (included in Polybios, 38.22.1-3) and Diodoros 32.24. Polybios, who was with him at the end, heard him cite from the *Iliad* the lines in which Hector foretells the destruction of Troy: 'there will come a day when sacred Ilion shall perish | and Priam, and the people of Priam of the strong ash spear' (6.448-9 Lattimore). Of course, Scipio Aemilianus' fatalistic fears were not realized until centuries later the Vandal Gaiseric brought the 'eternal city' to its knees. The western Roman world had just twenty-one more years to live. Kipling, in his 'Recessional', had likewise brooded over the possibility that the day would come when the British Empire would end and 'Lo, all our pomp of yesterday | Is one with Nineveh and Tyre!' (3.3-4). For Scipio Aemilianus' reflections, see Astin (1967), p.282-7.
2. Polybios 18.35.9.For the wealth of Carthage, see Lancel (1995), p.401-9.
3. *Qart Hadasht*, 'New City', as the Carthaginians called it, *Karchedôn* to the Greeks, *Carthago* to the Romans, and hence Carthage to us. These fledgling sites were invariably located on rocky promontories or offshore islets, at points where it was easy to berth and find protection from the winds and currents. Some would remain no more than hutted camps.
4. Timaios, *FGrHist* 566 F 60. The Sicilian-Greek Timaios lived in the third century BC, a time when it was still possible to draw directly on Punic sources for information, but little of his work remains. According to the Roman historian Velleius Paterculus (*Historiae Romanae* 1.2.3) Utica was founded by the Phoenicians in 1101 BC, though it must be said that excavations in the countries of North Africa have not touched strata earlier than the eighth century BC. Though today, as a result of the Oued Medjerda having changed its course and it mouth having silted up, Utica lies some 8km inland, at the time the site lay on the northern end of the long Djebel Menzel Roul ridge, which runs southwest to northeast before projecting well into the sea.
5. Around the beginning of the fifth century BC a divine couple, Tanit and Baal Hammon, gained a position of supremacy within the Carthaginian pantheon, a phenomenon probably connected with the political upheavals following the complete destruction of the Carthaginian forces at Himera (480 BC); in some text the goddess, who usually had supremacy over Baal Hammon in Carthage, is addressed as 'mother', but she is more frequently referred to as 'Mistress' or 'Face'. For the first material attestations at Carthage, see Lancel (1995), p.32-4.
6. Though the Annals of Tyre are an original source, recording the history of that city in two periods, tenth to eighth and sixth centuries BC, they have come down to us through a Graeco-Roman meditation-alteration in two of the works of Joseph ben Mathias, or Flavius Josephus, to give him

his Roman name. One is the *Antiquitates Iudaicae* (8.144-6, 324, 9.283-7), a history of the Jews from Adam to the Jewish revolt of AD 66, the other is *In Apionem* (1.116-25, 155-8), an impassioned but well-written and well-argued comprehensive *apologia* for the Jews and Judaism.
7. Justin, *Epitome* 18.4-6 *passim*. Justin's work is in fact an epitome of a world history written under Augustus by Pompeius Trogus, a Roman citizen of Gaulish origin. His *Philippic Historiae* is lost. Justin (*Epitome* 43.5.11) informs us that before turning his hand to history, Trogus had been a confidential secretary of Caesar.
8. Kition (biblical Chittim, modern Lárnaka), besides its lagoon and salt flats, was a Phoenician settlement. Originally colonized by the Mycenaeans in the thirteenth century BC, it had declined by about 1000 BC. It again emerged two centuries later, reestablished by the Phoenicians, and resumed its role as a port exporting copper from the Tróödhos Mountains.
9. Justin, *Epitome* 18.5.8. Apparently, the same trick was performed by the two Jutish warrior brothers, Hengest and Horsa, when they were given a grant of land from the Romano-British warlord, Vortigern. Traditionally the first amongst the Germanic mercenaries to land in Britain, they are said to have arrived in AD 449, a date derived from the Venerable Bede (*Historia Ecclesiastica* 1.15), and both appear in the *Anglo-Saxon Chronicle* (with notable economy of detail) in the years AD 449-488, with Horsa being slain in AD 455. Cryptic references to a certain Hengest in the Old English poem *Beowulf* (1069-1108) and a fragmentary Old English lay called *The Fight at Finnsburg* may be the same man. The archaeological record tells us the earliest Germanic settlements, beginning as early as AD 410-420, are found in eastern Britain north of the Thames, and are represented by cremation cemeteries in the Saxon and Anglian tradition, with a different group from Jutland settling in what is now Kent.
10. *Poeni*, a Latin adaptation of the Greek word *Phoinîkêios*, from which has come 'Punic'. The Greeks called the Canaanites 'Phoenicians' probably because of their monopoly of the only colourfast dye in antiquity, the purple-red (*phoínikeos*) extract from the molluscs of the *Murex* genus. This superb dye, which ranged from dark red to violet hues, went to colour the 'purple cloths' mentioned in Ezekiel 27:24. These fabrics were enormously popular for many centuries all over the Mediterranean, becoming, as we would say today, a status symbol, a sure sign of solid wealth and refined taste. The elder Pliny relates that in the days of Cicero 'double-dyed Tyrian purple fabric was impossible to buy for less than 1,000 *denarii* a pound' (*Historia Naturalis* 9.63.137), an outrageous price. At the time Caesar's legionaries were earning 225 *denarii* per annum.
11. Virgil's *Aeneid* is the story of Aeneas of Troy. Troy was besieged and sacked by the Greeks. After a series of adventures, Aeneas met and loved Dido, but obeyed the call of duty to his gods, his people and his family, particularly to his beloved son Ascanius (who was also called Iulus, which is why the Iulii attributed their ancestry to him), and left her to her death. Then, after long years of wandering the seas, he reached Latium, fought a bitter war against the locals and in the end formed an alliance with them, which enabled him to found his city of Lavinium, named for his new Latin wife, Lavinia. From these beginnings, 333 years later, in 753 BC, the city of Rome was to be founded by Romulus. The Romans had arrived in Italy. While Virgil allowed himself to be strongly inspired by Homer and included so many references and allusions to the *Iliad* and the *Odyssey* that his epic poem almost seems to mirror them, the atmosphere of the *Aeneid* is completely different. Aeneas too, whose role in the *Iliad* is rather modest, has a diametrically opposed character from the rorty-snorty Greek heroes with their hotheaded zest for fame and favour. Virgil often refers to him as 'pious Aeneas' (*sum pius Aeneas*), and indeed he is a godfearing, disciplined figure who, with his strong sense of duty and obedience, has a one-dimensional attachment to the task in hand, and the personality of breadmould.
12. According to the elder Pliny, Mago's agricultural manual was held to be of fundamental importance to the Romans, so much so that the Senate issued a decree to this effect: 'with a single exception it laid down that his twenty-eight books should be translated into Latin, in spite of the fact that the elder Cato had already written his treatise; and that the task should be undertaken by persons instructed in the Punic language; the person who got the best part was D. Silanus, a personage of noble

origins' (*Historia Naturalis* 18.5.22). The treatise of Cato mentioned here was, of course, his plain talking no nonsense *On Agriculture*, a work written in his old age (*c.* 165-160 BC). In his handbook on agricultural practices, likewise entitled *On Agriculture* in English, Varro says he took 'from Mago's writings an amount equivalent to eight books' (*On Agriculture* 1.1.10, cf. 2.1.27, 5.18, 3.2.13). With the exception of such surviving passages, this work unfortunately shared the oblivion that was the fate of the libraries of Carthage. As for slaves, in 310 BC, when Agathokles of Syracuse overran the Carthaginian camp near Tunis, he found thousands of shackles intended for the prisoners of war that the Carthaginians expected to capture. Indeed, three years later, when the tables of war had been turned, the Greek soldiers who had been taken captive were put to work to restore to cultivation lands that had been laid waste during the invasion (Diodoros 20.13.2, 69.5).

13. If we are to believe Diodoros, the planting of fruit trees in North Africa was a fairly recent event, for at the end of the fifth century BC Carthage, or so he claims (13.81.4-5, cf. 4.17.4), was still importing olives from Sicily. Maybe the change came with the agronomist Mago and his 'agricultural revolution'.
14. The Greek version of the Byrsa, *bursa*, literally means 'the skin stripped off'. See especially, Virgil, *Aeneid* 1.369.
15. Diodoros 32 fr. 13 (Cothon), Appian, *Bellum Punicum* 128, Diodoros 20.44.4-5 (buildings).
16. Diodoros 32 fr. 14, Appian, *Bellum Punicum* 95 (landward defences). A cubit (Greek *pêchys*, Latin *cubitus*) being the distance from the point of the elbow to the tip of the little finger, a unit of distance equivalent to 444mm. Polybios says (1.73.5) the promontory neck was about 25 stades in width, a stade (*stadion*, pl. *stadia*, whence our word 'stadium') being a Greek unit of distance that varied from place to place, and it is for this reason that we generally consider it to be roughly equivalent to 200m. But according to Strabo (7.7.4), however, Polybios counted 8.5 stades to the Roman mile, which gives his stade a length of 177.5m. It appears the Greek stade was rationalized to a length of one-eighth of a Roman mile by Artemidoros half a century after the Roman conquest of Greece. As a point of interest, the stade race was of great antiquity, being the distance that the 'superman' of Greek mythology, Herakles, ran flat out in a single breath at Olympia (Pindar, *Olympian Odes* 10.43). For the archaeological evidence concerning the fortifications see Lancel (1995), p.415-19.
17. Livy, *Periochae* 51. Livy (59 BC - AD 17) devoted his long life to writing his *Ab urbe condita libri*, *History of Rome*, which comprised 142 books (35 are still extant, with books 21 to 30 covering the Second Punic War) from the foundation of Rome down to 9 BC. The *Periochae* ('Tables of Contents', brief summaries of each book's contents added to the mediaeval manuscripts of his work), are all that survive of the lost books, including those dealing with the First and Third Punic wars. Livy had no personal experience in politics and warfare, and seems neither to have visited the places he wrote about nor consulted any documentary evidence, but apparently relied entirely on literary evidence to chronicle and glorify the story of Rome.
18. Some idea of the productivity of the Carthaginian hinterland can be gained from Livy's references to Carthage's prosperity immediately after the Second Punic War. In 200 BC, 200,000 *modii* of wheat, the *modius* being a Roman unit measure equivalent to 8.62 litres, were exported to Rome, and the same amount to Macedonia for the Roman expeditionary force operating there (31.19.2). In 191 BC, much larger quantities, including 300,000 *modii* of barley destined for the Roman army, were supplied by Carthage (36.4.9). In 170 BC, again, a similar supply of barley, plus 1,000,000 *modii* of wheat, were shipped to Macedonia to feed yet another Roman expeditionary force (43.6.11, 14). These were mass supplies, to say the least, and post-war Carthage thus appears to be an astonishingly prosperous city.
19. At the time of Saint Augustine of Hippo Regius (AD 354-430), when the Roman Empire was crumbling in the west, the Punic tongue was still spoken in his native North Africa and his compatriots were still calling themselves *Kena'ani*, Canaanites *(Epistulae ad Romanos* 13*)*. The bishop lived long enough to see the Vandals effectively walk into his fair province, with their women, baggage and dependents, but he was spared the destruction of Hippo Regius, dying a year

before the city was evacuated and partly burnt. Their king, Gaiseric (r. AD 428-477), a crippled son of a slave, was a proud ruthless leader, a gifted conspirator with a genius for political intrigue. In AD 429 Gaiseric had ferried his people across the Pillars of Hercules and led them east along the North African coast. One by one the Roman cities with their well-stocked granaries fell to the spear of the Vandal. After the fall of Roman Carthage in AD 439 the Vandals ruled as a quasi-independent state in Africa. The Vandals (Latin *Vandilii*) were thought by the Romans to be Germanic peoples, originating in lands to the east of the Rhine (e.g. Tacitus, *Germanica* 2.4).
20. E.g. Curtius (4.2.10, cf. 3.19) records a delegation of Carthaginians arriving just at the moment Alexander was about to besiege the island city (323 BC). *Melek Qart*, 'King of the City', whose name is to be found in those of Hamilcar and Bomilcar, was originally regarded as the founder and lord of Tyre, but later he became its protector and also the god of Phoenician colonization. Understandably, he was very early on identified with the Greek rover Herakles (Roman = Hercules), the eponymous hero of all the major routes in the Graeco-Roman world, and much of the information we have on this god and his worship has come down to us with that name (e.g. Diodoros 20.14.1-2, Arrian, *Anabasis* 2.16.1-6). As a point of interest, Hannibal visited the temple of Melqarth at Gadir (Cadiz before his invasion of Italy, 'and swore to express further obligations to that god, should his affairs prosper' (Livy 21.21.9, cf. 41.7).We also know that while serving as quaestor in Hispania Ulterior (69 BC) Caesar visited the same temple. It was there, according to Suetonius, Caesar gazed upon a statue of Alexander and sighed that at his age 'Alexander had already conquered the whole world' (*Divus Iulius* 7).
21. *Odyssey* 15.415 Lattimore.
22. Diodoros 5.20.1.
23. E.g. both Strabo (3.5.11) and Velleius Paterculus (*Historiae Romanae* 1.2.3) date the Phoenician foundation of Gadir (Greek Gadeira, Latin Gades, modern Cádiz) to circa 1100 BC. This means as one of the colonies of Tyre, Gadir was among the early centres of Phoenician expansion in the Mediterranean. However, excavations have not been possible in the original settlement since it lies under the modern conurbation, while the archaeological material found in the vicinity of the city suggests that Phoenician influence did not appear in Cádiz before 770-760 BC.
24. Herodotos 4.196.1.
25. Ibid. 196.2.
26. Consider only Cicero, *de re publica* 2.4.9 (piratical); Plautus, *Poenulus* 112-13, Cicero, *pro Scauro* 19.42, *de lege agrarian* 2.35.95, Valerius Maximus 7.4.4, Silius Italicus, *Punica* 3.233-4, Horace, *Odes* 4.4.52 (deceitful); Diodoros 20.14.4-6, Livy 23.5.12, Plutarch, *de superstitione* 13, Appian, *Bellum Punicum* 62 (cruel); *Odyssey* 15.415-16, Cicero, *de re publica* 3 fr. 3 (greedy); Livy 21.4.9, 22.6.11-12, 42.47.7, Appian, *Bellum Punicum* 62-4 (perfidious). What we are witnessing here, of course, is the construction, invariably through fear, of the idea of the 'Other' as an enemy. And so, ethnic, racial or national identities are defined via a system of differentiation that may or may not give rise to conflicts. It must be said, however, that before the Punic wars began, as far as we know, there was no racial hatred between the two peoples, though there certainly was by the end. The demonization of the Carthaginians in this way raises the question about what happens when we call someone 'bad' or 'evil' without taking a moment to consider that, in some cases, we might be wrong. To take a well-known example from English history, there are those who claim that Richard III, never a popular monarch admittedly, was not the personification of evil portrayed by that arch-propagandist of the Tudors, William Shakespeare.
27. Livy 21.22.3.
28. Walbank (1957), p.363, Lancel (1995), p.288.
29. Polybios 7.9.5, Diodoros 20.55.4.
30. E.g. Polybios 3.33.15.
31. During the First Punic War, according to Polybios, Carthage 'exacted from the peasantry, without exception, half of their crops, and had doubled the taxation of the townsmen without allowing exemption from any tax or even a partial abatement to the poor' (1.72.2). As the age-old adage goes 'death and taxes' are the dual constants of human existence.

32. E.g. Agathokles of Syracuse receives active support form the Libyans, who 'hated the Carthaginians with a special bitterness because of the weight of their overlordship'. (Diodoros 20.55.4).
33. Justin, *Epitome* 18.7-19.2, Orosius 4.6.
34. Piracy is as old as the maritime trade on which it preys. The economics of shipping, even in the ancient world, meant that merchant ships carried a relatively small crew, and this attention to profit naturally made such vessels vulnerable to predators.
35. Polybios 3.22.3.
36. Sallust, *Bellum Iugurthium* 19.2 (Altars off the Philaeni); Polybios, 3.3.9.1 (Pillars of Hercules).

CHAPTER 2

1. Aristotle, *Politics* 1273a2, cf. Polybios 6.51-56. By 'mixed', Aristotle means the Carthaginian constitution, like that of Sparta, 'partakes of oligarchy and of monarchy and of democracy'. The 'mixed constitution', the ideal of Greek political theory, was considered the natural condition for a civilised state.
2. Greek *basileús/basileîs*, Aristotle, *Politics* 1272b35. Punic *?ptm*, cf. the Hebrew *shophet/shophetim*, judge.
3. Aristotle, *Politics* 1272b35, 1273a15.
4. Ibid.1272b35.
5. The epigram is Voltaire's (*Candide ou l'optimisme*, ch. XXIII), referring of course to the fate of the unfortunate Admiral John Byng, shot on his own quarterdeck after the sea battle off Minorca in 1757. Compare, for example, the 'fate' of Caius Terentius Varro, the consul who fled from the field of Cannae (216 BC). On arriving at the gates of Rome he was met by senators who publicly thanked him in front of a great crowd for not having despaired of the Republic. As the Roman Livy sagely remarks, a 'Carthaginian general in such circumstances would have been punished with the utmost rigour of the law' (22.61.14). The lucky Varro was then appointed to the command of a legion at Picenum. Meanwhile, the unlucky survivors of the Cannae army, the common soldiers, were banished in utter disgrace to Sicily.
6. Diodoros 20.44.1-6.
7. Justin, *Epitome* 19.2.5.
8. Aristotle, *Politics* 1324b10.
9. E.g. Livy 21.18.3 (senate), Aristotle, *Politics* 1272b37, Diodoros 20.59.1 (*gerousia*).
10. Cf. Polybios 3.13.4, the popular election of Hannibal Barca.
11. Aristotle, *Politics* 1273a7, Polybios 6.56.3-8.
12. Cicero, *de re publica* 1 fr. 3.
13. Latin: *quinqueremis*, Greek: *pentêrês* ('five-fitted'). Larger and smaller were also used, for example, *triêrês*, triremes (e.g. Polybios 1.20.14), the two *hexêrêis* ('six-fitted') that served as the consuls' flagships at Ecnomus (ibid. 26.11), and the *heptêrês* ('seven-fitted'), which once belonged to Pyrrhos and served as the Carthaginian flagship at Mylae (ibid. 23.4). All these terms seem properly to refer to the number of files of oarsmen from bow to stern, on each side of the vessel, rather than to the number of banks of oars. In all likelihood no warship ever had more than three banks of oars, and so larger numbers of oarsmen were accommodated by doubling up on some or all of the oars. Thus a *hexêrês* could be rowed in the same fashion as a bireme, with three men per oar, or as a trireme, with two men per oar.
14. Morrison (1995), p.68. Here Morrison, a leading light in the *Olympias* trireme project, also points out that the quadrireme (*tetrêrês*, 'four-fitted') was invented after the quinquereme, and was developed by double-manning from a two-level pentaconter (i.e. warship with fifty oars, twenty-five per side in two banks). According to Aristotle (fr. 600 Rose) the Carthaginians built the first quadrireme, and there is no reason to doubt his authority. Most probably the invention was made after the middle of the fourth century BC. Ironically, quadriremes make their first historical debut at Alexander's siege of Tyre in 332 BC, both among the Tyrian ships (Arrian, *Anabasis* 2.21.9, 22.5)

NOTES

and in his own fleet (Curtius 4.3.14) largely supplied by his Phoenician allies (Arrian, *Anabasis* 2.20.1).
15. Polybios 1.26.7. In Herodotos' day a trireme consisted of a crew of 200, that is, 170 oarsmen and 30 marines and deck crew, the latter to handle the sails and rigging (3.14.4-5, 7.184.1, 185.1, 8.17).
16. Morrison (1995), p.68. In a trireme each oarsmen rowed one oar, casually confirmed by Thucydides' comment 'the oarsmen were each to take their oar, cushion, and rowlock thong' (2.93.2).
17. Cf. Morrison (1995), p.69, who says 90 oars a side, basing his calculation on an oar crew of 300.
18. It is easy to forget that though the bronze-sheathed ram could smash a hole in an enemy warship and so cripple her, it could not literally sink her. Ancient sources use terms meaning 'sink', but it is evident that ships so 'sunk' could still be towed away. For instance, the Greek word *kataduein*, which is almost invariably translated as 'sink', in fact means no more than 'dip' or 'lower'. So, when warships were holed in a sea fight, though they had become absolutely useless as fighting vessels, the combatants went to great lengths and some risk to recover the waterlogged wrecks. These could be towed home as prizes; after being repaired, equipped and re-named, they became part of the navy. According to Coates, a retired naval architect and the technical say-so behind the *Olympias* trireme project, for a warship to sink she needed to be burdened with sufficient freight to weigh in water enough to overcome the buoyancy of the hull structure and its furniture, 'roughly 40 per cent of the weight of the complete hull in air, assuming that its density is 0.6 tonnes per cubic metre', Morrison (1995), p.133.
19. Polybios 1.46.4-47.10.
20. Ibid. 51.4-9.
21. Appian, *Bellum Punicum* 96.
22. For the naval harbour see especially, Hurst (1979), p.19-49, (1993), p.42-51, Lancel (1995), p.172-8.
23. Theophrastos, *History of Plants* 5.7.1-5. Of course, since the earliest of times the Phoenician shipbuilders had easy access to these cedar supplies, for instance a bas-relief from the palace of Sargon II (r. 722-705 BC) at Khorsabad (now in the musée du Louvre) clearly depicts Phoenician merchantmen transporting cedar wood. Theophrastos himself was aware of this, saying elsewhere in his treaties that in 'Syria and Phoenicia triremes are made of cedar because pine is... in short supply' (ibid. 4.4).
24. Theophrastos, *History of Plants* 5.1.5.
25. Ibid. 4.4, cf. *Iliad* 13.389-91, 16.482-4.
26. Greek *terêdôn*, or *teredo navalis* as the Romans called it, and marine biologists still call it.
27. Pliny, *Historia Naturalis* 16.79.
28. Athenaios 5.207b.
29. Theophrastos, *History of Plants* 5.4.4.
30. Ibid. 9.2, Pliny, *Historia Naturalis* 16.56. The most common epithet for a warship in the Homeric epics after 'swift' is 'black' (e.g. *Iliad* 1.141, 2.524, 5.551, 15.424, *Odyssey* 3.365, 6.268, etc.), presumably a black coloured hull being the result of the pitch applied externally.
31. Polybios 1.51.8.
32. Ibid. 51.9.
33. Plutarch, *Timoleon* 29.4.
34. Ibid. 27.6, Diodoros 16.80.4.
35. Plutarch, *Timoleon* 28.9.
36. Thucydides 6.90.3.
37. It comes as no great surprise that in our classical sources Hamilcar is one of the commonest of Punic names, representing as it does 'Servant of Melqarth', the great god of Tyre and divine patron of Phoenician expansion in the west. Having said that, it is all too easy for us to get confused over our Carthaginian commanders, since the same names tend to pop up over and over again. Thus we will find the Carthaginian ranks crammed not only with Hamilcars, but also Hannos, Himilcos, Hasdrubals, and even a few Hannibals.

38. Herodotos 7.165, Diodoros 11.1.5 (480 BC), 13.44.1, 54.1 (409 BC), 80.2-4 (406 BC), 14.55.4 (397 BC), 95.1 (393 BC), 16.73.3 (341 BC), 19.106.2, 5 (311 BC).
39. Ibid. 20.29.6, cf. 31.1.
40. For an analysis of Timoleon's army at the Krimisos, see Parke (1933), p.173 n. 4. It is impossible to accept as literally true the estimates given by our sources for the numbers of the Carthaginians, but it remains sufficiently clear that the total of Timoleon's bantam-sized army was still much below that of the Carthaginian (cf. Plutarch, *Timoleon* 25.3).
41. Plutarch, *Timoleon* 30.3, Diodoros 16.81.4. Sicilian Greeks had in fact served in Carthaginian armies previously, but as allies not as mercenaries (e.g. Diodoros 13.54.6, 58.1).
42. E.g. Dareios III reckoned that 100,000 men should be enough to conduct his forthcoming fight with Alexander the Great as long as 'one third were Greek mercenaries' (Diodoros 17.30.3).
43. In Cicero's words: 'The sinews of war, unlimited money' (*Philippics* 5.2.5).
44. Diodoros 5.38.2. Of course, the downside of this policy, as Diodoros himself points out, is that the mercenaries employed by Carthage caused no end of trouble for the city by making it a habit to 'cause many and serious mutinies' (5.11.1).
45. Plutarch, *Timoleon* 28.6, Diodoros 16.81.3, 4.
46. Plutarch, *Timoleon* 27.3, 28.1, 3, Diodoros 16.80.3, 6. For the stelae, see Head (1982), p.140-2.
47. Pausanias 6.19.7.
48. Diodoros 16.80.2, Plutarch, *Timoleon* 28.2.
49. Diodoros 20.10.5-6 (310 BC), Polybios 15.11.2, Livy 30.33.5 (202 BC).
50. Polybios 15.33.3 (Hannibal's view), 31.21.3 (Polybios' view).
51. Diodoros 20.12.3, 7 (Sacred Band).
52. Ibid. 16.9, 38.6, 39.4-5.
53. Ibid. 69.3. More than 200 of Agathokles' mercenaries had previously deserted to Carthage (ibid. 34.7).
54. Xenophon, *Hellenika* 6.4.28.
55. Ibid. 1.5.
56. Polybios 3.109.6-7, 111.8-10, cf. 6.52.3-8, 11.28.7.
57. Ibid. 1.43.
58. Ibid. 2.7.6-10.
59. Ibid. 1.19.12.
60. Ibid. 2.5.4, 7.11.
61. Ibid. 1.77.4-5, 78.12, 86.4. Frontinus (*Strategemata* 3.16.2, 3) gives two other examples from the First Punic War of treacherous Gaulish mercenaries, the second of which is confirmed by Diodoros (23.8.3) and Zonaras (8.10), albeit involving a Carthaginian general named Hamilcar instead of Hanno.
62. Polybios 1.17.4, 19.2, 43.4, 48.3 (First Punic War), 67.7 (Mercenary War), 3.33.11, 16, 72.7, 83.3, 113.6, 11.1.2, 3.1, 19.5, 14.7.5, 15.11.1, etc. (Second Punic War).
63. Strabo 3.5.1, Diodoros 5.18.3-4, Florus, *Epitome* 1.43.5, Vegetius 1.16.
64. Diodoros 19.106.2 (310 BC), Polybios 3.56.4 (218 BC).
65. Griffith (1984), p. 232.
66. Polybios 3.87.3, 114.1, Livy 22.46.4.
67. Lazenby (1978), p.14, cf. Bagnall (1999), p.170.
68. Plutarch *Marcellus* 12.8. Of course Plutarch uses the term 'javelin' (*akóntion* in his Greek), but probably said with *pilum* in mind. Also, for 'Carthaginians' read 'Libyan spearmen', because in the same breath Plutarch talks of Iberians and Numidians deserting to Marcellus, and we know from the much more reliable Polybios that Libyans and Iberians made up the bulk of Hannibal's infantry force (e.g. 3.56.1).
69. Daly (2002), p.90. However, here he does argue for the notion that Hannibal's Libyans took the full Roman panoply, *pilum* as well as *gladius*. For the *gladius*, etc. see Appendix 2.
70. Frontinus *Strategemata* 2.3.7.

NOTES

71. Envelop, from the French *envelopper*, to wrap.
72. For the British the most notable example of this phenomenon must be Kitchener's Armies, the mass citizen force of volunteers who answered his personal appeal for recruits, boldly transmitted by billboards that carried his glaring face, its unflinching gaze emphasising his battle cry, 'Your Country Needs You'. On the first bloody day of the Somme, which turned out to be the most disastrous day in British military history, they were fated to be cut down in swathes: more than 19,000 killed and 35,000 wounded.
73. The mercenary (Latin: *mercenarius*, 'hired, paid', from *merces*, 'hire, pay, wages') is a professional soldier whose behaviour is dictated not by his membership of a socio-political community, but his desire for personal gain, viz. he owes no allegiance beyond the cash nexus. Here, the thorny questions of motive (money) and status (serving a foreign flag) are extraordinarily complex to decipher. Larousse, for instance, simply defines a mercenary as a '*soldat qui sert à prix d'argent un gouvernement étranger*'. Though much more verbose, even the official United Nations interpretation of a mercenary follows the neutral dictionary definition by classifying him as a person who 'is motivated to take part in the hostilities essentially by desire for private gain and, in fact, is promised, by or on behalf of a party to the conflict, material compensation substantially in excess of that promised or paid to combatants of similar rank and functions in the armed forces of that part' (UN Mercenary Convention, Article 1.1.b). In brief, therefore, the mercenary is commonly defined by three basic qualities: being a specialist, being stateless, and getting paid. Here the etymology and use of the word 'soldier' is worth a thought. When *La Marseillaise* speaks of '*ces féroces soldats*' (1.6), it must mean mercenaries taking the shilling of the various 'conspiratorial monarchies', as opposed to the citizens being called to arms: '*tout français est soldat*', the civic ideal of the French Revolution.
74. Isokrates (436-338 BC), an Athenian orator and pamphleteer, was tireless in his vilification of mercenaries, 'the common enemies of all mankind' (*Pax* 46) who are 'better off dead than alive' (*To Philip* 55). In his day Isokrates was sleekiest sarcasm, but such sentiments about hired professionals are still voiced to this day. Take, for instance, the banner headline from the 7 December 1981 edition of *The Nation*, the leading newspaper of the Seychelles, ran as follows: 'The only good mercenary is a dead mercenary. Let us make them all good ones'.
75. For some two centuries or so the unwritten rule that forbids the deployment of mercenaries in a European theatre of operations has come to be thought of, without any real justification, as almost a moral law. In their colonial and post-colonial skirmishes the European powers used, and still use, mercenaries: the much feared Gurkha regiments still employed by Britain and currently fighting in Afghanistan, or the legendary *Légion étrangère* still deployed by France in Chad. Incidentally we may remark that when quizzed why they swear allegiance to Her Majesty the Queen (Nepal, by the way, had its own monarchy until its abolition on 27 December 2007) Gurkhas will invariably reply in the following way: 'We have eaten your rations and taken your salt'.
76. Polybios 11.13.
77. *Mahâbhârata* 5.152.13-15.
78. Megasthenes, *Indika* fr. 35 ap. Aelian, *de natura animalium* 13.10.
79. Arrian, *Anabasis* 3.8.6, 15.6 (Gaugamela), 5.15.5, Curtius 8.13.6 (the Hydaspes).
80. Strabo 16.4.4, 7. Cut off from India by the Seleukid kingdom, the Ptolemies had to look closer to home for their pachyderms. According to the Adulis Inscription of Ptolemaios III Euergetes (r. 246-222 BC), originally set up in Adulis (Massawa, Ethiopia), elephants were hunted in the coastal belt of the Red Sea and in the interior of what is now the Sudan (Burstein 99). They were still to be found in those regions at the time of General Sir Robert Napier's punitive expedition to Magdala in 1868. Ironically, as they laboured across the plateau of Abyssinia, the British and Indian soldiers were aided by the 44 elephants shipped over with them from India.
81. E.g. at Paraitakene (317 BC) Antigonos Monophthalmos fielded 65 elephants against the 114 of Eumenes of Kardia, whilst at Ipsos (301 BC) he and his son, Demetrios, had 75 against the reputed 400 mustered by the Ptolemaic-Seleukid coalition (Diodoros 19.27.1, 28.4, Plutarch, *Demetrios* 28.3).

ROMAN CONQUESTS: NOTES

82. Beyond our geographical limits, of course, the armies of the Mogul emperors of India continued to employ elephants in a big way. Jahangir (r. 1605-1627), for example, used at least 300 of them, their crews armed with bows as well as firearms. Indeed, it was *de rigeur* for Mogul generals to be mounted on elephants; while largely for prestige reasons, this also made the general visible to his army, provided a good vantage point, and raised the great man above the vulgar brawl going on below. In the same period, war elephants were used by other Indian states, Muslim and Hindu alike, as well as in Burma, Siam, Cambodia and Java.
83. Herodotos 4.191.
84. Hasdrubal Gisgo was to obtain elephants from Mauretania in 205 BC (Appian, *Bellum Punicum* 9, cf. Frontinus, *Strategemata* 4.7.18), and we last hear of them in that area when Caius Suetonius Paulinus, the future governor of Britannia and vanquisher of Boudica, campaigned there in AD 41 (Pliny, *Historia Naturalis* 5.1.14). Its disappearance forms part of the Arab legend concerning Sidi Tayeb. This holy man was bitten by a deadly snake and, as he lay dying, called upon the animals in the name of Allah to leave the forested valley of Guir, which they did six days later: de Beer (1967), p.134.
85. Polybios 5.84.2-7.
86. Scullard (1974), p.240-5.
87. In our Greek sources drivers are invariably referred to as *Indói*, Indians (e.g. Polybios 1.40.15, 3.46.7, Diodoros 19.84.1).
88. Polybios 11.1.3.
89. Livy 27.49.1. Contemplating upon elephantine mayhem, Lucretius (c. 95-55 BC), a learned Epicurean, surmises that perhaps other wild animals were 'once enlisted in the service of war', with similar catastrophic results. The brute beasts, 'inflamed by the gory carnage of battle', must have slashed, snapped and stabbed their own masters with talons, teeth and tusks, 'just as in our own times war elephants sometimes stampede over their own associates' (*de rerum natura* 5.1298-1349). In this philosophical poem, which ran to six books no less, Lucretius was aiming to convert his fellow Romans to the philosophy of peace of mind; he was not a major influence in his life time.
90. Diodoros 16.80.2, 20.10.5.
91. Polybios 1.19.9-10.
92. Normally an elephant will walk at a speed of 6.4km/h (4mph), while at full tilt it can reach a speed of some 40km/h (25mph).
93. Polybios 1.34.1-8, 39.11-12, 40.3-15, cf. 38.2.
94. Livy 22.55.4-56.2, cf. Polybios 3.72.8, 74.7. According to Appian (*Hannibalica* 1.4), Hannibal crossed the Pyrenees with 37 elephants, and Polybios (3.42.10) has the same number being rafted across the Rhône, but unfortunately no source records how many survived the crossing of the Alps, though clearly he had enough left to play a significant part at the Trebbia.
95. Livy 30.33.4, 13-15, Polybios 15.12.1-4.
96. Diodoros (23.21) claims that a total of 60 were killed or taken, whereas Zonaras (8.14) has 120 being rounded up, while the elder Pliny (*Historia Naturalis* 8.16) gives the larger figures of 140 to 142.

CHAPTER 3

1. Though the Greeks with their 60 ships defeated the 120 of their enemies, their casualties were heavy: 40 vessels lost and the rest no longer battle worthy with their 'rams so badly bent as to render them unfit for service' (Herodotos 1.166.2).
2. Polybios 3.22.3. The Polybian date of 508 BC is hotly disputed, some scholars placing the treaty in 348 BC (i.e. Polybios' second treaty).
3. Ibid. 23.1.
4. Ibid. 24. Livy (7.27.2) and Diodoros (16.69.1) both date this treaty to 348 BC, but regard it as the first one between the two states. This second treaty was perhaps renewed, or at least informally reaffirmed, in 343 BC, since Livy (7.38.2) has Carthaginian envoys congratulating the Romans on

their recent victory over the Samnites and offering a gold crown to their chief god, Iuppiter Capitolinus.
5. Polybios 3.25.2, cf. Livy, *Periochae* 13. After discussing this treaty, Polybios (3.26) goes on to condemn the Sicilian-Greek historian Philinos for saying that there was also a treaty that obliged the Romans not to interfere anywhere in Sicily, and likewise the Carthaginians anywhere in Italy. This is often equated with the treaty mentioned by Livy under the year 306 BC, but all he actually says is that 'the treaty with Carthage was renewed for a third time' (9.43.26, cf. *Periochae* 14). See Lazenby (1996), p.32-3.
6. Justin, *Epitome* 18.2, Valerius Maximus 3.7.10.
7. Lazenby (1996), p.33.
8. Thucydides 6.2.6
9. Known to the Greeks as *Trinakria* (lit. 'three-pointed'), one of the most dramatic phases of Sicily's multi-faceted history came in the eighth century BC with the arrival of the Greeks. Bronze Age evidence shows the earlier existence of trade routes with mainland Greece, and in 735 BC the first colony was established at Naxos (below modern Taormina) by Greeks keen to exploit the island's agricultural potential; the olive and the vine were introduced. Sicily's fertility ensured the successful growth of this and subsequent colonies, which, along with those of southern Italy, came to rival the city states of the Greek mainland. Syracuse (Siracusa), the greatest and wealthiest of Sicily's Greek city states, became a significant power in the Mediterranean, although Greek Sicily was riven by inter-state warfare (the phenomenon of tyranny was strong here) and a century of antagonism between Greeks and Carthaginians.
10. Herodotos 7.167, cf. Diodoros 11.21-22. The Sicilian-Greek tradition that Gelon's victory took place on the same day as the sea battle of Salamis, as recorded here by Herodotos, thus places the victories of the Greeks over the 'barbarians' of the east (the Persians) and over those of the west (the Carthaginians) on the same level. As a final point here, we do not know the Punic name for Palermo, Panormus (signifying 'all port') being the name later given to it by the Greeks.
11. In Herodotos' version, Hamilcar commits suicide by throwing himself on the funeral pyre of his dead soldiers, having ordered that his ships be burned, while Diodoros says (11.25-26 *passim*) the survivors were used as slave-labour in a major building programme at Akragas, then ruled by Gelon's father-in-law and fellow tyrant, Theron.
12. It is interesting to note that there was no Bronze Age in sub-Saharan Africa. Apart from some limited copper smelting in West Africa, the earliest evidence of metal working is in iron. Smelting furnaces in Rwanda excavated by archaeologists have been dated to 800 BC, well before such technology was established in the British Isles and only marginally later than Greece or Italy.
13. Diodoros 13.85.1-91.1 (Akragas), 108.2-111.1 (Gela), 114.1-2 (peace treaty).
14. The non-torsion catapult (*katapéltes*, 'shield-piercer') was first deployed in the form of a simple *gastraphetes*, 'belly-shooter' (Diodoros 14.50.4, cf. 41.4). In essence an over-large crossbow, it acquired this seemingly homely and unthreatening name because a concavity at the rear of the wooden stock was placed against the stomach and the weight of the body was used to force back the bowstring to its maximum extension (Heron, *Belopoiika* 81). The revolutionary development of this mechanical propulsive device, which essentially accumulated and stored human strength, would eventually threaten fortifications by the sheer amount of force it could produce. Along with warships, catapults would come to epitomize the acme of ancient military technology.
15. It was probably during this war with Dionysios that the Carthaginians first became acquainted with the quinquereme. According to Diodoros (14.41.2) Dionysios' highly-paid military engineers built, along with the catapult, the first quinquereme. As for Motya, alas it never rose again. It was replaced by a new city, Lilybaeum, which was planted just to the south and across the water on the headland of present-day Capo Boeo, the western extremity of Sicily.
16. Diodoros 14.45-64 *passim*, 70-75 *passim*, 77. To identify this 'plague' with precision, along with the one that devastated the Carthaginian army in 405 BC, is impossible. Diodoros (14.70.4-71) at least offers a grim and graphic description of the symptoms of the appalling epidemic.

17. Justin, *Epitome* 4.2.
18. Diodoros 19.106-110 *passim*. To the unconstitutional or oppressive ruler the mercenary was especially profitable as the two fostered each other. It was mostly by the lavish use of mercenaries, for instance, that the Greek tyrants of Sicily held sway in their domains. Generally speaking, however, the early tyrants employed mercenaries as a personal bodyguard, while it was the later military tyrants who used them for territorial expansion, as well as for private protection. Nonetheless, despotism could only begin when a ruler was able to surround himself with a strong force of aggressive men whose desires and feelings were alien to those of the ruled. When the latter show signs of resistance, they are removed as a danger and, accordingly, a tyrant, says the ex-mercenary Xenophon, 'delights to make the mercenaries more formidable than the citizens, and these he employs as bodyguards' (*Hiero* 5.3). A military tyrant, and Agathokles is a prime exemplar, found his natural support in foreign, hired soldiery. Agathokles had served a stormy apprenticeship in the twin arts of tyranny and war. In the course of his early struggles he was twice exiled from Syracuse, the first occasion serving as a soldier of fortune in the pay of Taras, and the second recruiting his own private army of fellow exiles and mercenaries with a more immediate view to returning home by force (Diodoros 19.4-9 *passim*).
19. Ibid. 20.3-18 *passim*.
20. In 306 BC Agathokles assumed the title of king (*basileús* in Greek), comparing his rule to that of the Hellenistic (non-royal) princes who, in those same years, bickered among themselves for the kingdoms born of the carving up of the empire of Alexander the Great. In the course of one life he had been a soldier, captain, tyrant, and finally king.
21. In fact Pyrrhos was the last in a succession of soldiers of fortune invited by the Tarentines, intruders on Italian soil, to help them in their wars against the Italic peoples, whose history had taken them into mountainous regions of the peninsula instead of the plains, with consequent disadvantages and advantages to themselves. Agathokles, at the time banished from his native Syracuse, had served as a mercenary in Taras around 320 BC. By turning gold into iron Taras was hoping to contain and control the mounting pressure from a wide coalition of the indigenous populations, Lucanians, Bruttians and Messapians. Besides the larger-than-life Agathokles, these *condottieri* included Archidamos, Kleonymos and Akrotatos, all Spartan princes of royal blood, and Alexander of Molossia who, like Pyrrhos, was a blood relation of Alexander the Great. See Fields (2008C), p.10-14.
22. Plutarch, *Pyrrhos* 19.7.
23. There is a painted plate from Capena, Campania, now in the Museo Nazionale di Villa Giulia, Rome, showing a war elephant and calf. Unmistakably an Indian elephant (*Elephas maximus*), and possibly one of those brought to Italy by Pyrrhos: Florus describes (*Epitome* 1.13.12) how a cow-elephant, anxious for her offspring's safety, spread havoc among Pyrrhos' army. Some 3m high at the shoulders, this breed is large enough to carry a howdah, the Campanian plate showing a fine example complete with crenellations and containing two soldiers armed with javelins. These howdahs were wooden, that shown on the plate suggesting light slats over a heavier frame, and equipped with a large round shield hung outside (each side presumably) for additional protection. According to the great antiquarian Varro, 'the elephants with Pyrrhos shone (*relucebant*) with gilt shields attached to the howdahs on their backs' (*de lingua Latina* 7.40). Alternatively, the howdah was already in service in India. Megasthenes, who visited the court of Chandragupta shortly before 300 BC, describes the three-man fighting crew of a war elephant being carried 'either in what is called the tower, or on his bare back' (*Indika* fr. 35 *ap*. Aelian, *de natura animalium* 13.10).
24. Florus, *Epitome* 1.13.9. Not only were the legionaries unfamiliar with the tactics of the Macedonian phalanx, but they had never clapped eyes on war elephants before and with good soldierly humour, they called them *Luca bos*, 'Lucanian oxen' (Naevius, *Bellum Punicum* frs. 65-6 *ap*. Varro, *lingua Latina* 7.39). See Scullard (1974), p.104-5.
25. Plutarch, *Pyrrhos* 21.9, cf. Diodoros 22.6.3. The phrase 'Pyrrhic victory' is a much later development, appearing in English for the first time in an edition of *The Daily Telegraph* dated 17 December 1885. See Graeme (2008), p.221.

NOTES

26. After separating from Pyrrhos, Lanassa went on to marry Demetrios, the son and successor of the great Antigonos Monophthalmos (d. 301 BC). Ever flamboyant and impetuous, Demetrios would earn for himself the grand appellation 'Taker of Cities', Poliorketes.
27. After this victory, Malventum was happily renamed Beneventum.
28. Plutarch, *Pyrrhos* 23.8.
29. Florus, *Epitome* 1.13.25-28.
30. Ibid. 14.1.
31. E.g. Plutarch, *Pyrrhos* 1, 7.12, Pausanias 1.11.1.
32. Plutarch, *Pyrrhos* 24.8-12.
33. Ibid. 8.1.
34. Mentioned in passing by Plutarch (ibid. 21.8), Pyrrhos wrote his autobiography, of which a fragment survives (*FGrHist* 229), drawing upon his own official archives.
35. Juvenal, *Satires* 10.158 Green.
36. Livy 35.14.5-9.
37. Plutarch, *Pyrrhos* 8.5. Antigonos II Gonatas (r. 276-239 BC) was the grandson of Antigonos Monophthalmos and the son of Demetrios Poliorketes.
38. Justin, *Epitome* 25.4.5.
39. Plutarch, *Pyrrhos* 26.7, 9.
40. For Pyrrhos' actions at Sparta and Argos, see ibid. 27-34 *passim*, Pausanias 1.13.3-8, Justin, *Epitome* 25.4.6-5.2.

CHAPTER 4

1. Polybios 1.7.1-5.
2. Ibid. 7.6. As a subgroup of the Roman citizen body, 'citizens without the vote' (*cives sine suffragio*) had the same rights and duties as those with full Roman citizenship apart from not being allowed to vote in Rome assemblies or hold Roman office. The Campanians themselves were descended from Oscan-speaking highlanders who, during the course of the fifth and fourth centuries BC, harried the rich coastal settlements of Campania, many of them founded by Greeks. In this way they seized Greek Cumae and Etruscan Capua, merging with the existing inhabitants of Campania to give rise to the Campanians (Latin: *Campani*).
3. Polybios 1.9.7-9, cf. Diodoros 22.13.6.
4. Polybios 1.10.2.
5. Ibid. 10.9.
6. Livy, *Periochae* 14, Cassius Dio fr. 43 Boissevain, Zonaras 8.6, Orosius 4.3.1-2, Ampelius 46.2, cf. Livy 21.10.8, where Hannibal's rival, Hanno 'the Great' (still alive), refers to the incident when attempting to dissuade the Carthaginian senate from going to war in 218 BC.
7. Polybios 1.10.5-9, Cassius Dio 11.1-4, Zonaras 8.8. Polybios says (1.11.2) when the consuls came to persuade the people to vote for war, they used, in addition to this argument, the prospect of booty to be won. The actual profits in plunder from this war cannot be measured, but some idea of its scale can be inferred from the size of the enslavements made by the Romans: 25,000 at Akragas in 261 BC (Diodoros 23.9.1), 20,000 in Africa in 256 BC (Polybios 1.29.7), 13,000 at Panormus in 254 BC plus 14,000 who purchased their freedom at 2 *minae* (=200 *denarii*) each (Diodoros 23.18.3), nearly 10,000 at the Aegates Islands in 241 BC, just to mention the extreme cases.
8. Polybios 1.63.4.
9. Now known as the Isole Egadi (Favignana, Levanzo, Marettimo), the Greeks called the three islands the Aegusae and the Romans the Aegates.
10. Polybios 1.20.8.
11. Ibid. 20.13-14. These borrowed ships were pentaconters and triremes.
12. Ibid. 11.9-12.3. Cassius Dio (11.11-15), Zonaras (8.9), and Orosius (4.7.2-3) all agree with Polybios, whereas Diodoros (23.3) has Hiero hotfooting it to Syracuse believing he had been

betrayed by the Carthaginians, and Appius Claudius suffering a heavy reverse at a place he calls 'Aigesta'.
13. Polybios 1.17.4-6.
14. Ibid. 20.1-2.
15. Ibid. 20.7.
16. Pliny, *Historia Naturalis* 16.192 (60 days), Polybios 1.20.15 (model).
17. Frost (1973), p.229-30; (1974), p.35-54; (1982), p.42-50. Discovered by Honor Frost in 1971 off the Isola Longa in the shallow lagoon known as Lo Stagnone. The well-preserved stern was lifted from the seabed and the rest of the hull, 35m in length, was reconstructed in 1980. Manned by sixty-eight oarsmen, it is thought to have floundered on its maiden voyage sometime during the Third Punic War. The wreck is housed in the Museo Archeologico di Baglio Anselmi, Marsala.
18. *Odyssey* 5.244-8, 361.
19. In northern Europe, and here we just have to think of the Gokstad Ship, most wooden hulls have been made by a method called 'skeleton-first' or 'clinker-built'. The keel is first laid down, with a heavy, shaped beam ('keelson') on top of it, and the stem- and sternpost joined to it. Then vertical frames are attached at intervals, which determine the eventual shape of the hull. The outside shell of planks is then put on, starting with one either side of the keelson ('garboards'), each overlapping the one below by a small amount.
20. Polybios 1.21.1-2. This land-based nautical training has its parallels in Polyainos 3.11.7, Ennius, *Annales* frs. 227-31 Vahlen, Cassius Dio 48.51.5. As for the 300-strong crews for these ships, Polybios says (6.19.3) those Roman citizens who rated at less than 4,000 *asses* (400 *drachmae* in Polybios' Greek) worth of property (i.e. the *proletarii*) were liable for service in the navy. It has been argued that this meant as marines: Thiel (1954), p.77-8, but a more straightforward interpretation of Polybios' words is that he meant service in the crews. Of course, additional crews could be supplied by the *socii navales*, and we even hear of those fierce highlanders, the Samnites, being called up for a stint in the navy (Zonaras 8.11).
21. Polybios 1.22.3-8
22. Described in Latin as *manus ferreas* (lit. 'iron hands'), which derives from the Greek word *harpágones* meaning 'snatchers': Frontinus, *Strategemata* 2.3.24, Florus, *Epitome* 1.18.9, Zonaras 8.11, Anon. *de viribus illustribus* 38.1.
23. Wallinga 1956, cf. Thiel (1954), p.101-28. The real uncertainty with Polybios' description is whether the gangplank was hinged where it intersected with the pole. But Polybios does not mention hinges, which would have been a structural weakness anyway, and if it was so there would have been no point in having a groove when a simple round hole would have done. In constructing his working model, Wallinga faithfully followed Polybios.
24. Polybios says 'with the loss of fifty ships' (1.23.10), which might be a case of round reckoning as the secondary sources give 31 captured and 13 crippled (Orosius 4.7.10), or 31 captured and 14 crippled (Eutropius 2.20), or 30 captured and 13 crippled (Anon. *de viribus illustribus* 38).
25. *CIL* 12.2.25 (abridged).
26. Polybios 1.23.4. The *columna rostrata* was adorned with the beaks (*rostra*) of captured Carthaginian ships and originally set up in the Forum. Ironically, the monument was destroyed by lightning during the interval between the Second and Third Punic wars. A new column was erected by Claudius and an inscription placed upon it. Some would argue that either the original column had no inscription at all, or else a short and simple one; some of the verb forms contained in it are too antique, while others are too modern, for the age in which it professes to have been written; curiously, the emperor was known as somewhat of an antiquarian. Also the inscription records, unlike the Polybian narrative, the land operation first and the sea battle second. Anyway, a portion of the *columna rostra* is now in the Musei Capitolini, Palazzo di Conservatori, Rome.
27. Though it is often claimed that Leyte Gulf (October 1944) deserves the title 'the largest naval engagement in history', fewer than 200,000 men took part (compared with over 285,000 at Cape Ecnomus), manning only 282 American, Japanese and Australian ships.

28. Polybios 1.25.7, 9 (fleet sizes), 26.7 (marines), 28.14 (losses). The figures for the losses are repeated, with slight variations, in the secondary sources (Orosius 4.8.6, Eutropius 2.21.1, Anon. *de viribus illustribus* 40.1).
29. In Greek: *prôton stratópedon*, Polybios 1.30.11. We know for certain that by the time of the Second Punic War a standard consular army consisted of two Roman legions, plus two *alae* from the Latin and Italian allies, the *socii*.
30. Ibid. 29.
31. Ibid. 31.4-6. The other sources, however, are unanimous that it was the Carthaginians who took the initiative (Diodoros 23.12, Livy, *Periochae* 18, Eutropius 2.21.4, Orosius 4.9.1, Zonaras 8.13), with some saying Regulus' command was prolonged against his wishes (Frontinus, *Strategemata* 4.3.3, Valerius Maximus 4.4.6). As Lazenby (1996), p.101 points out, unless he was terribly ill, it seems somewhat irregular for a Roman general to surrender his command willingly. To date Regulus' career had been a series of unbroken success, and surely he wanted to finish his current command with yet another. He had already served as consul back in 267 BC, when he defeated the Salentines and captured Brundisium (Florus, *Epitome* 1.15).
32. Polybios 1.32.1, cf. Diodoros 23.16.1.
33. A much later story (Cicero, *de re publica* 3.29, Livy, *Periochae* 18, Horace, *Odes* 3.5, Florus, *Epitome* 1.18.23-26, Eutropius 2.25, Orosius 4.10.1, cf. Diodoros 23.16) tells how Regulus, having been captured in battle, was sent by his captors to Rome to negotiate, but instead of trying to persuade the Senate to accept the Carthaginian peace terms, he urged them to continue the struggle. True to the oath he had sworn, the honourable proconsul then returned to Carthage to face hideous torture and horrendous death. Since Polybios makes no mention of this incident, it appears to have been an attempt by the Romans to whitewash what in truth was a humiliating beating, and it seems Regulus was a victim of his own puffed-up ambition and not one of the greatest of generals.
34. Polybios 1.37.2. According to Diodoros (28.18.1), Hiero of Syracuse looked after the survivors, providing them with food, clothing and other essentials, before assisting them on their way to Messana.
35. It has been estimated that 100,000 souls may have been lost at sea, though Thiel (1954), p.235-6, without quoting any figures, implies that it could have been considerably less as the ships were undermanned. Whatever the true figures, and it is still hard to think of a greater maritime disaster, the Roman loses for the entire African *débâcle* must have been horrendous.
36. Polybios 1.38.6.
37. Ibid. 38.7 (fleet), 9-10 (siege).
38. Ibid. 39.1-7. Polybios does not give us a precise location, but Orosius says (4.9.11) the storm hit the fleet off Cape Palinurus (Capo Palinuro), in Lucania.
39. According to Polybios (1.44.2) this relief force amounted to 10,000 men, while Diodoros (24.1.2, cf. Zonaras 8.15) reduces the number to 4,000 and has it under the command of a general named Adherbal. Probably, as Lazenby (1996), p.126 suggests, there were two relief expeditions, the first being commanded by Adherbal and the second by Hannibal, who was, as Polybios says, a 'most intimate friend of Adherbal' (1.44.1). As Polybios (1.46.1) has Adherbal stationed just up the coast in Drepana, all this hangs together nicely.
40. The modern visitor to Marsala will find that the harbour lies to the south of the town, but the ancient one was to the north. It was here one encountered, as Virgil so elegantly writes, 'the dangerous shoals and hidden rocks of Lilybaeum' (*Aeneid* 3.708 West).
41. Polybios 1.46.4-47.10. Such nicknames were not uncommon among the Carthaginians, who, after all, were a cosmopolitan lot. Thus we hear later of Mago 'the Samnite' and Mago 'the Bruttian' from Polybios (9.25.4, 36.5.1). Lazenby (1996), p.129 suggests that Hannibal's moniker may have been given in recognition of superlative seamanlike skills, for the Rhodians at this time were regarded as being among the finest seafarers in the Mediterranean.
42. Publius Claudius, the first to bear the cognomen 'Pulcher', meaning 'good looking', has not been kindly dealt with by history. Polybios himself says (1.52.2-3) the consul was held personally to

blame for the disaster, while Diodoros (24.3) describes him as a man of choleric temperament and mental instability, who denounced his predecessors as drunken amateurs, and looked down on everyone with patrician disdain. Neither Polybios nor Diodoros, however, says anything about the infamous story concerning the sacred chickens. Apparently, when they refused to eat, Publius, with true Claudian arrogance, snapped 'Well, let them drink!' The unfortunate birds were tossed overboard, an act of gross impiety, and the battle fought and lost. (Cicero, *de natura deorum* 2.7, *de divinatione* 1.29.2, 20, 71, Livy, *Periochae* 19, Valerius Maximus 1.4.3, 8.1.6, Suetonius, *Tiberius* 2.2, Florus, *Epitome* 1.18.29, Eutropius 2.26).
43. Polybios 1.51.4-9.
44. Ibid. 52.5-54.8.
45. Orosius 4.4.9.
46. Appian, *Iberica* 4 (moniker), Diodoros 24.10, Polybios 1.73.1 (Hekatompylos). For Hanno's capture of Hekatompylos and the consequences, see Lancel (1995), p.259.
47. Polybios 1.74.7.
48. Ibid. 67.1, 72.3.
49. Hanno, victor of Hekatompylos and unscrupulous rival of Hamilcar, is the sizeable antihero in Flaubert's exotic novel *Salammbô* (1862).
50. Polybios 1.56.3. Monte Castellaccio, some 10km northwest of Palermo, is an escarpment overhanging the coast with a flattop summit that is crowned by a kind of natural keep (cf. the Greek *heirktê*, a prison). Another possibility for Mount Heirkte is Monte Pecoraro, west of Monte Castellaccio, were traces of a camp, with pottery of the first half of the third century BC, have been found. Nearby, at Terrasina, was also found a merchantman with amphorae and two swords of Roman type, dated to the mid-third century BC. See especially, Giustolisi 1975.
51. Polybios 1.56.10.
52. Ibid. 58.1-2. Though the Romans had troops both on the summit at an ancient temple there, and at the foot of the hill facing towards Drepana, Hamilcar took the town in between the two. The temple was dedicated to the goddess the Romans knew as Venus Erycina, supposedly founded by her son, Aeneas (Virgil, *Aeneid* 5.760-1). But the ritual prostitution practised there suggests a Punic origin, and the Carthaginians venerated the goddess as Astarte.
53. Hamilcar's name was given to a Second World War British glider, appropriately first deployed during Operation Husky (10 July 1943), the Allied invasion of Sicily. Constructed of wood and metal, it was designed to carry heavy loads: 17-pounder anti-tank gun and tractor; 25-pounder field gun and tractor; a light tank; or two Bren carriers.
54. Polybios 1.59.7-8.
55. Ibid. 59.9-12.
56. Ibid. 60.3.
57. Ibid. 60.4-9.
58. Ibid. 61.2. Polybios does not say how many Carthaginian warships there were, but Diodoros says (24.11.1) that there were 250, and there is no real reason to doubt him.
59. Polybios 1.61.6.
60. Diodoros 24.11.1.
61. Zonaras 8.17 (Hanno), Polybios 1.62.3 (Hamilcar). Incidentally, Zonaras says in his account that just before the fleets engaged 'a meteor had appeared above the Romans, and after rising high on the left of the Carthaginians plunged into their ranks'.
62. Polybios 1.63.1-3, cf. 62.8-9, Zonaras 8.17. The talent, a Greek monetary unit of international worth, was a fixed weight of silver equivalent to 60 *minae* (Attic or Euboian *tálanton* = 26.2kg, Aiginetan *tálanton* = 43.6kg). The *mina* was a unit of weight equivalent to 100 Attic *drachmae* or 70 Aiginetan *drachmae*, a Greek *drachma* being more or less the same as a Roman *denarius*. Thus 3,200 Euboian talents were more than 80 tons of silver or 12 million *denarii*, which was equivalent to the total annual expenditure of the Roman state.
63. Polybios 1.63.6.

NOTES

64. Ibid. 32.2-9. Lazenby (1996), p.103 suggests that Xanthippos may have seen elephants in action when Pyrrhos invaded the Peloponnese and attacked Sparta (272 BC). It is, of course, possible.
65. Polybios 1.33.1.
66. Ibid. 30.15. See Lazenby (1996), p.104 for a discussion on the possible location of the battle.
67. Polybios 1.33.9.
68. See Fields (2007), p.44-5.
69. Polybios 1.33.10.
70. Ibid. 34.2-3.
71. Ibid. 34.3-6.
72. Ibid. 34.9-10.
73. Ibid. 35.4. This was a line from Euripides' *Antiope*, of which only fragments survive.
74. Polybios (1.36.2-3) thought that Xanthippos sailed for Sparta soon after his victory rather than incur the jealousy that, as a foreigner, was likely to become his lot. But he adds that there was another story to be told, which he would 'endeavour to put forth on an occasion more suitable than the present' (1.36.4). The other story was presumably the rather dubious one told by many other sources; the Carthaginians had him drowned on his way home (Diodoros 23.16, Zonaras 8.13, Valerius Maximus 9.6.1, Silius Italicus, *Punica* 6.682, Appian, *Bellum Punicum* 4). On the other hand, Ptolemaios III is said (Hieronymus *in Daniel* 11:7-9) to have appointed a Xanthippos as governor of a newly won territory, in 245 BC, and if this is our man, Polybios may have told the other story in a lost part of his work, in the context of something to do with Egypt, perhaps the events of the Third Syrian War (246-241 BC) when Ptolemaios invaded Anatolia hoping to secure the Seleukid throne for his nephew.

CHAPTER 5

1. The fact that most of the German army was allowed to march back across the Rhine without being disarmed gave rise to *Dolchstaßlegende* (lit. 'Dagger-stab-legend'). This was the social theory that attributed Germany's defeat in the Great War not to the Allies but to the German public's failure to respond to its patriotic calling at the most crucial of times, and to intentional sabotaging of the war effort, particularly by Jews, Socialists and Bolsheviks. The legend had been popularized almost five decades before in Wagner's *Götterdämmerung* where the invincible Teutonic dragon-slaying hero, Siegfried, is fatally stabbed in the back by Hagen, the sinister son of the arch-villain, Alberich. And that is the twist, of course, the hero cannot be overcome by fair means or external forces, but only by someone close to him resorting to treachery (e.g. Samson, Herakles, Agamemnon, Jesus). Wagner, like any good bard, had himself cherry-picked his plot device from the most famous of German medieval epics, the *Nibelungenlied*, created circa 1200 by some anonymous Homer-like tale-teller from the many current Germanic and Norse tales; he thus manages to combine into a single complex of events the Ostrogoth Theodoric, king of Italy from AD 493 to 526, Attila the Hun, who invaded Italy in AD 452 and died the following year, twoscore years before the accession of Theodoric, and a certain Pilgrim, who was Bishop of Passow from AD 971 to 979.
2. Polybios 1.66.1-6.
3. Ibid. 67.4. Polybios describes the Greeks as 'half-breeds, mostly deserters and slaves' (1.67.7). Incidentally, he uses a rare term here, *mixhéllênes* (lit. 'mix-Greeks').
4. Ibid. 67.13.
5. Ibid. 70.7, 9. Griffith (1984), p.219-20 moots the possibility that the Libyans to be counted amongst the mutineers were mercenaries as opposed to subject levies.
6. In Greek: *aspondos polémos* (lit. 'a war that admits no truce'), Polybios 1.65.6, 88.7.
7. Ibid. 73.1. Polybios says (1.75.2) that when Hamilcar Barca was appointed to the command, the Carthaginian army was no stronger than 10,000, consisting of citizens, both horse and foot, and of the mercenaries they had recruited, and deserters from the enemy. There were also 70 elephants.

Roman Conquests: Notes

Later, as Polybios also says (1.78.13), Hamilcar armed with weapons taken from the enemy those of the prisoners of war who volunteered - some 4,000 of them - to join his own army.
8. Ibid. 79.
9. Ibid. 3.28.2.
10. Ibid. 1.88.7-12.
11. Ibid. 69.4-5 (Spendios), 6 (Mathos), 77.1, 5, 80.5-7 (Autaritos). Frontinus makes a similar point with regards to Hannibal's army in Italy, which contained soldiers who had picked up the Latin tongue 'as a result of long experience in the war' (*Strategemata* 3.2.3). On the other hand, interpreters certainly seem to have been part and parcel of a Carthaginian army, and there are occasional scattered references to them in our sources (e.g. Diodoros 23.16.1, Polybios 1.67.9, 3.44.5, 15.6.3, Livy 30.30.1, 33.12).
12. Ibid. 69.6-7.
13. Ibid. 1.70.8-9, 73.3.
14. Ibid. 72.5-6.

CHAPTER 6

1. Ibid. 2.1.5-9, 13.1-7, 36.3, 3.10.5-6, 39.3-4.
2. Nepos, *Hamilcar* 4.1.
3. Polybios 2.36.3, cf. 3.13.3. According to Diodoros, Hasdrubal too had been 'acclaimed as general by the army and by the Carthaginians alike' (25.12.1).
4. Livy 24.41.7, Silius Italicus, *Punica* 3.97-105. Silius names the bride as Imilce, a Punic name, and gives her a royal pedigree. Hannibal's brother-in-law, Hasdrubal the Splendid, after the death of his first wife, the second daughter of Hamilcar Barca, had married a local girl too.
5. Polybios, in his detailed analysis of the root causes of the Second Punic War, identifies three salient reasons for the conflict: first, 'the wrath (*thymós*) of Hamilcar, surnamed Barca, the father of Hannibal' (3.9.6); 'the second and greatest cause of the war', the 'bitterness' (*orgé*) of their fellow Carthaginians at Rome's villainous behaviour during the mutiny of mercenaries, the 'truceless war', which broke out after the end of the First Punic War (3.10.4); and third, the 'success' (*eúroia*) of the activities of Hamilcar Barca and his successors in Iberia (3.10.6).
6. Ibid. 11.7. Being Greek, of course, Polybios (3.11.5) has Hamilcar performing a sacrificial ceremony devoted to Zeus (Roman = Iuppiter).
7. E.g. Livy 21.1.4-5, 5.1, Nepos, *Hannibal* 2.3-6, Valerius Maximus 9.3.2. Though later, Livy (35.19) does supply the Polybian version of the boyhood oath, which does not, of course, automatically imply active enmity between Carthage and Rome.
8. Virgil, *Aeneid* 4.626-7 West.
9. Polybios 2.13.7, cf. 3.30.3. Greek Iber, Latin Iberus, nowadays the Ebro.
10. Ibid. 2.22.9-11.
11. Ibid. 3.30.1, cf. Livy 21.2.7.
12. In the territory controlled by Rome there were essentially two broad groups of people, Roman citizens and their allies, *socii*. Of the latter around one-quarter were 'Allies of the Latin Name' (*socii nominis Latini*), made up of a handful of old Latin states that had not been incorporated into the Roman state after the war with Rome (Latin War, 340-338 BC), and thirty Latin colonies planted at strategic points throughout Italy. All these communities enjoyed special rights, such as the rights of intermarriage and commerce with Roman citizens, and their citizens could even become Roman citizens by migrating to Rome. The other broad group was made up of the ordinary allies of Rome, what we call the Italians. Some of these had joined the Roman confederacy more or less voluntarily, others only after lengthy and often-bitter conflict. The main obligation of both Latins and Italians was to furnish Rome with troops.
13. According to Livy (21.7.2) Saguntum was regarded as a Greek colony founded by citizens of Zakynthos (Zante), but this appears to be a fable born of the resemblance of the two place-names.

14. Some 400km south from the mouth of the Iberus and sitting on a peninsula commanding one of the best harbours in the Mediterranean, New Carthage (presumably called *Qart-Hadasht* by the Carthaginians like their home city) had recently been founded by Hasdrubal the Splendid to serve as a military and naval base. The Romans called it Carthago Nova (lit. 'New New-City'), whence our name, but Polybios says (2.13.1) it was either known as *Karchedôn* (i.e. Carthage) or *Kaine Polis* (i.e. New City), and in fact uses both names himself (e.g. 3.13.7, 10.6.8). Another attraction of the site was the rich silver mines that lay in the immediate vicinity of the city. Polybios says (34.9.8-11) in his day 40,000 slaves were working there to the benefit of the Roman state, bringing in a revenue of 25,000 *drachmae* per day, the Polybian *drachma* being the equivalent of the *denarius*. By way of a comparison, we know from Polybios (6.39.12) that the Roman legionary received an allowance of 1 *denarius* every three days (120 *denarii* per annum), while his centurion received double this amount.
15. Ibid. 3.14.10.
16. Ibid. 21.1, 29.1-3, 30.3.
17. Ibid. 6.2.
18. See ch. 6 n.5 for his three 'greatest causes'.
19. Polybios 3.33.1
20. Ibid. 2.24.16.
21. Ibid. 3.33.4, 41.2, Livy 21.17.3, 22.4, 49.2, 4.
22. Polybios 3.40.2, 41.2, Livy 21.17.5, 8.
23. As you can well imagine, the modern literature on this particular Hannibalic hot potato is voluminous, and the ink continues to flow from the pens of professional historians, amateur buffs, and erudite locals alike. Do look at, however, de Lavis-Traffort 1956, de Beer 1967, (1974), p.120-82, Procter 1971, Lazenby (1978), p.34-48. For what Polybios calls 'the ascent towards the Alps' (3.50.1, cf. 39.9) there are two main contenders for the honour of having been Hannibal's route from the basin of the Rhône to the watershed pass: by marching up the valley of the Isère in the north he used an 'Isère Pass', viz. Col du Petit St. Bernard (2,188m), Col du Mont-Cenis (2,083m), or Col de Clapier (2,482m); or by marching up the middle reaches of the valley of the Durance in the south he used a 'Durance Pass', viz. Col de Montgenèvre (1,854m), Col de la Traversette (2,947m), Col de Mary (2,654m), Col de Roure (2,829m), or Col de Larche, sometimes Col de l' Argentière (1,991m). As a point of interest, the Col du Mont-Cenis is the pass Napoléon thought Hannibal used, the Col de Montgenèvre is the pass Pompey used making his way to Iberia in 77 BC (Sallust, *Historiae* 2.98) and Caesar used hotfooting it to Gaul in 58 BC (Caesar, *Bellum Gallicum* 1.10.3-5), while the Col de l' Argentière is the pass François I crossed, in June 1515, with horse, foot, artillery and baggage train en route to his bloody victory over the Swiss at Marignano (now known as Melignano), on the Milan-Lodi road. On 20 May 1800, the First Consul himself swept over the Alps into Italy, astride a mule, using the Col du Grand St. Bernard (2,469m).
24. Polybios 3.70-74, Livy 21.54-56 (Trebbia), Polybios 3.82-84, Livy 22.4-6 (Trasimene), Polybios 3.111-117, Livy 22.46-49 (Cannae). The historic battlefield of Cannae was to be the scene of a number of battles: here in AD 861 the Lombards fought the Salernese, and a decade later the Arabs; in 1018 the Byzantines defeated the hopelessly outnumbered Lombard rebels and their Norman allies, who took their revenge under William de Hauteville, the Iron-Arm, some 23 years later; while in 1083 Robert de Hauteville, known to history as Guiscard, captured and destroyed the town of Cannae after it had rebelled against his rule.
25. Euripides, *Supplicant Women* 481-3.
26. Capua had been founded about the late sixth century BC by the Etruscans just south of the Volturnus (Volturno), on the site of present-day Santa Maria di Capua Vetere, then a century later subdued by the Samnites of the highlands to its east, who turned it into a city to rival Rome. It came into Rome's orbit soon after the middle of the fourth century BC, during the upheavals of the Latin War. Since 334 BC every Capuan had enjoyed the right of full Roman citizenship, and, as well as its official language, Oscan, the city had preserved its municipal magistrates. Even if, on the right

bank of the Volturnus, it had lost the *ager Falernus* and its celebrated vineyards, annexed by Rome, the city soon became the western capital of copiousness and opulence through the industries of gladiators, prostitutes and perfumers. Before Capua's senate, according to Livy, Hannibal deliberately flattered its members by promising that the city would soon be 'the capital of Italy, whence Rome, like every other Italian community, would seek her laws' (23.10.2). During the winter following Cannae' Hannibal's soldiers took up quarters in Capua and, according to Livy (23.18.10-15), the Carthaginian army lost its body and soul in those steamy delights the city had to offer. Later the Roman historian would put into the mouth of Marcellus the famous, but false, adage, 'Capua was Hannibal's Cannae' (23.45.4).

27. Tarentum was established in an exceptionally fine location, on a slender promontory stretching from east to west between an outer bay (mare Grande) and an inner lagoon (mare Piccolo). Between the western extremity and the mainland opposite was a channel, which overlooked by the citadel as it ran north into the lagoon. This magnificent body of water was some 26km in circumference and provided the best harbour in southern Italy. Tarentum was thus surrounded by water on three sides: the circular lagoon in the north, by the narrow sound in the west, and by the deep bay and open sea to the south. It was understandably small, covering an area of about 16ha.
28. Livy 25.15.7, Appian, *Hannibalica* 35.
29. The elderly mastermind developed an array of formidable weapons, from catapults that hurled fireballs to gargantuan cranes that dropped heavy stones onto Roman ships or even lifted them bow first out of the water. Byzantine tradition (e.g. Zonaras 9.4) would later ascribe to Archimedes the installation of batteries of parabolic mirrors on the heights of Syracuse capable of frying the Roman ships below by focussing the sun's rays onto their rigging. Like burning paper with a magnifying glass, the intense heat of the concentrated rays caused the sails and ropes to catch fire instantaneously. The Roman fleet was reduced to ashes. Legend, perhaps, but one which the wizardry of the man who discovered spheroids, as well as the cone and Archimedes' screw pump, does not render totally improbable. He was, of course, destined to die amid the noise and fury created by the sacking of the city. Completely engrossed in the figures he had traced in the dust, Archimedes was cut down by a soldier who did not recognize the man (Livy 25.31.9).
30. Livy 25.32-36 *passim*.
31. Cicero, *pro Balbo* 34.
32. Livy 27.9.1-6, 10.3-4. According to Polybios (2.24.10) in 225 BC the Latins could furnish 80,000 foot and 5,000 horse. The twelve dissenters were Ardea, Nepete, Sutrium, Alba, Carseoli, Sora, Suessa, Circeii, Setia, Cales, Narnia, and Interamna. Apart from Carseoli, Suessa and Cales, the others were remote from the fighting. The eighteen loyalists, all remoter colonies and staunch in their support, were Signia, Norba, Saticula, Fregellae, Luceria, Venusia, Brundisium, Hadria, Firmum, Ariminum, Pontiae, Paestum, Cosa, Beneventum, Aesernia, Spoletium, Plancentia, and Cremona. One reason for this may be the fact that the manpower of the inner colonies was employed for overseas campaigns, which was one of their main complaints, whereas the manpower of the remoter colonies was retained to defend the colonies themselves.
33. Polybios 11.1-3 *passim*, Livy 27.47-49 *passim*.
34. Polybios 10.37.5. According to Livy (27.36.2) and Appian (*Hannibalica* 52), Hasdrubal followed his brother's footsteps over the Alps. However, nothing obliged Hasdrubal to make the detours that cost Hannibal and his army such suffering, and it is believed that he took the shorter Durance route and crossed via the Col de Montgenèvre, e.g. de Sanctis (1968), p.561. He reached Gallia Cisalpina in fine weather and with a much fitter army.
35. Hannibal, on the other hand, invariably showed the utmost respect for the bodies of dead enemy commanders. For example, the bodies of Aemilius Paullus, Gracchus, and Marcellus were all recovered and cremated with due ceremony, the ashes of Marcellus being sent to Marcellus' son in a silver urn (Livy 22.52.6, 25.17.5, 27.28.2, Plutarch, *Marcellus* 30.1-4, cf. Livy 22.7.5).
36. Livy 27.51.12, Frontinus, *Strategemata* 2.9.2, Zonaras 9.9.
37. Ovid, *Fasti* 6.770.

NOTES

38. Polybios 11.2.1.
39. Horace, *Odes* 4.4.41-44.
40. Appian, *Hannibalica* 59.
41. Polybios 15.9-14 *passim*, Livy 30.32-35 *passim*.
42. Polybios 15.18.4-10, Livy 30.37.2-6, cf. 42.23.3, Appian, *Bellum Punicum* 54. According to one secondary account (Cassius Dio 17 fr. 57.82 Boissevain), there was a clause in this treaty forbidding the recruiting in future of any mercenaries whatever (though this clause is not mentioned by either Polybios or Livy).
43. Livy 35.14.5-8, cf. Plutarch, *Flamininus* 21.4.
44. Nepos, *Hannibal* 13.3, cf. Cicero, *de oratore* 2.18.75.
45. Zonaras 8.21, Livy 21.4.3-5, 8, Nepos, *Hannibal* 3.1, Appian, *Iberica* 6.
46. Polybios 1.64.6, Plutarch, *Cato major* 8.14.
47. Polybios 1.56.3.
48. Florus, *Epitome* 1.22.9.
49. Polybios 3.71.6.
50. Livy 22.5.5.
51. Polybios 11.19.3, 5. During the time that Hannibal was in Italy, as far as we know, there were two occasions only when he lost men through desertion. The first occasion was in 215 BC when 272 Numidian and Iberian horsemen went over to the Romans three days after Hannibal suffered a reverse outside Nola (Livy 23.46.6). The second occasion was in 213 BC when 1,000 Iberians of the Carthaginian garrison deserted after the Romans recaptured Arpi in Apulia (ibid. 24.47.8-9). As Lazenby (1978), p.106 points out, these two desertions are a sign of the times, the virtual deadlock in Italy offering few chances of booty for Hannibal's men.
52. du Picq (1946), p.165.
53. In Latin: *O formosum spectaculum*!: Seneca, *de ira* 2.5.4.

CHAPTER 7

1. Polybios 1.37.7.
2. Livy 23.25.7, 31.2-4, 24.18.9, 26.1.9-10, 28.10, 27.7.12-13, 22.9, 28.10.13, 29.13.6. We also know from Livy (22.50.3, 54.1, 4) that these survivors amounted to some 14,550 men.
3. Ibid. 29.24.13, 14.
4. Ibid. 25.1-4.
5. Before he left, Hannibal put on record what he and his army had achieved since setting out from Iberia well-nigh sixteen years ago. The record, written in Punic and in Greek, the international language of Hannibal's day, and either in the form of an inscribed column or a bronze tablet (or both?), was set up at the temple of Hera Lacinia (Roman = Iuno Lacinia) on the cliff edge of the Lacinian promontory (Capo Colonne) 12km south of Kroton, his final headquarters. A generation later the inscription was seen and read by the Greek soldier-historian Polybios (3.56.4, cf. 2.24.17, 3.33.18, Livy 21.38.2, 28.46.16, 30.20.6), who took from it the figures for the strength of Hannibal's army when it first entered Italy - 20,000 foot (12,000 Libyans, 8,000 Iberian) and 6,000 horse. There is no mention of elephants, the thing Hannibal's march is remembered for today, but Appian says (*Hannibalica* 1.4) that he set out with thirty-seven, and Polybios (3.42.10) has the same number being rafted across the Rhône, but unfortunately no source records how many survived the crossing of the Alps.
6. Polybios 15.5.3, summarised by Livy 30.29.2.
7. Scullard (1970), p.142-55, Walbank (1970), p.445-51, Lazenby (1978), p. 218, Lancel (1999), p.173-4, Hoyos (2008), p.107-8. The other locations bearing the name Zama are: one perhaps at Sidi Abd el Djedidi, some 45km northwest of Kairouan; one or possibly two more at Jama. Of course, it is important for us to remember that though Zama now gives its name to the battle, it was only an encampment on Hannibal's march. The mistake was Nepos', who said the subsequent battle

was fought 'at Zama' (*apud Zamam, Hannibal* 6.3). It is clear from Polybios' narrative that the battle was not fought there, but some distance away, and within 5km of Scipio's camp. Polybios locates this at a site he calls 'Margaron' (15.5.4) but Livy calls 'Naraggara' (30.29.9). The latter is thought to be near modern Sakhiet Sidi Youssef on the Tunisian-Algerian frontier. The most widely held view is that the actual battle was fought on a plain some 25km to southeast of Sakhiet Sidi Youssef and not far from the site of today's El Kef airport.
8. Polybios 15.6.1-8.14, Livy 30.29.9-31.10, cf. Frontinus, *Strategemata* 1.1.3, 6.2.1, 2.
9. Polybios 15.9.2.
10. Ibid. 3.6, 11.1, 14.9.
11. Appian, *Bellum Punicum* 41.
12. Polybios 15.5.12, Livy 30.29.4.
13. Polybios 15.11.1.
14. Livy says the second line also included 'the one legion from Macedonia' (30.33.5), presumably the 4,000 men under the command of Sopater he mentions earlier (30.26.3), and whom he later alleges were rounded up by the Romans and clapped in irons (30.42.4-5). Frontinus also has 'Macedonians' (*Strategemata* 2.3.16) deployed in the second line, but in view of Polybios' silence, we can dismiss them as their presence at Zama probably derives from Roman annalistic propaganda against Philip V of Macedon. The First Macedonian War between Rome and Hannibal's ally Philip had ended in 205 BC, but the Second War was due to commence two years after Zama and it appears that the annalists wished to show that Rome's hostile attitude to the king was justified. See especially, Lazenby (1978), p.222.
15. Polybios 15.11.2.
16. Livy 30.33.6, Appian, *Bellum Punicum* 40.
17. Polybios 15.11.7-9, 16.4. Frontinus, on the other hand, says these men were 'Italians, whose loyalty he [Hannibal] distrusted and whose indifference he feared, inasmuch as he had dragged most of them from Italy against their will' (*Strategemata* 2.3.16). Frontinus, in all likelihood, has used Livy as his source here. Livy, believing Hannibal's third line was composed of unenthusiastic Italians, has him place them there 'since their doubtful loyalty might prove them either friend or foe' (30.35.9). It seems safest to follow Polybios' account.
18. Polybios 15.11.1.
19. As Polybios himself once explained, 'for the cavalry was the arm on which he [Hannibal] relied above all others' (3.101.8).
20. Ibid 15.9.7-10.
21. Ibid. 12.2-5.
22. Livy 30.34.3, Polybios 15.13.1.
23. Polybios 15.14.6.
24. Ibid. 6.6, quoting *Iliad* 4.300.
25. Polybios 15.14.9, Livy 30.35.3, Appian, *Bellum Punicum* 48.
26. Polybios 15.16.2-4
27. Ibid. 15.14.7. Here Polybios uses the term *daimonios* (lit. 'marvellously [time]'), but Livy omits the qualifying adjective. Naturally, our Roman historian patriotically overlooks the extreme uncertainty of the final stages of the contest.
28. Though Livy, our authority here, says he was unable 'to find out how it became current - through the army's devotion to their general, or from popular favour; or it may have started with the flattery of his close friends, in the way, in our fathers' time, Sulla was called 'Felix' and Pompey 'Magnus'. What is certain is that Scipio was the first general to be celebrated by the name of the people he conquered' (30.45.6-7). Seneca, however, states (*de brevitate vitae* 13.5) that the consul Marcus Valerius Maximus, who captured Messana (263 BC), adopted the name 'Messana', which was afterwards changed to 'Messala'. As for Sulla and Pompey, the first solemnly adopted the name Felix, which his many flatterers had for some time applied to him, when he heard of the defeat of Marius minor at Sacriportus (82 BC), while the second, on returning to Italy after having defeated

NOTES

the Marians in Sicily and Africa (80 BC), was greeted by Sulla, perhaps half in jest, as Cnaeus Pompeius Magnus. The title stuck.
29. Polybios 10.4.5, cf. Livy 25.2.6-8. However, Polybios was incorrect with the date of Scipio's aedileship, it being 213 BC not 217 BC as he implies.
30. Polybios 10.3.3-7, Livy 21.46.7-8.
31. Livy 22.52.4, 53.1, cf. Frontinus, *Strategemata* 4.7.39, Valerius Maximus 5.6.7, Silius Italicus, *Punica* 10.426-8.
32. Livy 26.18.9.
33. Ibid. 35.14.9, cf. Plutarch, *Flamininus* 21.3-4.

CHAPTER 8

1. Polybios 1.1.5. It must be said, however, there was a great historian in Livy. With his flypaper mind, he had the right imagination that knew just how far it was safe to stray from the truth and just how far to colour it so as to change its shape for his own purposes.
2. Ibid. 1.3.7, 15.9.2-4, cf. 5.104.4-10.
3. E.g. Cicero, *de finnibus* 4.9.22, *Philippics* 1.5.11, Juvenal, *Satires* 6.290, cf. 10.156.
4. Livy 22.51.5,6. Three centuries later Juvenal (*Satires* 7.160-4) would write satirically of schoolboys doomed to discuss as rhetorical exercises whether Hannibal ought to have followed his victory at Cannae by a march on Rome. Hoyos, intriguingly perhaps, floats the suggestion that the Maharbal story does not belong to the aftermath of Cannae, it having been displaced from Trasimene, 'a battlefield 85 miles, four days' march, from Rome, not 300 miles like Cannae' (2008), p.53, cf. 60.
5. The so-called Servian wall, which actually belongs to the period immediately after the occupation of Rome by the Gaul Brennos (390 BC), ran for some 11km and enclosed an area of roughly 426ha. See Fields (2008A), p.6-11.
6. Livy 22.57.7-8.
7. Cf. Demosthenes, *On the Crown* 246-7.
8. Cf. Livy 26.7-8, 11 *passim*, Frontinus, *Strategemata* 3.18.2-3, Valerius Maximus 3.7.10.
9. Livy 23.15.1-6, Cassius Dio 15.37.30, 34, Zonaras 9.2.
10. Cf. Livy 29.6, the siege of Locri.
11. Polybios 3.96.9.
12. Livy 23.13.7, 41.10, 43.6.
13. Polybios 3.107.9, cf. Livy 22.36.2-4. See Fields (2007), p.65.
14. Brunt (1971), p.419-22.
15. Plutarch *Pyrrhos* 19.7.
16. Livy 22.49.15. As for the size of the Roman army at Cannae, Livy (22.36.2-4) reports that it was made up of 8 beefed-up legions, each of 5,000 foot and 300 horse (instead of 4,000 and 200 respectively), supported by an equal number of Latin-Italian *alae*, each of 5,000 foot and 600 horse. Thus, by Livy's reckoning, there would have been 80,000 foot and 7,200 horse. According to Polybios (3.113.5, 117.8), there were 80,000 foot, 10,000 of whom served as the garrison of the main camp, perhaps one legion and its corresponding allied *ala*, and over 6,000 horse. Like Livy, Polybios says (3.107.9-15, cf. 6.20.6-7) the army was organised into 8 legions and 8 *alae*, each of 5,000 foot supported by 300 and 900 horse respectively. Appian (*Hannibalica* 17) and Plutarch (*Fabius Maximus* 14.2) support these figures, the former claiming there were 70,000 foot and 6,000 horse excluding camp garrisons, while the latter notes that the combined force amounted to 88,000 men. These estimates are generally favoured by Walbank (1957), p.439-40, Lazenby (1978), p.75-6, 79-80, Goldsworthy (2001), p.95-6, Daley (2002), p.25-9, but are disputed by de Sanctis (1968), p.131-5, Brunt (1971), p.419 n.2, 672.
17. Polybios 2.24.16-17, cf. 3.33.17-18, 56.4.
18. Livy 22.58, cf. 26.11.
19. In Latin: *Qui vincit non est victor nisi victur fatetur*, Ennius, *Annales* fr. 493 Vahlen.

Roman Conquests: Notes

20. Livy 22.49.16, 23.12.1-2. Later, in a dramatic scene, Hannibal's brother, Mago, was to pour out on the floor of the Carthaginian senate house these aureate bands, 'and that long war, whose spoil was heaped so high with rings of gold, as Livy tells, who errs not' (Dante, *Inferno* 28.10 Sayers).
21. Polybios 18.28.7.
22. Brunt (1971), p.28.
23. Polybios 3.77.3-7, 85.1-4, cf. Frontinus, *Strategemata* 4.7.25.
24. In Latin: *de dignitate atque imperio*, Livy 22.58.1-2, 3. Compare here the Roman anecdote, as related by Valerius Maximus, in which Hamilcar Barca, watching his three sons playing, exclaimed: 'These are the lion cubs I am rearing for the destruction of Rome!' (9.3.2).
25. Polybios 7.9.12-15. The text of the treaty as reproduced by Polybios is a Greek translation, made in Hannibal's chancellery, of the Punic original; it contains turns of phrases that jar with Polybios' customary Greek, and was probably captured by the Romans from Philip's chief envoy Xenophanes. The version of the treaty given by Livy (23.33.11) in a not very credible résumé is distorted and misleading.

Chapter 9

1. Livy 32.2.1.
2. Ibid. 33.46.1-47.2.
3. Ibid. 36.4.7. According to Aurelius Victor, a fourth century AD writer from Roman Africa, Hannibal had even turned his soldiers to agriculture. He writes Hannibal 'replanted much of Africa with olive trees, using his soldiers, whose idleness he considered problematic for Carthage and its leaders' (*Liber de Caesaribus* 37.3).
4. According to Livy (37.1.7-10, cf. Cicero, *Philippics* 11.17), a public announcement by Scipio Africanus that he was going to serve as his brother's legate secured the Asian command for Lucius Cornelius Scipio (*cos.* 190 BC), particularly as it was widely known in Rome that Hannibal was in Antiochos' court. This highly organized man, of rare precocity, comes over as an all-time manipulator of public opinion. In fact the old adversaries did not encounter each other again in battle, nor was Scipio Africanus present at Magnesia. See Scullard (1970), p.210-44.
5. Livy 33.47.4. Here Livy summarizes the speech delivered in the Senate by Scipio Africanus and here apparently follows Polybios, whose text is unfortunately missing for the years 196-192 BC.
6. Nepos, *Hannibal* 7.6-7, Livy 33.45.6-7, 47.3-49.8.
7. According to Cicero, when in Ephesos Hannibal was once invited to attend a lecture by one Phormio, and after being treated to a lengthy discourse on the art of generalship, was asked by his friends what he thought of it. 'I have seen many old drivellers', he replied, 'on more than one occasion, but I have seen no one who drivelled more than Phormio' (*de oratore* 2.18.75). Of course the story may be apocryphal, but it should certainly cause those of us who pose as experts in matters military to pause for thought. As Polybios (12.25e.1-25h.6) himself explained, the good historian, above all, must have personal experience of political life (which in his day included warfare).
8. Livy 34.60.3-6, cf. Appian, *Syrica* 7, Justin, *Epitome* 31.3.7-10.
9. Frontinus, *Strategemata* 1.8.7, cf. Livy 35.14.1-2, Nepos, *Hannibal* 2.2.
10. There is another tradition, not recorded by Nepos in his mini-biography of Hannibal; that the footloose military genius went to the newly independent kingdom of Armenia before going on to Crete. Here, according to both Strabo (11.14.6) and Plutarch (*Lucullus* 31.4-5) the satrap-turned-king, Artaxias, having no military tasks for Hannibal, had him survey a site for his new capital on the River Araxes, the soon-to-be Artaxata (present-day Artashat, 32km of Yerevan).
11. Nepos, *Hannibal* 9.
12. Cf. Nepos, *Hannibal* 10-11 *passim*, Justin, *Epitome* 32.4. Frontinus (*Strategemata* 4.7.10) has Hannibal suggesting this diabolical stratagem to Antiochos. Please yourself.
13. Plutarch, *Flamininus* 21.1.
14. Livy 39.51.9, cf. Plutarch, *Flamininus* 20.5, Nepos, *Hannibal* 12.

CHAPTER 10

1. Sallust, *Bellum Iugurthinum* 5.4-5.
2. Livy, *Periochae* 47, Appian, *Bellum Punicum* 69, Plutarch, *Cato major* 27.2. Whatever the subject, be that the grain supply, or the coinage, or citizenship, Cato always managed to relate it to Carthage and end his speech with the same idiomatic expression (in indirect speech of course): '*Censeo etiam delendam esse Carthaginem*'; 'It is my firm opinion that Carthage must be destroyed', though we have the habit of writing this Catonian phrase as *delenda Carthago*. Marcus Porcius Cato (237-149 BC) is known also as the Orator, the Censor, Cato major, or the Elder, to distinguish him from his great-grandson Marcus Porcius Cato Uticensis (aka Cato minor, or the Younger), the steadfast, stoic opponent of Caesar.
3. Entering upon his military service at the age of 17, Cato served with distinction in the Second Punic War, and devoted the following 26 years of his life to military affairs. In 204 BC, despite his opposition to the African adventure, he served as quaestor in Sicily and Africa under Publius Cornelius Scipio, and as praetor, in 198 BC, he governed Sardinia. As a military tribune he was to see action against Antiochos III at Thermopylae in 191 BC, even though the tribunate was on the bottom rung of the *cursus honorum*, it was a prestigious post that was indeed sometimes filled by established senators like Cato here. In the field of literary composition Cato was prolific. This output not only included his well-known agricultural manual, but also an account on the Second Punic War, in which he apparently sung the praises of a certain Surus, 'the Syrian', bravest elephant of the Carthaginian army who had lost a tusk, presumably in combat (Pliny, *Historia Naturalis* 8.5.11). It is almost certain that Surus was an Indian elephant, and very possible that he came to Carthage from Syria via Egypt. Hannibal's elephants, therefore, included at least one Indian. Moreover, after the Trebbia, the weather was so inclement that all his elephants died except one, on which Hannibal rode when he led his army across the floodwaters of the upper Arno (Polybios 3.74.11, 79.12, Livy 21.58.11, 22.2.2, Zonaras 8.24). Was this sole survivor Surus, the bravest of the brave? Later it seems the Romans captured Surus, who set him out to pasture on an estate near Rome. He was famous in his day and his name was the source of puns by Ennius in *Annales* (fr. 234 Vahlen, with *surus* 'stake', since he had but one tusk) and Plautus in *Pseudolus* (1215, 1218, with *Surus* 'Syrian' and *sura* 'ankle'). See especially, Scullard (1974), p.174-7.
4. Plutarch, *Cato major* 27.1, cf. Florus, *Epitome* 1.31.5.
5. Appian, *Bellum Punicum* 69, cf. Augustine, *City of God* 1.30.
6. Cf. Cicero, who would write Scipio Aemilianus 'overthrew two cities, both extremely hostile to this empire, and thus extinguished not only present but also future wars' (*de amicitia* 3). The two cities, of course, were Carthage and Numantia.
7. Polybios 36.2.1.
8. Ibid. 38.21.1.
9. The first two provinces were prizes of the First Punic War, Sicily and Sardinia-with-Corsica, Citerior Iberia and Ulterior Iberia of the Second, and Africa (meaning the bit we know as Tunisia) of the Third. Eastward expansion began with Macedonia, taken over the year before Carthage fell. The province of Africa, as we shall discover, would serve as the base of operations in the war with Iugurtha.
10. Polybios 36.6.7, Appian, *Bellum Punicum* 80.
11. Appian, *Bellum Punicum* 97-8.
12. Cicero, *de re publica* 6.9.
13. Of this turncoat, Polybios has kind words, saying 'the Carthaginian general was in the prime of life, of great valour, and what is most important in a soldier, a good and bold rider' (36.8.1).
14. Appian, *Bellum Punicum* 112.
15. Ibid. 121. Lacking Iberian broom for making cordage, the admirals of the fleet, or so says Frontinus (*Strategemata* 1.7.3), employed the hair of their women as a substitute. Having earlier furnished the springs for the city's catapult, we might wonder how much hair the poor ladies of Carthage had left to give.

16. Excavations in this area have revealed such large apartment buildings, many with central courtyards, built on a regular grid pattern of streets in the Hellenistic manner. Finds of human bones amongst the ruins of this area suggest that Appian's lurid account of the street fighting is not all that farfetched. For the archaeology of this area see Lancel (1995), p.156-72, 425-6.
17. Appian, *Bellum Punicum* 128.
18. For the Third Punic War we have to almost totally rely on Appian's account, supported by the few snippets of Polybios.
19. Eshmun is portrayed in our Graeco-Roman sources, all of which identify him with the healing divinity Asklepios, as a god who dies and then returns to life: e.g. Pausanias (7.23.6), who quotes a Sidonian source, describes the Phoenician Asklepios as the son of a sun god and an immortal woman and has a specific health-giving nature.
20. Polybios (38.7.1-8.15) offers us an unflattering sketch of Hasdrubal, whom he considered a poltroon.
21. Pliny, *Historia Naturalis*. The archaeologists discovered 'little plaques' of bitumen in the thick layer of ashes covering Punic Carthage.
22. Polybios was concerned above all with the aetiology of events, making careful distinction between true causality (*aitía*), pretexts (*prosphaseis*), and beginnings (*archai*). In 3.6, for the benefit of his readership, he dwells upon this subject at some length.
23. Plutarch, *Philopoimen* 21.5. As the leading soldier and statesman of the Achaian League, which include Achaia proper and much of Polybios' mountainous homeland of Arcadia, along with the city states of Corinth, Argos and Sikyon, Philopoimen saw fit to transform the cavalry of the coalition forces from a worthless body into an impressive fighting arm (ibid. 7.2-5). The corps was clearly blue-blooded and better-off as Plutarch describes its members as 'the most esteemed of citizens' (ibid. 18.4). It was probably with this corps that Polybios earned his spurs.
24. Polybios 31.23.4.
25. Thus Scipio Aemilianus was not a Cornelii by blood but by adoption. Born in 184 BC (or 185 BC), he was the second son of Lucius Aemilius Paullus (viz. minor), the victor of Pydna. When his father remarried, the two sons by his first marriage had been given away in adoption to the Fabii (Fabius Maximus Aemilianus) and the Scipiones (Publius Cornelius Scipio Aemilianus). Such adoptions were not uncommon among the Roman nobility.
26. Polybios 3.48.12.
27. According to Cicero (*Epistulae ad familiares* 5.12.2) Polybios wrote a monograph on the Numantine War.
28. Polybios 1.19.14-15, Diodoros 23.9.1. According to Tacitus, the Roman custom was that 'when a city was stormed, its booty fell to the troops; when surrendered, to the commanders' (*Historiae* 3.19.2, cf. Caesar *Bellum civile* 1.21.2).
29. Polybios 10.15.5-6.
30. Ibid. 1.14.3-4. Philinos was probably contemporary with the first war: indeed, Polybios' account of the siege of Lilybaeum is so graphic (1.41.4-48.11) that it is thought to be based on an eyewitness account by Philinos, while Fabius Pictor was a contemporary of the second.
31. Polybios 1.27.7-11, 20.12, 6.52.1.
32. Ibid. 9.22.8-10, 24-26 *passim*.
33. Ibid. 24.5-8.
34. Livy 21.4.
35. E.g. Polybios 3.26.1-2 (treaties preserved on bronze tablets in Rome), 12.4c.4-5 (importance of personal investigation).
36. Ibid. 1.6.3.
37. Ibid. 6.6.
38. A Greek of this period referred to himself as a *Hellene*. The Romans, intolerant at the best of times, did not extend that simple courtesy. Instead, a Roman would call a Greek a *Graecus* (whence our modern term), which was known to be belittling. Far more belittling was *Graeculus*, 'Greekling' (a Carthaginian likewise could be branded a *Poenulus*).

39. Pausanias 8.37.2.
40. Pseudo-Lucian, *Macrobioi* 23.

CHAPTER 11

1. In its literal sense *l-Maghrib* means 'the west', viz. the lands to the west of *Misr*, Egypt. During the first half of the second millennium AD Arab armies gradually drove the Berbers from the fertile lowlands to the rugged mountain valleys and desert regions where they live today, scattered across North Africa in isolated groups from Siwa Oasis, close to the Egyptian-Libyan border, to the High Atlas Mountains of Morocco, some 3,000km to the west. It must be said that modern Berbers are a very diverse group of peoples whose main connections are linguistic. See Brett-Fentress (1996), p.3-4, 81-7.
2. Polybios 1.78.1-11. This unnamed daughter of our historical sources is indebted to Flaubert for having come down the centuries under the esteemed adopted name of Salammbô, springing fully ornamented from the novelist's head.
3. Gsell (1928), p.362, Brett-Fentress (1996), p.24-5, Lancel (1998), p.158-9. Also, Law (1978), p.176-7 notes that the Graeco-Roman sources refer to Numidian leaders as 'king' (Greek *basileús*, Latin *rex*) or 'prince' (Greek *dunástes* Latin *dynastes*), in an effort to render the indigenous title *gld*.
4. Pliny, *Historia Naturalis* 5.1.
5. Livy 29.32-33 *passim*.
6. Ibid. 28.35.
7. Ibid. 27.4.5-9. A Roman pound, *libra*, equates to 323 grams or thereabouts.
8. More correctly Sophoniba, but she is better known as Sophonisba, a form found in fifteenth century MSS and early printed editions. The name is not uncommon in Punic inscriptions where it appears as the equivalent of *Safonbaal* (= 'she whom Baal has protected'). After praising her beauty and musical and literary gifts, Cassius Dio adds that 'she was so charming that the mere sight of her or even the sound of her voice sufficed to vanquish every one, even the most indifferent' (34 fr. 61). Such a lulu sounds as unquestionably irresistible as that *femme fatale sans pareil*, Helen of Troy, whose dreadful beauty and adulterous flight with Paris started the Trojan War.
9. Livy 29.23.
10. It is around this time, according to Livy (30.21.3), that Carthaginian recruiting officers, loaded with money, were arrested in Saguntum.
11. Ibid. 29.23.4. Diodoros (27.7) believed that Hasdrubal, before he gave preference to the marriage with Syphax, had first promised his daughter to Masinissa, although he had never seen her. This version, of which Livy is ignorant, is questioned by some.
12. Caesar, *Bellum civile* 2.24.
13. Sallust, *Bellum Iugurthinum* 18.7 (*mapalia*).
14. Polybios 14.4-5 *passim*, Livy 30.5-6 *passim*, Frontinus, *Strategemata* 2.5.29. Polybios (14.5.15) does not hesitate to say that, of all the acts of war undertaken by Scipio, this was the finest and most daring.
15. This has been tentatively identified as the plain of Souk el Kremis, near Bou Salem and beside the upper reaches of the Oued Medjerda (the ancient Bagradas) about 110km southwest of what was once the city of Utica.
16. The tribal chief Tychaios, a kinsman of the fallen Syphax, would rally to Hannibal with 2,000 horsemen, reputed to be the best in Africa (Polybios 15.3.5-7, Appian, *Bellum Punicum* 33), while Masinissa rode into the Roman camp with double that number (Polybios 15.5.12, Livy 30.29.4).
17. Livy's narrative concerning the Great Plains and its immediate aftermath derives from Polybios, but then the surviving manuscript breaks off. Modern commentators are divided on the question whether the romantic episode of Sophonisba's marriage and death (Livy 30.12.11-15.10) is also Polybian or from the later annalists such as Claudius Quadrigarius, Valerius Antias or Quintus Fabius Pictor. Plays have been written on her tragic story by Trissino (1515), John Marston (1606),

ROMAN CONQUESTS: NOTES

Nathaniel Lee (1676), Pierre Corneille (1663), and James Thomson (1730). Of the latter playwright, one line at least of his play survives: 'Oh! Sophonisba! Sophonisba! Oh!' A wall painting at Pompeii probably depicts her death, and much later she would become the heroine of so many paintings of the European classical age.

18. *Amore captivae victor captus*, as Livy (30.12.18) charmingly puts it.
19. On receiving the cup, according to Livy, she said, 'I accept this bridal gift - a gift not unwelcome if my husband has been unable to offer a greater one to his wife. But tell him this: that I should have died a better death had not my marriage bed stood so near my grave' (30.15.7). Like Cleopatra after her, Sophonisba preferred death to being taken to Rome where she would be forced to walk in Scipio's triumphal parade. Doubtless the fall of the Queen of the Nile, which had occurred in Livy's lifetime, was vivid in his memory as he composed this account of Sophonisba. As a complete contrast, we can mention the example of Septimia Zenobia, the fallen queen of conquered Palmyra, who lived to walk in Aurelian's triumph (autumn AD 274) and ended her life as a very fashionable Roman hostess with a pension and a villa (*SHA* Aurelian 30.27).
20. Or so believed Livy, though he does report that 'Polybios, an authority by no means to be despised, relates that Syphax was led in the triumph' (30.45.5, cf. Polybios 16.23.6, Tacitus, *Annales* 12.38). This is Livy's sole reference to his great Greek predecessor, and his cavalier acknowledgment of his great debt to him is somewhat shabby to say the very least.
21. Strabo 17.3.15 (agriculture). It is interesting to note that these Numidian coins usually show (obverse) Syphax and Masinissa (bearded profiles) wearing a diadem, the Hellenistic symbol of kingship, tied round the head, and (reverse) a cantering Numidian horse or horseman.
22. Polybios 14.7.9.
23. Ibid. 8.11.
24. Ibid. 8.13.

Chapter 12

1. The chief missile of all North African peoples was unquestionably the broad-bladed javelin rather than the bow, although the Numidian contingent sent to support the Romans during their siege of Numantia (134-133 BC) included a dozen elephants (African forest) 'and a body of archers and slingers who usually accompanied them in war' (Appian, *Iberica* 16.89). According to Caesar (*Bellum Gallicum* 2.7, 10), Numidian archers and slingers served under him in Gaul. However, though he employed archers in his tactical armoury, he rarely used them in large numbers. In Africa, at Ruspina, he mustered just 150 bowmen alongside 30 cohorts of legionaries (Anon. *Bellum Africum* 12). Some weeks later, at the Cercina islands, he received reinforcements from Italy, which included two more legions, 800 Gallic horsemen and 1,000 slingers and archers (ibid. 34).
2. A second-century BC prince's tomb at Es Soumâa near El Khroub, Algeria, contained, along with some iron javelin heads and pointed iron butt-spikes, a sword with a blade approximately 60cm long: Connolly (1998), p.150. According to Feugère (1993), p.79-81 the sword was originally 70.5cm long (now actually 67cm) and should perhaps be included among the group of known Roman republican swords, viz. the classic legionary sword, *gladius Hispaniensis*. Perhaps it was taken in battle, thus providing its new owner with a trophy of war. The tomb, which also contained an iron conical helmet, with ears embossed at the sides, and an iron mail shirt, dates from between 130-110 BC, close to the time of Iugurtha and Marius.
3. Livy 35.11.7, Polybios 3.71.11, Herodotos 4.175, Strabo 17.3.7.
4. Spring (1993), p.30, 43.
5. Sallust, *Bellum Iugurthinum* 80.2 (training discipline), 38.6, Appian, *Numidica* fr. 3 (Thracians, Ligurians), Sallust, *Bellum Iugurthinum* 56.2, cf. 38.6, 62.6 (deserters).
6. Livy 21.46.5, 35.11.7, Anon. *Bellum Africum* 48.1, 61.1, Silius Italicus, *Punica* 1.215-19, Lucan, *Pharsalia* 4.685.

7. Polybios 3.71.10, Appian, *Bellum Punicum* 2.11, 10.71.
8. Polybios 1.47.7, cf. Sallust, *Bellum Iugurthinum* 54.4, 74.3, Frontinus, *Strategemata* 2.1.13.
9. Livy 25.41.4, 28.44.5, 29.23.4, 30.12.18.
10. Aelian, *de natura animalium* 3.2.
11. For a description of the small Barbary horse common in North Africa before the arrival of the Muslim Arabs and their horses, see Hyland (1990), p.12.
12. Livy 35.11.7. Note here too an appliqué terracotta plaque of south Italian origin, circa mid-third century BC, depicting a Numidian horseman (Paris, musée du Louvre, inv. 5223), and a series of pre-Roman stelae from Algeria showing bearded men on horseback armed with two or three javelins and a small, round, boss-less shield (*Encyclopédie Berbère* 1: sv 'Abizar').
13. Strabo 17.3.7, *CIL* 4.10047, 10053.
14. Sallust, *Bellum Iugurthinum* 75.3. Use of a pack train was the most mobile logistical method, but it was still slow and unwieldy. It was also of limited duration, a pack mule would eat all the grain it could carry in around twenty days.
15. Xenophon, *Hipparchikos* 1.3.
16. Ewer (1982), p.118.
17. Hyland (1990), p.40.
18. Dixon-Southern (1992), p.209.
19. *P. Amh.* 107.
20. Davies (1989), p.187.
21. Varro, *On Agriculture* 1.31.4-5, Columella, *On Agriculture* 2.10.31, Pliny, *Historia Naturalis* 18.142.
22. Polybios 6.39.13 with Hyland (1990): 90, cf. Roth (1999), p.64.
23. E.g. Suetonius, *Divus Augustus* 24.2, Frontinus, *Strategemata* 4.1.37, Plutarch, *Antony* 39.7, Vegetius 1.13.
24. Fink 1, 2 (Doura-Europos), 70, 80 (Egypt).
25. Strabo 11.13.7.
26. Hyland (1990), p.41.
27. Columella, *On Agriculture* 2.10.25.
28. Strabo 17.3.19.
29. Napoléon, *Military Maxims* I.
30. Cf. Xenophon, *Kynegetikos* 12.
31. Livy 30.7.11, 8.8.
32. Appian, *Bellum civilia* 2.45
33. Caesar, *Bellum civile* 2.25.4
34. Anon. *Bellum Africum* 69.5
35. Ibid.78.2
36. Napoléon, *Military Maxims* L.
37. du Picq (1946), p.92.
38. Keegan (1988), p.83.
39. Napoléon, *Military Maxims* LI.

CHAPTER 13

1. Sallust says the two brothers 'died of disease' (*Bellum Iugurthinum* 6.1).
2. Ibid. 8.1. This theme is repeated again by Sallust, viz: 'everything at Rome had its price' (ibid. 20.1).
3. Ibid. 11.6, cf. 9.3.
4. Ibid. 20.3.
5. Ibid. 21.5.
6. Ibid. 23.1.
7. Cf. the notice in Livy, *Periochae* 64 makes the killing of Adherbal the reason for war, there being

no mention of the slaughtered Italians. Cirta was an important centre for the grain trade, hence the number of Italians resident there.
8. Sallust, *Bellum Iugurthinum* 35.10: 'A city for sale and doomed to speedy destruction if it finds a purchaser', repeated almost verbatim by both Appian (*Numidica* fr. 1) and Florus (*Epitome* 1.36.18).
9. Sallust, *Bellum Iugurthinum* 44.
10. Ibid. 45.6.
11. Caesar, *Bellum civile* 2.31.6.
12. Sallust, *Bellum Iugurthinum* 48-53 *passim*.
13. Ibid. 56.3.
14. As Sallust make clear, 'many Italians used to settle there for purposes of trade' (*Bellum Iugurthinum* 47.1). Direct beneficiaries of the exploitation of the growing empire were those bankers and commercial entrepreneurs who took advantage of the fact that it was impossible for members of the senatorial order overtly to obtain money by usury or commercial speculation. Such activity in fact contradicted the system of aristocratic standards on which their prestige and authority relied. It was certainly not due to lack of keenness on their part. But since they were unable to get rich (or richer) directly by these means, they were obliged to deal through associates who represented them in all matters, even the shadiest, in which they had interests. Thus the bankers, usurers, shipowners, large and small commercial entrepreneurs who dealt in wheat, olive oil, wine or slaves, the *negotiators* (sing. *negotiator*) whose numbers and importance always increased, who spread through the provinces as early as the second century BC. These individuals did not need any specific civic qualifications as they looked after functions that had no direct relationship with the management of the state's interests. They might or might not be Roman citizens, viz. equestrians (e.g. ibid. 65.4), and there were many Italians among them. Thus we find in the pages of Sallust Italian traders not only in Cirta and Vaga, but in Utica too (ibid. 64.5). See Badian (1972) chapters 3 & 5.
15. Rutilius was very much interested in the science of warfare, and was to gain a well deserved reputation as a military theorist and author; the excellent narration (*Bellum Iugurthinum* 48-53 *passim*) of the Muthul battle strongly suggests Sallust used him as the source here, though sadly for us Rutilius' memoirs have been extinguished by the malevolence of time. Rutilius, as one of the consuls for 105 BC, was to introduce the methods of the gladiatorial schools into military training (Valerius Maximus 2.3.2). The following year, while he was busy making preparations for the war against the Cimbri and Teutones, Marius was so impressed by the soldiers trained by Rutilius that he preferred them to his own, choosing 'the army of Rutilius, though it was the smaller of the two, because he thought it was the better trained' (Frontinus, *Strategemata* 4.2.2). Of course it should not be forgotten that Rutilius had seen service in the field, beginning, like so many who come into the story of Iugurtha, at Numantia (Appian, *Iberica* 88). Apart from Marius, Caius Memmius (*tr. pl.* 111 BC) was also there (Frontinus, *Strategemata* 4.1.1), and, perhaps, Marcus Aemilius Scaurus (*cos.* 115 BC) too (cf. Anon. *de viris illustribus* 72.3).
16. Here Sallust (*Bellum Iugurthinum* 50.2) actually uses the term *cohortes* and not *manipuli*. Whether or not this is an inconsistency on Sallust's part, for Marius is supposed to have introduced this change after the Iugurthine War, not during it.
17. Ibid 51.3. Cohorts of legionaries are referred to once more by Sallust (ibid. 100.4), this time during Marius' second campaign.
18. Ibid. 53.1.
19. Ibid. 53.4.
20. Livy, *Periochae* 65, Velleius Paterculus, *Historiae Romanae* 2.11.2, Florus, *Epitome* 1.36.10-12, Eutropius 4.27.2.
21. Ibid. 56-60 *passim*. Iugurtha had strengthened the garrisoned at Zama with deserters from the Roman army, desperadoes who dare not fail in their mission to defend the place knowing full well the terrible punishment meted out to those who forsake Rome.

22. Ibid. 61.2.
23. Ibid. 62.10.
24. Ibid. 70-72 *passim*. In fact, Metellus had begun his African campaign with an attempt to ensnare or to liquidate Iugurtha, tampering with envoys of the king before he took the field (ibid. 46.4). He tried again after the occupation of Vaga (ibid. 47.4). According to Frontinus (*Strategemata* 1.8.8), Metellus urged the envoys sent to him by Iugurtha to deliver their master prisoner to him, and for the same purpose kept up a correspondance with them after they had left him until Iugurtha, discovering it, grew so suspicious of them that he put them to death - on one pretence or another.
25. Sallust, *Bellum Iugurthinum* 73.1.
26. Ibid. 81.2.
27. Ibid. 82.2. Of course, little did the horrified Metellus realize at the time that this consulship proved to be the first of seven, more than any man, let alone a *novus homo*, had ever held before. What is even more startling is that five were held in consecutive years between 104 BC and 100 BC, whilst the seventh he seized, along with Rome, with armed force in 86 BC. In many ways the spectacular career of Marius was to provide a model for the great warlords of the last decades of the Republic. He came from the local aristocracy, *domi nobiles*, of the central Italian hill-town of Arpinum (Arpino), which had received Roman citizenship only thirty-one years before his birth. See Fields (2008B), p.37-40, 50.
28. Sallust, *Bellum Iugurthinum* 6.1.
29. Polybios 3.116.5, Appian, *Bellum Punicum* 11, Caesar, *Bellum civile* 2.41, Anon. *Bellum Africum* 14-15 *passim*, 70.2, 71.2, Frontinus, *Strategemata* 1.5.16.
30. Sallust, *Bellum Iugurthinum* 48.2-50.6, 54.9-10, 55.8.
31. Ibid. 84.4.
32. Plutarch, *Marius* 9.1, cf. Sallust, *Bellum Iugurthinum* 86.4, Aulus Gellius, *Noctes Atticae* 16.10.10.
33. Appian, *Bellum civilia* 1.57. See Fields (2008B), p.48-52.
34. Sallust, *Bellum Iugurthinum* 88.3.
35. Ibid. 91.6-7, 92.3 cf. 54.6, 55.4-6.
36. Ibid. 89-91 *passim*.
37. Ibid. 92.1.
38. Ibid. 90.1.
39. Ibid. 92.5, also at 19.7, 110.8. With the geography of North Africa, Sallust, erstwhile Caesarian governor of Africa Nova (former eastern Numidia), is economical, specifying only three rivers and seven settlements in the theatre of operations covered by the marches and battles of Metellus and Marius. We assume this was all for brevity and not wishing to overburden the narration. The Moulouya forms the frontier between Algeria and Morocco.
40. Ibid. 94.7.
41. Ibid. 95.1.
42. Ibid. 97.5.
43. Ibid. 101.1, 102.1.
44. Plutarch, *Marius* 7.5.
45. Pliny, *Historia Naturalis* 37.1.9, Plutarch, *Marius* 10.4.
46. Sallust, *Bellum Iugurthinum* 113.6.
47. Whereas Marius prided himself on being provincial, his now bitterest foe Sulla was a patrician, not merely an aristocrat or a noble. However, his branch of the Cornelii had long fallen into obscurity and straitened circumstances. Sulla had thus entered politics relatively late in his life, indeed first seeing action as Marius' quaestor in Africa.
48. Gsell (1930), p.264.
49. Harris (1986), p.151.
50. Pliny, *Historia Naturalis* 5.19.
51. Anon. *Bellum Africum* 25.2. Having rendered signal service to him, Caesar was to give Cirta to Sittius, who then ruled there like a native vassal. Sittius was to be killed by a Numidian princeling soon after the Ides of March (Cicero, *Epistulae ad Atticum* 15.17.1).

ROMAN CONQUESTS: NOTES

CHAPTER 14

1. In Latin: *metus hostilis*, Sallust, *Bellum Iugurthinum* 41.2.
2. Harris (1986), p.127-8, 266-7.
3. E.g. Livy 1.9.4, 2.32.6, 39.7, 54.2, 3.9.1, etc.
4. Ibid. 22.37.8, 24.15.3, 20.16.
5. Justin, *Epitome* 21.4.7, Polybios 38.7.9, Appian, *Bellum Punicum* 111. We also know that back in 406 BC the Carthaginian army that landed in Sicily had included Moors (and Numidians) 'who were their allies' (Diodoros 13.80.3).
6. Law (1978), p.188.
7. Polybios 15.11.1.
8. Livy 22.37.8-9. Polybios says (3.75.7) the Senate actually appealed to Hiero for these mercenaries, and adds they amounted to 500 Cretan archers and 1,000 javelineers. The patriotic Livy obviously prefers to overlook what he considered an abase act.
9. Strabo 17.3.9, cf. Anon. *Bellum Africum* 25.2, Appuleius, *Apologia* 24.1.
10. Pliny, *Historia Naturalis* 5.17, cf. Law (1978), p.143, Brett-Fentress (1996), p.42.
11. Livy 23.18.1.
12. E.g. Anon. *Bellum Africum* 32, 56, 61.
13. Sallust, *Bellum Iugurthinum* 18.1-2, cf. Cassius Dio 53.26.2.
14. E.g. Sallust, *Bellum Iugurthinum* 13.5-8, 15.1, 3, 15.5-16.1, 3-4, 20.1.
15. Ibid. 25.4, Pliny, *Historia Naturalis* 8.223.
16. E.g. Cicero, *pro Murena* 16, 36, *Brutus* 112.
17. Sallust, *Bellum Iugurthinum* 28.5.
18. Ibid. 40.
19. Ibid. 65.5. The five are named in Cicero, *Brutus* 128.
20. Sallust, *Bellum Iugurthinum* 40.4.
21. Syme (2002), p.168.
22. Sallust announces this, his main theme, in *Bellum Iugurthinum* 5.1.
23. In Latin: *avidus belli gerundi*, ibid. 35.3.
24. Livy, *Periochae* 64.
25. Sallust, *Bellum Iugurthinum* 38.
26. Sallust, amongst other crimes, talks of Iugurtha's 'skilful agents who worked night and day to corrupt the Roman army, bribing *centuriones* and *decuriones* either to desert or to abandon their posts at a given signal' (ibid. 38.3).

EPILOGUE

1. Virgil, *Aeneid* 1.437 West.
2. Polybios 36.9.
3. Plato, *Laws* 3.698b-c, Aristotle, *Politics* 1334a. Of course, we are all familiar with the famous dictum of Lord Acton: 'Power tends to corrupt, and absolute power corrupts absolutely', letter to Bishop Mandell Creighton, 3 April 1887.
4. Sallust, *Bellum Iugurthinum* 41.2-42.2
5. Sallust was called the Roman Thucydides (Velleius Paterculus, *Historiae Romanae* 2.36.2, Quintilian 10.1.101), and his style is certainly Thucydidean, with its pessimism, satire, and subversion. With Rome replacing Athens, it was a style fit for a story of imperial decline. However, as we have already touched upon, this decline for Sallust is moral not political, the corruption of virtue by ambition and greed.
6. Sallust first airs this, one of his pet themes, in *Bellum Catilinae* 10.
7. Florus, *Epitome* 1.47.2.

APPENDIX 1: ROMAN POLITICS

1. Messalla, *ap.* Aulus Gellius, *Noctes Atticae* 13.15.4.
2. Cicero, *pro Murena* 38. For the function of a consul, see especially, Polybios 6.12. Cicero was consul in 63 BC, the year of the so-called conspiracy of Catiline. See Fields (2008B), p.72-6.
3. Festus 290 Lindsay.
4. Cf. Polybios 6.13-14 *passim.*
5. In Latin: *Senatus consultum,* and abbreviated as *SC,* as on coinage from the mint at Rome under the Senate's control.
6. Gibbon, *Decline & Fall,* vol. I, p. 23.

APPENDIX 2: THE ROMAN ARMY

1. It was the doyen of modern military historians, Hans Delbrück (1975: 275), who first characterised the Roman legion as a phalanx with joints.
2. Polybios 6.11-18 *passim* (constitution), 19-42 *passim* (army).
3. Polybios 6.26.7.
4. Ibid. 26.9. According to Livy (9.30.3), the latest possible date for the regular number of legions to double to four was 311 BC. Polybios (3.109.12) has Rome levying and supporting four active legions each year for annual service, which were supplemented by an equal number of soldiers provided by the *socii.*
5. Polybios 6.19.2.
6. Ibid. 21.1.
7. Ibid. 20.8-9. Elsewhere Polybios refers to the standard complement of 4,000 infantry and 300 cavalry (1.16.2) and of 4,000 infantry and 200 cavalry (3.107.10), and does suggest that there were sometimes fewer than 4,000 infantry per legion (6.21.10).
8. Ibid. 21.7.The same order for the three lines appears elsewhere in Polybios' narrative (14.8.5, 15.9.7), and in Livy's also (30.8.5, 32.11, 34.10) as well as in other antiquarian sources (e.g. Varro, *de lingua Latina* 5.89).
9 Polybios 6.21.7, 24.4
10. Cicero, *Tusculanae disputationes* 2.16.37.
11. Vegetius 1.1.
12. Polybios 6.25.10.
13. Ibid. 23.6.
14. Cf. Dionysios of Halikarnassos says 'cavalry spears' (20.11.2), viz. hoplite spears, were still being employed in battle by the *principes* during the war with Pyrrhos (280-275 BC).
15. Polybios 2.33.4.
16. Livy 10.39.12, cf. Plutarch, *Pyrrhos* 21.9, Polybios 1.40.12
17. Ibid. 6.23.9-11.
18. Polybios fr. 179 with Walbank (1957), p.704.
19. Livy 31.34.4.
20. Polybios 3.114.2-4, Livy 22.46.6.
21. Polybios 6.23.14-15.
22. Ibid. 23.12-13.
23. Ibid. 23.8, Arrian, *Ars Tactica* 3.5.
24. Walbank (1957), p.703-4, Cornell (1995), p.170.
25. Polybios 6.23.2-5, Connolly (1998), p.132.
26. Livy 38.21.15.
27. Polybios 6.22.1-3.
28. Livy 26.4.4, Lucilius, *Satires* 7.290.
29. Polybios 6.20.8-9, 25.1, cf. 2.24.13, Livy 3.62.

Roman Conquests: Notes

30. Polybios 6.25.1-2.
31. Ibid. 20.9.
32. Plutarch, *Cato major* 1.3.
33. Livy 23.7.2, 24.13.1.
34. Polybios 6.39.14-15.
35. Ibid. 25.3-8.
36. In Latin: *equestris parma*, Livy 2.20.10, cf. 4.28.
37. Ibid. 31.34.4.
38. The saddle was certainly a part of Roman cavalry equipment in the time of Caesar, a concession, so he says (*Bellum Gallicum* 4.4.2), considered effete by the Germans. The padded saddle with four horns made by internal bronze stiffeners appears for the first time on Roman sculptures (Arc d' Orange, Mausoleum at Saint-Rémy-de-Provence) of the early Principate. Like most equestrian equipment, it was almost certainly of Celtic origin as it is depicted on the Gundestrop cauldron (which probably pre-dates the first century BC).
39. Hyland (1990), p.130-4.
40. Livy 8.8.5.
41. E.g. Adcock (1940), p.9, Keppie (1998), p.39, Goldsworthy (2000A), p.44.
42. Keppie (1998), p.38-9.
43. Ennius, *Annales* fr. 284 Vahlen.
44. Polybios 15.12.8, cf. 1.34.2.
45. Ibid. 18.30.6-8.
46. Plutarch, *Cato major* 1.4.
47. Polybios 6.23.6-7.
48. Bishop-Coulston (1993), p.53, Feugère (1993), p.79.
49. Polybios 18.30.6.
50. Vegetius 1.12.
51. Tacitus, *Annales* 2.14, 21, 14.36, *Historiae* 2.42, *Agricola* 36.2.
52. Polybios 2.30.9.
53. Ibid. 33.6.
54. Ibid. 6.23.4.
55. Livy 8.8.9.
56. Polybios 15.15.7-10
57. du Picq (1946), p.53.

Bibliography

ABBREVIATIONS

Burstein: S.M. Burstein, *Translated Documents of Greece and Rome 3: The Hellenistic Age from the battle of Ipsos to the death of Kleopatra VII* (Cambridge, 1985)

CIL: T. Mommsen *et al.*, *Corpus Inscriptionum Latinarum* (Berlin, 1862-)

FGrHist: F. Jacoby, *Die Fragmente der griechischen Historiker* (Berlin/Leiden, 1923-1958)

Fink: R.O. Fink, *Roman Military Records on Papyrus* (New Haven, 1971)

P. Amh.: B.P. Grenfell & A.S. Hunt, *The Amhurst Papyri* (London, 1900-1901)

SHA: *Scripturae Historiae Augustae* (London, 1932)

Adcock, F.E., *The Roman Art of War under the Republic* (Cambridge, MA: Harvard University Press, 1940)
Ardent du Picq, C., (trans. Col. J. Greely & Maj. R. Cotton 1920, repr. 1946) *Battle Studies: Ancient and Modern* (Harrisburg, PA: U.S. Army War College, 1903)
Astin, A.E., *Scipio Aemilianus* (Oxford: Clarendon Press, 1967)
Astin, A.E., 'Saguntum and the origins of the Second Punic War', *Latomus* 26 (1967), pp.577-96
Badian, E., *Foreign Clientalae* (Oxford: Clarendon Press, 1958)
Badian, E., *Publicans and Sinners: Private Enterprise in the Service of the Roman Republic* (Dunedin: University of Otago Press, 1972)
Bagnall, N., (repr. 1999) *The Punic Wars: Rome, Carthage and the Struggle for the Mediterranean* (London: Pimlico, 1990)
Barker, G.W.W. & Jones, G.D.B., 'The UNESCO Libyan valleys survey 1980', *Report of the Society for Libyan Studies* 12 (1980), pp.9-48
Bath, T., *Hannibal's Campaigns* (Cambridge: Patrick Stephens, 1981)
de Beer, G., *Hannibal's March* (London: Sidgwick & Jackson, 1967)
de Beer, G., *Hannibal* (London: Thames & Hudson, 1969)
Bishop, M.C. and Coulston, J.C.N., *Roman Military Equipment from the Punic Wars to the fall of Rome* (London: Batsford, 1993)

Braudel, F., (trans. S. Reynolds 2001) *The Mediterranean World in the Ancient World* (London: Penguin, 1998)

Brett, M. & Fentress, E.W.B., *The Berbers* (Oxford: Blackwell, 1996)

Brunt, P.A., *Italian Manpower 225 BC - AD 14* (Oxford: Oxford University Press, 1971)

Brunt, P.A., *Social Conflicts in the Roman Republic* (London: Chatto & Windus, 1982)

Camps, G., *Aux origines de la Berbérie: monuments et rites funéraires protohistoriques* (Paris: Arts et métiers graphiques, 1962)

Carey, B.T., Allfree, J.B. & Cairns, J., *Warfare in the Ancient World* (Barnsley: Pen & Sword, 2005)

Carney, T.F., 'Plutarch's style in the *Marius*' *Journal of Hellenic Studies* 80 (1960), pp. 24-31

Carney, T.F., *A Biography of Caius Marius* (Assen: Royal van Gorcum, 1962) (Proceedings of the African Classical Association 1)

Claassen, J-M., 'Sallust's Jugurtha - Rebel or Freedom Fighter? On Crossing Crocodile-Infested Waters' *Classical World* 86 (1993), pp.273-97

Connolly, P., (repr. 1988, 1998) *Greece and Rome at War* (Mechanicsburg, PA: Stackpole, 1981)

Cornell, T.J., *The Beginnings of Rome* (London: Routledge, 1995)

Cornell, T.J., Rankov, N.B. & Sabin, P. (eds.), *The Second Punic War: A Reappraisal* (London: University of London Press, 1996) (Bulletin of the Institute of Classical Studies 67)

Crawford, M.H., (2nd edn.) *The Roman Republic* (London: Fontana, 1993)

Daly, G., *Cannae: The Experience of Battle in the Second Punic War* (London: Routledge, 2002)

Davies, R.W., *Service in the Roman Army* (Edinburgh: Edinburgh University Press, 1989)

Dawson, D., *The Origins of Western Warfare* (Boulder, CO: Westview, 1996)

Delbrück, H., (trans. W.J. Renfroe, 1975) *History of the Art of War within the Framework of Political History*, vol. 1 (Westport, CT: Greenwood Press, 1920)

Dixon, K.R. & Southern, P., *The Roman Cavalry, from the First to the Third Century AD* (London: Batsford, 1992)

Errington, R.M., *The Dawn of Empire: Rome's Rise to World Power* (London: Hamilton, 1971)

Ewer, T.K., *Practical Animal Husbandry* (Bristol: John Wright & Sons, 1982)

Feugère, M., *Les armes romains de la république à l'antiquité tardive* (Paris: Editions du Centre national de la recherché scientifique, 1993)

Fields, N., *The Roman Army of the Punic Wars 264 – 146 BC* (Oxford: Osprey, 2007) (Battle Orders 27)

Fields, N., *The Walls of Rome* (Oxford: Osprey, 2008A) (Fortress 71)

Fields, N., *Warlords of Republican Rome: Caesar versus Pompey* (Barnsley: Pen & Sword, 2008B)

Fields, N., *Tarentine Horseman of Magna Graecia 430 – 190 BC* (Oxford: Osprey, 2008C) (Warrior 130)

Frost, H., 'The Punic wreck off Sicily', *Mariner's Mirror* 59 (1973), pp.229-30

Frost, H., 'The Punic wreck in Sicily', *International Journal Nautical Archaeology* 3.1 (1974), pp.35-54

Frost, H., 'La réconstruction du navire punique de Marsala', *Archeologia* 170 (1982), pp.42-50

Garouphalias, P., *Pyrrhus, King of Epirus* (London: Stacy International, 1979)

Giustolisi, V., *Le nave romane di Terrasina e l'avventura di Amilcare sul Monte Heirkte* (Palermo, 1975)

Gaebel, R.E., *Cavalry Operations in the Ancient Greek World* (Norman, OK: University of Oklahoma Press, 2002)

Goldsworthy, A.K., *Roman Warfare* (London: Cassell, 2000A)

Goldsworthy, A.K., *The Punic Wars* (London: Cassell, 2000B)

Goldsworthy, A.K., *Cannae* (London: Cassell, 2001)

Goldsworthy, A.K., *The Complete Roman Army* (London: Thames & Hudson, 2003)

Grainger, J.D., *The Roman War of Antiochus the Great* (Leiden/Boston: Brill, 2002) (Mnemosyne Supplementa)

Graeme, D., *Fighting Talk* (Oxford: Osprey, 2008)

Griffith, G.T., (repr. 1984) *The Mercenaries of the Hellenistic World* (Chicago: Ares Publishers, 1935)

Gsell, S., (3e éd.) *Histoire ancienne de l'Afrique du Nord*, vol. 2 (Paris, 1928)

Gsell, S., *Histoire ancienne de l'Afrique du Nord*, vol. 7 (Paris, 1930)

Hammond, N.G.L., (repr. 1992) *The Macedonian State: the Origins, Institutions and History* (Oxford: Clarendon Press, 1989)

Harris, W.V., *War and Imperialism in Republican Rome, 327 – 70 BC* (Oxford: Clarendon Press, 1986)

Head, D., *Armies of the Macedonian and Punic Wars 359 BC – 146 BC* (Worthing: Wargames Research Group, 1982)

Hopkins, K., *Conquerors and Slaves* (Cambridge: Cambridge University Press, 1978)

Hoyos, D., (repr. 2004) *Hannibal's Dynasty: Power and Politics in the Western Mediterranean, 247 – 183 BC* (London: Routledge, 2003)

Hoyos, D., *Hannibal: Rome's Greatest Enemy* (Exeter: Bristol Phoenix Press, 2008)

Hurst, H., 'Excavations at Carthage, 1977-8. Fourth interim report', *Antiquaries Journal* 59 (1979), pp.19-49

Hurst, H., 'Le port militaire de Carthage', *Dossiers d'Archéologie* 183 (1993), pp.42-51

Hyland, A., *Equus: the Horse in the Roman World* (London: Batsford, 1990)

Jones, B.W., 'Rome's relationship with Carthage: a study in aggression', *The Classical Bulletin* 49 (1972), pp.5-26

Keppie, L.J.F, (repr. 1998) *The Making of the Roman Army: From Republic to Empire* (London: Routledge, 1984)
de Kistler, J.M., *War Elephants* (Westport, CT: Praeger Publishers, 2005)
Lancel, S., (trans. A. Nevill 1995) *Carthage* (Oxford: Blackwell, 1992)
Lancel, S., (trans. A. Nevill 1998, repr. 1999) *Hannibal* (Oxford: Blackwell, 1995)
Law, R.C.C., 'The Berber kingdoms in North Africa', in J.D. Fage (ed.) *Cambridge History of Africa*, vol. 2 (Cambridge: Cambridge University Press, 1978) pp.176-91
Lazenby, J.F., *Hannibal's War: A Military History of the Second Punic War* (Warminster: Aris & Phillips, 1978)
Lazenby. J.F., *The First Punic War: A Military History* (London: University College London Press, 1996)
Lind, L.R., 'The tradition of Roman moral conservatism', in C. Deroux (ed.) *Studies in Latin Literature and Roman History*, (Brussels: Latomus, 1979), pp.7-58
McEvedy, C., (2nd ed.) *The New Penguin Atlas of Ancient History* (London: Penguin, 2002)
Mattingly, D.J., 'War and peace in Roman North Africa: observations and models of state-tribe interaction', in R.B. Ferguson and N.L. Whitehead (eds.) *War in the Tribal Zone: Expanding States and Indigenous Warfare* (Oxford: James Currey, 2000), chapter 2
Morrison, J. (ed.), *The Age of the Galley: Mediterranean Oared Vessels since pre-classical Times* (London: Conway Maritime Press, 1995)
Moscati, S. (ed.), (repr. 2001) *The Phoenicians* (London: I.B. Tauris, 1997)
Nillson, M.P., 'The introduction of hoplite tactics at Rome', *Journal for Roman Studies* 19 (1929), pp.1-11
Nossov, K.S., *War Elephants* (Oxford: Osprey, 2008) (New Vanguard 150)
Parke, H.W., *Greek Mercenary Soldiers: From the Earliest Times to the Battle of Ipsus* (Oxford: Clarendon Press, 1933)
Parker, H.M.D., (repr. 1958) *The Roman Legions* (Cambridge: Heffer & Sons, 1928)
Paul, G.M., *A Historical Commentary on Sallust's* Bellum Iugurthinum (Liverpool: Francis Cairns, 1984) (Classical and Medieval Texts, Papers and Monographs 13)
van Ooteghem, J., *Gaius Marius* (Brussels: Latomus, 1964)
Picard, C. G. & C., (trans. D. Collon, 1969) *The Life and Death of Carthage* (London, 1968)
Proctor, D., *Hannibal's March in History* (Oxford, 1971)
Rawson, E., 'The literary sources for the pre-Marian Roman army', *Papers for the British School at Rome* 39 (1971), pp.13-31
Ridley, R.J., 'Was Scipio Africanus at Cannae?' *Latomus* 34 (1975), pp.161-5
Roth, J.P., *The Logistics of the Roman Army at War (264 BC – AD 235)* (Leiden: Brill, 1999)

Rostovtzeff, M., 'Numidian horsemen on Canosa vases', *American Journal of Archaeology* 50 (1946), pp.263-7 with pls. 11 & 12

de Sanctis G., (2nd ed.) *Storia dei Romani*, vol. 3.2 (Florence, 1968)

Scullard, H.H., *Scipio Africanus, Soldier and Politician* (London: Thames & Hudson, 1970)

Scullard, H.H., *The Elephant in the Greek and Roman World* (London: Thames & Hudson, 1974)

Seibert, J., *Hannibal* (Darmstadt: Wissenschaftliche Buchgesellschaft, 1993)

Spring, C., *African Arms and Armour* (London: British Museum Press, 1993)

Sumner, G.V., 'Roman policy in Spain before the Hannibalic War', *Harvard Studies in Classical Philology* 72 (1967), pp.205-46

Sumner, G.V., 'The legion and the centuriate organization', *Journal of Roman Studies* 60 (1970), pp.61-78

Syme, R., (repr. 2002) *Sallust* (Berkeley & Los Angeles/London: University of California Press, 1964)

Thiel, J.H., *A History of Roman Sea-Power before the Second Punic War* (Amsterdam: North-Holland, 1954)

Walbank, F.W., *A Historical Commentary on Polybios*, vol.1 (Oxford: Clarendon Press, 1957)

Walbank, F.W., *A Historical Commentary on Polybios*, vol.2 (Oxford: Clarendon Press, 1970)

Wallinga, H.T., *The Boarding-Bridge of the Romans* (Groningen: J.B. Wolters, 1956)

Warry, J., *Warfare in the Classical World* (London: Salamander, 1980)

Wiedemann, T.E.J., 'Sallust's *Jugurtha*: Concord, Discord, and the Digressions', *Greece & Rome* 40.1 (1993), pp.48-57

Wise, T. & Healy, M., (repr. 2002) *Hannibal's War with Rome: The Armies and Campaigns 216 BC* (Oxford: Osprey, 1999)

Zhmodikov, A., 'Roman Republican Heavy Infantryman in Battle (IV-II centuries BC)', *Historia* 49 (2000), pp.67-78

Index

Adherbal (Carthaginian admiral) 40, 161 n. 39
Adherbal (son of Micipsa) 103, 104-5, 115, 116, 119
Aegates Islands 39, 42, 159 n. 9
    battle of (241 BC) 34, 42, 159 n. 7
Aelian 96, 98
Aemilius
    Lucius Aemilius Paullus (cos. 218 BC) 83, 166 n. 35
    Lucius Aemilius Paullus minor 138, 172 n. 25
    Marcus Aemilius Scaurus (cos. 115 BC) 116, 176 n. 15
Aeneas xix, xxv-xxvi, 2, 50, 121, 149 n. 11, 162 n. 52
Aeneid, the xvii, xxv, 121, 149 n. 11
Africa *passim*
Agathokles of Syracuse xxv, 15, 17, 24, 28, 29, 30, 33, 67, 150 n. 12, 152 n. 32, 154 n. 53, 158 nn. 18, 20 & 21
ager Falernus 166 n. 26
Ahenobarbus, Domitius, Altar of 138
Akragas (Agrigentum) 18, 35, 84, 157 n. 11
    siege of (262-261 BC) 18, 24, 84, 157 n. 13, 159 n. 7
Akrotatos of Sparta 158 n. 21
ala/alae 52, 69-70, 71, 90, 108, 126, 127, 135, 161 n. 29
Alalia (Aleria) 8, 25
Alaric (the Visigoth) 68
Albinus
    Albinus, Aulus Postumius (brother of below) 119-20
    Albinus, Spurius Postumius (cos. 110 BC) 118, 119
Alexander the Great 13, 22, 31, 56, 57, 67, 74, 144, 151 n. 20, 152 n. 14, 154 n. 42, 158 nn. 20 & 21

Alexander of Molossia 158 n. 21
Alexon (Greek mercenary) 18
Alps 1, 23, 52, 57, 76, 84, 85, 117, 156 n. 94, 165 n. 23, 166 n. 34, 167 n. 5
Altars of the Philaeni (Arae Philaenorum) 7, 152 n. 36
Antigonos I ('Monophthalmos') 155 n. 81, 159 nn. 26 & 37
Antigonos II of Macedon ('Gonatas') 31-2, 159 n. 37
Antiochos III of Syria ('the Great') xv, 50, 74, 75, 77, 170 nn. 4 & 12, 171 n. 3
Apamea 22, 146 n. 28
Appian 3, 62, 65, 82, 100, 111, 166 n. 34, 167 n. 5, 169 n. 16, 172 nn. 16 & 18, 176 n. 8
Apulians 30
Archimedes 53, 166 n. 29
Archidamos (Spartan king) 158 n. 21
Ardent du Picq, Charles 59, 101, 144
Aristotle 9-10, 13, 121, 152 nn. 1 & 14
Arno, river 171 n. 3
Artaxata 170 n. 10
Artaxias (Armenian king) 170 n. 10
Asculum, battle of (279 BC) 26, 29
Aspis (Clupea, Kelibia) 38, 44
Atilius
    Marcus Atilius Regulus (cos. 255) 24, 38-9, 40, 42-4, 55, 67, 161 nn. 31 & 33,
Aufidus, river 66
Augustus (Octavianus) xvi, xvii, xxi, xxiii, xxv-xxvi, 129, 130, 146 n. 35, 147 nn. 37 & 42, 49 n. 7
Autaritos 19, 47, 48, 163 n. 11

Baal Hammon 92, 148 n. 5,
Baal Shamaim, temple of 50
Baecula, battle of (208 BC) 54
Baetis (Guadalquivir), river 49

186

INDEX

Bagradas (Medjerda), river/valley/plain 1, 3, 6, 43, 67, 106, 173 n. 15
Balearic Islands, slingers 19, 62, 65, 115
Bocchus 109, 112-13, 114
Bomilcar (renegade general) 10
Bomilcar (admiral, Second Punic War) 72
Bomilcar (friend of Iugurtha) 107, 109, 119
Bon, Cap (Hermaia Promontory, Rass Adder) 25
Boudica, Queen xxv, 156 n. 84
Britons xxi, xxii, xxv
British Empire xxii, 147 nn. 38, 40 & 41, 148 n. 1
Bruttians 30, 62, 158 n. 21
Burning of the Camps (203 BC), the 88-90
Byrsa, the 2, 81, 82, 150 n. 1

Caesar xxii, 88, 100-1, 112, 113, 145 n. 12, 149 nn. 7 & 10, 151 n. 20, 165 n. 23, 171 n. 2, 174 n. 1, 177 n. 51, 180 n. 38
Caecilius
    Lucius Caecilius Metellus (cos. 251 BC) 24, 39
    Quintus Caecilius Metellus ('Numidicus') 96, 105-10, 111, 120, 177 nn. 24, 27 & 39
Calgacus xxiv, xxv
Campanians 15, 33, 45, 47, 113, 139, 159 n. 2
campus Martius 130, 132
Cannae, battle of (216 BC) 17, 20, 52, 53, 59, 60-1, 62, 63, 66, 67, 68-70, 72, 83, 134, 139, 152 n. 5, 165 n. 24, 169 nn. 4 & 16
Capsa (Gafsa) 111
Capua 53, 54, 69, 159 n. 2, 165-6 n. 26
Caratacus (Caractacus) xxiv, xxv, 148 n. 45
Carthage, Carthaginians passim
    army 14-17, 19-20, 164 n. 11
    city 2-4, 12-13, 23, 81-2
    constitution 9-10, 73, 152 n. 1
    empire 6-8, 49, 71-2
    foundation 1-3, 9, 148-9 n. 6
    navy 7-8, 11-14, 17, 31, 34-6, 40, 56, 69
    treaties with Rome 7, 12, 25-6, 42, 46, 50, 55-6, 73, 74, 77, 156 n. 2, 156-7 n. 4, 157 n. 5, 167 n. 42,
    senate 10, 51, 53, 72, 73-4, 75, 91, 159 n. 6, 170 n. 20

carvel construction 35-6
castra Cornelia 88
cavalry tactics 101-2
Celtiberians 19, 45, 88, 90-1, 137
Celts 10, 15, 19, 96, 140, 142
Centenius
    Marcus Centenius Paenula 55
Cercina, island (Kerkennah) 75, 174 n. 1
Claudius
    Appius Claudius Caudex (cos. 264 BC) 34, 160 n. 12
    Marcus Claudius Marcellus (cos. 222 BC etc.) 55
    Caius Claudius Nero (cos. 207 BC) 54
    Publius Claudius Pulcher (cos. 249 BC) 40, 161-2 n. 42
Claudius, emperor xxi-xxii, xxiv, 146 n. 33, 147 n. 36, 160 n. 26
Cicero xvi, xviii, xix, xx, 10, 53, 116, 118, 127, 128, 136, 147 n. 37, 149 n. 10, 154 n. 43, 170 n. 7, 171 n. 6, 172 n. 27, 179 n. 2
Cirta (Constantine) 86, 87, 91, 104-5, 109, 111, 112, 113, 116, 117, 119, 176 nn. 7 & 14, 177 n. 51
Clapier, Col du 165 n. 23
Columella 97-8
Cornelius
    Cnaeus Cornelius Scipio Calvus (cos. 221 BC) 53-4, 66, 86, 88
    Publius Cornelius Scipio (cos. 218 BC) 53-4, 66, 71, 86, 88
    Publius Cornelius Scipio ('Africanus')
        early career 53, 66-7
        later career 74, 170 nn. 4 & 5
        in Africa 61-6, 87-92
        at Great Plains 90-1
        at Zama 62-6, 83
    Lucius Cornelius Scipio (cos. 190 BC) 170 n. 4
    Publius Cornelius Scipio Nasica (cos. 162 BC etc.) 77-8
    Publius Cornelius Aemilianus Scipio (cos. 147 BC etc.)
        adoption 83, 172 n. 25
        in Africa 1, 3-4, 78, 81-2, 83-4, 119, 148 n. 1, 171 n. 6
        in Iberia 84, 102, 111, 171 n. 6
    Lucius Cornelius Sulla ('Felix') 110-11, 112, 125, 126, 168-9 n. 28, 177 n. 47

187

Corsica 7, 8, 15, 25, 46, 68, 171 n. 9
corvus 36-7, 38, 40, 160 n. 23
Cumae 41, 159 n. 2
Cyprus 2

Demetrios I of Macedon ('Poliorketes') 155 n. 81, 159 nn. 26 & 37,
Diodoros xxv, 3, 4, 6, 14, 15-16, 42, 84, 88, 148 n. 1, 150 n. 13, 154 nn. 44 & 61, 156 nn. 96 & 4, 157 nn. 11, 15 & 16, 159-60 n. 12, 161 nn. 34 & 39, 161-2 n. 42, 162 n. 58, 164 n. 3, 173 n. 11
Dionysios of Syracuse 28, 157 n. 15
Dionysios of Halikarnassos 179 n. 14
Dolchstaßlegende ('Dagger-stab-legend') 163 n. 1
Dido xxv-xxvi, 2, 50, 148 n. 53, 149 n. 11
diekplous, the   12, 13-14, 40
Drepana (Trapani) 39, 41, 161 n. 39, 162 n. 52
    battle of (249 BC) 14, 34, 40, 42, 44
Duilius, Caius (cos. 260 BC) 37-8
Durance, river 165 n. 23, 166 n. 34

Ecnomus, battle of (256 BC) 34, 38, 152 n. 13, 160 n. 27
Egesta (Segesta) 37
elephants
    use in war 21-4, 155 nn. 80 & 81, 156 nn. 82, 89 & 92
    of Carthage 3, 42-4, 54, 55, 56, 62-3, 65, 69, 156 nn. 84 & 94, 163 n. 7, 167 n. 5, 171 n. 3
    of Iugurtha 107, 108, 117, 118, 174 n. 1
    of Pyrrhos 29, 30, 31, 32, 158 nn. 23 & 24, 163 n. 64
Eryx (Monte San Giuliano) 18, 41, 86
Eshmun 82, 172 n. 19
Etruscans 16, 19, 25, 85, 165 n. 26
equites
    Servian class 131, 133
    citizen cavalry 135, 139- 40
Eumenes II of Pergamon 76

Fabius
    Quintus Fabius Pictor (historian) 84, 172 n. 30, 173 n. 17
Fair Promontory (*Pulchri Promontorium*, Rass Sidi Ali el Mekki) 25, 88

Flaminius, Caius (cos. 223 BC etc.) 58, 69
Flaubert, Gustave 162 n. 49, 173 n. 2
Florus 30-1, 57, 123, 158 n. 23
Fulvius
    Cnaeus Fulvius Centumalus Maximus 55
    Marcus Fulvius Flaccus 122

Gadir (Gades, Cádiz) xviii, 8, 55, 87, 151 nn. 20 & 23
Gaia (Maesulii king) 86, 87
Gallia Cisalpina 52, 55, 62, 73, 166 n. 34
Gallia Narbonensis 146-7 n. 36
Gauls xx, xxi, xxii, 15, 18, 19, 30, 35, 45, 47, 50, 55, 60, 62, 65, 66, 73, 85, 154 n. 61, 174 n. 1
Gaetulians xx, 109, 115
Gelon of Syracuse 16, 27, 28, 157 nn. 10 & 11
Gesco (general, First Punic War) 45, 47-8
Gibbon, Edward xvi, 130
Great Plains, battle of (203 BC) 90-1, 99, 173 n. 17
Greeks xx, xxi, xxiv, 2, 5, 10, 25, 26, 27, 59, 68, 83, 85, 134, 149 n. 11, 156 n. 1
    mercenaries 15-16, 17, 19, 45, 163 n. 3
    of Italy 29, 30, 34, 159 n. 2
    of Sicily 7, 14, 15, 28, 30, 154 n. 41, 157 nn. 9 & 10
Gulussa (son of Masinissa) 80, 101, 119

Hadrumentum (Sousse) 61
Hamilcar (son of Hanno) 15, 27, 157 n. 11
Hamilcar (general in Sicily) 15, 17
Hamilcar (general, First Punic War) 39, 154 n. 61
Hamilcar Barca (father of Hannibal) 18, 19, 41-2, 45, 46, 47-8, 49-50, 52, 56, 57, 72, 86, 162 nn. 49, 52 & 53, 163-4 n. 7, 164 nn. 4, 5 & 6, 170 n. 24
Hamilcar (general, Second Punic War) 73-4
Hannibal (Barca) *passim*
    as general 56-9
    Hannibal's oath 50, 164 n. 7
    '*Hannibal ad portas*' 68
Hannibal (grandson of Hamilcar [son of Hanno]) 15, 27-8
Hannibal (son of Hamilcar [general, First Punic War]) 39
Hannibal 'the Rhodian' 12, 40, 41, 161 n. 41

188

Hannibal Monomachos 85
Hanno (admiral, First Punic War) 41-2, 154 n. 61
Hanno ('the Great') 41, 45, 48, 159 n. 6, 162 nn. 46 & 49
Hasdrubal (son of Mago) 7
Hasdrubal the Splendid 49, 50, 57, 164 nn. 3 & 4, 165 n. 14
Hasdrubal Barca 23, 53, 54, 64, 66, 166 n. 34
Hasdrubal Gisgo (general, Second Punic War) 53, 87, 88-91, 92, 156 n. 84, 173 n. 11
Hasdrubal (general, Third Punic War) 78, 79, 80, 81, 82, 172 n. 20
hastati 63, 91, 135-6, 141, 143
Heirkte (Monte Castellachio) 72, 162 n. 50
Hekatompylos (Tébessa) 41, 162 n. 46
heptêrês 37, 152 n. 13
Hera Lacinia, temple of 167 n.5
Herakleia 29, 53
  battle of (280 BC) 26, 69
Herdonea, battle of (212 BC) 61
Herodotos 94, 121, 153 n. 15, 157 nn. 10 & 11
hexêrêis 152 n. 13
Hiempsal (son of Micipsa) 103, 104, 115, 119
Hiero II of Syracuse 33, 35, 42, 50, 115, 159-60 n. 12, 161 n. 34, 178 n. 8
Himera, battle of (480 BC) 16, 27, 148 n. 5
Himilco (son of Hanno) 15, 28
Himilco Phameas 79, 80, 171 n. 13
Hippo Acra (Bizerta) 48
Hippo Regius (Bône, Annaba) 87,
hoplites 15-16, 17, 19, 136, 179 n. 14
Horace xvii, xxi, 54

Iarbas, king 2
Iberia 4, 15, 19, 25, 45, 50, 51, 71, 88, 98
Iberians xx, xxi, 15, 19, 60, 62, 136, 137, 138, 142, 154 n. 68, 167 nn. 51 & 5
Iberus (Iber, Ebro), river 25, 51, 52, 164 n. 9, 165 n. 14
  treaty (226 BC) 50, 51
Ibiza 8
Iugurtha 95, 103-5, 107-8, 109-10, 111, 112, 115-20, 176 n. 21, 177 n. 24, 178 n. 26
Ilipa, battle of (206 BC) 67, 87, 90-1
Imilce 164 n. 4
Isère, river 165 n. 23

Italians
  allies (*socii*) 52, 63, 69-70, 71, 90, 95, 126, 127, 135, 161 n. 29
  traders 105, 117, 175-6 n. 7, 176 n. 14
Iuppiter xvii, xxvi, 129, 146 n. 33, 156-7 n. 4, 164 n. 6

Jason of Pherai 17
Josephus, Flavius xviii, 2, 148-9 n. 6
Justin 2, 26, 28, 31, 149 n. 7
Juvenal 21, 31, 146 n. 28, 169 n. 4

Kleonymos of Sparta 31-2, 158 n. 21
Kipling, Rudyard xxii, 147 nn. 38 & 41, 148 n. 1
Kition (Lárnaka) 149 n. 8
Krimisos, battle of the (341 BC)
Kroton 54, 55, 167 n. 5

Lacinian promontory (Capo Colonne) 167 n. 5
Lacumazes 87
Laelius, Caius 63, 66, 90, 91
Larche (l' Argentière), col de 165 n. 23
Latins 52, 54, 63, 69-70, 71, 85, 90, 122, 126, 127, 135, 161 n. 29, 164 n. 12, 166 n. 32
Lee, Robert E. 67
legionaries 19, 20, 24, 36, 43-4, 61, 63, 95, 100, 136-8, 140-4, 147 n. 36, 149 n. 10, 158 n. 24, 174 n. 1, 176 n. 17
legions
  legiones Cannenses (*legiones V et VI*) 61, 62
  consular (*legiones* I-IIII) 38, 52, 66, 69-70, 80, 108, 127, 135, 161 n. 29
  pay 149 n. 10, 165 n. 14
  Polybian 134-6
Leyte Gulf, battle of (1944) 160 n. 27
Libyan War (240-237 BC) 45-8
Libyans
  levies/mercenaries 15, 19-20, 45, 48, 60, 62, 154 nn. 68 & 69, 163 n. 5, 167 n. 5
  people 2, 3, 6, 7, 41, 46, 48, 152 n. 32
Libyphoenicians 6, 7, 62
Ligurians 15, 19, 45, 62, 65, 95,
Lilybaeum (Marsala) 15, 30, 41, 88, 157 n. 15, 161 n. 40
  siege of (250-241 BC) 18, 39-40, 172 n. 30

189

Livius
    Marcus Livius Salinator (cos. 219 BC etc.) 54
Livy *passim*
Locri 41, 57, 69, 169 n. 10
'Lucanian oxen' 158 n. 24
Lucanians 29, 30, 158 n. 21
Lutatius
    Caius Lutatius Catulus (cos. 242 BC) 41-2

Macedonian War, Second (200-197 BC) 168 n. 14
Macedonian War, Third (172-168 BC) 83
Macedonians 29, 30, 56, 71, 83, 137, 140, 142, 158 n. 24, 168 n. 14
Maesulii 86, 88
Mago (tyrant) 7
Mago (agronomist) 3, 149-50 n. 12, 150 n. 13
Mago (general) 15
Mago (admiral) 26
Mago Barca 53, 54, 55, 62, 91, 115, 170 n. 20
Magnesia, battle of (190 BC) 24, 74, 75, 76, 145 n. 1, 170 n. 4
Maharbal 68, 169 n. 4
Malchus (tyrant) 6-7
Malventum, battle of (275 BC) 26, 30, 159 n. 27
Mamertini 31, 33-4, 35
Marius, Caius (cos. I 107 BC)
    army reforms 111, 176 nn. 15, 16 & 17
    early career 103, 128, 147 n. 36, 177 n. 47
    his consulships 177 n. 27
    in Africa 107, 108, 109, 110-12, 120
Marius, Caius minor (son of above) 168 n. 28
Mars 33
Marsala wreck, the 35-6, 160 n. 17
Mary, col de 165 n. 23
Masaesulii 86
Masinissa 86
Massalia (Massilia, Marseille) 25, 50
Massiva (son of Gulussa) 119
Mastanabal (son of Masinissa) 101
Mathos 47-8, 164 n. 11
Mazaetullus 87
Melqarth 2, 4, 151 n. 20, 153 n. 37

mercenaries
    modern 20-1, 155 nn. 73, 74 & 75
    nature of, 17-9, 21
Messana (Messina) 3, 34, 35, 37, 161 n. 34, 168 n. 28
Metapontion 53
Metaurus, battle of the (207 BC) 23, 54
Micipsa (son of Masinissa) 103, 104, 114, 119
Mont-Cenis, col du 165 n. 23
Montgenèvre, col de 165 n. 23
Moors 19, 62, 65, 114-15, 178 n. 5
Motya (Mozia) 27, 28, 157 n. 15
Muluccha, battle of the (106 BC) 112
    river 113, 115
Mylae, battle of (260 BC) 34, 37, 152 n. 13

Napoléon 64, 98, 101, 102, 165 n. 23
Naraggara (Margaron, Sakhiet Sidi Youssef) 168 n. 7
Naravas (Numidian prince) 86, 87
Nepheris (Bou-Beker) 79, 80, 81
New Carthage (Cartagena) 51, 165 n. 14
Nola 167 n. 51
Numantia, siege of (134-133 BC) 84, 103, 104, 111, 137, 171 n. 6, 174 n. 1, 176 n. 15
Numidians
    horse 96-7, 98
    horsemen 62, 63, 86, 90, 93, 94-6, 97, 99, 100, 101, 107, 109, 175 n. 12
    allies/levies 19, 62, 63, 69, 80, 90-1, 94, 103, 154 n. 68, 167 n. 51, 174 n. 1, 178 n. 5
    people 6, 41, 86-7, 92-3, 94, 99
    warfare 92-3, 94-101, 107, 109

Olympias, the 152 n. 14, 153 n. 18
Orwell, George 147 n. 41
Oscans 19, 29, 159 n. 2, 165 n. 26
Ovid 54, 130

Pachynon (Passero), Cape 40
Palinurus (Palinuro), Cape 161 n. 38
Panormus (Palermo) 27, 41, 157 n. 10
    siege of (254 BC) 39, 159 n. 7
    battle of (250 BC) 24, 39
Pausanias 16, 116, 172 n. 19
pax romana xv-xvi, xvii-xviii, xix, xxii
penteconter 152 n. 14, 159 n. 11
Pergamon 74, 76

INDEX

periplous, the 12, 13-14, 40
Petit St. Bernard, col du 165 n. 23
Philinos of Akragas (historian) 84, 157 n. 5, 172 n. 30
Philip II of Macedon 56, 57, 69
Philip V of Macedon 53, 71, 72, 74,168 n. 14, 170 n. 25
Philopoimen 83, 172 n. 23
Phoenicians 4-5, 7, 6, 8, 9, 16, 26, 27, 28, 75, 148 n. 4, 149 nn. 8 & 10, 151 n. 23, 152-3 n. 14, 153 nn. 23 & 37
Pillars of Hercules (Straits of Gibraltar) xxiii, 5, 8, 150-1 n. 19, 152 n. 36
Plancentia (Piacenza) 57, 73
Plato 121
Pliny (the elder) xv-xvi, xvii, xxi, 13, 82, 86, 97, 115, 146 n. 28, 149 n. 10, 149-50 n. 12, 156 n. 96
Plutarch 14, 15, 16, 20, 76, 78, 110, 154 n. 68, 169 n. 16, 170 n. 10
Po, river 57
Poeni 149 n. 10
Polybios passim
  on elephants 23
  on *gladii* 142
  on Hannibal 59
  on mercenaries 18, 21
  on *pila* 137
  on Rome's rise 85
  on Second Punic War 49-51
  on Zama 62, 65, 68
Popilius
  Publius Popilius Laenas (cos. 132 BC) 118
Porcius
  Marcus Porcius Cato (the elder) xvi-xvii, xxi, 57, 74, 77-8, 139, 141, 146 n. 31, 149-50 n. 12, 171 nn. 2 & 3
  Caius Porcius Cato (cos. 114 BC) 117, 118
principes 63, 90, 135-6, 141, 143
proletarii 110, 131, 160 n. 20
Prusias I of Bithynia 76
Pyrenees 57, 156 n. 94
'Pyrrhic victory' 158 n. 25
Pyrrhic War (280-275 BC) 26, 140, 179 n. 14
Pyrrhos of Epeiros 23, 26, 29-30, 31-2, 55, 56, 67, 70, 85, 152 n. 13, 158 nn. 21 & 23, 159 nn. 26 & 34, 163 n. 64

quadrireme 40, 152-3 n. 14
quinquereme 11-14, 35-6, 38, 39-40, 41, 42, 52, 152 n. 14, 157 n. 15
Rhegion (Reggio di Calabria) 31, 33
Rhodes, Cecil John xxii, 147 nn. 38 & 39
Rhodes (island) 74
Rome, Romans passim
  army 69, 105, 134-44, 169 n. 16
  constitution 124-33
  manpower 54, 70-1, 110, 146 n. 35, 147 n. 36, 166 n. 32, 169 n. 16
  Senate xxii, 26, 29, 33-4, 38, 46, 51-2, 53, 55, 61, 71, 77-8, 88, 90, 104, 105, 108, 110, 112-13, 115-19, 122, 124, 126, 127, 129-30, 132, 135, 146-7 n. 36, 149-50 n. 12, 161 n. 33, 178 n. 8, 179 n. 5
Rhône, river 156 n. 94, 165 n. 23, 167 n. 5
Roure, col de 165 n. 23
Rutilius
  Publius Rutilius Rufus 107-8, 176 n. 15
Sacred Band (of Carthage) 14, 15, 17
saddle, Celtic 96, 140, 180 n. 38
Saguntum (Sagunto) 50-1, 164 n. 13, 173 n. 10
Salammbô 173 n. 2
Sallust passim
Samnites 29, 30, 71, 85, 138, 156-7 n. 4, 160 n. 20, 165 n. 26
Sardinia
  Punic 4-5, 7, 8, 14, 15, 25, 46-7,
  Roman xxv, 47, 49, 72, 126, 171 nn. 3 & 9
Scribonius
  Caius Scribonius Curio 100, 101, 106
scutum/scuta 19, 136, 138, 143
Sempronius
  Tiberius Sempronius Gracchus 55
Seneca xxi-xxii, 59, 147 n. 37, 168 n. 28
'Servian system' 131-2
'Servian wall' 169 n. 5
Servius Tullius, king 131, 132
Sicca (La Kef, El Kef) 45, 87, 106
Sicily *passim*
Siga (Takembrit) 86
Silenos 56-7, 75
Sophonisba 88, 91-2, 173 n. 8, 173-4 n. 17, 174 n. 19
Sosylos 56, 75
Souk el Kremis, plain 173 n. 15
Spendios 47, 48

191

Strabo (geographer) 94, 96, 98, 147 n. 42, 150 n. 16, 151 n. 23, 170 n. 10
Surus, 'the Syrian' 171 n. 3
Syphax (Masaesulii king)
    campaign against Scipio 88-91
    clash with Masinissa 87, 91, 173 n. 11
    dealings with Rome 88
    fate 65, 92, 174 n. 20
    kingdom of 86
    marries Sophonisba 88
Syracuse (Siracusa) 15, 17, 28, 29, 33, 53, 54, 157 n. 9, 166 n. 9
    siege of (213-212 BC) 53, 72
Syrtis, Minor (Gulf of Gabès) 87
swords
    Celtic 142
    falcata 19, 137
    gladius 19, 20, 136, 137-8, 139, 140, 142-3, 154 n. 69, 174 n. 2
    kopis 137

Tacitus
    on the Lyon Tablet 147 n. 36
    on imperialism xvii, xix, xxii, xxiv-xxv, xxvi, 78
    on swords 142
Tanit 2, 148 n. 5
Taras (Tarentum, Taranto) 29, 30-1, 34, 53, 69, 72, 139, 158 nn. 18 & 21, 166 n. 27
Terentius
    Caius Terentius Varro (cos. 216 BC) 152 n. 5
    Caius Terentius Varro (antiquarian) xvi, 97, 149-50 n. 12, 158 n. 23
Teuta, Queen 19
Thapsus (Rass Dimasse) 75, 100
Thourioi 53
Thugga (Dougga) 86
Timaios of Tauromenion (historian) 1, 2, 148 n. 4
Timoleon 14, 15, 16, 23, 28, 154 n. 40
Trasimene, battle of Lake (217 BC) 52, 58-9, 62, 69, 72, 134, 139
Traversette, col de la 165 n. 23
Trebbia, battle of the (218 BC) 19, 24, 31, 52, 57-8, 62, 72, 134, 156 n. 94, 171 n. 3
triarii 63, 90, 135-6, 141, 143
triplex acies 43, 63, 90, 91, 135-6, 141
trireme 12, 35, 37, 56, 81, 152 n. 13, 153 n. 23, 159 n. 11

Tunis 38, 45, 48, 150 n. 12
    battle of (255 BC) 24, 38-9, 42-4
turma/turmae 139
Tyndaris, battle of (257 BC) 34
Tyre 1-2, 4, 9, 148 n. 1, 148 n. 6, 151 nn. 20 & 23, 152-3 n. 14, 153 n. 37

Utica 1, 6, 26, 48, 79, 88, 90, 91, 114, 148 n. 4, 173 n. 15, 176 n. 14
Vegetius 136, 142
velites 24, 43, 63, 135, 136, 139, 141
Vespasianus, emperor xviii, 146-7 n. 36, 148 n. 52
Vidal, Gore xviii
Virgil xv, xvi-xvii, xix, xxii, xxv, 2, 50, 121, 149 n. 11, 161 n. 40
Vitruvius xvii
Voltaire 152 n. 5

weapons
    catapults 28, 79, 81, 157 n. 14, 166 n. 29
    daggers 94-5, 138
    javelins 19, 22, 29, 62, 93, 94, 107, 109, 139, 141, 154 n. 68, 158 n. 23, 174 nn. 1 & 2, 175 n. 12
    pilum/pila 19-20, 136-7, 141, 142, 154 nn. 68 & 69
    spears 19, 20, 43, 79, 94, 119, 141, 179 n. 14
    see also swords

Xanthippos 24, 39, 42-4, 163 nn. 64 & 74
Xenophanes 170 n. 25
Xenophon 96, 158 n. 18
Xerxes 25, 27

Zama, battle of (202 BC) 17, 24, 31, 55, 60-7, 68, 71, 83, 91, 111, 115, 167-8 n. 7, 168 n. 14
Zama Regia 188, 176 n. 21
Zanfour 62
Zonaras 154 n. 61, 156 n. 96, 159 n. 12, 162 n. 61